READINGS OF DŌGEN'S
TREASURY OF THE TRUE DHARMA EYE

COLUMBIA READINGS OF BUDDHIST LITERATURE

COLUMBIA READINGS OF
BUDDHIST LITERATURE

SERIES EDITOR: STEPHEN F. TEISER

This series is published with the sponsorship
of the Dharma Drum Foundation for Humanities
and Social Science Research.

Readings of the Lotus Sūtra, Stephen F. Teiser
and Jacqueline I. Stone, editors

Readings of the Platform Sūtra, Morten Schlütter
and Stephen F. Teiser, editors

Readings of the Vessantara Jātaka, Steven Collins, editor

Readings of Śāntideva's Guide to Bodhisattva Practice,
Jonathan C. Gold and Douglas S. Duckworth, editors

READINGS OF DŌGEN'S *TREASURY OF THE TRUE DHARMA EYE*

Steven Heine

COLUMBIA UNIVERSITY PRESS   NEW YORK

Columbia University Press
Publishers Since 1893
New York   Chichester, West Sussex
cup.columbia.edu
Copyright © 2020 Columbia University Press
All rights reserved

Library of Congress Cataloging-in-Publication Data
Names: Heine, Steven, 1950- author.
Title: Readings of Dōgen's Treasury of the true dharma eye / Steven Heine.
Description: New York : Columbia University Press, [2020] | Series: Columbia readings of Buddhist literature | Includes bibliographical references and index.
Identifiers: LCCN 2019042597 (print) | LCCN 2019042598 (ebook) |
ISBN 9780231182287 (cloth) | ISBN 9780231182294 (paperback) |
ISBN 9780231544085 (ebook)
Subjects: LCSH: Dōgen, 1200-1253. | Dōgen, 1200-1253. Shōbō genzō.
Classification: LCC BQ9449.D657 H46 2020 (print) | LCC BQ9449.D657 (ebook) |
DDC 294.3/85—dc23
LC record available at https://lccn.loc.gov/2019042597
LC ebook record available at https://lccn.loc.gov/2019042598

Cover image: Detail of cover page of a manuscript in a rare
woodblock edition of the *Treasury*, c. 1800

CONTENTS

List of Illustrations vii
Preface ix

PART I. Textual Sources and Resources

1. Creativity and Originality: Orientations, Reorientations, and Disorientations 3

2. Receptivity and Reliability: Numerous Levels of Significance 33

3. Multiplicity and Variability: Differing Versions and Interpretations 60

PART II. Religious Teachings and Practices

4. Reality and Mentality: On Perceiving the World of Sentient and Insentient Beings 91

5. Temporality and Ephemerality: On Negotiating Living and Dying 119

6. Expressivity and Deceptivity: To Speak or Not to Speak 145

7. Reflexivity and Adaptability: The Functions and Dysfunctions of Meditation 175

8. Rituality and Causality: On Monastic Discipline and Motivation   201

Appendix 1: Titles of Treasury *Fascicles*   227
Appendix 2: Comparison of Versions of the Treasury   231
Appendix 3: Timeline for Dōgen and the Treasury   235
Appendix 4: Complete Translations of the Treasury   239
Character Glossary   243
Notes   259
Bibliography   277
Index   289

ILLUSTRATIONS

Calligraphy for the title, "Treasury of the True Dharma Eye (*Shōbōgenzō*)"   *viii*

Figure 0.1. *Treasury* cover   *xii*

Figure 0.2. *Treasury* text   *xiii*

Dōgen's Temples and Travels   *xv*

Figure 3.1. A *Treasury* sermon at Lord Hatano's residence   *76*

Figure 4.1. View of awakening   *96*

Figure 5.1. Spiritual transformation   *127*

Figure 5.2. Reality   *129*

Figure 7.1. Dōgen's view of *kōan*s and *satori*   *192*

Figure 8.1. Dignified demeanor   *204*

FRONTISPIECE Calligraphy for the title, "Treasury of the True Dharma-Eye (*Shōbōgenzō*)," by Kazuaki Tanahashi

PREFACE

THE *TREASURY OF THE TRUE DHARMA EYE* (*Shōbōgenzō* 正法眼蔵, hereafter *Treasury*) was written by the master Dōgen (1200–1253) during the first half of the thirteenth century as a guidebook for his growing assembly of monks, who were studying meditation at the time of the emergence of the Sōtō Zen institution as a major component of religion in medieval Japan. Dōgen's text has long been recognized as a masterpiece of traditional East Asian Buddhist literature for combining in thought-provoking ways Chinese sources he studied during a pilgrimage to the continent with Japanese grammatical constructions. Since being introduced to the English-speaking world about a half-century ago, the *Treasury* has been gaining increasing international acclaim for its innovative approach to expressing the Zen view of spiritual awakening. The past few decades have seen an impressive flow of translations and scholarly studies produced by specialists and comparative scholars, in addition to numerous publications geared primarily to the interests of Zen practitioners.

It seems clear that the *Treasury* is now appreciated perhaps as much as any other single work in the history of Buddhism. However, despite this widespread attention and acclaim, the *Treasury* remains particularly difficult to comprehend and is subject to diverse and sometimes conflicting interpretations. One of the main translators, Gudō Wafu Nishijima, confesses in *Understanding the Shōbōgenzō*, "The first time that I picked up a copy of the *Shōbōgenzō*, I found that I could not understand any of it, although I was reading a book written in my own native language." This is a common reaction, he points out, because "Dōgen wrote using many phrases and quotations from Chinese Buddhism which are relatively unknown to the layman, and difficult to render into other languages."

In light of the intertwined attitudes of exhilaration and frustration that many new readers may feel in approaching the *Treasury* for the first time, my aim is to clarify the complexity of Dōgen's writing by dealing with several main issues. First, this book explores the religious and cultural context, as well as the personal striving and aspiration, that led Dōgen to compose the *Treasury*, which was edited by the author and prominent followers. Second, it explains the basis for Dōgen's use of inventive rhetorical flourishes in disclosing the foundation of contemplative experience. Third, it aims to elucidate the various versions and editions that have been constructed over the centuries by monks of the Sōtō Zen sect in terms of how these have been analyzed by premodern and modern commentators. Fourth, the book explicates the philosophical implications of Dōgen's views on attaining and sustaining enlightenment by evaluating the role of meditation and other forms of monastic discipline in terms of the relation between Zen practice and societal concerns.

Readings of Dōgen's Treasury of the True Dharma Eye contains two main divisions. The first section, consisting of three chapters, discusses the historical background and intellectual significance of the *Treasury*, especially involving the connections between different manuscripts that were not fully completed at the time of the master's death and are still very much debated and disputed by scholars today. The second section considers five main thematic topics that form the basis of Dōgen's approach to Zen theory and training, including the meaning of reality or Buddha nature, the impact of temporality and impermanence, the role of expressivity and language, deliberations on reflexivity and meditation, and the moral consequences of karmic causality. In addition, there are several supplementary sections, including a brief review in appendix IV of current complete translations.

Although numerous translations are available in English and other languages, it is fair to say that there is as yet no definitive rendition and that creating such a work is an elusive goal, given the incredible degree of intricacy and ambiguity embedded in Dōgen's compositions. Therefore, in consultation with the editors at Columbia University Press, I have decided to use my own translations from the following source: *Dōgen Zenji zenshū* 道元禪師全集 (*Dōgen's Collected Works*), edited by Kawamura Kōdō 河村孝道, et al. (Tokyo: Shunjūsha, 1988–1993), vols. 1 and 2 (of 7 vols.); this will be referred to in parentheses as "Dōgen," with volume and page number provided. In the bibliography there are a couple of other Japanese compilations edited by Ōkubo Dōshū with the same title.

Since my translations contain brief passages culled from a much longer text, for each translated passage I reference four bits of information:

a) the romanized version of the Japanese title of that fascicle (see appendix I for a list of all the fascicles with Japanese in characters and romanization plus my translation of the titles, which may vary from the versions of other translators although the romanization generally does not);
b) the page number(s) in *Dōgen Zenji zenshū*, referred to as "Dōgen";
c) the page number(s) in complete translation #1, referred to as "Nearman";
d) the page number(s) in complete translation #2, referred to as "Tanahashi."

The first complete translation cited by Hubert Nearman is *Shōbōgenzō: The Treasure House of the Eye of the True Teaching, A Trainee's Translation of Great Master Dōgen's Spiritual Masterpiece* (Mount Shasta, CA: Shasta Abbey Press, 2007). The Nearman edition has the advantages of being reliable throughout and readily available as a single, searchable PDF located at https://www.shastaabbey.org/pdf/shoboAll.pdf. The second complete translation cited, by Kazuaki Tanahashi and a long list of cotranslators, including associate editor Peter Levitt and more than thirty others, is *Treasury of the True Dharma Eye: Zen Master Dogen's Shobo Genzo* (Boston: Shambhala, 2010). This is also a readable and reliable translation that is available in a single volume and also in digital editions; it features outstanding introductory and supplementary materials for understanding the history and philosophy of the text.

There are, however, a couple of important caveats in citing these two translations. Both the Nearman and Tanahashi renderings follow a different sequence of *Treasury* fascicles than I use, and they often select wording, including for the titles of fascicles, that is quite distinct from my choices. Therefore, readers should not be surprised in numerous cases to find that the three translations (mine along with Nearman and Tanahashi) vary considerably. Comparing the variable renderings will hopefully be a central part of the process of learning to understand Dōgen's complicated text. Also, foreign terms are italicized for their first usage only. Moreover, the sequence of the fascicles is different in the Japanese edition I follow than in the versions used by Nearman and Tanahashi, which also vary to some extent.

I am very pleased to have the opportunity to contribute to the Columbia Readings of Buddhist Literature series. This book has been in the works for over four years since my initial discussions with the series academic editor, Stephen F. Teiser, and the executive editor at Columbia University Press, Wendy Lochner. Yet, for me, the process of researching and writing began over forty years ago when I first studied the *Treasury* in graduate school with my mentor, the late Charles Wei-hsun Fu, and also gained knowledge from various scholars at Komazawa University in Tokyo, whose profound and detailed studies of the masterpiece continue to inspire my efforts.

In addition, I thank Kaz Tanahashi for providing the brilliant calligraphy of "*Shōbōgenzō*" used as the frontispiece. I also thank Professors Ishii Shūdō, Ishii Seijun, and Matsumoto Shirō of Komazawa for their sage advice, in addition to the spirit of their late colleague, Yoshizu Yoshihide, may he rest. I greatly appreciate that Carl Bielefeldt shared a series of drafts

FIGURE 0.1 Cover page of a manuscript in a rare woodblock edition of the *Treasury*, c. 1800

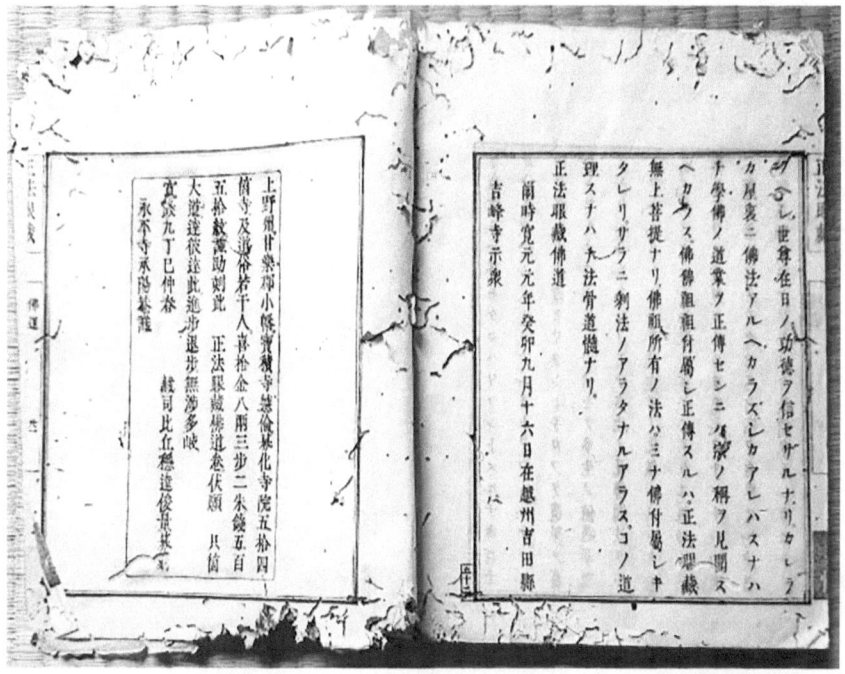

FIGURE 0.2 The final page of the manuscript shown above

of the wonderful annotated translation of the *Treasury* currently being prepared by the Sōtō Zen Translation Project. I am also very grateful to Rachel Levine for helping edit the manuscript, Michaela Prostak for her capable assistance with the glossary and index, and Maria Sol Echarren for her creative work in helping provide the images.

While conducting research for the current book I was led to acquire or examine several older versions of the *Treasury* that I had not previously scrutinized in depth. Figures 0.1 and 0.2, which show respectively the cover and final page, are from a weathered manuscript I purchased at an auction that was originally part of a rare twenty-volume woodblock print edition published around 1803 that includes seven of the more than ninety fascicles in the whole work.

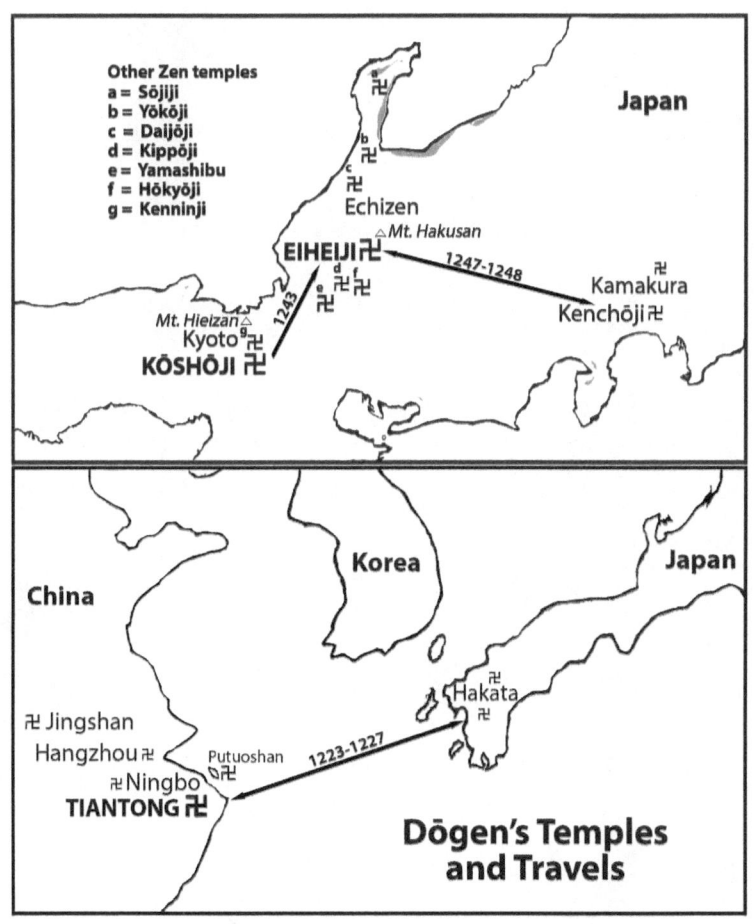

PART I

TEXTUAL SOURCES AND RESOURCES

{ 1 }

CREATIVITY AND ORIGINALITY

ORIENTATIONS, REORIENTATIONS, AND
DISORIENTATIONS

INTRODUCING DŌGEN'S *TREASURY*

"If you wish to pursue the Buddhist way (*butsudō*), then you must first cultivate the way-seeking mind (*dōshin*). Those who know this principle are rare, so you need to learn from a trusted teacher who understands it clearly based on their own experience" (Dōshin: Dōgen 2.530, Nearman 1088, Tanahashi 886).[1] Thus reads a thought-provoking passage about navigating the path to enlightenment composed by the Zen (Ch. Chan) Master Dōgen (道元, 1200–1253) in his celebrated work titled the *Shōbōgenzō* (正法眼蔵), or *Treasury* (*zō*) *of the True Dharma* (*shōbō*) *Eye* (*gen*, or "insights").[2] This text is generally considered the best introduction to Dōgen's lifetime of teachings as well as crucial reading for understanding various theoretical and ritual developments in the history of Zen Buddhism that continue to have important implications and resonances with worldwide examples of religious literature. According to *The Princeton Dictionary of Buddhism*, "The essays are renowned for their subtle and elliptical style, clever wordplay, and enigmatic meanings. Part of their difficulty arises from the fact that Dōgen quotes liberally from Buddhist sūtras and the works of Chinese masters, but also interprets these passages quite ingeniously."[3]

For Dōgen, who founded the Sōtō (Ch. Caodong) sect in early medieval Japan, derived largely from teachings he learned while training and attaining enlightenment in China during the 1220s, refining the mind necessarily involves the creative use of appropriate words and phrases to evoke the intricacy of the process of Zen realization. This is highlighted by a prominent scholar who notes, "Dōgen was a wordsmith who crafted compositions with poetic precision. His writings invite the reader to analyze the significance of each word."[4] This quality is illustrated by the double-edged use of "way" (dō, Ch. dao) to indicate both an attribute of an individual's intellectual activities in seeking enlightenment and the ultimate goal of those efforts by apprehending unity with Buddhist truth. The passage also features an injunction about the need to avoid falsity and fabrication while learning directly from an authentic adept who teaches the value of self-discipline and self-reliance.

The term "Treasury of the True Dharma Eye" (Shōbōgenzō), which is also the title of several notable texts written by Chinese masters in addition to a couple of other writings by Dōgen and his followers, portrays the Zen school as the culmination of the long expansion of the Buddhist tradition stemming from India and spreading throughout China and Japan.[5] Zen is characterized by methods of teaching that utilize language inventively, yet "do not depend on words and letters" (furyū monj, Ch. buli wenzi) because the school constitutes a "special transmission outside traditional teachings" (kyōge betsuden, Ch. jiaowai biechuan). As the name of Dōgen's text, long regarded as one of the most interesting and important treatises produced in the East Asian canon, "Treasury of the True Dharma Eye" further implies an exhaustive explanation of an advanced teacher's view of Zen's theoretical foundations in relation to copious instructions for the daily practices of an assembly of monks.[6]

The foremost training method emphasized in the *Treasury*'s approach to capturing and conveying true insight is the continuing and concentrated commitment to perform *zazen*, or seated meditation, through making "sustained exertion (or effort)" (gyōji). Dōgen also refers to this technique as the act of "just sitting" (shikan taza or tada suwaru) in unencumbered yet altogether mindful awareness that lacks any preoccupation with a fixed aim, sense of purpose, or anticipated outcome as the aftermath of meditative exercises. As he writes in "Discerning the Way," which appears as the opening section of a commonly cited version of the *Treasury* that contains a total of 95 fascicles (maki or kan, Ch. juan) or nonsequential chapters, "Even though it may last for just a moment, when someone sitting steadfast in meditation realizes the seal of the Buddha through three types of volitional actions, including those of body, speech, and thought, the entire universe and everything in it manifests the Buddha's seal. Moreover, all of space throughout the whole universe becomes one with and reflects enlightenment" (Bendōwa: Dōgen 2.462–463, Nearman 4, Tanahashi 5). According to Dōgen, hankerings that are typical of instrumentalist approaches to zazen performed in pursuit of a set goal diminish an appreciation of the immediacy and fullness of instantaneous yet simultaneous experience realized by contemplative consciousness.

Dōgen maintains that the practice of zazen does not merely refer to a single, simple physical posture. Even though sitting cross-legged in the upright position without back support is required for monks several hours each day, the term "just sitting" encompasses a determined yet eminently flexible and adaptable state of mind that reflects the power of "nonthinking" (*hishiryō*), regardless of which kind of deportment is being carried out. Nonthinking indicates mental attentiveness and attunement beyond the dichotomy of thought versus the absence of cogitation, or of logic and reason in opposition to the illogical and irrational. Whether someone is "walking around, standing still, sitting straight, or lying down" (*gyōju zaga*), when nonthinking is perpetually actualized, various postures adopted during the course of twenty-four hours reflect savvy alertness and discerning anticipation realized by virtue of single-minded dedication. In fostering an integrated and applied understanding of the fundamental unity of all aspects of human and natural existence based on the emptiness of conceptual categories, through embracing contradictory perspectives regarding diverse levels of experience, the method of just sitting functions as the trigger and fulfillment of the realization of nonthinking. This training technique serves as the touchstone for a Zen practitioner's approach to speaking and acting while renewing the regulations of a rigorous reclusive routine, including daily chores such as bathing, cooking, cleaning, and scrubbing floors in addition to listening to sermons, wearing robes, reciting scriptures, and many other kinds of daily monastic rites and yearly ceremonies.

Distinctive Discursive Style

The *Treasury* consists of a lengthy series of erudite essays and insightful sermons on diverse topics regarding Buddhist philosophy and clerical behavior produced by Dōgen over the course of a couple of decades after he returned to Japan in 1227 from a four-year journey to study Zen in China. The passage cited above regarding apprehension of the way is one of many dozens of intriguing examples in which Dōgen challenges those standpoints that tend to deemphasize the role of language for seeming to represent a distraction that invariably detracts from the quest to attain awakening. His focus on the utility of various types of expression for spiritual attainment is illustrated by additional instances of purposely puzzling sayings that reflect a fundamentally paradoxical view of reality. The maxims include:

a) "To study the way is to study the self, and to study the self is to forget the self."
b) "Life is a continuous mistake, or a series of misunderstandings one after another."
c) "'Mountains are mountains' does not mean 'mountains are mountains,' yet it does."
d) "Only the painting of a rice cake can satisfy one's hunger; no other remedy applies."
e) "Vision is dependent on dimness, which is the main feature enabling us to see."
f) "The question posed, 'What are you thinking?' truly means, 'This is what you think.'"
g) "We disentangle entangled vines by using those very intertwined creepers."
h) "Buddha nature never arrives in the future, as it is always already here."
i) "A full instance of time that is half known is a half instance that is fully known."
j) "Some do not accept 'a head above the head,' but there is always one more head."[7]

These cryptic yet illuminating adages demonstrate the distinctive discursive style found throughout the *Treasury*. All highlight difficulties and challenges to overcoming delusion and ignorance by showing that nearly anywhere one turns can reveal a sense of being trapped by partial perspectives, misleading assumptions, circular thinking, uncertainty, deception, or blunder. Yet each of the dictums, if properly understood, also emphasizes a contrary standpoint in that the Zen approach to realizing enlightenment surpasses illusion by embracing the comprehensive unity of all forms of existence as well as endless variability perpetually manifested in everyday life. That enigmatic view can be summed up by paraphrasing some of Dōgen's main ideas as, "Reality is one, but as soon as you try to explain a particular thing, any utterance appears at first to be limitlessly misguided. However, from within the midst of such a series of errors and fragmentations, a genuine understanding of the wholeness of true reality can instantaneously emerge, even though an expression of this level of insight still needs to be continually clarified and modified depending on particular pedagogical circumstances." Carrying out that ongoing interpretative task requires an innovative way with words chosen carefully so as to articulate the fundamental contradictions embedded in human experience that lead from misunderstanding to genuine spiritual awareness.

Because people generally function through deficient habits that are further obstructed by conceptual blinders and other self-imposed fetters to understanding, the basic level of discernment evident in all of the enigmatic expressions cited above remains hidden from view. According to Dōgen, the perceptiveness needed must be disclosed by the unfathomable teachings of a compassionate but demanding instructor in a manner appropriate and precisely fitted to the degree of knowledge of the learner plagued by persistent misconceptions. Even when truth is displayed, however, there likely remain oversights and entanglements to be overcome. As Dōgen says of the innate yet self-surpassing limitations of human perception, "When one side of a phenomenon is illumined, [this means] the other side remains obscure" (Genjōkōan: Dōgen 1.3, Nearman 32, Tanahashi).

Therefore, all articulations of Zen realization are subject to revision and alteration. Dōgen comments, for example, on the mysterious occurrence of synesthesia evoked by the Chinese Master Dongshan (807–869, Jp. Tōzan), an important predecessor in his lineage who once suggested that people truly see sights with their ears and hear sounds with their eyes. "Because the voice heard by the eyes must be the same as the voice heard by the ears," Dōgen argues, this expression can be flipped to indicate, "the voice heard by the eyes is not the same as the voice heard by the ears" (Mujō seppō: Dōgen 2.11, Nearman 663, Tahahashi 555). He concludes by cautioning against misreading the original expression: "We should not take Dongshan's remark to mean that there is an ear functioning in our eye, or that the eye becomes the ear, or that there are voices occurring within the eyes" (Mujō seppō: Dōgen 2.11, Nearman 663, Tanahashi 555).

This passage highlights what translator Gudo Nishijima (1919–2014) refers to as four kinds of contradictions evident in the *Treasury*: between fascicles, between paragraphs in a fascicle, between sentences, and within sentences.[8] What exactly these sets of incongruity should be taken to mean is left up to each reader to determine for him- or herself based on their own level of awareness and aspiration to transcend misunderstanding. For his part, Nishijima advises readers not to take a "halfway" approach that admires some ideas while criticizing others or cherry-picks only what is preferred, but instead to fully accept the merit of Dōgen's teachings prior to entertaining various kinds of skeptical attitudes.

The *Treasury* is particularly renowned for being composed in vernacular script or *kana*, an innovative accomplishment during Dōgen's stage of Japanese Buddhist textual history when the standard procedure was to write entirely either in classical Chinese or in a hybrid form of Sino-Japanese known as *kanbun*.[9] Nevertheless, Dōgen's text is not strictly composed in the native tongue, since it is based primarily on his extensive citations and groundbreaking interpretations of voluminous Chinese Chan records of enlightenment. He learned these materials while staying on the continent, where he attained an experience of awakening known as "casting (or dropping) off body-mind" (*shinjin datsuraku*), or a psychophysical release of attachments gained by training rigorously in the practice of zazen. The prominence of the *Treasury*, which is appreciated perhaps even more today than in the past, reflects Dōgen's freewheeling facility in crossing effortlessly between the idioms and grammars of Chinese and Japanese. These linguistic alignments and cultural reconstructions are interwoven to create a unique vision and vocabulary for conveying the multiple layers of meaning of the Zen realization of indivisible truth, divulged in terms of manifold human perspectives. As Dōgen writes, "The methods for explaining enlightenment are inexhaustible, so that a teacher's efforts are never finished, as he may at any time encounter a new disciple in need of a wholly different way of having truth explained" (Kattō: Dōgen 1.419, Nearman 580, Tanahashi 481).

Dōgen's discursive skill is perhaps the main key to understanding the historical importance of the *Treasury* as well as the surging impact the text has been exerting in modern times. Because of its creative and resourceful disclosure of Buddhist notions in ways that strongly resemble current theoretical and rhetorical standpoints that similarly emphasize the role of self-reliance in attaining spiritual insight, Dōgen's text is not seen merely as an antiquated body of writing that evokes a bygone era. Rather, as Puqun Li suggests in a recent study examining numerous Asian classics, "Over the past thirty years, Dōgen has become the most renowned and most studied figure in Buddhist history in the West, and the *Treasury* has also secured a place among the masterworks of the world's religious and philosophical literature."[10]

Moreover, the distinguished historian of Zen Buddhism Heinrich Dumoulin maintains that Dōgen is preeminent for the pure integrity of his character, which places him among the great thinkers of mankind based on a "unique blend of lofty religious achievement and uncommon intellectual gifts."¹¹ These qualities helped produce "a literary work of exceptional quality and unique experience . . . without equal in the whole of Zen literature."¹² The *Treasury*, according to Dumoulin, "shows a fluency of style of unmistakable uniqueness that is branded with Dōgen's own language."¹³ It is invaluable for guiding the mystical training or subjective experience of sectarian practitioners and also for inspiring the speculative observations or objective analysis of academic researchers. Dumoulin further argues that both insiders and outsiders to the legacy of the Sōtō Zen tradition are able to appreciate reading the text in a contemporary context, for somewhat different yet overlapping reasons.

From another angle of interpretation, numerous scholars suggest that Dōgen's speculative reflections are noteworthy for offering insight into key aspects of medieval Japanese society. Although Dōgen's main audience was an assembly of monks, his writings address ideas that pertain to the concerns of laypeople, who no doubt attended the temple lectures that, after editing, came to form the *Treasury*. They were intrigued by topics such as the role of women in Buddhist practice, the compassionate doctrines of Mahāyāna sūtras, and the efficacy of worshipping local deities in relation to meditating and attaining merit while avoiding transgressions and mitigating the effects of karmic retribution. Many of these themes remain relevant and continue to attract a broad audience today. According to the synopsis on the back cover of a recent Spanish edition that includes various appendices and glossaries as guides to deciphering the *Treasury*, the study of supplementary reference materials "facilitates and enriches the reading of this vast and complex work that fascinates not only Buddhist studies researchers but also all those interested in ecology in addition to the psychology of enlightenment as reflected in Japanese philology, literature, history, gender issues, and theory."¹⁴

Many modern readers, however, may feel that it is a formidable task to untangle the sheer density of philosophical ideas and religious ideals presented through Dōgen's exceedingly complicated—or perhaps convoluted—literary methods. The complex rhetorical style of the *Treasury* has long been considered difficult to comprehend for anyone whose knowledge is less than that of a true adept. Even experts eminently familiar with the subject matter find Dōgen's discourse perplexing. The cumulative effect of uncertainties creating obstacles to accessing the obscure body of writing was probably first pointed out by the monk Giun, a fifth-generation Sōtō follower of the founder who helped edit several fascicles in 1279 and fifty years later wrote one of only two Kamakura-era (1185–1333) commentaries on the *Treasury*. According to Giun's introductory observations to his verse remarks on each of the fascicles:

> After returning from China, where he thoroughly investigated Chan lineages, Dōgen decided to spread the teachings in a revitalized way by evoking grandmotherly kindness in combining Japanese grammar with Chinese characters. This was very beneficial in that it expressed the Dharma but did not lead to a reliance on language, like constructing a jade pagoda higher than the tallest mountain peak. Yet, most followers were still not able to smash the barriers to gain an understanding of his main purpose in using vernacular discourse, so that the true Dharma was not penetrated and the great teachings of First Patriarch Bodhidharma were not seen even in a dream.[15]

Moreover, in a study of Menzan Zuihō (1683–1769), the single most famous early modern commentator on the master's life and works, David Riggs notes persistent problems of interpretation. "It is true that Dōgen is not now, and probably never was very approachable," Riggs points out. "His powers of language and his ability to inspire are not in question, but it is a daunting challenge to grasp what those inspiring words actually mean, much less put into practice the path he indicated."[16] Over the centuries, the supporters of Giun and Menzan have at times strenuously argued about the merits of interpretation with rival standpoints, thus giving rise to a plethora of views about the origins and levels of meaning of Dōgen's masterwork that may also confuse contemporary readers.

The aim of this book is to generate a balanced interpretative approach that opens up an appreciation for the magnitude of the *Treasury* while also clarifying reasons for its contested and at times misjudged legacy. By maintaining that various approaches to assessing the work, traditional and modern in addition to sacred and secular perspectives, can be seen as complementing and reinforcing rather than opposing one another, I examine the multiple implications of Dōgen's stimulating writing while clarifying why students often feel a sense of inspiration as well as exasperation in trying to make sense of his dense ruminations.

In doing this, a series of important questions are raised. First, which factors led to the initial composition of Dōgen's masterwork that was always greatly respected yet somewhat overlooked for much of its history, and how have they contributed to the incredible revival of interest in the modern period? Next, what is the basis of the ongoing appeal of and widespread acclaim for the *Treasury*, despite considerable obstacles to reading and comprehending its multifaceted layers of meaning since it is filled with many arcane allusions and abstract wordplay regarding obscure scrolls and scripts? Third, what are some of the major scholarly theories currently being promulgated for interpreting the content and meaning of the *Treasury* in light of its medieval context as well as manifold current theoretical ramifications? Furthermore, how do we assess, in terms of the appeal of readability adjusted to standards of reliability, various English translations and interpretations, part of a growing list that includes at least half a dozen complete renditions of the text? Some fascicles have been translated over a dozen times each, and there are entire volumes dedicated to presenting a single fascicle or analyzing a particular theme to disclose Dōgen's religious philosophy and/or views of practice.[17]

The remainder of the current chapter offers an overview of the fundamental historical orientations of the *Treasury*'s discursive style by examining briefly how Dōgen's intense interest in Buddhist spirituality led him to achieve a realization of enlightenment in China, amid the broader religious and cultural trends of thirteenth-century East Asian society. It also discusses rhetorical reorientations in terms of Dōgen's remarkably innovative literary approach that weaves together continental sources with Japanese interpretations by virtue of various kinds of punning and other examples of inventiveness. The chapter concludes with a consideration of key aspects of the sense of conceptual disorientation that is often felt during the initial stages of reading the elegant but contradictory discourse that characterizes nearly every fascicle. This effect can lead to difficulties and challenges felt not only by relatively uninformed readers but also by many specialists who have developed competing and often conflicting theories about the text's significance.

HISTORICAL ORIENTATIONS

The narrative of Dōgen as a reluctant religious aspirant born in the capital who eventually became a charismatic monastic leader in the provinces begins with his aristocratic upbringing and renunciation of secular life in Kyoto. It continues with Dōgen's sense of doubt while investigating Buddhism as a teenager and his travels to China beginning in 1223 to attain enlightenment before coming home "empty-handed" to establish the Sōtō branch of Zen. For more than twenty years after his return, first in his hometown and then in the spectacular mountainous region of Echizen province (currently Fukui prefecture), where the prestigious Eiheiji temple was established, Dōgen crafted the various fascicles that are included in the *Treasury*.[18]

The transmission and transplantation from China of two Zen schools, Sōtō and Rinzai (Ch. Linji), gained popularity during an extraordinary phase of religious diversity and experimentation in the turbulent "upside-down age" of Kamakura-era Japan.[19] At this time the shogunate and attendant samurai class had ascended to leadership of the country, replacing the centuries-old nobility of the Heian era (794–1185) that supported the Tendai Buddhist sect. That denomination was based primarily at temples situated on Mount Hiei (or Hieizan), a sacred peak located to the northeast of Kyoto, in order to help ward off evil spirits lurking at the city's "demon gate" (*kimon*), according to the traditional beliefs of geomancy (*fusui*, Ch. *fengshui*) used for city planning. In addition to profound sociopolitical changes caused by military conflicts that overturned conventional societal status and moral ideals while depreciating the value of outdated principles and property, the dawn of medieval Japan was characterized by an ongoing series of natural catastrophes that disrupted life in the capital. These events in the midst of an unstable worldview exacerbated a sense of decline and reminded dedicated religious seekers like Dōgen of the urgency of the quest to gain liberation from the chains of karma.

By the end of the first half of the thirteenth century, several novel schools emerged in Japan that are often referred to collectively as the New Kamakura Buddhism (Shin Kamakura Bukkyō), even though many of the changes unfolded over several centuries. This designation includes the devotional Pure Land and scriptural-based Nichiren sects in addition to Sōtō and Rinzai Zen, which developed varying approaches to the practice of meditation. Like the founders of other major Buddhist denominations, such as Eisai (1141–1215, Rinzai), Hōnen (1133–1212, Pure Land), Shinran (1173–1253, True Pure Land), Ippen (1234–1289, Momentous Pure Land), and the eponymous school of Nichiren (1222–1282), Dōgen first trained in the Tendai sect as a young acolyte beginning in 1213 before eventually breaking away to explore newly formed religious ideals and practice techniques.

Born to a noble family, because of his deep emotional response to the evanescence of life when he was orphaned at the age of seven and witnessed the smoke wafting from the incense at his mother's funeral pyre that symbolized incessant impermanence, Dōgen abandoned a possible career in the imperial court recommended by a prominent uncle in order to become an ordained priest prior to reaching adulthood. Dōgen reports that shortly after he began studies at Mount Hiei he felt a "great doubt" (*taigi*) about what he considered to be an unsolvable inconsistency embedded within Tendai teachings and sought an authentic Zen instructor who could help overcome his spiritual impasse. For nearly a decade, while still training in Japan, Dōgen pondered a basic but recurring quandary: If all beings are supposed to possess as a natural endowment the innate potential for gaining illumination, according to the widely accepted "theory of original enlightenment" (*hongaku shisō*) supported by the Mahāyāna Buddhist doctrine of an all-inclusive Buddha nature, then why is religious practice of any kind deemed necessary? Tendai's notion of original enlightenment would seem to vitiate the need to make any effort to achieve realization, but the still youthful Dōgen already felt that a determined commitment to the sustained effort of meditative practice was a crucial component of monastic behavior and, thus, a main component of the pathway to awakening.

Following the pattern of other charismatic leaders of Kamakura Buddhism, at the age of fourteen Dōgen split from the esoteric ritualism of the hegemonic Tendai institution, which functioned as protector of the state, in order to pursue a more personalized path to salvation. The intellectual approach he adopted, based on idiosyncratic yet innovative elucidations of classical Buddhist texts reflecting his distinctive religious vision, was in league with an interpretative method utilized by other sectarian leaders known as "changed readings" (*yomikae*) of scriptural writings. This involved adapting the Chinese syntax of sūtras to native grammar in a way that enabled a creative commentator to forge hybrid linguistic constructions featuring fresh spiritual interpretations of long-standing source materials.

Resolving the Great Doubt

In seeking to come to terms with his doubt, Dōgen became the second main Zen pioneer who traveled to learn the practice of seated meditation in Southern Song-dynasty (Nan Song) China (1127–1279), following the four-year journey of Eisai from 1187 to 1191.[20] Eisai found that Chan had become the leading tradition in a highly competitive religious environment involving rivalry with various other Buddhist schools in addition to Confucianism and Daoism. Chan's esteemed status was primarily the result of the massive production of creatively composed historical, theoretical, and poetic writings. These works explicate the efficacy of contemplative consciousness realized through zazen by propagating a multigenerational and multibranched set of lineages incorporating an ongoing succession of captivating masters, whose initially oral teachings were later transcribed and preserved in ample recorded documents.

In 1202 Eisai established the first Zen monastery in Kyoto at Kenninji temple, which proved instrumental in the early stages of Dōgen's meditative practice before he made the trip to China. According to traditional accounts, Dōgen studied with Eisai for a brief but intense intellectual exchange prior to the Rinzai leader's death in 1215. After spending nine years at Kenninji, in 1223 Dōgen journeyed to the mainland in the company of Eisai's main disciple and successor, Myōzen (1184–1225). Myōzen died from exhaustion after just two years of travel and was commemorated in China by Dōgen before he returned his senior colleague's ashes to Japan. This trip occurred during the decade Genghis Khan (1162–1227) conquered vast northern territory as the Mongol empire was rapidly advancing and would, just a half century later under the charge of the conqueror's grandson Kublai Khan (1215–1294), overtake the Southern Song to establish the Yuan dynasty (1279–1368), which controlled China for nearly a century. In Japan, warriors greatly appreciated the Zen path of contemplative discipline that provided a vehicle for resistance during the Mongol invasions in 1274 and 1281.

At first wandering to try out meditation methods at various temples in China, Dōgen quickly gained a sense that the golden age of Chan Buddhism was fading, so that the current institution was in many ways a pale shadow of what he imagined it to have been a couple of centuries earlier. Disappointed and disillusioned during the first two years of his journey because he felt that the teachers he initially encountered lacked a genuine spiritual outlook, Dōgen was on the verge of returning home unfulfilled in the spring of 1225. His odyssey changed dramatically when he started intensive training during the annual summer retreat under the tutelage of Rujing (Jp. Nyojō, 1163–1228). Sectarian biographies indicate that several fateful occurrences led Dōgen to meet his mentor. Both the prospective teacher Rujing, who was hoping to gain a truly determined disciple before the end of his life, and the anticipatory student Dōgen, then on the verge of a spiritual collapse while seeking a forthright and inspiring master, experienced prophetic dreams foretelling their fortuitous encounter.[21]

Known for a strict and uncompromising approach to meditative training, Rujing was a leader of the Caodong lineage who had become abbot during the last phase of his life at the respected Mount Tiantong (Jp. Tendō) monastery, located in current Zhejiang province near the port city of Ningbo, where the incoming seafarers from Japan and other Asian countries disembarked. Tiantong was one of the cloisters that belonged to the highly cultured district of intellectuals and artists located in the nearby Southern Song capital of Hangzhou, which served as the center for the major temples in the Chan school known collectively as the Five Mountains (Gozan, Ch. Wushan).[22]

At their initial meeting, Dōgen and Rujing immediately sensed that they were taking part in an auspicious encounter based on an intimate connection involving master and disciple that is immortalized in the "Face-to-Face Transmission" fascicle of the *Treasury*. This passage asserts that transmission can only take place through personal interaction with an enlightened master, rather than by reciting and copying sūtras or adhering to other training methods. Dōgen writes, "Patriarchs, as successive heirs for generation after generation, have passed on face-to-face transmission in accord with a disciple being 'seen' by a master and the master 'recognizing' the disciple." Moreover, "If even a single patriarch, master, or disciple had failed to confirm face-to-face transmission, there would not be buddha after buddha or patriarch following patriarch" (Menju: Dōgen 2.55–56, Nearman 836, Tanahashi 571).

Just two months after they met, Dōgen attained an experience of casting off body-mind. In a conversation in the abbot's quarters the evening after he experienced an awakening upon hearing the teacher scold another monk for falling asleep during meditation, Rujing confirmed that Dōgen's realization represented spontaneous liberation from all hindrances to realizing the Dharma or Buddhist truth. This occasion was further highlighted by the mentor's use of two impromptu proclamations that greatly influenced Dōgen's teaching method. One was the rhetorical reversal of Rujing declaring, "Body-mind is cast off!" (*datsuraku shinjin*), thus indicating that any notion of authentic selfhood should not be ossified and must be dropped, lest it become an object of attachment. The other saying that capped the conversation was Rujing's tautology, "Cast off casting off!" (*datsuraku datsuraku*), further suggesting that the release of obstacles is a temporary act to be renewed by continually letting go of any subtle clinging to presumptive liberation. Dōgen's sudden breakthrough highlighting the oneness of corporeal and mental components (*shinjin*), realized through a process of shedding (*datsuraku*) or overcoming deficiencies and self-imposed barriers to insight, inspired the rest of his teaching career.

Several ideas evident from the account of Dōgen's spontaneous breakthrough are crucial for the development of the *Treasury*'s discursive patterns. A key point involves an emphasis on the inseparability of body and mind that perpetually work together as a single experiential unit and are thereby liberated simultaneously in one holistic function, as stressed in several *Treasury* fascicles such as "Learning the Way Through Body-Mind." For Dōgen, mental functions are not part of an immaterial realm standing over and above concrete physical activities; rather, the mind is fully and irrevocably intertwined with all aspects of bodily behavior (Shinjin gakudō: Dōgen 1.45, Nearman 491, Tanahashi 423).

An important issue related to this notion of unity is that Rujing was not known from his writings to use the phrase, "casting off body-mind." Instead we find the expression, "casting off dust from the mind" (心塵脱落), mentioned in just one instance in a poem contained in his recorded sayings.[23] This utterance is homophonic in Japanese (*shinjin*) with the phrase "casting off body-mind" (身心脱落), even though the pronunciation in Chinese of the first two characters is distinct (*xinchen* for "dust from the mind," compared to *shenxin* for "body-mind").[24] It seems that Dōgen, as a nonnative speaker who had difficulty deciphering the mentor's words precisely, either misconstrued what Rujing said or, more likely, deliberately altered the wording to reflect an indirect critique of his teacher. Rujing's saying seems to indicate a subtle duality in that ignorance is caused by physical objects collecting in the mind as the source of sensations, just as dust alights and blurs the surface of a mirror. Therefore, Dōgen revises the mentor's standpoint by stressing the oneness of body-mind as a holistic entity purified through the unceasing practice of zazen, without any need to constantly wipe away the dust.

Another major theme connected with Dōgen's awakening is that the technique of just sitting takes precedence over all other forms of religious practice, which are not necessarily rejected or replaced but are clearly eclipsed in terms of their significance for prompting realization. According to Rujing's dictum, cited by Dōgen in the "Discerning the Way" fascicle and elsewhere, "Take no recourse to burning incense, making bows, reciting the name of Buddha, performing acts of repentance or reciting sūtras. Just practice sitting meditation and attain the casting off of body-mind" (Bendōwa: Dōgen 2.462, Nearman 4, Tanahashi 5). Dōgen mentions Rujing's admonition frequently in the *Treasury* and some of his other texts, and the phrase "casting off" (*datsuraku*) appears by itself dozens of times in various works, referring to thoughts and actions that are extricated from self-imposed barriers. However, in another of the numerous apparent incongruities that must be kept in mind when evaluating his writings, the monastic life that Dōgen supervised did not forego but instead used extensively the various techniques Rujing dismissed.[25] Dōgen found creative ways to justify the functions of these practices by viewing them as manifestations of the core spiritual experience of nonthinking.

Two years after his breakthrough, Dōgen turned down an offer to become Rujing's successor at Tiantong monastery and decided instead to return home to spread Zen teachings. Rujing bid farewell and bestowed full transmission at the time of Dōgen's departure by handing over a robe, seal, staff, and ritual portraiture as emblematic of the authority of office and authenticity of experience. Then the mentor, who died shortly after this event, urged his foremost foreign follower to instruct novices in Japan to embrace dedication to just sitting while taking care to steer clear of secular distractions. Whether or not Dōgen deliberately altered his teacher's expression, the foundational experience of casting off body-mind became the benchmark of the *Treasury*'s detailed practical directives for enacting contemplative exercises connected to wide-ranging speculative reflections, postulated in an inventive literary style.

Sometime after his return Dōgen spoke of "coming back empty-handed" (*kūshu genkyō*) from China because, other than receiving a few ceremonial items from Rujing, he showed little regard for gathering continental relics and regalia and was not concerned with transporting sacramental objects as trophies of the trip, a custom typical of many other pilgrims. As Hee-Jin Kim writes, "Unlike other Buddhists who had previously studied in China, Dōgen brought home with him no sūtras, no images, and no documents. His sole 'souvenir' presented to his countrymen was his own body and mind, his total existence, which was now completely liberated and transformed. He himself was the surest evidence of Dharma."[26] In droll fashion, Dōgen proclaims that the only knowledge he gained overseas was, "Rains pouring down and clouds floating above the mountains ... Every four years is a leap year, and roosters crow at dawn."[27] In typical Zen style, Dōgen suggests that the less there is a focus on external paraphernalia, the greater the degree of interior awareness revealed. However, this transpires without neglecting the outer trappings of practices involving bells, bowls, robes, scrolls, seals, and staffs, which in their respective ways at once complement and embody the meaning of interior awareness.

Dōgen's literary records show that he was by no means empty-headed, although he may have had a head full of "emptiness," so to speak, since his body-mind was crammed full of new ideas based on interpreting a variety of religious texts as entryways to the attainment of awakening, reflecting his understanding of the Buddhist notion of emptiness or nothingness. It is clear that Dōgen gained an extraordinary familiarity and facility with diverse genres of Zen writings, which he cited extensively yet critically and creatively in his sermons and other works. His profound knowledge of Chinese literature, especially commentaries on *kōan* (Ch. *gongan*) case stories of exchanges leading to a trainee's spontaneous self-realization, is symbolized by the legend of the "One Night *Blue Cliff Record*" (Ichiya *Hekiganroku*).

According to this tradition, just before leaving China Dōgen copied a version of the most famous Song-dynasty kōan collection, the *Blue Cliff Record* (Ch. *Biyanlu*, Jp. *Hekiganroku*), which was first published in 1128 but was lost or destroyed by a rival a decade later, then recovered around 1300. It seems that Dōgen may have been given access to a special, private edition of this text during his visit. As supportive lore, it is said that the deity that guarded Eiheiji temple, known as Hakusan Gongen, the avatar from the sacred peak Mount Hakusan located close to the temple, showed up in China and assisted him in completing this mysterious project. This tale is no doubt dubious, despite some text-historical evidence to the contrary that includes an alternate manuscript still claimed by some proponents to represent Dōgen's own version of the *Blue Cliff Record*, but the legend highlights the extent to which the master's continental learning was admired and appreciated for nearly singlehandedly initiating the study of kōan literature in Japan during the thirteenth century.[28]

In any event, Dōgen seems to have memorized a vast amount of written material from the capacious Chinese Chan canon that included four main categories: (a) illumination records explaining various lineal transmissions establishing the history of the multiple branches of the flourishing Chan school; (b) recorded sayings of eminent individual masters providing their life story as well as transcribed records of the main oral teachings and dialogues; (c) eloquent commentaries composed in poetry and prose on kōan narratives, such as the *Blue Cliff Record*—in some respects, the *Treasury* represents a variation of this genre; and (d) monastic regulations for governing each and every aspect of temple rituals and practices carried out on a daily, seasonal, and yearly basis. Dōgen distilled and presented the essence of all of these kinds of works in a summative yet highly imaginative and critical fashion by writing the *Treasury* in Japanese vernacular, instead of Sino-Japanese syntax or kanbun, a style he saved for most of his other works.

RHETORICAL REORIENTATIONS

Back in Japan, Dōgen quickly introduced continental writing styles and methods of practice to a growing group of monastic followers eager to learn, but for the most part unaware and uninformed of Zen teachings that were being disseminated for the first time. In helping to spread this novel outlook, Dōgen demonstrated an exceptional ability to explicate complex ideas about the true nature of nondual reality as the basis for the religious ideal of achieving immediate insight to gain illumination. This rhetorical quality is reflected at nearly every turn in the inventive prose writing of the various fascicles of the *Treasury*, which became the greatest literary accomplishment of a prolific author and thoughtful exegetist known for ingeniously employing a wide variety of resourceful discursive devices. Dōgen's primary aim is to explicate the impact of his own knowledge of the Dharma attained in China by introducing expeditiously yet construing analytically numerous theoretical notions and meditative methods to edify neophyte trainees. The Sōtō patriarch realized that his emergent assembly of followers was enthusiastic about joining the fledgling Zen movement but had little background in its vast scriptural foundations.

Dōgen used the Japanese kana syllabary for semantic purposes, to provide connective phrases and verb conjugations that are juxtaposed with and sometimes intentionally intrude into citations of Chinese sources, which in the original are much more truncated than Japanese counterparts in terms of the use of grammatical markers. This distinctive manner of expression enabled Dōgen to navigate seamlessly between the two languages in productive and fascinating ways. But his eclectic approach to combining idioms can make for extremely difficult reading for those unfamiliar with the linguistic complexities of the Japanese constructions, especially when read in translation. Today's Japanese readers find the task of studying the *Treasury* a bit like English-speaking students trying to comprehend Chaucer in the original, which is rather close to archaic French, so they turn to translations into modern Japanese syntax (*gendaiyaku*) for guidance, along with related interpretative and reference materials.

In the highly contested religious context of the Kamakura era, the *Treasury* was designed to stake out positions carefully distinguishing Dōgen's teaching methods from those of other Buddhist schools, particularly but not limited to Rinzai Zen, by using a rhetorical style that borrowed heavily from, yet often revised and recast a vast storehouse of bewildering anecdotes, dialogues, and sayings featuring obscure allusions to remote teachers and texts. Throughout a career marked by numerous occasions of editing and polishing the *Treasury* fascicles right up until the time of his death, when he still considered the text unfinished, Dōgen was involved in an ongoing process of transmitting Chan expressions transformed into visionary but sometimes grammar-defying Japanese constructions. He developed many unique interpretations through clever turn-of-the-phrase remarks, crossing between languages that share a written script of glyphs or characters but have very distinct patterns of pronunciation and parsing.

In many cases, Dōgen appears to deliberately distort the original Chinese syntax in order to support conjectural arguments with eccentric appropriations of continental compositions. His method of writing includes intentional adjustments or inversions of typical verbal indicators to produce a bold new speculative standpoint or, in complementary fashion, to deconstruct and disentangle what he considers an outmoded motif. Dōgen proves himself capable of citing verbatim from a storehouse of Chan textual resources. But he also feels confident in reinterpreting or revising these in irreverent fashion through original elucidations that frequently modify wording to the extent that some critics have accused him of misrepresenting, unwittingly or not, the non-native tongue of the cited materials. Other interpreters praise his ability to foster intentionally "creative misunderstandings" of the sources.

The latter group of proponents claims that Dōgen purposely takes license with passages in Chinese so as to reveal metaphysical distinctions underlying everyday verbal expressions that reflected his personal experience of awakening. For example, the scholar Frédéric Girard, who has translated Dōgen's writings into French, analyzes an instance in which Dōgen rewrites a poem by Rujing that is cited in the fascicle, "The Perfection of Great Wisdom," and elsewhere, about the sounds made by a wind bell (Makahannya haramitsu: Dōgen 1.11, Nearman 28, Tanahashi 27). Dōgen's revision carefully preserves the rules for Chinese prosody used in the original passage, including rhyming and tonal patterns as well as lyrical imagery typical of continental verse. Girard argues, "We can conclude from this that [Dōgen] never commits error nor modification by ignorance nor omission by always knowing exactly what he is doing. The modifications of Dōgen are intentional, as in other cases when he modifies quotations of Rujing."[29]

Girard further suggests, "In the well-known example of *shinjin datsuraku* [casting off body-mind]: it is not an auditory misunderstanding which made him replace 'mental dusts' with 'body-mind' but a deliberate intention" to shift the meaning of the phrase.[30] Another modern scholar, He Yansheng, a Chinese national working in Japan who translated the *Treasury* into Mandarin and also published a book written in Japanese analyzing Dōgen's appropriations of Chinese sources, supports Girard's thesis by referring to Dōgen as a "genius of misreading" (*godoku tensai*).[31] He notes that Dōgen's text consistently stresses that some key expressions, such as "making the right mistake" (*shoshaku jushaku*, lit. "mistake piled on mistake") or "disentangling entanglements through the evocation of entanglements" (*kattō*, lit. "twining vines"), suggest the creative use of language as a liberating tool instead of a mental trap or a debilitating conceptual knot, in contrast to what the meanings of these phrases tend to imply.

Through embracing the standpoint of oneness that incorporates rather than rejects or suppresses a plurality of views, Dōgen's interpretative perspective is endlessly playful yet profoundly astute in exploring a tremendous diversity of Chinese sources he brought to Japan. His writing is replete with ingenious phrasings and philosophical wordplay that stimulate readers by continually overturning their expectations and fixed opinions with groundbreaking notions that, depending on circumstances, provoke either a positive or a negative evaluation of the topic under consideration. A seventeenth-century commentator once said of the *Treasury*'s intricate rhetoric, "Dōgen had the remarkably flexible ability to praise and celebrate or to criticize and censure various predecessors and ideas as he saw fit. This was based on a style of writing that is eminently accomplished in conveying oneness yet invariably ironic and paradoxical in articulating multiple pathways for realizing truth."[32]

Recasting Conventional Expressions

A principal instance that represents just one of dozens of examples showcasing Dōgen's rhetorical creativity in service to Zen theoretical insight is his radical interpretation of an everyday word normally indicating "sometimes" (*uji* 有時, also pronounced *arutoki* in Japanese). For Dōgen, the usual expression at once conceals and reveals a conjectural view of the essential harmony of "being-time," which he argues means that "all times (*ji* 時 or *toki*) are essentially all beings (*u* 有 or *aru*) and, conversely, all beings are all times" (Uji: Dōgen 1.240, Nearman 109, Tanahashi 104). Dōgen begins a fascicle of the *Treasury* titled "Being-Time," which is dedicated to examining thoroughly the topic of temporality, including the intricate relation between momentariness and continuity, by citing a traditional Zen saying attributed to the Chinese Master Yaoshan (745–827, Jp. Yakusan) about the relation between times and beings.

In this passage, Yaoshan suggests that all aspects of reality, ranging from standing on the highest mountain peak to plunging to the depths of the ocean, or from the seeming stability of a stone pillar to the motion of a teaching staff being wielded by a deft instructor, exist "sometimes," "at a particular time," "for the time being," or as an "existential moment."[33] Dōgen argues that the underlying connotation of the term *uji* suggests that each of these expressions reflects an instantiation of the indivisibility of being-time. Therefore, there is really no need to resort to an unnecessary use of wording, such as referring to incidences taking place "at," "for," "in," or "during" a temporal occasion, since using those supposedly commonsense dictions for ordinary happenings implies that time is merely an abstraction conceived of as a container holding separable entities that are somehow passing, one by one, through its invisible boundaries. Dōgen's analysis recalls St. Augustine's saying in *On Genesis* and in book XI of *The Confessions*, "What then is time? If no one asks me, I know; but if I want to explain it to a questioner, I do not know,"[34] in that the reference to not knowing evokes the profound complexity of the topic. On another level, according to some modern interpretations Dōgen's view resembles Einstein's critique of Newtonian physics in developing the theory of relativity by redefining the significance of the spacetime continuum.[35]

For Dōgen, typical axioms in many languages suggesting that time "flies like an arrow" or "flows quickly by like rushing water" are delusory because temporality is really no different than the projectile or the river itself, or any other fleeting object, since all things are invariably manifestations of being-time instead of entities that exist in time. His deceptively simple comments about the meaning of being-time are justifiable in that the multivalent term *u*, which can mean "has," also indicates "is" and further suggests "being" or "beings" in a more general sense. That implication would not be apparent from a typical conversation but nevertheless undergirds the function of customary speech patterns, even though that level of understanding usually remains unrecognized. He further maintains that flowers should not be seen as blooming in spring, as if the season were a fixed unit bearing diverse external items. Rather, blossoms themselves are spring in that each and every appearance of any given phenomenon participates in temporality by means of an assimilating process of incessant change, regardless of conventional designators that tend to carve the passage of time into segmented phases of past, present, and future.

In introducing his rendering of the *Treasury* fascicle, translator Hubert Nearman suggests that the notion of being-time is very much connected with the Zen master's existential situation based on his enlightenment attained in China: "Underlying the whole of Dōgen's presentation is his own experience of no longer being attached to any sense of a personal self that exists independent of time and of other beings, an experience that is part and parcel of his 'casting off body and mind.'"³⁶ Time and being are but two aspects of the selfsame dynamic reality in a view that is distinctively expressed by Dōgen but also basically consistent with traditional Buddhist notions suggesting that enlightenment reflects "the interrelationship of *anicca* (Skr. *anitya* Jp. *mujō*), 'the ever-changing flow of time,' and *anatta* (Skr. *anatman*, Jp. *muga*), 'the absence of any permanent self that exists within or independent of this flow of time.'"³⁷

In supporting while also revising key elements of basic Buddhist thought, Dōgen criticizes forcefully what he considers the single most insidious obstacle to attaining enlightenment that affects many approaches to Zen practice, including those of numerous Chinese and Japanese teachers he otherwise admires. Referred to as the "Senika (Skr. Śreṇika) heresy" (*Senni gedō*) in several fascicles of the *Treasury*, especially "Discerning the Way," "This Mind Itself Is Buddha" and "Buddha Nature," this term indicates an erroneous view derived from pre-Buddhist or Brahmanic Indian sources that infiltrated legitimate Buddhist thought. The Senika heresy suggests that the integrated essence of the intangible mind or soul abides forever, while the evanescent body and other tangible forms of existence must perish. Such a timeless or eternal view of substantive reality, also labeled the "naturalist heresy" (*jinen gedō*) by detractors, seems to have led practitioners to either adopt quietism or withdrawal from meditative practice or attempt to legitimate all activities as enlightened, rather than engaging with contemplative consciousness each and every moment. That view stands in contrast to Dōgen's emphasis on seeing nonthinking as an eminently dynamic approach reflecting the trainee's involvement with particular perspectives that continually shed light on the fundamental unity of being-time. Dōgen further argues in the fascicle "The Moon" that "only foolish people would look at the moon and clouds or at a boat drifting from shore and presume that one of the objects observed is stationary while the other is moving, since both partake of the unimpeded dynamism of reality" (Tsuki: Dōgen 1.265, Nearman 550, Tanahashi 456). All elements of existence are constantly shifting relative to one another, so that the appearance of being static or motionless is illusory and must be cast aside.

The notion of being-time as an example of extensive uses of inventive rhetorical techniques, such as ironies, reversals, and chiasmic expressions in addition to tautologies and axioms evoked in distinctive ways, was designed by Dōgen to rapidly expose his readers in Japan to a new body of imported continental religious literature and, more important, to immerse them in the topsy-turvy, through-the-looking glass standpoint of Zen teachings. Apparent inconsistencies abound and are to be embraced for representing a higher level of awareness, instead of rejected for apparent insufficiency according to ordinary logic. This alteration of awareness helps dissuade trainees from falling back on staid and stereotypical viewpoints so as to stimulate self-reflection that challenges conventional conceptual boundaries.

In thought-provoking remarks on being-time, Dōgen proposes that the usual distinctions between now and then, the fleetingness of the present moment versus the constancy of the realms of past and future, or the manifestations of a flower in contrast to the mental construct of spring as a cyclical occurrence, no longer apply from an awakened outlook that apprehends the truly vibrant, never-stagnant nature of existence as the locus of all experience. By making this argument Dōgen refutes commonly held assumptions, including those he considers deficient forms of Zen that betray an underlying attachment to the Senika heresy, in order to carve out distinguishing ideological positions vis-à-vis rival schools of thought.

The effect of Dōgen's approach based on imaginative interpretations of Chinese writings deliberately bewilders his reader so as to shift drastically their mode of thinking from everyday reason to the wisdom of the realm of nonthinking, which is unbound by the rules of logic yet can operate freely in terms of rationality when that level of discourse is appropriate to the pedagogical needs of a disciple. The *Treasury* frequently uses novel allusions and metaphorical expressions involving ingenious puns in addition to purposeful grammatical distortions of both Chinese and Japanese sources. These unusual discursive methods uncover the normally concealed levels of spiritual significance underlying experience even—or especially—when this stance upsets and inverts the typical sense of words and phrases. To cite a Chinese Chan saying that epitomizes Dōgen's outlook, a genuine teacher should try to startle his audience by "overturning the great ocean, kicking over Mount Sumeru [a mythical cosmic peak], scattering the white clouds with shouts, and breaking up empty space; straightaway, with one device or one object, he cuts off the tongues of everyone on earth!"[38]

CONCEPTUAL DISORIENTATIONS

The *Treasury* has long been seen as the touchstone of the Sōtō Zen sect's method of monastic training and as one of the hallmarks of premodern Japanese literature written to express religious truths. For several centuries after its composition the text was used mainly as a practical manual or sectarian guide for advanced meditative specialists, and it was often considered so complex that novices were warned not to try to read the disruptive work, lest they succumb to a sense of hopeless confusion and misapprehension. The trend of maintaining an exclusive sectarian focus in regard to studies of the *Treasury* was dramatically challenged in the early twentieth century by Watsuji Tetsurō (1889–1960), a well-known theorist of traditional Japanese culture associated with the nonsectarian Kyoto School of modern Japanese philosophy. Watsuji argues against the priority of the Sōtō tradition as the lens for appropriating the *Treasury* by advocating the universal significance of Dōgen's thought, a claim that was applauded by many secular readers yet criticized by orthodox proponents.

In his seminal book, *Monk Dōgen* (*Shamon Dōgen*), published in 1926 as the initial major nondenominational study of the Zen master's life and thought for a broad audience both in Japan and throughout the world, Watsuji maintains that Dōgen's writing is best understood as the philosophical expressions of a prominent religious thinker who should be appreciated by all of humanity.[39] He argues that Dōgen should no longer be regarded merely as the patriarch of the Sōtō sect, as if he were a relic of a medieval denomination whose members are often stubborn about explaining the words of the founding figure as exemplary of their vision of absolute truth. Watsuji's harsh critique of what he considers the corruption of modern Zen for being unworthy of upholding the authentic legacy of Dōgen was contested by factional advocates such as Etō Sokuō (1888–1958), who in 1939 published the first inexpensive paperback edition of the *Treasury* targeting a readership much broader than clerical specialists. A few years later Etō crafted a spirited defense of the role of zazen instruction as the central intellectual component of Dōgen's writing in the lengthy monograph, *Master Dōgen as Founder of a Religious Sect* (*Shūsō toshite no Dōgen Zenji*). He disputes trying to see the *Treasury* mainly as a record of philosophical reflections carried out separate from religious aspirations, as suggested in Watsuji's interpretation.[40]

Whether Watsuji's skeptical stance toward Sōtō-based understanding is accepted or Etō's apologetic view is preferred, the former's fresh perspectives helped bring international attention to the *Treasury*, so that its reputation now seems just as strong among a variety of nonmonastics as among religious affiliates. Tanabe Hajime (1885–1962), a prominent thinker from a Pure Land Buddhist background who was also affiliated with the Kyoto School and was influenced by Watsuji's book, generously praised Dōgen a decade later. In a slim volume titled *My Views on the Philosophy of the Treasury* (*Shōbōgenzō no tetsugaku shikan*) published in 1939, Tanabe declares he "is greatly impressed by the depth and accuracy of Dōgen's speculation," which he claims "strengthens my belief in the Japanese people's capacity of philosophical thinking."[41] For Tanabe, Dōgen is the most sophisticated Buddhist intellectual in the history of Japan and in many ways a direct precursor to contemporary global approaches to examining reality through the method of dialectical reasoning that explores various modes of thinking, including both premodern and modern theoretical standpoints, without being fixated on a particular mode of conceptualization belonging to a specific ideological movement.

In the near century since Watsuji's opus, the production of scholarly investigations and spiritual explanations of the *Treasury* has continued unabated in both Japan and the West. Because of resonances with present-day worldviews ranging from existential phenomenology and quantum physics to literary modernism and deconstructive social theory, all of which express in respective ways an understanding of the vitality of reality coupled with a surpassing of the borders of ordinary human perception and rationality, Dōgen's text is even more popular and widely read now than ever before. A Japanese term, *Genzō-ka*, referring to a "*Shōbōgenzō* aficionado" or "Genzōnian," was coined as early as the eighteenth century, which witnessed a major Sōtō Zen renewal of efforts to decipher the complexity of Dōgen's work. This term applies today to many kinds of readers on both sides of the Pacific with sectarian or unaffiliated backgrounds.

The term *Genzō-ka* suggests all who are knowledgeable about the status of Dōgen's text in relation to traditional Japanese Buddhism or comparative religious thought and ethics yet remain boundlessly eager to keep learning and polishing their interpretative skills through ongoing philological studies and theoretical investigations. This includes a continually enlarging group of enthusiasts involved in appreciating and appropriating Dōgen from different angles and for diverging purposes. Therefore, the medieval musings of a lineal patriarch have begun to realize their full significance now that the work is examined by a wide range of *Genzō-ka* for its intricate rhetorical flair in elucidating the long-lasting value of contemplative consciousness based on nonthinking.

The archives at Eiheiji along with the resources of the Buddhist studies department and related research institutes at Komazawa University in Tokyo, which was first established in the 1880s as the Sōtō Sect University (Sōtōshū Daigaku), are the central scholarly organizations supporting studies of the founder's main work.[42] Every year, there is a steady flow in Japan of densely researched scholarly tomes that investigate the origins and implications of the *Treasury* and its obscure Chinese references through evidential textual studies. In addition, researchers regularly publish translations of Dōgen's medieval syntax into contemporary semantic arrangements that try to make opaque phrasings accessible to nonspecialist readers.

Also featured among Japanese approaches to the *Treasury* over the past century are diverse methods of disseminating Dōgen's thought. These include: summer intensive retreats known as *Genzō-e* (lit. "*Treasury* meetings") each year at major monasteries for in-depth readings of selected portions of the text; Dharma talks (*hōgo*) or popular sermons by dozens of priests at various outlets, including temples and museums throughout the country, to explicate the work's diverse implications; and a highly condensed version called *Principles of Practice and Realization* (*Shushōgi*) recited during the performance of various Sōtō Zen rituals, such as funerals and memorial ceremonies. The *Principles* was first compiled in 1891 by a small group of leading lay practitioners who were responding in part to new competition from Christian missionaries. In order to make the *Treasury* accessible for uninformed readers and usable in rites, it includes from the entire text just thirty-one paragraphs with about 4,000 words divided into five thematic sections.

Among the newer avenues for popularizing Dōgen's masterwork and its contemporary significance, there is now available a wide range of introductory, how-to-read, and even *manga*-style illustrated presentations. A well-received Kabuki play and a recent high-profile biopic film highlighted the Sōtō founder's life and teachings around the time of the 800th death anniversary in 2003.[43] In addition, many dedicated readers in the West today are taking part in *Genzō-e* discussion sessions that are spreading worldwide as the transmission and translation of the *Treasury* continues to gain momentum. This is taking place after centuries during which the sheer difficulty of phrasings left the work more or less neglected except for a relative handful of experts knowledgeable about Dōgen's continental sources.

Receptions Mixed with Rejections

Despite the tremendously high standing and widespread acclaim it now receives on both sides of the Pacific, for various reasons the *Treasury* has had a surprisingly unsteady reception during much of the history since it was first composed by Dōgen. Over the centuries the text was well known primarily to a relative handful of Sōtō Zen institutional leaders or head priests at some of the main training temples, but not distributed or read throughout the denomination or beyond the sect except among a select group of Rinzai monk-scholars who often criticized the work. There was a lengthy period in late medieval Japan during which the *Treasury* was disregarded outside of a small circle of specialists, and many monasteries that owned a copy apparently used the manuscript more as a prestigious and powerful iconic possession than a text to be studied diligently. Serious investigations, it seems, were only conducted at Eiheiji, where copies were carefully kept in confidential status and occasionally made available to visitors.

Considerable interest in commenting on the *Treasury* in the Edo period (1603–1868) gave rise to dozens of detailed philological and philosophical commentaries created by leading Sōtō priests, who also studied other writings by Dōgen and early sect leaders. However, this development was accompanied by a prohibition on publishing the text that lasted for most of the eighteenth century. The ban was supported by the shogunate in conjunction with sectarian institutional administrators, who were hoping to avoid what they considered misrepresentations of the founder's major text. These distortions reflected sharp criticisms of Dōgen's use of Chinese sources promulgated by prominent commentators from both the Rinzai and Sōtō sects.[44] Because of the prohibition, interpreters who supported Dōgen's methods had to produce their annotations of the *Treasury* somewhat surreptitiously. Therefore, it is important to clarify the extent to which the work's reputation has waxed and waned over the centuries prior to a phenomenal modern revival that has resulted in ever-expanding global interest in reading this opaque tome that has always proved challenging for audiences.

Explaining this rocky reception acknowledges that basic difficulties, discrepancies, and disorientations involved in understanding the full significance of the *Treasury*'s arcane prose often arise because of several factors. The first is the lack of an authoritative edition of the text, since Dōgen was continually revising the manuscript and was still indecisive about the final edition by the time of his death. We simply cannot gauge the author's true intentions, and this has led to endless speculation on the part of traditional and contemporary researchers. Dōgen left behind several versions that were further edited by his trusted disciple and scribe, Ejō (1198–1280), who joined Dōgen's assembly in 1234 and succeeded him as abbot of Eiheiji, in collaboration with other prominent followers such as Gien (?–1314) and Giun (1253–1333). By the middle of the 1250s there existed several different manuscripts, including compilations containing 75, 60, 28, and 12 fascicles. Additional configurations with 83, 84, and 89 fascicles were developed by subsequent generations. Each of these versions had at least a couple of variants, although during the late medieval period the 60-fascicle edition prevailed.

Eventually, a comprehensive edition consisting of 95 fascicles was compiled in the 1690s by organizing all the available sections in the chronological order in which they were originally composed, even though dating is difficult or unknown in more than a few cases. This edition, considered definitive at the time, was long delayed and not completed until 1816. It was officially published in a commercial edition released to the public a century later, in 1906. Known as the Main Temple (Honzan) Edition because it was based on manuscripts held at Eiheiji, the 95-fascicle version was considered standard for much of the twentieth century and has served as the basis for most of the complete English translations (see appendix 4). However, nearly all Japanese scholarship since the 1970s has preferred to use an edition consisting of a combination of 75 fascicles and 12 fascicles in addition to miscellaneous fascicles, thus creating a text referred to as the Original (Kohon) Edition. Nevertheless, the matter is not entirely settled, as there remain significant debates among researchers about the validity and relative significance of the various editions.

The second factor causing disorientation in reading the *Treasury* pertains to Dōgen's extensive reliance on obscure citations interpreted in idiosyncratic fashion, some of which were probably intentionally misread but, in any case, are not easy to reconstruct and interpret in a meaningful way. For example, in a single sentence in the fascicle on "Disclosing a Dream Within a Dream," Dōgen uses the key phrase self-referentially six times in three grammatical modes (subject, object, action) and two tenses: "You should recognize that yesterday's explaining a dream within a dream was explaining a dream within a dream as explaining a dream within a dream, and today's explaining a dream within a dream is explaining a dream within a dream as explaining a dream within a dream" (Muchū setsumu: Dōgen 1.298, Nearman 504, Tanahashi 434). Some interpreters wonder whether this unusual form of expression helps clarify or further obfuscates the meaning of the term in question.

A third factor that puzzles numerous readers is apparent inconsistencies between fascicles dealing with a common topic that either were meant to target varying audiences, such as advanced monks, novices, or lay followers, or were written at different stages of Dōgen's career as his views apparently changed over time.[45] Some of the fascicles composed on distinct occasions or for disparate readerships may seem overlapping and repetitive or, conversely, unrelated and contradictory. Perhaps the single main example of such a discrepancy, to be discussed in greater detail in chapter 8, involves a traditional Zen dialogue known as the Fox Kōan, which deals with the issue of whether an adept remains subject to the law of karmic causality. In the fascicle on "Great Cultivation" written in 1244, Dōgen seems to agree with the mainstream view that causality and noncausality are of equal value, thus deemphasizing the moral consequences of action in favor of maintaining a transcendental meditative state. Despite this approach, in a later interpretation of the kōan included in the fascicle on "Deep Faith in Causality" written almost a decade later, he adamantly denies that standpoint and insists that the consequences of moral cause and effect invariably prevail and can never be avoided.

One of numerous inconsistencies implicit in studying his complex writings is that Dōgen is primarily known as the founding patriarch of the Sōtō sect, but the *Treasury* strongly disavows factional labels. So although he transmitted the Zen tradition to Japan, he was not necessarily interested in being considered the originator of a movement. That status was attributed to him through subsequent institutional initiatives that sought to gain prestige for the denomination by asserting that the eminent Master Dōgen was its formative leader. According to a prominent passage in the fascicle on "The Buddhist Way," which denies an emphasis on the notion of a single correct lineage, Dōgen maintains that seated meditation was always characteristic of authentic Buddhism since the time of Śākyamuni Buddha, regardless of superficial denominational discrepancies (Butsudō: Dōgen 1.471, Nearman 622, Tanahashi 501). Adamant about the universality of the experience of all Buddhist practitioners, he denies a special capacity for his own school and strongly discourages followers from contributing to contentious sectarian polemic while insisting they forego schismatic disputes. Denying factionalism by refuting the independence of Zen in favor of the uniformity of the Dharma eye as the essential component of all forms of Buddhism, regardless of labels, Dōgen writes: "In India and China from ancient times down to the present day, no one has ever spoken of 'the Zen sect,' which is the term by which foolish people arbitrarily refer to themselves. Such monks are demons out to destroy the Buddhist way; they are a divisive crowd who are enemies of buddhas and ancestors" (Butsudō: Dōgen 1.472, Nearman 623, Tanahashi 502).

Dōgen goes on to point out that Linji, the putative founder of the Chinese lineage that eventually became the rival Rinzai sect in Japan, bequeathed to his main disciple after he died not a separate school, only the repository of genuine insights (*shōbōgenzō*) that is uniformly shared by all Buddhist teachers. In "The Ancient Buddha Mind," he suggests by using intriguing chiasmic phrasing that self-realization based on casting off body-mind is at once the root and result of all lineages from time immemorial: "Prior to the appearance of all buddhas, the mind of ancient buddhas (*kobusshin*) blossoms; after the appearance of all buddhas, the mind of ancient buddhas bears fruit." Dōgen concludes the passage by proclaiming, "Prior to the mind of ancient buddhas, the ancient Buddha mind is cast off (*datsuraku*)" (Kobusshin: Dōgen 1.91, Nearman 570, Tanahashi 472).

Nevertheless, Dōgen frequently wields a scathingly critical rhetorical sword toward those Zen leaders, especially from the Linji/Rinzai faction but also including a few members of his own Caodong/Sōtō lineage, whom he considers deceptive teachers or falsifiers of genuine enlightenment. Dōgen even questions the legitimacy of enlightenment in commenting on Dahui (1089–1163), one of the most prominent Chinese Linji school thinkers of the Southern Song dynasty, who was probably the first to use the term *Shōbōgenzō* (Ch. *Zhengfayanzang*) as the title of a major collection of commentaries on kōan cases. This attack is included in a controversial passage in the fascicle on "Samādhi of Self-Realization," which was left out of some editions of Dōgen's masterwork by later editors to avoid misunderstandings about the author's views.[46] Even Dōgen's mentor, Rujing, is not altogether immune from skeptical reactions and is occasionally subjected to critiques or rewritings proffered by his former student.

In this vein, modern interpreter Thomas Kasulis suggests, "To read the *Shōbōgenzō* carefully is hard work,"[47] because various linguistic and historical as well as Buddhist complexities make it seem indecipherable. Even with diverse reference materials piling up on one's desk, or as PDF files accumulating on a laptop, including annotations, chrestomathies, citation lists, chronologies, commentaries, concordances, critical editions, dictionaries, glossaries, grammars, historical narratives, indexes, maps, and timelines, "individual [passages] assume unfathomable depth, but somehow the basic meaning is still elusive."[48] Puqun Li remarks, "One must read selected chapters from the *Shōbōgenzō* extremely slowly. Dōgen's ideas are profound and radical; his writing style is pithy, poetic, but often notoriously difficult."[49] The master's exacting manner of communication, which is key to the captivating quality of the *Treasury*, often enthralls and arouses but may also frustrate and discourage many readers. That was one of the reasons medieval Sōtō novices, who lacked a strong foundation in Chinese sources, tended to either overlook the text or become hypercritical of it. This difficulty applies to sectors of the contemporary audience with considerably less linguistic background than is needed to interpret the work's multifaceted themes.

Due to the various aspects of disorientation, including the incomplete and inconclusive quality of textual construction as well as difficulties in deciphering the meaning of the writing, some modern Japanese scholars have referred to the *Treasury* as "a tentative or provisional (*toriaezu*) and thus contested text."[50] Many of the passages were composed for dissimilar purposes and at different times and places during Dōgen's career. Somewhat unusual among the masterpieces of philosophy of religion, this feature nevertheless contributes to an appreciation for the spontaneity and open-endedness of the original work.

In order to analyze the value of the composition that was crafted by Dōgen for wide-ranging pedagogical purposes, it is necessary to clarify the overall historical context in addition to the author's life story. Therefore, a careful study surveys objectively diverse developmental and structural issues regarding the planning and organization of the *Treasury* so as to capture the richness and vitality permeating Dōgen's high-minded discursive efforts, which in recent decades have garnered considerable international praise. This analytic outlook links the skeptical concerns of impartial researchers, who highlight the text's apparent inconsistencies or discontinuities, with the subjective beliefs of enthusiastic meditators, who focus on its underlying unity, by showing that those perspectives are not necessarily opposing modes of thought when it comes to unraveling the complexity and originality of this work.

Looking at the hermeneutic situation from Dōgen's own standpoint, when the overall interpretative context of Zen sayings is properly understood, all the words of participants in various kōan dialogues or verbal exchanges, whether seeming to be enlightened and self-realized or unenlightened and deluded, are of equal value in communicating the true Dharma. The extensive battery of discursive devices used by Dōgen in support of a purposely ambiguous approach to expounding Buddhist theory and practice encourages the audience to read the text in a self-reflective way that continually involves "constructive entanglements" (*kattō*). As a modern expert once suggested to a colleague who was having difficulty in interpreting the *Treasury*, "In the final analysis, no one—not any commentary, not I, no other scholar—can teach you. The correct Dharma (*shōbo* [as in the work's title]) is you."[51]

{ 2 }

RECEPTIVITY AND RELIABILITY

NUMEROUS LEVELS OF SIGNIFICANCE

STATUS OF THE TEXT

The *Treasury of the True Dharma Eye* is widely recognized as one of the greatest representatives of worldwide religious literature because it absorbs and reflects, yet also surpasses and outshines, so many different East Asian Buddhist textual and cultural influences that Dōgen incorporated into his teachings about the theory and practice of seated meditation for new followers of Zen. To appreciate the text's singular status, we can turn to an ancient Zen saying cited by Dōgen in the postscript to the fascicle "Spring and Autumn": "There are many beasts with horns, but having just one unicorn (*kirin*, Ch. *qilin*) is more than enough" (Shunjū: Dōgen 1.415, Nearman 754, Tanahashi 637). In other words, a single outstanding composition at once encompasses and stands apart from the crowd of other available materials.

The main reason for the *Treasury*'s towering reputation involves the complex ways that Dōgen draws creatively yet critically from voluminous Chinese records of enlightenment experiences contained in kōan cases with copious commentaries. In addition, he offers evaluations of key passages culled from seminal Mahāyāna Buddhist scriptures, especially the *Flower Garland Sūtra* (Ch. *Huayan jing*, Jp. *Kegonkyō*), *Lotus Sūtra* (Ch. *Fahuajing*, Jp. *Hokkekyō*), *Nirvāṇa Sūtra* (Ch. *Niepan jing*, Jp. *Nehangyō*), and *Vimalakīrti Sūtra* (Ch. *Wéimójiéjing*, Jp. *Yuimagyō*), which provide parables and doctrinal enunciations about the attainment of insight based on awakening the true Dharma eye. Modern Japanese researchers have carefully documented the basis for almost every direct citation or indirect reference to previous Zen teachers and Buddhist texts, as well as the writings of secular literati, that appear in the printed pages (originally handwritten scrolls) of the *Treasury*. They also offer various explanations of Dōgen's interpretative methods in quoting and recasting these multifarious sources.

One of the most important works in this research category is *Dōgen's Citations of Recorded Sayings and Sūtras* (*Dōgen Zenji no in'yō kyōtengoroku*), published in 1965 by Kagamishima Genryū (1912–2001), the leading postwar scholar in the field of Dōgen studies.[1] Kagamishima shows that the words of Śākyamuni Buddha, with nearly seventy citations mainly from various sūtras, and of Rujing, with more than forty mentions from his recorded sayings in addition to Dōgen's recollections of his mentor's sermons, are by far given the most attention.[2] Dozens of other Zen leaders are also quoted extensively, including First Patriarch Bodhidharma (n.d.), Sixth Patriarch Huineng (638–713, Jp. Eno), Rinzai school founder Linji (d. 866, Jp. Rinzai), Sōtō school founder Dongshan (807–869, Jp. Tōzan) and additional prominent masters featured in numerous kōan narratives such as Zhaozhou (778–897) and Yunmen (862–949, Jp. Unmon). Dōgen's facility with citing so many continental religious leaders originally discussed in diverse textual genres, along with his mastery in summoning rhetorical resources for innovatively rendering and ingeniously interpreting these materials, enables the *Treasury* to weave effortlessly through a wide range of literary extractions and associations evoked to explicate diverse Zen topics.

Indian Buddhist writings redacted in Chinese translations also figure prominently in the *Treasury*. Citations from these sources include theoretical expressions of the temporal conditions and causal factors of human and natural existence, in addition to morality tales concerning miracles or exorcisms symbolizing the effects of karmic retribution carried out by protective deities, advanced practitioners, or inspired converts. Furthermore, various types of Chinese folklore, in addition to secular poetry that was often very much interactive with Buddhist writings, are well integrated into the *Treasury*. This category includes numerous references to examples of Confucian and Daoist thought, even though in the fascicle "Four Meditative Stages of a Monk" Dōgen strongly disapproves of the then-common motif of identifying Zen with the essence of all three Chinese religious traditions (Shizen biku: Dōgen 2.464, Nearman 601, Tanahashi 863).

Other East Asian materials cited by Dōgen range from imperial legends concerning the impact of generosity or compassion and deceit or treachery, which are conjured in several fascicles as exemplary of how the Buddhist Dharma affects secular life, to references to famed Chinese poets from different epochs, such as Bai Juyi (772–846) and Su Shi (a.k.a. Su Dongpo, 1037–1101), who were both said to have been awakened by encounters with Zen teachers. In the fascicle "Refrain from Committing Evil," Dōgen discusses a cryptic dialogue about making moral choices that took place between Bai Juyi and the wise Chan meditator Daolin (741–824), who was said to have resided in the branches of a tree for so many years that he became known as the Bird's Nest Monk (Shoaku makusa: Dōgen 1.349–352, Nearman 85–88, Tanahashi 101–103). In "Sounds of Valleys, Colors of Mountains," Dōgen offers an intriguing interpretation that calls into question the symbolism of a celebrated verse by Su Shi about an insight he realized while meditating one night at a temple located in a beautiful natural landscape that, in his reverie, came to signify the physical features of the Buddha during the act of preaching (Keisei sanshoku: Dōgen 1.274–276, Nearman 66–68, Tanahashi 85–87).

Dōgen's text also features allusions to indigenous literary traditions, especially regarding the topic of the poignancy of impermanent existence symbolized by the changing of the four seasons as expressed in thirty-one-syllable *waka* poetry and various prose sources, including epic (*monogatari*) and self-reflective (*zuihitsu*) writings. Dōgen's corpus exerted a strong influence on the theoretical works of Zeami (1363–1443), one of the founders of Noh theater, and also left a lasting impression on haiku poet Bashō (1716–1783), who refers to going out of his way to visit secluded Eiheiji temple in his celebrated travel journal, *Narrow Road to the Deep North* (*Oku no hosomichi*). Moreover, in "Spring and Autumn" (Shunjū: Dōgen 1.411–412, Nearman 748–749, Tanahashi 633) and other fascicles such as "Disentangling Vines" and "Ocean Seal Samādhi," Dōgen cites examples of strategies for playing competitive games of chess (*go*), in which the movement of pieces on the game board becomes a metaphor for the strategic interpersonal dynamics of master-disciple relationships. In the fascicle "Disclosing a Dream Within a Dream," he evokes the image of scales used to weigh items for sale as symbolic of trying to achieve impartiality and fairness (Muchū setsumu: Dōgen 1.299–300, Nearman 506–507, Tanahashi 435–436) in ethical decision making.

In addition to equaling or exceeding in esteem many of its major influences, the eminence of the style and content of the *Treasury* has long eclipsed the impact of successive writings produced by Zen thinkers over the past eight centuries. Dōgen's masterwork remains the premier text in the history of the Sōtō sect and medieval Japanese Buddhism more generally. In Edo-period Japan, various scholar-monks composed dozens of in-depth commentaries and produced many new editions. Even though some Rinzai Zen priests such as Mujaku (1653–1744) were sharply critical of Dōgen's apparent misreading of Chinese sources, the most renowned Rinzai master of the era, Hakuin (1686–1768), who otherwise was skeptical of rival Sōtō thinkers, lavishly praised the magisterial creativity of Dōgen's text.[3] Whether appropriated today by sectarian teachers of meditation abiding in a training monastery, secular scholars and comparative philosophers of religion working in the academy, or other enthusiasts with a strong interest in studying traditional mystical writings, the *Treasury* consistently receives nearly unmatched acclaim. It generates countless practical applications as well as learned studies examining the text from diverse homiletic and analytic perspectives, part of a long-term disseminative trend that has been increasing in recent years.

This chapter explores various aspects of the *Treasury*'s significance in light of manifold ways the work has been construed by commentators, including critics and skeptics along with supporters and guardians who cherish its legacy. It shows that Dōgen was at once a caretaker or protector and a destabilizer or disruptor by preserving and transferring, yet altering what he considered the strengths and weaknesses of the Zen tradition to suit his idiosyncratic, unwavering vision of truth. Current scholarship on Dōgen is similarly subject to the twofold function of creative appropriations that uphold and unravel the merits of his classic. The main areas of importance include: (a) the historical and doctrinal impact of the *Treasury* on the overall development of East Asian religion and society; (b) the personal and spiritual implications of this work for understanding Dōgen's life and career choices; (c) levels involving lineage and pedagogy; (d) the philological and philosophical ramifications of the master's rhetorical methods evoked to articulate his distinctive view of spiritual awakening; (e) the behavioral and moral repercussions of Dōgen's approach to employing meditative discipline in ritual routines and moral crises; and (f) the global and topical implications of applying the *Treasury* to wide-ranging contemporary social and philosophical issues.

HISTORICAL AND DOCTRINAL LEVELS

Even though the lofty status of the *Treasury* in its original Japanese setting was not fully appreciated for centuries, it seems clear that Dōgen himself recognized during his lifetime the influential role his work would eventually play, serving as a primary fulcrum of intellectual advancement at a critical turning point in the historical trajectory of Buddhism in East Asia. Dōgen's writing contributed to the transplantation of the incipient Zen movement just when medieval Japanese society was shifting away from aristocratic regency and toward the leadership of the recently empowered samurai.[4] The function of Buddhism made a drastic transition from the pageantry and ritualism of Tendai esoteric teachings to a focus on the personal quest for salvation characteristic of the Kamakura Buddhist emphasis on individual soteriological goals. Dōgen understood that the *Treasury* would be seen as the major crossover work implementing an innovative approach to the diffusion of continental religious writings and observances. That is why he devoted so much time and energy to editing and revising different versions of the manuscript, to the extent that this task was still in progress when he died.

When compared to the other emerging sects of the medieval period, all of which recommended that their followers make the "selection" (*senjaku*) of a particular method for attaining enlightenment, Dōgen is noted for advocating the path of just sitting, which is usually seen in contrast to the Rinzai Zen emphasis on kōan investigation (*kanna zen*, Ch. *kanhua chan*) or introspection based on solving the puzzle of particular case narratives. Nevertheless, the common view of contemplation supported by the Sōtō and Rinzai sects can be differentiated from the recitation of Buddha's name (*nembutsu*) used in the Pure Land school, the act of giving thanks for the grace of Amida Buddha preached in True Pure Land, and venerating the title of the *Lotus Sūtra* evoked in Nichiren. None of these multifaceted religious standpoints can or should be reduced to a single or simple idea. Dōgen's teachings, therefore, must be examined for their extensive references to many different aspects of Zen Buddhist theory and practice based on, but by no means limited to, the function of seated meditation without necessarily excluding some of the religious principles endorsed by non-Zen sects, especially appreciation for the *Lotus Sūtra*.

By virtue of his advanced knowledge and ability to coordinate key aspects of imported and indigenous Buddhist teachings, Dōgen's writing in the *Treasury* constructs novel philosophical explorations of the meaning of sentient and insentient existence, of momentary experience in relation to the continuity of time, and of overcoming delusion through creative uses of language. Major doctrinal themes expressed in the text concern lofty ruminations on the concept of the all-encompassing Buddha nature, advocated in varying ways by all East Asian Buddhist schools, seen in terms of how apprehending impermanence inspires an individual's striving to gain spontaneous illumination (*satori*). Other issues include an analysis of the nondual or unified nature of reality linked to disparities of human knowledge; coming to terms with contingency and mortality that affect the urgency of the quest for awakening; and identifying the capacities as well as limitations of perception and expression in order to divulge the quality of realization liberated from ordinary conceptual fetters.

The *Treasury* also provides detailed guidelines for maintaining a steadfast resolve to sustain daily monastic activities that support contemplative consciousness. The same body of writing that speculates about how to perceive the movement of time by radically adjusting the typical view of anticipation and resolve switches abruptly to specific instructions for clerical conduct. Dōgen's masterwork is unusually detailed in its practical guidelines regarding how to read and recite sūtras or to prepare food, scrub floors, take baths, and perform numerous other rites of behavioral etiquette as examples of spiritual renewal that contribute to perpetuating mindfulness within the confines of the monastery gates. Guidelines cover such practices as washing one's face, brushing teeth, folding robes (which he says he learned to do properly for the first time by observing monks on the mainland), and rinsing after going to the toilet so as not to despoil the same fingers used for eating meals, cleaning the body, or handling sacred objects.

In the fascicle "Washing the Face," which was delivered on three separate occasions at different sites (Kōshōji in 1239, an Echizen mountain retreat in 1243, and Eiheiji in 1250), highlighting its importance for guiding novices, Dōgen shows how the simple act of cleaning one's teeth is correlated with cleansing the mind in maintaining mystical as well as physical purity. He writes extensively about chewing the willow twig, a device used in Buddhist monasticism that was one of a few hygienic practices not followed strictly enough in China, where monks often grew long fingernails to imitate Confucian lords eager to show their disdain for menial labor.

By evoking Mahāyāna scriptures, Dōgen describes the length and thickness of the twig, how to chew on and clean it, and ways to store and discard this tool so that it will not soil one's clothes or befoul the environment (Senmen: Dōgen 2.44, Nearman 672–673, Tanahashi 63). The *Treasury* also treats extensively the link between meditative exercises and devotional rites, such as venerating sūtra scrolls or stupas, that similarly manifest or reveal the experience of awakening. Several fascicles address the ethical consequences of Zen's utopian mystical teachings related to the functions of karmic retribution and repentance while negotiating moral decision making in regard to troublesome personal and conflictive societal situations.

Zen monastic regulations (*shingi*) stipulated in various *Treasury* fascicles deal with holding services for penitential rites and petitions, convening funerals and memorial services, celebrating anniversaries and other commemorative occasions, participating in annual summer retreats, and distributing blessings or opportunities to earn merit to novice and lay disciples or hosting donors for banquets held as fundraisers in temple halls. Each and every activity is considered an essential component of the comprehensive state of nonthinking that must be cultivated with the same sense of enduring commitment that is applied to contemplative practice. The proper ways of eating meals, bathing, and carrying out every task on the temple grounds represent direct, unimpeded manifestations of Zen insight.[5]

The *Treasury* is celebrated for its remarkable literary value as the first major Buddhist work written in the vernacular. The text is largely based on inventive appropriations of Chinese materials that Dōgen was translating, and thereby transforming, for a native audience by casting the original paradox-laden expressions into Japanese constructions. Despite its idiosyncratic style, Dōgen's text has affinities with other Buddhist self-reflections while living in the midst of evanescent reality (*mujō*) that were written during the Kamakura era. These works include the prestigious collection of waka poetry titled the *New Collection of Old Verses* (*Shinkokinshū*) and the short but powerfully symbolic eremitic essay *An Account of My Hut* (*Hōjōki*) by Kamo no Chōmei (1155–1216), both of which were produced in the early 1200s. Another example of this genre from a century later is the diverse musings on temple life related to secular society in *Essays in Idleness* (*Tsurezuregusa*) by Yoshida Kenkō (1284–1350). During a historical period ravaged by civil war and the effects of numerous natural disasters, including typhoons, earthquakes, and fires, Japanese culture gave priority to expressing truth through literary and visual arts rather than philosophical reasoning. Dōgen's rhetoric reflects a worldview that embraces with equanimity the profoundly ephemeral, egoless quality of all aspects of human and natural existence. As in the writings of his contemporaries, this outlook provides the basis for overcoming attachments and desires that impede a realization of religious truth underlying yet surpassing the limitations of ordinary self-awareness.

Beyond the local context, Dōgen's approach is appreciated for helping to frame wide-ranging discussions of Buddhist theory from the standpoint of Zen meditative practice. Reading and interpreting the *Treasury* helps develop a broader understanding of the overall spread of Buddhism in Asian societies, where it has been influenced by, yet also competed with, various indigenous religions. Dōgen frequently discusses themes that are central to all Buddhist schools, ranging from the doctrines of karma and causality used in analyzing the roots of suffering to the redemptive practices of confession and devotion through daily rites and chants based on following monastic precepts. His views on the unqualified identity of impermanence and Buddha nature, a topic usually analyzed in terms of a stark contrast between the temporal and the eternal, draw on long-standing debates among factions of Indian philosophy as well as Chinese and Japanese thought. Dōgen's approach to shaping human perception and perspectives through contemplation reflects inspirations absorbed from Confucian, Daoist, and Shinto spirituality along with the world of secular letters and calligraphic arts.[6]

PERSONAL AND SPIRITUAL LEVELS

In addition to serving as a vehicle for understanding many of the sweeping changes in religiosity that affected the development of a Japanese epoch, the *Treasury* is an important resource for understanding key aspects of Dōgen's personal life and career transitions. This is particularly the case with regard to his retrospective reflections concerning the spiritual reasons for and results of his travels to China, as well as his reactions to residing in Kyoto and Echizen province, where his informal sermons were delivered and edited as fascicles.

On the one hand, neither Dōgen nor his immediate followers were especially concerned with producing an accurate record of his exploits that would be considered acceptable according to modern historiographical standards. Much of what we know about his biography beyond the basic facts of birth, death, and travels, some aspects of which are contested, comes from sectarian accounts produced half a century or more after his demise that incorporated and thus legitimated numerous myths and legends then in circulation. Although considered interesting and illuminating from a religious standpoint, these records are unreliable hagiographies or pseudo-histories that function in ways typical of earlier Chan chronicles produced in China by mixing some facts with a lot of fiction. For example, when he was preparing to leave the mainland in 1227, Dōgen supposedly scared away a threatening tiger through the power of meditation; received medicine for an upset stomach from a Japanese folk deity who magically appeared in his path; copied a major kōan collection in a single night with the aid of another divinity just before his departure; and was saved during a typhoon by the appearance in the Sea of Japan of the mysterious bodhisattva Kannon (Ch. Guanyin) floating on a single leaf. Another major flaw of premodern accounts is that Dōgen and his profilers fail to explain clearly the basis of some of his most important career choices, such as the move from the capital to the provinces in 1243 or the trip four years later to the temporary urban center in Kamakura, where he apparently declined an offer from the shogun to lead a new temple. How and why these events transpired remains unclear.

Some important answers to basic questions about Dōgen's motivations and impulses are revealed within the discursive innovations of the *Treasury*'s theoretical explications. He was clearly intent on creating the contours of a spiritual autobiography reflecting a dramatic tale of self-doubt and uncertainty followed by experiences of renewal and redemption that won the respect and appreciation of both followers and rulers. Dōgen was greatly influenced by Song-dynasty Chinese narratives about the religious development of pioneering Chan monks, who often overcame numerous challenges and obstacles, including periods of exile from the capital, before becoming eminent teachers recognized and rewarded by the secular rulers of society. In particular, his writings convey vividly the grave doubt he felt while first training at Mount Hiei and Kenninji temple in Japan and the firm resolution he attained in China under Rujing's tutelage, as well as his mixed feelings regarding reclusion in relation to organizations. This account is designed to stimulate the pursuit of awakening among potential disciples by showing that Dōgen journeyed to the mainland in the spring of 1223 because he felt the true Dharma (*shōbō*) was not available in his native land. Based on what he learned from Eisai and Myōzen, he expected that only Chinese monasteries were imbued with enough authentic practice to provide access to genuine Zen teachings. Various passages of the *Treasury* along with other works are useful for understanding the transformative experiences Dōgen realized through the diligent practice of seated meditation and applied to building a sustainable Zen institution.

In "Discerning the Way," the initial fascicle composed while he still lived in a small hut in Kyoto for a couple of years before opening Kōshōji temple, his first of two major training monasteries, in 1233, Dōgen puts in perspective the purpose of his overall religious path. He states in the postscript, "This was recorded on the mid-autumn day of 1231 by the mendicant monk Dōgen, who went to Song China so that he might receive and bring back to Japan the transmission of the Dharma" (Bendōwa: Dōgen 2.481, Nearman 24, Tanahashi 22). In the opening section Dōgen succinctly sums up in a confessional tone the crucial period leading up to, through, and following his pilgrimage:

> After the aspiration for enlightenment arose in me, I began to search for the Dharma by visiting teachers at various places in our country. Then I went to Kenninji temple and began training with Master Myōzen. The autumn dews and spring flowers went by quickly for nine years, during which I learned the teachings of the Rinzai Zen school. Only Myōzen, as Eisai's senior disciple, had authentically received transmission of the unsurpassable Buddha Dharma. No one else in Japan could match what he alone accomplished.
>
> Then I went to Song China [with Myōzen], where I visited learned elders on both sides of the Yangzi River in Zhejiang province and heard the teachings of the Five Houses of Chan. Finally, I became a student of Master Rujing of Mount Tiantong and was able to fully resolve the great doubt that stimulated my quest. After a couple of years, I came back to Japan with the vision of spreading the Dharma to all sentient beings. I understood that this was quite a heavy burden to bear, so I decided to bide my time until I was free of all traces of the discriminating mind. (Bendōwa: Dōgen 2.461, Nearman 2–3, Tanahashi 4)

In the fascicle "Face-to-Face Transmission," Dōgen reminisces about the intense feelings of anticipation at the time of the first meeting with his mentor, and how this experience dramatically affected the rest of his odyssey in China and subsequent lifelong teaching mission (Menju: Dōgen 2.60, Nearman 841, Tanahashi 569–570). Based on the direct personal encounter with Rujing in the fifth month of 1225 that was presaged by dreams and heralded through an intuitive mutual recognition by both parties, Dōgen was allowed the rare privilege, almost unheard of for a foreign practitioner, of being given entrée from 1225 to 1227 into the private quarters of the master to receive the most advanced teachings. An account of these conversations is contained in the *Record of the Hōkyō Era* (*Hōkyōki*), although there is a debate about whether Dōgen compiled the record at the time or created it retrospectively later in his career.

Dōgen held Rujing in the highest regard among the Chinese masters he read of or studied with. This is especially expressed in several fascicles composed in 1243, about a year after Dōgen received via messengers arriving from the continent a copy of Rujing's freshly edited collection of recorded sayings (*goroku*, Ch. *yulu*). *Treasury* writings in response to this text mainly were composed while Dōgen's assembly was staying temporarily in small hermitages for nine months of hardship over the long winter in the Echizen mountains while awaiting the construction of Eiheiji. Eager to trumpet some of the key passages from Rujing's sayings, Dōgen apparently felt that the official version did not adequately convey the grandeur of his mentor's style of teaching, so he amplified the record by including additional citations and making various observations that were not part of the compilation he received. In the fascicles "Plum Blossoms" and "Eyeball," both composed during this pivotal period, Dōgen quotes Rujing's maxims and poems more than half a dozen times each, including a number of examples he recalled being spoken that were left out of the official record.

In another tribute to his mentor, the fascicle "True Form of All Dharmas" offers a detailed description of the enthusiasm felt by disciples whenever Rujing presented a sermon in the hallowed halls of Mount Tiantong. According to this account, near the fourth watch on a night in the third month of 1226, Dōgen heard "three beats from the summoning drum. Putting on my robe and taking my sitting mat," he reports, "I left the Cloud Hall [a dormitory for itinerant monks] and saw that a sign inviting entrance to the master's room for a private meeting (nyūshitsu, Ch. rushi) had been hung" (Shohō jissō: Dōgen 1.468, Nearman 605, Tanahashi 528).[7] After describing various buildings on the monastic compound linked by passageways, staircases, and entries, Dōgen reports that other members of the assembly were lined up to offer incense and make prostrations while the abbot's quarters were screened off to ensure privacy.

Rujing's lecture that night, Dōgen recalls, offered a vivid and inspiring description of an esteemed Tang-dynasty Chan recluse, Damei (752–839), whose deep commitment to strict ascetic practice left him wearing dried leaves and eating pine nuts. This speech brought the crowd of followers to tears. Rujing concluded with a verse, "The golden-faced Gautama [Buddha] explicates the true form of things. / Even if you want to buy this, it is priceless. / The song of a cuckoo flying by is heard far above a solitary cloud" (Shohō jissō: Dōgen 1.467, Nearman 604, Tanahashi 527). When the poem was finished, Rujing struck the right arm of his meditation seat with his hand and announced, "Enter my room for your personal session." His topic for each monk's meeting held that auspicious evening was, "The night bird cries out and the bamboo on the mountain splits open" (Shohō jissō: Dōgen 1.469, Nearman 606, Tanahashi 528), but Rujing offered no commentary, and most members of the large assembly were unable to respond quickly as they were simply awed by the teacher's presence. Since there was no fixed schedule while the assembly remained standing, interviews took place with whichever monk felt prepared and volunteered to engage with Rujing's pedagogical acumen. When a session was finished the monk departed through the door of the abbot's quarters, but those who remained could see and hear everything taking place. Eighteen years after an occasion he remembered so vividly, Dōgen suggests that this method of conducting an innovative spiritual consultation was not used anywhere else in China. Only his late teacher Rujing performed the function authentically.

The relatively simple but highly effective instructional model based on intense spiritual consultations that was established by Rujing and recalled by Dōgen motivated the rather unusual way the *Treasury* was created, as a loosely knit compilation of sermons initially delivered without a systematic organizational structure. According to fascicle postscripts, Dōgen presented some of the talks in the middle of the night because of a unique inspiration or in response to the current teaching situation. For example, the fascicle "Mountains and Rivers Proclaiming the Sūtras," in which Dōgen emphatically supports the clarity of Zen sayings that suggest such radical ideas as "mountains walk or flow like waters" (Sansuikyō: Dōgen 1.319, Nearman 144, Tanahashi 158), was originally given at midnight during the tenth month of 1240 in reply to questions raised by disciples about how to interpret various kōan case narratives.

Similarly, "Radiant Light," featuring fantastic images of illumination understood to be symbolic of spiritual experience rather than a physical force, was a lecture delivered at 2 a.m. in the summer of 1242, during one of the darkest and most dreary nighttime skies of the year when "a drenching storm caused rain to pour down and gush from the temple's eaves" (Kōmyō: Dōgen 1.144, Nearman 490, Tanahashi 421). The postscript notes that members of the assembly were invited to discover their own brightness by resolving a case attributed to Yunmen suggesting that everyone possesses an interior light. In addition, "Plum Blossoms" was presented during a three-foot blizzard in the early winter of 1243, shortly after Dōgen moved from Kyoto to the northerly mountains. This fascicle interprets several verses authored by Rujing and other teachers that evoke natural symbolism associated with the onset of spring, when the budding of beautiful, fragrant plum flowers is intertwined with but prevails over the last traces of snow.

According to a Rujing poem giving words of encouragement and hope for renewal in the midst of winter, "The thornlike old plum tree / Suddenly bursts forth, first with one or two blossoms, / Then with three, four, five, and ultimately a countless array of blossoms.... Their scattering represents a springtime tableau as petals are blown over the grass and trees" (Baika: Dōgen 2.69, Nearman 683–684, Tanahashi 581). Dōgen comments:

> Blossoms of the old plum tree suddenly bursting into bloom seemingly from out of nowhere ... reflect spontaneous spiritual transformations in ways that are inexhaustible. This reveals that the great earth and the heavens above, alongside the luminous sun and clear moon, function with the merit of those ancient trees that represent entwining entanglements (*kattō*) within [and, thereby, liberation from] entanglements. (Baika: Dōgen 2.70, Nearman 684, Tanahashi 582)

LINEAL AND PEDAGOGICAL LEVELS

Around the time he moved to establish Eiheiji temple in the early to mid 1240s, Dōgen started the long, ultimately unfinished process of revising the lengthy manuscript. For the first time, he used the term *Treasury of the True Dharma Eye* as the main title for all the accumulated fascicles being transcribed in freshly produced handwritten scrolls. Each section was from then on known, for example, as "*Treasury* 'Plum Blossoms.'" This title was based on a long-standing legend about the origins of Zen Buddhism transpiring through a silent mind-to-mind transmission that is said to have occurred spontaneously between Śākyamuni and one of his ten main disciples, Mahākāśyapa, who was known as the leading adept of ascetic training. After the death of Śākyamuni, Mahākāśyapa assumed the leadership of the monastic assembly and compiled the Buddha's sayings with the assistance of five hundred followers, becoming the first disciple to propagate those teachings. As indicated by his gentle, all-knowing smile, Mahākāśyapa was the only student attending an assembly on Vulture Peak who fully understood the significance of the Buddha simply holding up a single flower while giving a sermon instead of relying on ordinary language to explain his ideas. In recognition of Mahākāśyapa's intuitive insight indicated by his insightful grin, Śākyamuni said that he entrusted to him the treasury of the eye of (or insights into) the true Dharma (*shōbōgenzō*, Ch. *zhengfayanzang*) and the wondrous mind of *nirvāṇa* (*nehan myōshin*, Ch. *niepan miaoxin*), or the true form of the formless and subtle entry through the passages of the Dharma gate.

The legend of Vulture Peak is recorded in numerous Chinese Chan texts, especially case 6 of the collection of kōan commentaries titled the *Gateless Gate* (Ch. *Wumenguan*, Jp. *Mumonkan*), first published in 1229 by Wumen

(Jp. Mumon) and later a mainstay of the Japanese Zen curriculum. According to the text's ironic comments that playfully equate Śākyamuni's approach with the greatest deceptions needed to get across the unique quality of his transmission beyond ordinary language: "Gold-faced Gautama insolently degrades noble people to commoners. He sells dog meat under the sign of mutton and thinks it is quite commendable. Suppose that all of the monks at the time had smiled—then how would the treasury of the true Dharma eye (*shōbōgenzō*) have been transmitted? Or suppose that Mahākāśyapa had not smiled—how could he have been entrusted with the legacy?"[8] By emphasizing in tongue-in-cheek fashion the Buddha's duplicity and the assembly's lack of competence, this verse highlights the paradoxical quality of Zen expressions that at once reveal and conceal the Dharma.

The transmission received by Mahākāśyapa was later disseminated to successive ancestors. These included Bodhidharma, the Twenty-Eighth Patriarch in India, who was said to have first brought the Chan style of meditation to China in the sixth century, and the Sixth Chinese Patriarch Huineng, who initiated the notion of sudden awakening as the key method of attaining enlightenment, subsequently accepted by almost all Zen factions including Dōgen's lineage. Chan teaching continued to spread throughout China. Although available to everyone, this standpoint is truly understood only by those who have "an intimate knowledge of sounds" (*chi'in*, Ch. *zhiyin*), a phrase that symbolizes appreciating the "tune" (*in/yin*) of true teaching that can be heard by the initiated. According to the title of a *Treasury* fascicle that is borrowed from a passage in the *Lotus Sūtra*, truth is communicated intimately, "Only Between a Buddha and a Buddha."

Eventually, the entrusted transmission was inherited from Rujing and transported to Japan by Dōgen, who declared that his view is fundamentally identical to that of every preceding ancestor beginning with Śākyamuni. By this time in Zen history, *Treasury of the True Dharma Eye* (Ch. *Zhengfayanzang*) had already been used as the title of several prominent Chinese texts, including an important anthology of kōan cases produced by Dahui, a major exponent of Linji Chan. Dōgen admired and emulated Dahui in many ways, although he occasionally harshly attacked him in various writings. The use of this title seems to demonstrate Dōgen's commitment to seeing his own collection of essays dealing largely with kōan cases as a means of propagating the Dharma by transcending lineal affiliations.

A primary aim of the *Treasury* is to capture and convey the state of mind of the primordial moment of Mahākāśyapa's wise reticence, based on

Dōgen's own experience of casting off body-mind. He evokes words and phrases that appropriately reveal the power of creative discourse to disclose an illuminative form of commentary beyond the conventional distinction of speech and silence, so as to master the paradox of expressing the inexpressible truth. In the fascicle "Expressing the Way" Dōgen argues, "Expressing what one has realized is an ability that is not to be gained by following the thoughts of others and is also not an innate talent that some have but others do not. Instead, it occurs whenever a practitioner thoroughly realizes the way of the buddhas and ancestors and is able to explain the same truth they have attained" (Dōtoku: Dōgen 1.374, Nearman 510, Tanahashi 439).[9]

While Dōgen emphasizes that the Dharma is revealed through language used properly, he also highlights the value of exploiting nonverbal symbols as a pedagogical device, such as the Zen master's walking staff (*shakujō*) and ceremonial fly whisk (*hossu*), which are waved in the air while speaking, or a temple pillar and stone lantern, which represent seemingly solid yet fundamentally ephemeral objects. Sometimes Dōgen says that the ultimate teaching tool simply involves the raising of a fist or pointing to the eyes, nose, or top of the head, all actions that signify the authority and authenticity of a master's subjective realization better than an external pedagogical device. Nevertheless, Dōgen is more adamant than other Zen teachers of the period about the need for in-depth study of all Zen written records in addition to Mahāyāna scriptures. These works contain vast expressions of Buddhist teachings that are of equal value to the practice of seated meditation.

Dōgen also used the term "Treasury of the True Dharma Eye" in the title of two other important works produced in the 1230s, before he had the idea to collect his informal vernacular sermons into a single volume. One of these was the *300-Case Treasury* (*Shōbōgenzō sanbyakusoku*, also known as the *Mana Shōbōgenzō* to distinguish it from the *Kana Shōbōgenzō*, or the masterwork written in colloquial language). This was a *kanbun* compilation of kōan narratives without any prose or poetic commentary. Written at Kōshōji temple in 1235, this text greatly influenced many of Dōgen's later writings by serving as a storehouse of case records that he cited and interpreted throughout the *(Kana) Treasury*. The other main work with the title was *Treasury of Miscellaneous Talks* (*Shōbōgenzō zuimonki*, also known as *Record of Things Heard*), a six-volume compendium of informal evening sermons delivered during the mid 1230s and recorded by Ejō that were designed to help win over some recent converts to Dōgen's emerging Sōtō Zen temple.[10]

By evoking the key term in all of these texts, Dōgen asserts a reverence for the "True Dharma" (*shōbō*) that can be grasped through the path of self-power (*jiriki*), or the capacity to attain the highest state of realization by means of meditative discipline, at the time in the thirteenth century when various new forms of Kamakura Buddhism, especially the Pure Land and Nichiren sects, believed strongly in the view of other-power (*tariki*). This contrasting yet more commonly held conviction reflected a long-standing prophecy that East Asian society had entered a period of irreversible "Decline of the Dharma" (*mappō*) around the year 1000 CE. According to a commonly held prediction, this historical phase rendered people incapable of attaining illumination through individual effort alone due to their accumulated collective deficient karma. Instead, they must accept the salvific capacity of Buddha's grace received through the recitation of either Amida's name or the title of the *Lotus Sūtra*.

In expressing a belief in self-reliance based on the continuing practice of seated meditation while also studying kōan cases and following strict monastic regulations, Dōgen's approach was in accord with the main teaching methods of the leaders of the Rinzai sect. However, from a polemical stance seeking to distinguish his own outlook from that of rivals, Dōgen at times criticizes key aspects of Rinzai teaching by claiming a different emphasis in terms of how the goal of awakening should be achieved. In the fascicle "Going Beyond Buddha," for example, he argues that the Chinese Caodong school initiator Dongshan's views are far superior to those of Linji and Deshan (780–865, Jp. Tokusan). On the other hand, in "Sustained Exertion" he offers high praise by maintaining that "Linji should not be lumped in with the herd . . . since his training activities were pure and single-minded, and his unremitting practice was particularly outstanding" (Gyōji: Dōgen 1.165, Nearman 397, Tanahashi 350).

Switching perspectives yet again, in "Expressing Mind, Expressing Nature" Dōgen criticizes one of Linji's most prominent notions, that all followers must learn to discover within themselves "a true person who is without (or beyond any) rank (*shinjin mui*)." According to Dōgen's typical rhetorical method of inversion, he says this phrase should be recast as "a true person with (or who has) a rank" (*shinjin ui*) (Sesshin sesshō: Dōgen 1.455, Nearman 535, Tanahashi 499). Otherwise, Linji's view may sound nihilistic in a way that indicates he never realized genuine enlightenment. An important implication of this censure is that Dōgen stresses the quality of assertion as much as negation as part of the overall value of language used to disclose spiritual realization. The role of words and phrases, he argues, necessarily reflects the extent to which a speaker articulates his or her own level of expressing true mind and nature. In "Mountains and Rivers Proclaiming the Sūtras," Dōgen rebukes an instrumentalist approach to the use of language that he feels is taken by many Linji/Rinzai thinkers, who view words only as a means of reaching the end point of realization represented by silence. This outlook fails to understand the fundamental unity of action and motivation, or practice and realization, that links intimately the possibilities of speaking or not speaking (Sansuikyō: Dōgen 1.319–320, Nearman 146–147, Tanahashi 157–158).

Another key example of criticism related to non-Sōtō lineage ancestors occurs in the fascicle "Four Meditative Stages of a Monk," when Dōgen reprimands the doctrine of "seeing one's true nature" (*kenshō*, Ch. *xiansheng*) attributed to Sixth Patriarch Huineng in the *Platform Sūtra* (Ch. *Tanjing*, Jp. *Dankyō*) (Shizen biku: Dōgen 2.427, Nearman 1058, Tanahashi 865), a seminal text Dōgen suggests at one point must have been a fabrication because of its inauthentic doctrines. The notion of "own nature," which became a mainstay of Rinzai sect teachings, implies for Dōgen a facile attempt to attain a state of mind that appears eternal and unchanging, and therefore is susceptible to the charge of reflecting the Senika heresy.

In contrast to a linear progression leading directly to the attainment of permanent selfhood, Dōgen writes in "Realization Here and Now" of the dialectical, or endlessly back-and-forth, learning process that he believes characterizes true Zen practice: "To study the Buddha Way is to study the self. To study the self is to forget the self. To forget the self is to be illumined by myriad things. Being illumined by myriad things is to cast off the body-mind of self as well as to cast off the body-mind of others. No trace of enlightenment remains, and the traceless state is endlessly maintained" (Genjōkōan: Dōgen 1.3, Nearman 32, Tanahashi 30). Dōgen's circular approach to self-reflection as the key to gaining comprehension, which represents a virtuous or productive rather than a vicious or defective cycle of awareness, maintains that the realization of genuine selfhood unified with all things in the universe transpires through continually overcoming egotistical attachment to a false sense of personal identity. He further indicates that the condition of authentic or traceless awakening must be perpetuated when it would appear to have been completed from a conventional view, according to Linji/Rinzai school teachings, since there is no end to the process of spiritual renewal.

RHETORICAL AND THEORETICAL LEVELS

In numerous fascicles Dōgen interprets freely a broad assortment of Chinese writings, particularly the recorded sayings of prominent Chan teachers and other historical, philosophical, and ritual materials regarding monastic life and lineal transmission, in addition to doctrines expressed in various Mahāyāna sūtras. The *Treasury* thereby demonstrates an encyclopedic quality and serves as a remarkable reference tool for understanding a wide variety of textual sources from the Song dynasty and earlier eras, especially when modern scholars track the manifold instances in which Dōgen cites, yet usually revises or rewrites, various sayings attributed to a multitude of teachers. He generally does not try to present these passages in an objective or straightforward way, since his main purpose is to put forth a distinctive evaluative interpretation assessing how and to what extent Zen sayings genuinely contribute to the attainment of awakening. As he learned from diverse East Asian literary traditions, the primary aim of creative discourse in deciphering previous works is to link fidelity to whatever original source is interpreted with a sense of flexibility and flair that takes license to rethink and recast its underlying meaning through subtle changes of wording. In quoting texts, therefore, there is no strict opposition between faithfulness or exactitude and inaccuracy or unreliability. Such an artificial contrast is replaced by a willingness to continually modify and improvise based on the interpreter's particular degree of intuitive insight.

The *Treasury* features an inventive and intricate method of discourse in addressing an array of Chinese notions for a new audience of Japanese practitioners. Dōgen is especially proficient in quoting—while amending and adapting through interlinear (or line-by-line) commentary—impenetrable stories included in kōan case narratives of how a trainee or rival once upon a time attained awakening by undergoing a puzzling interaction with a teacher, fellow student, or adversary. In the original dialogues it often seems that one interlocutor in the competitive exchange is defeated in a battle of wits, but Dōgen typically seeks to show that the expressions of the seemingly lesser party are just as viable as those of the presumed victor.

In contrast to instrumentalist interpretations that stress the difference between winners and losers based on supposedly right versus wrong responses given in kōan records, Dōgen develops what Hee-Jin Kim calls a "realizational" model by maintaining that all participants in Zen dialogues are equally meritorious in their utterances regardless of any initial impression that one is superior or inferior.¹¹ Interlocutors can take full advantage of the fact that everyone at any time possesses the potential to reveal at least a partial, ultimately very useful understanding, regardless of rank, seniority, or other external considerations. Instead of endorsing a sequential interpretative standpoint, whereby a wise master illuminates by exposing the deficiency of a learner who thereby progresses from ignorance to enlightenment, the *Treasury* presents both parties as inherently enlightened and engaged in mutually awakening each other without concern for hierarchical standing or degree of experience.

Moreover, Dōgen emphatically argues that each imaginative commentator must be able to interpret the specific dialogue being discussed in a distinctive way by suggesting his or her own unique understanding of what could or should have been said in order to create a more complete understanding. All exchange partners are partly right, but nobody can claim the whole truth. In undertaking this kind of analysis, the *Treasury* argues that the mundane realm has metaphysical significance while the ethereal is embodied in tangible existence. Also, the parts reveal the whole, so that the ideal is fully divulged in the particularities of everyday reality, and the seemingly static world is really dynamic with momentariness, harboring the manifestations of truth since the realms of past and future are contained in the present.

Another main principle emphasized by Dōgen is that what appears to form an inquisitive sentence in Chinese, such as "What is this?" or "What are you thinking?" (according to the fascicle "The Lancet of Zazen," to be discussed more fully in chapter 7), can be recast in the Japanese context as a declarative utterance like, "It is what," or "This is what it is," thus signifying, "This is what you think" (Zazenshin: Dōgen 1.104, Nearman 336, Tanahashi 303). Similarly, in the fascicle "Bodhisattva Kannon," when an inquirer says in response to a teaching, "I get it," and the master probes, "What did you get?" Dōgen interprets this apparent query to mean, "You get it," which is the same as saying, "I [master] get it," because after all, "You get what I get" (Kannon: Dōgen 1.217, Nearman 462, Tanahashi 400).

To cite another of the numerous creative comments throughout the *Treasury*, Dōgen interprets a famous saying attributed to Chan Master Mazu (709–788), "This mind itself is Buddha" (*soku-shin-ze butsu* 即心是佛), by rearranging the four characters (*kanji*) or lexical components so that it becomes a deliberately awkward yet provocative form of discourse indicating "Mind-this-Buddha-is" (*shin-soku-butsu-ze* 心即仏是), "Buddha-this-is-mind" (*butsu-soku-ze-shin* 仏即是心), "This-mind-Buddha-is" (*soku-shin-butsu-ze* 即心仏是), and "Is-Buddha-mind-this" (*ze-butsu-shin-soku*

是仏心即) (Sokushin zebutsu: Dōgen 1.57, Nearman 50, Tanahashi 46). Each of these four expressions (out of twenty-four possible variations that were identified by later Sōtō commentators, only a few of which seem to make grammatical sense in translation), represents "a single dharma's total exertion which is absolutely discrete from all others, yet bears all others in it, without falling into atomism or monism."[12] However, in a passage in "The Ancient Buddha Mind," Dōgen argues against any sense that abstraction pervades the process of intellection by emphasizing its identity with concrete entities in citing a saying of Nanyang Huizhong (d. 775), "The ancient Buddha mind is nothing other than tiles, stones, and pebbles used for walls and fences, which are neither immediately apparent nor not immediately apparent.... Not a single mote of dust has ever defiled this" (Kobusshin: Dōgen 1.90, Nearman 569, Tanahashi 471).[13]

BEHAVIORAL AND MORAL LEVELS

By heeding Rujing's injunction that he spread the Dharma widely, free of the world of secular conflicts, Dōgen was ever mindful of the need to maintain a focus on the ethical implications of his teaching mission. In a kanbun-style poem composed in 1231, while he was residing alone in a small hermitage in the countryside village of Fukakusa (lit. "deep grass") on the outskirts of the capital and was just starting the process of writing the *Treasury*, Dōgen succinctly proclaims the value of propagating Zen in the ephemeral world:

> How pitiful is the ceasing and arising of life and death!
> I lose the way yet find my path as if awakening from a dream.
> Even so, there is still one thing I must never forget—
> While listening to the sound of evening rain in the deep grass of my Fukakusa hut.[14]

The first two lines of the verse convey the dialectics of traversing the dualities of the comings and goings of living and dying, as well as the intricate process of losing yet finding one's true identity that is involved in choosing between illusion and reality, which are invariably intertwined possibilities that depend on each other for reconciliation. The second half of the poem shows that even the serenity of the meditative state encompasses complex choices by highlighting the imperative to avoid solipsism and ensure that the Dharma is transmitted effectively to all interested followers. This is poignantly evoked in the third line focusing on the value of compassionate commitment.

Throughout the *Treasury*, Dōgen emphasizes that Zen trainees must understand and disseminate the oneness of practice-realization (*shushō ittō*), which is also referred to as the undivided nature of cultivation and enlightenment (*fuzenna no shushō*). All notions about spiritual attainment spring from, and every expression should be true to, the ongoing exercise of seated meditation, understood in the broader sense of reflecting the state of nonthinking regardless of which physical posture is adopted. Dōgen's primary goal is to demonstrate that the disparate realms of speculative ideas and routine clerical deeds are inextricably interrelated. In "Discerning the Way," written in the same year as the Fukakusa verse, Dōgen maintains:

> To think that practice and realization are distinct from each other is a non-Buddhist view or a basic misunderstanding of the way. In Buddhism practice-realization is completely one and the same experience. Because this view refers to practice based on being spiritually awakened at this very moment, the diligent training that arises from one's initial resolve (*hosshin*) to seek the way is, in itself, the fulfillment of realization. For this reason, you should not hold in mind any expectation of being enlightened as something that stands apart from constant dedication to training, since practice itself points directly to realization. (Bendōwa: Dōgen 2.470, Nearman12–13, Tanahashi 12)

The oneness of practice-realization enables a ritualized orchestration of deeds conducted during the three phases of time, consistently confirmed by the sustained effort of meditation that advances and enhances spiritual awakening by never pausing on the path or stopping at a set goal. The experience of enlightenment does not represent a final destination but is a continuing process of interior refinement demonstrated through exterior actions. All elements of practice are thereby fully amalgamated with the essentials of theoretical reflection by virtue of an all-encompassing standpoint that is renewed every moment.

The *Treasury* shows Dōgen fully engrossed in defining methods for maintaining contemplation while following a variety of day-to-day clerical procedures, including engaging in ceremonies, chants, chores, and other observances or responsibilities. In several fascicles and in the *Extensive Record* (*Eihei kōroku*), a compilation of over five hundred formal sermons composed in kanbun, Dōgen asserts that he was the first person in Japan to establish rules for Zen monastic rituals and offices. These include the principles of meditation (*zazengi*), the requisite lifestyle of the monks' hall (*sōdō*) where zazen takes place, and ways of presenting evening lectures (*bansan*) in addition to sermons delivered in the Dharma hall (*jōdō*) by an abbot who wields the symbolic walking staff or ceremonial fly whisk in order to make emphatic gestures. Dōgen's innovations also include providing instructions for the chief cook (*tenzo*) and other activities in the kitchen and refectory that are considered part of the bundle of contemplative training methods.

GLOBAL AND TOPICAL LEVELS

Since an interest in Dōgen as a universal thinker was promulgated in the twentieth century by nonsectarian interpreters such as Watsuji Tetsurō and Tanabe Hajime, and the *Treasury* was thereby lifted from the obscurity of being considered an antiquated phenomenon of historical interest epitomizing a stage of the legacy of Japanese Buddhism, the masterwork has garnered admiration and praise from worldwide interpreters. The seemingly incomprehensible medieval manuscript is now seen as a distinctively creative masterpiece of premodern religious rhetoric that holds great appeal on multiple levels for a new readership intrigued by the current relevance of traditional forms of contemplation. A vibrant contemporary discourse involves divergent methods of analyzing and applying Dōgen's sophisticated discursive style to various social themes as well as intellectual topics and literary motifs.

In Japan, research efforts by sectarian scholars in addition to unaffiliated historians, philosophers, and cultural critics have developed innovative ways of reconstructing the multifaceted contents of the *Treasury*. As Zen meditation has spread globally in the post-World War II period, translations of the *Treasury* have appeared in English and various other languages, including a version produced in modern Chinese that seeks to return some of the interpretative verbiage to its original linguistic status.[15] Some of the text's major fascicles have now been rendered into English dozens of times, although these translated versions tend to be of varying quality in terms of balancing the concerns of readability and accuracy. Beginning in the 1970s there has also been a steady flow of books, scholarly articles, and conference sessions, in addition to more informal communications about the *Treasury* via websites, listservs, and blogs. Well over fifty volumes on Dōgen studies have been published in English, which makes the Sōtō founder the most extensively studied East Asian Buddhist leader in the West.

Perhaps the main area of emphasis involves associating Dōgen's compositions with some of the great works of religion and philosophy throughout the history of Western thought, ranging from the metaphysical writings of Aristotle or Aquinas and the mystical reflections of Meister Eckhart or the Jewish text, the *Zohar*, to the modern existential musings of Søren Kierkegaard or Albert Camus, the poetic eloquence of T. S. Eliot or Gary Snyder, and the theoretical elements of Martin Heidegger's phenomenology or Jacques Derrida's deconstructionism. These names represent just a handful of the many thinkers, authors, and forms of expression that have been evoked as part of a long list of intellectual movements also encompassing quantum mechanics and environmental revisionism. Some commentators suggest that Dōgen's prowess in capturing medieval Japanese Buddhist thought presaged various crucial modernist trends by focusing on each individual's spiritual striving with a sense of great urgency in the quest to realize authentic understanding. That goal is to be attained while being aware of occupying an ephemeral position in dynamic spacetime, as depicted by Einstein's theories, and comprehending the relativist quality of the universe, which highlights the multiplicity of human perspectives coming to grips with the fundamental unity of momentary and continuing existence, as in Nietzsche's notion of eternal recurrence.

An individual's religious development is conveyed in the *Treasury* through creative forms of communication that highlight the need to make difficult moral choices in light of the basic contingency of human discourse. By constantly casting aside a conventional view of self-identity based on ego, according to Dōgen, one can prepare and perpetuate a more deep-seated sense of self-reliance that maintains constancy and consistency in the midst of ever shifting, unstable conditions. A recent blog by an American Sōtō Zen priest teaching in Japan refers to Dōgen as a kind of jazz poet, who is "riffing and free expressing-reexpressing-bending-straightening-unbinding-releasing the 'standard tunes' of the Sutras and Koans. The untrained ear can't make head or tail of its complex rhythms, notes flying, wild tempo."[16]

Dōgen's notion of the oneness of being-time (*uji*) and its emphasis on the fullness of the present is comparable to the philosophy in Martin Heidegger's magnum opus, *Being and Time* (*Sein und Zeit*). This work, in turn, greatly influenced Kyoto School philosophers such as Nishitani Keiji (1900–1990), who was engaged in explicating traditional Zen thought from a modern perspective when Heidegger's work was first translated into

Japanese, shortly after its initial German publication in the late 1920s.[17] According to Heidegger, "Temporalizing does not signify that ecstasies come in a 'succession.' The future is not later than having been and having been is not earlier than the present. Temporality temporalizes itself as a future which makes present in the process of having been."[18] This complex standpoint recalls Dōgen's formidable expression, "Mountains are time, and seas are time. If they were not time, there would be no mountains and seas. So, you must not say there is no time in the immediate now of mountains and seas. If time is destroyed, mountains and seas are destroyed. If time is indestructible, mountains and seas are indestructible" (Uji: Dōgen 1.245, Nearman 116, Tanahashi 109–110). Dōgen's view of temporality also recalls the opening lines of T. S. Eliot's No. 1 of *Four Quartets*, "Time present and time past / Are both perhaps present in time future, / And time future contained in time past."[19]

In a fascinating variation on the theme of temporal existence, Ruth Ozeki, a Japanese American author and ordained Zen practitioner, published a prize-winning novel titled *A Tale for the Time Being*, an intricate narrative concerning the effects of the Triple Disaster (earthquake–tsunami–nuclear meltdown) that struck Fukushima prefecture in 2011. This work craftily utilizes Dōgen's theories in a story with multiple meanings that captures the effects of magical realism as evoked in the novels of Murakami Haruki and other postwar Japanese authors. In an appendix to the novel Ozeki further suggests affinities with science. "If Zen Master Dōgen had been a physicist," she reflects, "I think he might have liked quantum mechanics. He would have naturally grasped the all-inclusive nature of superposition and intuited the interconnectedness of entanglement. As a contemplative who was also a man of action . . . he would have appreciated the unbounded nature of not knowing,"[20] which is crucial to understanding the principles of subatomic particles.

Furthermore, the *Treasury*'s view of expressivity as a self-disentangling entanglement (*kattō*) has been compared to Jacques Derrida's poststructuralist analysis of the semiotic functions of language. In the monograph *From Derrida to Dōgen: Deconstruction and Casting off Body-Mind* [*Derrida kara Dōgen e: datsu-kochiku to shinjin datsuraku*], Japanese scholar Morimoto Kazuo, who also wrote a comparative analysis of Dōgen and Jean-Paul Sartre, shows affinities based on the keyword *datsu* (脱) between Derrida's notion of deconstructionism, which is translated into Japanese as *datsu-kōchiku*, and *shinjin datsuraku*.[21] This term is often used as a prefix indicating "de-," and it implies escaping, shedding, falling, or abandoning in a way that resonates with another verb evoked by Dōgen, *suteru*

(捨てる, to renounce or resign). In addition, the modern French philosopher Jean-Francois Lyotard, one of the few major Western thinkers who studied parts of the *Treasury* in translation, developed his own approach to the awakening (*éveil*) of mind that was influenced by appropriating Dōgen's view of the melding of seer and seen, particularly in his analysis of the image of a broken mirror that is discussed in the fascicles "The Ancient Mirror" and "Great Awakening."[22] Lyotard likens this philosophical notion to the enigma of a flame constituting the event of its own manifestation of destructiveness.

Another area of emphasis in comparative religious thought involving both denominational and nondenominational scholars pertains to concrete applications of Dōgen's premodern teachings to a variety of current social issues. The *Treasury* comments frequently on topics of contemporary significance, such as the role of women and lay practitioners in relation to male monastics or the struggle between institutional authority and individual authenticity in Zen training, as well as the underlying unity of humans and nature in a world characterized by diverse challenges and conflicting perspectives.[23] Modern interpreters try to tease out the societal significance of Dōgen's eloquent writings by noting that some of his doctrines are clear and straightforward but others seem ambiguous or contradictory. For example, he affirms the capacity of lay and female participants to study Zen in fascicles written early in his career in the capital, yet seems to question or even undermine this argument in sections of the text written later in the remote mountains.[24]

An important instance of connecting Dōgen's thought to communal concerns stems from the methodological movement known as Critical Buddhism (*Hihan Bukkyō*), which was initiated in the late 1980s by a group of scholars at Komazawa University, long the bastion of Dōgen studies in Japan.[25] The impetus for their approach, to be examined in chapter 8, was an attempt to respond to an urgent crisis that was affecting many traditional Buddhist orders, including the Sōtō sect, regarding temple rituals' discriminatory tendencies toward the outcast group known as *Burakumin* (lit. "village people"). Critical Buddhists argued that certain ethical defects embedded in Zen notions of unity, which promoted a view of oneness or nondifferentiation in a fashion that tended to suppress distinctions, often led to a reprehensible disregard for the plight of exceptional or marginalized peoples. These scholars suggested that a renewed focus on a genuine sense of egalitarianism and inclusiveness, as expressed in some passages of the *Treasury* highlighting the inevitability of karmic retribution for those committing moral transgressions, provides a useful template for social reform efforts concerning the inequitable functions of religious institutions in Japanese society. In addition, Critical Buddhists dealt with the implications of Dōgen's thought for overcoming problematic trends of Japanese nationalism and nativism, even as some prominent commentators criticized many aspects of modern Zen that contributed to prewar imperialism and related violations of human rights.[26]

Additional weight has been given to the ecological implications of the *Treasury* for engaging the world in a compassionate espousal of the oneness of humans and the environment while recognizing discrepancies between species. Dōgen instructs that because a genuinely beneficent Buddhist outlook is all encompassing and without restriction or partiality, "You should contribute to the well-being of friend and enemy equally. This is done to assist self and others alike. If carried out with a contemplative attitude that does not seek any reward, beneficial action for the sake of grasses, trees, wind, and water as well as for those who are foolish and incorrigible is spontaneous and unremitting" (Bodaisatta shishōbō: Dōgen 2.513, Nearman 574, Tanahashi 475–476).

In *Mountains, Rivers, and the Great Earth: Reading Gary Snyder and Dōgen in an Age of Ecological Crisis*, Jason Wirth reflects on the notion of the unity of people and nature that is often referred to by Dōgen as the "Great Earth" (*daichi*), similar to the idea of the "Wild" suggested by Beat poet Gary Snyder, who in the early 1950s trained in meditation at Rinzai Zen temples in Kyoto and also studied the writings of the Sōtō founder. The primary aim of Dōgen and Snyder, Wirth suggests, is to portray a life in harmony with the environment through adopting attitudes of profound respect for and concern about preserving the integrity of all aspects of existence. According to this analysis, the views of Dōgen and Snyder "can illuminate the spiritual and ethical dimensions of place . . . culminating in a discussion of earth democracy, a place-based sense of communion where all beings are interconnected and all being matters [in the] radical rethinking of what it means to inhabit the earth."[27]

The last section of this chapter has spotlighted a small sampling of comparative studies of Dōgen and multifarious Western counterparts, ranging from figures in philosophy of religion and spirituality to those in literary studies, as well as the ideals of science and applications of technology. Known primarily as the patriarch of a medieval Zen sect, Dōgen has had a peerless influence on contemporary Japanese culture since Watsuji's analysis in the 1920s. The *Treasury* has been attracting Western interpreters eager to demonstrate how the master's insights about the unity of being-time and practice-realization have profound implications for the way contemporary people can conduct their lives in an authentic fashion amid the chaos and contradictions of modern society. This approach highlights compassionate behavior toward those people who are less fortunate in addition to nonhuman beings, including insentient entities that compose the environment, based on contemplative consciousness that is continually cultivated.

{ 3 }

MULTIPLICITY AND VARIABILITY

DIFFERING VERSIONS AND INTERPRETATIONS

MYTHS ABOUT THE TREASURY

The importance of the *Treasury* is demonstrated by citing one of the main Sōtō sect masters of the middle of the fourteenth century, about five generations after Dōgen, a monk named Daichi Sokei (1290–1366) mainly known for his composition of Zen poetry expressing the various meanings of Zen awakening. Daichi hailed from the southern island of Kyushu and traveled to China for more than a decade, beginning in 1314, in order to study with several prominent Chinese Chan monk-poets from the Caodong and Linji lineages. Before and after this trip he visited Eiheiji and other Sōtō temples in Echizen, and eventually returned to Kyushu to establish a monastery near his hometown. In the following *kanbun* verse, Daichi reflects "On Receiving a Copy of Dōgen's *Treasury of the True Dharma Eye*" while residing there:

> The enlightened mind expressed in the *Treasury*
> teaches us the innermost thoughts of all the various Zen ancestors.
> A mystical path stemming from Eiheiji temple reaches my remote village,
> Where I see anew an ethereal mist rising from among remarkable shoots.[1]

This stanza, which highlights the spiritual inspiration and rejuvenation that Daichi felt, reveals much about the complex history of Dōgen's masterwork in the medieval period. During this epoch the *Treasury* was not being circulated widely because the leaders of Eiheiji temple wanted to maintain a single primary edition and prevent too many different versions from being read by followers, who would not be able to understand some of the text's arcane mixture of Chinese and Japanese scripts. Monks interested in studying the work needed to visit the head temple to gain permission to view the manuscript. However, Daichi was an exceptional figure who was sent a copy of the *Treasury* in a distant place, where he wrote several poems celebrating "This Very Mind Is Buddha" and other fascicles.

Part of the reason for the anxiety leaders at Eiheiji felt about giving access to Dōgen's text was the tentative quality of its construction. According to the postscript written in 1255 for the fascicle "The Eight Realizations of a Great Person," the final passage Dōgen composed about a year before his death, Ejō refers to the incomplete nature of the manuscript:

> This fascicle represents a first draft of what was to be the twelfth fascicle of the New Draft. After this our master's illness worsened and, as a result, he stopped working on the writing or editing of these passages. Therefore, this draft is the final teaching he left behind. It is deeply regrettable that we will never see his completed version of one hundred fascicles. Those who admire and miss our late master should certainly make their own copies in order to study and preserve this twelfth fascicle, for it contains the final instructions of Buddha and represents the lasting legacy of Dōgen's work. (Hachidainingaku: Dōgen 2.458, Nearman 1105, Tanahashi xcii)[2]

Monks like Daichi who were knowledgeable in Chinese no doubt understood how the tremendous transfer of voluminous continental prose and poetic writings was expedited by the *Treasury* in addition to Dōgen's other major works.[3] This process contributed to the introduction and implementation of the Zen school's groundbreaking approaches to theory and training in the reform-minded environment of Kamakura-era Buddhism. While teaching the technique of just sitting as the core method of practice, Dōgen also adopted and adapted many different Chan literary styles, rites of passage, forms of discipline, and instructional stratagems to local customs and circumstances. These same methods are still diligently maintained in cloisters of the contemporary Sōtō sect, especially at more than two dozen highly specialized monastic training centers (*senmon dōjō*), including Eiheiji and other temples throughout Japan. However, there are thousands of smaller Sōtō temples that are primarily dedicated to rituals for funerals or memorials and various types of prayer or devotion.

Half a decade after his return from China, Dōgen began to present the lectures that were eventually incorporated into the *Treasury* as a collection of discrete or originally disconnected, though stylistically complementary, fascicles that are sometimes thematically consistent and sometimes seem contradictory. The different sections contained in the text were written during various stages of Dōgen's career as a temple abbot. The author and/or Ejō, who succeeded Dōgen as leader of Eiheiji and continued the editing process, kept careful records of each fascicle. Nearly all fascicles contain a postscript or colophon that provides some basic information about when and where it was composed. Occasionally an additional anecdote describes the situation of the lecture by referring to the time of day or the author's state of mind. However, the writings were usually preserved in multiple and frequently updated or revised manuscripts, so it is often unclear today which is the authoritative version.

In some instances, Dōgen prepared the sermon in advance and read aloud a written version instead of speaking extemporaneously and having his words transcribed. Any follow-up discussions with members of the assembly were not recorded, although occasionally there is an addendum following the postscript that contributes remarks on the main theme and was probably composed in response to an inquirer.[4] The primary audience consisted of resident monks and possibly some senior nuns who were among the master's students. A handful of foreign monks, such as Jakuen (1207–1299, Ch. Jiyuan), came from China to join Dōgen's assembly, along with various construction specialists, and after the patriarch's death Jakuen founded Hōkyōji temple in the vicinity of Eiheiji. Laypeople, including prestigious donors as well as laborers working on monastery building and maintenance projects, were also in attendance but seated separately. Like other medieval Buddhist teachers who believed that propagators of the Dharma could be either human or divine, Dōgen considered there to be a spiritual audience present that comprised heavenly beings, including bodhisattvas, who responded or perhaps even contributed to his choice of words.

Any reader of Dōgen's masterpiece must come to terms with the fact that this text is surrounded by a number of long-standing controversies concerning issues of origin, contents, goals, and intended audience. The process of composition and techniques established for editing and analyzing the work over the centuries were very much conditional and contingent on various personal, historical, institutional, and interpretative factors. Many aspects of the *Treasury*'s structure and significance remain obscure and disputed so that some basic features, such as how and when it was written as well as ways it was organized by editors and investigated by commentators, are often discussed in partial or conflicting ways. Because of this complicated hermeneutic situation, widespread myths about textual construction frequently get repeated and reinforced and thus need to be rectified. This remains the case despite—or perhaps because of—the considerable fanfare Dōgen's text has received.

According to typical explanations of its textual history, the following features that will be clarified and corrected in this and subsequent chapters characterize the *Treasury*:

a) the text consists of a total of 95 fascicles, all of which are written in the vernacular;
b) these were composed over a period of nearly twenty-five years, from 1231 until just before the time of Dōgen's death in 1253;
c) the text best reflects Dōgen's teachings conducted at his most famous temple, Eiheiji, located in the Echizen mountains;
d) it represents Dōgen's single most important body of writing, far outranking any other work, even if it was recorded and edited by Ejō;
e) nevertheless, the *Treasury* was inexplicably neglected for many centuries as part of a so-called "dark age of medieval sectarian studies";[5]
f) its philosophical significance is usually interpreted by modern Japanese commentators in terms of a central debate concerning whether and to what extent the master may have suffered a decline as a thinker or, contrariwise, had a spiritual renewal in his later years.

The last point pertains to the fact that Dōgen's production of fascicles trailed off as he began to emphasize other kinds of monastic activities focusing on practice rather than theory. While all the above notions dealing with issues of what, where, when, who, how, and why the *Treasury* was written are not necessarily untrue in that each bears a degree of merit for helping to explicate the formation of the work, to a large extent all six views reflect misconceptions rather than facts, which are often difficult to determine. When taken together in uncritical fashion, these opinions contribute to a picture of textual construction and interpretation that is partial and in many ways misleading because some fundamental ideas are unclear or falsely disclaimed. The primary aim of this chapter is to overcome prevalent myths about the development of the *Treasury* by providing an accurate account of how it was composed and revised for hundreds of years, incorporating recent research that has led to multiple methods for investigating diverse views concerning its construction.

This effort is possible because of vigorous scholarly advances in Japan over the past half century. The period around 2003, which marked the 750th anniversary of Dōgen's death, was a special occasion in the history of scholarly approaches to the *Treasury*. As with previous semicentennial memorial remembrances, which began in 1453 with the 200th commemoration when the main traditional biography, the *Record of Kenzei*, was composed, the recent celebration was an opportunity for Japanese scholars and practitioners—that is, diverse *Genzō-ka*—to enhance the number and quality of publications. These included edited versions with commentaries that interpret the master's teachings in light of new resources.[6]

PROVISIONALITY OF THE TEXT

The *Treasury* is a multifaceted and open-ended compilation comprising primarily a series of informal, often impromptu sermons (*jishu*) delivered and recorded in Japanese vernacular (*kana*), based largely on citations of Chinese texts featuring Dōgen's unique translations and elucidations. The informal sermon is a free-form style of Zen orating that could take place at any time of the day and in any temple location other than the Dharma hall, or wherever the abbot decided to convene his assembly. This genre stands in contrast to another category known as formal sermons (*jōdō*), which, according to Song-dynasty Chan monastic guidelines, are presented exclusively in the Dharma hall on a prescribed schedule that follows a weekly routine. Dōgen delivered formal sermons in Sinitic syntax (kanbun) over the course of fifteen years, beginning in 1236, that are included in the first seven sections of his ten-volume *Extensive Record*.

In some instances, the written version of a *Treasury* fascicle preceded the delivery of the lecture. But in most cases Ejō, as chief transcriber, made a record sometime after the oral presentation. Additional editing transpired either sometime before Dōgen's death or during the quarter century until Ejō died in 1280. The *Treasury* talks were originally offered as modes of instruction to serve the needs of followers whom Dōgen supervised at two major monasteries he led for about ten years each: Kōshōji temple situated on the outskirts of Kyoto, where he was founding abbot from 1233 to 1243; and Eiheiji temple in the Echizen mountains north of the capital, established in 1244. There was also an important nine-month interval from the late summer of 1243 through the spring of 1244, when the transition from the capital to the provinces was being undertaken, that proved to be remarkably productive. During this stage, while awaiting completion of the construction of the new temple, Dōgen's assembly was housed at small mountain hermitages, Kippōji and Yamashibu-dera, where he delivered as many as twenty-nine—or nearly one third—of the total number of sermons in the *Treasury*.

Therefore, the *Treasury* is considered a provisional, rather than a fixed and final, body of work. As William Bodiford notes, its composition is more tentative than comparable works by leading Buddhist authors or Japanese religious thinkers whose approaches to textual organization were more preplanned and systematic, although Dōgen's approach is in accord with the recorded sayings genre of Chinese Chan and later Japanese Zen teachers:

> The *Shōbōgenzō* is not just a single text, or even just different versions of one text. It consists of many different books (*maki* or *kan* 巻), which are bound together as ordered fascicles (*sasshi* 冊子) of the whole. Dōgen composed the books not as independent works, but as related parts of a larger whole that consists of a beginning, middle, and end. Dōgen repeatedly revised the individual books, and he rearranged their order at least two or three times. Subsequent generations compiled new versions of Dōgen's text, adding or rejecting individual books and rearranging them thematically or chronologically.[7]

Persistent questions and puzzling uncertainties about the formation of the *Treasury* caused by the lack of a standard edition are further exacerbated by the discovery over the past century of numerous lost manuscripts in Sōtō temple archives that are now recovered and housed in university libraries, museums, or research institutes. By revealing heretofore unconfirmed or unknown versions of some passages in addition to at least one important edition of the collection containing 12 fascicles, archival research and textual archaeology has triggered ongoing debates and competing theories about the work's basic construction as a key to unlocking the spiritual meaning and philosophical import of Dōgen's obscure rhetoric.

There are currently available over half a dozen editions of the *Treasury*, including the best-known but nevertheless unreliable version that contains 95 fascicles and, as previously mentioned, is often referred to as the Main Temple (Honzan) Edition.[8] In addition, there are the 75-fascicle and 60-fascicle editions, apparently planned by Dōgen himself and preserved at Eiheiji, plus the 28-fascicle and 12-fascicle editions, edited by Ejō to supplement the larger compilations. Also, editions containing 83, 84, or 89 fascicles were fashioned by subsequent editors during the fifteenth through seventeenth centuries. None of these is set in stone; indeed, all of them feature variations and discrepancies because, over time, different redactions were compiled. In explaining the reasons for this improbable degree of multiplicity, it is clear that leading Japanese scholars today consider the authentic version of the *Treasury* to be the Original Edition, which was formed over the past half century by combining the 75-fascicle and 12-fascicle versions with several miscellaneous fascicles. These include "Discerning the Way," which was the first passage Dōgen wrote in 1231 but was not included in either the 75-fascicle or 12-fascicle editions, yet serves as the opening passage of the Main Temple Edition. However, there remains considerable debate about the overall meaning and significance of the Original Edition.

Because of editorial complexities, in some instances two or more versions of a fascicle are now available with different contents. A prime example is "Attaining the Marrow Through Veneration," which deals primarily with whether nuns and other female practitioners have the capacity to realize enlightenment in a tradition that generally restricted such freedom. Legitimating the spiritual attainment of women, forbidden by male-oriented East Asian religious and cultural trends through notions expressed in various Buddhist scriptures such as the *Lotus Sūtra*, was an ideal promoted by many reform leaders in the Kamakura era. In China, Dōgen saw that this trend was also supported by numerous Song-dynasty Chan masters who ministered regularly to nuns and female lay followers. What was Dōgen's position on this matter? Was he a puritanically strict monastic leader who rejected social innovation or a freethinking philosopher preaching full universality and willing to overturn conventional social behavior? Whereas the best-known version of this fascicle contained in both the Main Temple and the Original editions offers a positive though still somewhat ambiguous assessment, the recommendation concerning women in an alternative manuscript (*beppon*) initially contained in the 28-fascicle edition provides a more emphatic endorsement of female enlightenment. In addition to complementing or reinforcing an idea in this case, there are several instances in which different versions of a fascicle are at odds with one another thematically.

The variability in manuscripts causes considerable disagreement among experts hoping to explicate the author's objectives. One of the main topics concerns whether and to what extent, over the course of a long teaching career that encompassed several transitional phases, Dōgen may have taken opportunities to rethink and thereby revise or even radically change his attitudes toward major religious themes. On the issue of women, for example, it can be asked if Dōgen was liberal while residing in cosmopolitan Kyoto but became more conservative in the remote setting of Eiheiji. This is one of several contested subjects concerning the development of Dōgen's ideology. Assuming some degree of alteration did take place, the next question is whether this represents a decline or a renewal in Dōgen's overall religious outlook. Or, is there a fundamental consistency underlying his writings from different career stages that needs to be highlighted despite any apparent discrepancies?

Scholarly speculations are often just as inconclusive as the text itself. In summing up a detailed argument about the relation between various editions of *Treasury* fascicles and how these can be appraised in terms of correctness or unreliability, Tsunoda Tairyū, one of the foremost contemporary Dōgen specialists, admits that he is the first to express hesitancy and doubt about the merits of his approach. "So, this is how I have understood the development of four main versions [with 75, 60, 28, or 12 fascicles] of the *Treasury*," Tsunoda suggests in a summative statement. "Although there are parts [of my theory] that cannot be proved, this is the way I have estimated the general point. Hopefully the study of the construction and development of the *Treasury* will continue, and newly discovered materials will shed new light on the understanding of the issue."[9]

Tsunoda's reluctant comments point to the fact that Dōgen's teachings are not altogether coherent, consistent, and easy to grasp; rather, they are complicated, subversive, and multifaceted, so that generations of scholars have been trying to comprehend them from different standpoints. Nevertheless, such a convoluted interpretative context has much value in that the greater the number of commentaries about the work of a pivotal thinker like Dōgen, the more this trend helps clarify for careful readers, in an open-ended and challenging fashion, the significance and depth of his words. As Dōgen himself might indicate, in-depth research is bound to make the "right mistake" by disentangling the entangled vines of misunderstanding.

STAGES OF DEVELOPMENT

The provisional nature of the *Treasury* is based on several factors involving Dōgen's unique yet uncertain style of authorship in addition to varied methods of editing and annotating the work undertaken by Ejō and later generations of medieval and modern interpreters reflecting diverse commentarial perspectives. The construction of the *Treasury* as a collection of assorted fascicles can best be understood by delineating its main stages of composition in relation to five periods of Dōgen's life and career:

(1) Formative (1200–1213) stage: his early upbringing, when he first studied Chinese classics and, impressed by an awareness of transiency after being orphaned at age seven, decided as an adolescent to become a spiritual seeker;
(2) Informative (1213–1223) period of initial religious practice: when Dōgen experienced a profound sense of doubt about the concept of Buddha nature as he studied the entire Buddhist canon in Kyoto while also practicing seated meditation that stimulated his trip to China;
(3) Transformative (1223–1233) stage of attaining enlightenment by casting off body-mind: when Dōgen conversed extensively with Rujing at Mount Tiantong in China and began the process of writing the first few of his own works included in the *Treasury*;
(4) Reformative (1233–1243) period: when Dōgen established Kōshōji temple in the capital as his first monastic center for recruiting disciples and composed nearly half of the total number of fascicles while experimenting extensively with other styles of writing;
(5) Performative (1243–1253) period at Eiheiji temple in the deep mountains: when he edited different drafts of the *Treasury* and wrote some additional fascicles without reaching a clear conclusion or completion of the structure of the multifaceted work.

The first two periods, the Formative and Informative stages, provided Dōgen with a firm educational background in both secular letters and Mahāyāna doctrines. This was a starting point for his eventual appreciation of Zen teachings as a culmination in the history of Buddhist thought transmitted from South to East Asia. Dōgen grew up in an aristocratic but troubled family at a crucial moment in Japanese history that revealed to him the meaning of impermanence. His father was a powerful general of a fading regime who died when Dōgen was two, and his mother, a beautiful mistress of his father, passed away five years later. Born to nobility, he demonstrated prodigious intellectual skills and was well educated in Chinese classics as early as age four. Bereaved at seven during a turbulent epoch of social upheavals, the already erudite prodigy abandoned a possible career in the court system offered a few years later by a wealthy uncle in order to take Buddhist vows and become ordained as a Tendai priest on Mount Hiei, the point of departure for most leaders of new Kamakura Buddhist movements. A year after his ordination he abruptly abandoned the then-dominant Tendai sect to study elsewhere, and this searching led him to try the path of Zen.

Over the course of the decade of the Informative period, in order to resolve his fundamental spiritual conundrum regarding the relation between original enlightenment and the need for everyday practice, Dōgen is said to have studied the entire Buddhist canon multiple times. After leaving Mount Hiei, he visited another Tendai site at Onjōji temple near the shores of Lake Biwa. In addition, he probably met Eisai briefly before the latter's death in 1215 and devoted more than half a dozen years to zazen training and other Zen rites at Kenninji temple under the tutelage of Myōzen. Dōgen demonstrated his scholastic prowess by challenging various authority figures he met who were unable to respond meaningfully to his sense of doubt, but he had not yet begun to write his own work. He also advocated that Myōzen make the journey to China, even though the senior colleague's teacher was dying at the time, because Dōgen felt that the goal of realizing the Buddhist Dharma took priority over the demands of Confucian-based filial piety.

The Transformative period covers Dōgen's pilgrimage to China in 1223 to overcome uncertainty and gain enlightenment under Rujing, as well as his return to Japan four years later to establish his distinctive role as a leader of the rapidly expanding Zen movement. The 1220s was a remarkable time in East Asian social and religious history. While Genghis Khan was paving the way for eventual Mongol rule of China by first conquering Beijing, then part of a northern dynasty ruled by Jin tribes who had defeated part of the Song Chinese empire a century before, the Hōjō clan was solidifying its shogunal power in Japan. This would soon result in strong support for the growth of Zen, beginning with the meditative practice of Hōjō Tokiyori (1227–1263), who, in 1247, offered Dōgen the chance to lead a new temple to be built in the garrison town of Kamakura.

Among significant Buddhist developments in Japan during the critical third decade of the thirteenth century, in 1220 the Tendai abbot Jien (1155–1225) published an influential history of Japanese Buddhism, *Jottings of a Fool* (*Gukanshō*), and in 1224 Shinran, founder of the True Pure Land sect, crafted his masterwork, *Teaching, Practice, Faith, and Realization* (*Kyōgyōshinshō*). Moreover, Zen priests Enni (1202–1280) and Kakushin (1207–1298) both reached key turning points in their respective religious development before they eventually undertook pilgrimages to China in the 1230s and 1240s, respectively. Both monks returned to Japan to become influential propagators of Chan theories and training methods among Japanese followers.

During the decade Dōgen visited the mainland, several of the most important kōan collections were being composed, including Caodong Master Wansong's (1166–1246) *Record of Serenity* (Ch. *Congronglu*, Jp. *Shōyōroku*) covering 100 cases with commentary, written in 1224 in Beijing; the *Collection of Commentaries* (*Sŏnmun yŏmsongjip*) with over one thousand cases with extensive remarks, compiled in 1226 by Hyesim (1178–1234), the successor to Chinul (1158–1210), who initiated the Zen (Kr. Sŏn) school in Korea; and Linji Master Wumen's *Gateless Gate* (Ch. *Wumenguan*, Jp. *Mumonkan*) with 48 cases with comments that was published in 1229 and has become the best known and most frequently translated work of this genre. It is highly unlikely that Dōgen would have been aware of any of these compilations, however, since the first and second examples were composed in faraway places and the *Gateless Gate* was not completed until after he had returned from China (it was transported by Kakushin on his return to Japan in 1254). Nevertheless, it is clear that Dōgen was fully immersed in reading many of the same voluminous illumination records and texts of recorded sayings that were being utilized by various Chinese and Korean kōan commentators as sources of anecdotes, dialogues, narratives, and sayings about attaining enlightenment.

Writings by Dōgen that stem from the first four years of the third career stage when he was still in China include: a short inscription memorializing Myōzen's relics, which he carried back to Japan; a collection of more than fifty poems written in Chinese, included in the tenth volume of the *Extensive Record*, that demonstrate Dōgen's mastery of this continental writing style as another important literary accomplishment; and *The Record of the Hōkyō Era*, a compendium of conversations held in Rujing's inner chambers, a rare privilege for a foreign student.[10] There is also a long-standing tradition that Dōgen copied the "One Night *Blue Cliff Record*" shortly before departing from China in 1227. Although exaggerated despite some degree of plausibility based on manuscripts discovered in the twentieth century, this account highlights Dōgen's singlehanded introduction of Chinese styles of kōan commentary to the Japanese Buddhist setting.

After his return home Dōgen first stayed at Kenninji temple, which he felt had deteriorated since losing the leadership of Eisai and Myōzen, and then resided at hermitages in the town of Fukakusa, a semirural retreat just outside the city limits of Kyoto. There he crafted two main works that help define the basic approach to the practice of just sitting as key to the resolution of his doubt about original enlightenment. One was the short but highly influential essay written in masterful formal kanbun calligraphy in 1227 and revised in 1233 called the *Universal Recommendation of* the *Principles of Zazen* (*Fukanzazengi*), a manifesto on the capacity everyone possesses to meditate effectively, along with brief instructions on how to carry out this practice.

The other main early work was "Discerning the Way," written as a kana discourse in 1231, discovered at a layman's home in the seventeenth century. This essay, which includes biographical and philosophical reflections on Chinese Chan practice in addition to Dōgen's responses to a series of eighteen hypothetical queries about the significance of zazen, was not included in any of the early *Treasury* manuscripts, including the 75-fascicle and 60-fascicle editions. However, "Discerning the Way" became the opening section of the 95-fascicle edition, which was designed in the Edo period as a comprehensive collection of vernacular writings in chronological order. Because of this, the fascicle is often regarded as an ideal introduction to the entirety of Dōgen's work.[11]

Dōgen's teachings in "Discerning the Way" at once build on the conceptual edifice of Tendai doctrinal formulations about the notion of original enlightenment in relation to the universality of Buddha nature, and radically reorient or revamp key aspects of that standpoint based on his unique vision of Zen meditative training as the true way of the Dharma. The text explains in a variety of literary styles that, by casting off body-mind in China, Dōgen came to understand that enlightenment is based on realizing the authentic meaning of Buddha nature as neither an innate potentiality rooted in the past nor a set goal to be reached in the future. Rather, Buddha nature represents an all-inclusive form of comprehension that is experienced in terms of the dynamism and immediacy of unified practice-realization actualized each and every moment of being-time. As Dōgen maintains in the fascicle "Realization Here and Now," written two years later, the absolute present "at once embraces and is cut off from before and after (*zengo saidan*)" (Genjōkōan: Dōgen 1.4, Nearman 13, Tanahashi 30). He further argues that this temporal view of awakening should not be conflated with the misleading tendencies of Tendai or other forms of Mahāyāna thought, which caused his doubt about original enlightenment by reflecting the Senika heresy's emphasis on eternal truth disconnected from everyday practice.

The Writing Explosion

The composition of the *Treasury* began at the end of the third, Transformative stage. Nevertheless, the major developments in the formation of *Treasury* manuscripts took place during the subsequent Reformative and

Performative stages that transpired at Dōgen's two major temples, with three important caveats. The first is that the transitional phase, lasting three quarters of a year from fall 1243 until spring 1244, when Dōgen's assembly was residing temporarily at mountain hermitages, was the single most productive phase of writing. Another caveat is that Dōgen spent six months visiting Hōjō Tokiyori in 1247 and 1248 and apparently did not write any fascicles during that time. Third, 11 fascicles that are undated were no doubt composed during Dōgen's final few years after he returned to Eiheiji temple from Kamakura, and most are included in the 12-fascicle edition.

Dōgen first preached at Kōshōji temple, then located on the outskirts of Kyoto (the cloister was moved in the seventeenth century to the town of Uji, southeast of the capital), from 1233 until the summer of 1243. He led a rapidly growing band of disciples who occupied a thriving monastic compound with newly constructed Song Chinese-style edifices erected in 1236. The buildings include a monks' hall used for meditation and sleeping and a Dharma hall for public sermons and other ceremonies. Prior to that, just two fascicles of the *Treasury* were written in 1233. One was "The Perfection of Great Wisdom," which includes a Rujing verse Dōgen admired about the ringing of a wind bell. The second was "Realization Here and Now," the only section of the *Treasury* that consists of a letter to a lay disciple from Kyushu rather than a sermon for monks; the recipient may have been the boatman who guided Dōgen's ship to and from China. This fascicle was placed first in the most important medieval versions of the text, including the 75-fascicle and 60-fascicle editions. It joins "Discerning the Way" in helping to introduce Dōgen's main overall themes and methods of argumentation, even though the fascicles are distinct in structure and style.

By the middle of the 1230s, Dōgen had taken a five-year hiatus from further *Treasury* compositions, during which he entered a tremendously prolific phase in which he tried his hand at several styles of writing in order to find appropriate ways to attract and appeal to his growing assembly. A number of Dōgen's followers, including Ejō, who served as head monk at both temples and recorded or edited almost all of the *Treasury* lectures, had converted to Dōgen's lineage from a small clique of early Japanese Zen devotees called the Daruma school (Daruma-shū). Its name was based on Zen founder Bodhidharma (Jp. Bodaidaruma), who supposedly came to China "from the west (India)" in the middle of the sixth century to introduce the practice of zazen. Even though the Daruma school adhered to many basic Zen principles followed by Eisai and Dōgen, it earned the ire of both leaders for failing to demonstrate a core commitment to meditative training, out of a misguided belief that enlightenment is accessible to anyone without having to make an effort to achieve it. According to Dōgen's analysis, this made the wayward school yet another example of the Senika heresy. His mid-1230s writings in kana and kanbun styles were mainly designed to convince former Daruma school followers of the merits of just sitting, as well as other features of monastic discipline including adherence to the traditional Buddhist precepts.[12]

The primary text dedicated to the conversion of Daruma school followers is a six-volume collection of informal sermons recorded by Ejō entitled the *Treasury of Miscellaneous Talks*. Other works from this phase include the short philosophical essay *Essentials of Learning the Way* (*Gakudōyōjinshū*) written in 1234; the *300-Case Treasury* (*Mana Shōbōgenzō*), a compendium of kōan cases without commentary written in 1235; a collection of 90 kōan cases with kanbun verse comments composed in 1236 and included as volume 9 of the ten-volume *Extensive Record*; and a key essay on *Rules for the Chief Cook* (*Tenzokyōkun*) written in 1237, which deals extensively with Dōgen's experiences in China and is one of six chapters of *Dōgen's Monastic Rules* (*Eihei shingi*) compiled in the seventeenth century.

Once the Dharma hall was established at Kōshōji temple in 1236, Dōgen began to deliver the formal sermons included in the first seven volumes of the *Extensive Record*. Many of these lectures express fundamental doctrinal themes that are consistent with *Treasury* teachings regarding the role of seated meditation, the experience of casting off body-mind, and the philosophy of karmic causality. Some of the doctrines dealt with extensively in *Treasury* fascicles are treated more briefly or elliptically in formal sermons contained in the *Extensive Record*.[13]

In 1238 Dōgen wrote the next *Treasury* fascicle, "One Bright Pearl," which was the fourth section thus far, beginning with "Discerning the Way" in 1231. He followed this with three more fascicles the next year, including two on daily chores, "Cleaning" and "Washing the Face," which were composed on the same day. The year 1240 featured the composition of eight new fascicles and marked the beginning of the remarkable period of Dōgen's *Treasury* productivity that lasted until 1245. During those six years, at Kōshōji temple and also at several hermitages in Echizen, as well as during the earliest phase at Eiheiji, Dōgen wrote 74 fascicles, or 80 percent of the grand total. This basic quantitative analysis certainly has a significant, though often overlooked, impact on understanding the formation of the text. It shows that a spurt of creativity occurred in the last couple of years at Kōshōji, when Dōgen's fame was increasing in the capital and he composed more than a third of the fascicles, including some of the best-known ones such as "Buddha Nature," "Being-Time," and "Mountains and Rivers Proclaiming the Sūtras," which highlight the underlying unity of all forms of human and natural existence in an unsteady but ever renewable world.

During the early 1240s Dōgen once again gained an additional group of followers from the defunct Daruma school who had studied Chinese texts, and he also received a copy of the recorded sayings of Rujing. Despite the emphasis most *Treasury* fascicles put on works imported from the mainland, Dōgen does not accept at face value all Chan teachings but frequently reworks and recasts their significance. He is rarely straightforward about the legacy of his school and often indicates mixed feelings in regard to the continental roots of the tradition. Dōgen lavishly praises its towering achievements as superior to anything that was taking place in the relative backwater of his native country, yet harshly censures some of Chan's main exponents as well as many average monks for being inauthentic or misguided, failing to grasp the true meaning of the oneness of practice-realization.

In addition to attacking the preaching methods of Dahui and other prominent Chinese leaders, including Linji and Yunmen, all of whom he at times applauds, Dōgen condemns many anonymous rank-and-file priests who failed, for instance, to properly fold their clerical robes, brush their teeth, wash their face, clip their fingernails, or crop their hair. Even though his discursive firepower is saved mainly for rival lineages or irregular practitioners whom he sometimes criticizes severely, even Rujing and other Caodong/Sōtō school predecessors are occasionally subjected to disapproval or recasting by this irreverent former student. That effort is usually carried out indirectly and in subtle or tongue-in-cheek fashion. Among many other instances of revisionism, Dōgen revises creatively several poems by Rujing and by another major Chinese Caodong predecessor, Hongzhi (Jp. Wanshi, 1091–1157).[14]

While exceptionally respectful of the etiquette and procedures dictated by the arduous eremitic lifestyle he advocated, in impertinent fashion typical of Zen iconoclasm, Dōgen is famously flippant about any particular doctrine, teacher, or manner of practice that he feels might become a source of either an untamable attachment or an unseemly disregard for ethical principles, rather than a trigger of genuine spiritual purification and application to activities. He sometimes lambastes the positions of various lineages to the point that later editors deleted those passages from some editions of the *Treasury*, especially the 60-fascicle version, apparently out of embarrassment regarding their high-pitched diatribe. But Dōgen is also consistently willing and eager to challenge and encourage the audience to overturn the views he puts forward based on each follower's level of confidence, as reflected in expressions of realization derived from their original thinking.

Further Writing and Editing After Relocation

The final, Performative period of Dōgen's career had an unexpected start with his sudden move to Echizen province pending the construction of Eiheiji temple. In the seventh month of 1243 Dōgen made a dramatic decision to relocate. Although this must have taken considerable advance planning, the specific reasons for the move are never mentioned, let alone explained clearly, in either Dōgen's corpus or later biographical materials. In 1689 the haiku poet Bashō in *Narrow Road to the Far North* (*Oku no hosomichi*) remarked on traveling nearly fifty miles out of the normal route in order to visit Eiheiji: "Dōgen apparently wanted to escape life in the capital, and must have had his reasons for moving to such a remote locale."[15] It is usually assumed that the Sōtō founder was chased out of Kyoto by Tendai rivals, who were threatened by his increasing popularity and may have torched Kōshōji temple, or he felt humiliated because a magnificent new Rinzai Zen monastery called Tōfukuji temple was being built near Kōshōji with the backing of the Fujiwara clan for another prominent pilgrim, Enni, who traveled to China in 1236, a decade after Dōgen. The construction of Tōfukuji commenced in 1243, around the time Dōgen left for the provinces. Both scenarios suggest negative or defensive reasons for fleeing the capital based on reactions to unfortunate sectarian rivalries.

In a more positive light, Dōgen may have been eager to seize the opportunity to preach to a new flock that combined rural monks along with those who accompanied him or, in a couple of instances, had arrived from China to join his assembly. By settling in the deep mountains, Dōgen fulfilled Rujing's final injunction to stay free from secular distractions in the capital. Furthermore, Dōgen's departure from Kyoto had the financial and moral support of his samurai patron, Hatano Yoshishige, for whom he had given a couple of sermons while still in Kyoto that are included as *Treasury* fascicles.

These lectures were presented in the early 1240s either at the warrior's residence in the case of "Total Activity," as shown in figure 3.1, or at a local temple in the Rokuhara district near Kōshōji, where Hatano and his

FIGURE 3.1 A *Treasury* sermon at Lord Hatano's residence. A scene depicting the delivery of "Total Activity." Dōgen and his scribes sit to the bottom right before a censer; at the top sit Hatano and his entourage, including women, while facing Dōgen are various lay devotees.

Patterned after the Edo-period drawing in Nara, *Your Principles of Practice and Realization* (Tokyo: Shōgakukan, 2001), 103, and drawn by Maria Sol Echarren entourage listened to "The Ancient Buddha Mind." Hatano's clan from western Japan owned a large estate near the sacred site of Mount Hakusan and the Tendai temple Heisenji, which was offered to Dōgen along with funds for temple construction. Another reason for the move is that the last major Daruma school outpost, Hajakuji temple, was located near the site of Eiheiji, and monks from this movement who had recently joined Dōgen probably encouraged the relocation to their former area.

The transitional phase lasting from the late summer of 1243 to the spring of 1244 saw twenty-nine, or nearly one-third of the total number of fascicles in the *Treasury* composed. Dōgen's assembly faced difficult conditions staying in temporary temples while enduring an unfriendly climate with less than favorable conditions for housing and rituals. This inspired the master to communicate intensively with his assembly about the role of meditation in relation to monastic discipline. Frequent preaching provided a stimulating and informative way to guide followers during a challenging time for the displaced community. Following this phase of productivity, Dōgen did not write for about a year after the new temple (initially named Daibutsuji) was opened in the fourth month of 1244, but he composed five fascicles in 1245 and completed two more in 1246. This marked the end of the compositions that are included in the 75-fascicle edition, although additional editing of this version continued to take place. Except for his six-month journey to Kamakura to visit shogun Hōjō Tokiyori, it seems that Dōgen remained active in writing for the *Treasury* during the late 1240s and early 1250s. The fascicles produced then are relatively few and are generally undated.

Even though the vast majority of the *Treasury* fascicles were completed by 1245, it seems that Dōgen did not combine the initially unorganized assortment of informal sermons he had been delivering on an irregular, often impromptu basis to constitute a single publication until he was settled at Eiheiji temple and began with some sense of urgency to focus on shaping his legacy. It is ironic that even though Dōgen is best known for the abbacy in the last major stage of his teaching career, only a small number of *Treasury* fascicles were composed at this location, most of which constitute the 12-fascicle edition. Moreover, many of the materials from the Eiheiji period are written in a different style from fascicles that are better known but were composed during the Kōshōji period. Nevertheless, Dōgen was very much involved in the process of revising and polishing the entire work until the end of his life in an unrealized effort to complete 100 fascicles, according to a remark made by Ejō.

Through the final phases of editing, Dōgen started working on several different compilations and separated the *Treasury* manuscripts into two main divisions. The first division is referred to as the Old (or Early) Draft (*kyusō*) and contains 75 fascicles composed mostly before the Eiheiji period. An alternate version of the Old Draft containing 60 fascicles deletes some sections for being overly critical of rival schools but incorporates nine fascicles not contained in the 75-fascicle edition, including seven from the 12-fascicle edition and two miscellaneous fascicles. The second division of the *Treasury* is the New (or Later) Draft (*shinsō*) consisting of 12 fascicles, 10 of which were completed near the end of Dōgen's life, although most lack specific dates of composition. All of the fascicles from the various drafts are included in the 95-fascicle or Main Temple Edition, first compiled in the early Edo period and distributed openly during the late Meiji era.

Crafting the New Draft fascicles was apparently instigated when Dōgen returned to the seclusion of the Echizen mountains in the spring of 1248 following a six-month visit in the company of Hatano to Kamakura, where Dōgen preached to shogun Hōjō Tokiyori, who had become a Zen meditator seeking to repent and gain solace for a lifetime of committing violence. This final main creative burst was based on Dōgen's critical reaction to the warrior's request for him to lead a new temple in Kamakura.[16] That complicated episode caused the Zen master to put a new focus on the basic Buddhist notion of the inevitability of karmic causality. The emphasis on cause and effect was further supported by the arrival at Eiheiji, as a gift from Hatano, of an edition of the Buddhist canon featuring Indian writings dealing with the doctrines of retribution and repentance that Dōgen had probably not studied thoroughly before. In 1250 he delivered the lecture on "Washing the Face" for the third time, and in 1252 he completed the final editing of "Realization Here and Now," written two decades before. In the last year of his life Dōgen wrote "Eight Realizations of a Great Person," which is included in the 12-fascicle edition, as well as "Three Stages of Karma," which is included as the eighth fascicle in the 60-fascicle edition and, in another version, as the eighth fascicle of the 12-fascicle edition.

During the decade at Eiheiji, Dōgen wrote several texts in Sino-Japanese or kanbun script that complement the *Treasury* in reflecting aspects of his rhetorical acumen. The most important is the *Extensive Record*, a collection of 531 formal sermons (*jōdō*) delivered in the Dharma hall along with other kinds of sermons plus poetry composed for various occasions, including comments on kōan cases and reflections on solitary meditation. The sermons are quite different in style from the *Treasury*'s informal vernacular sermons and include brief remarks that feature gestures and demonstrations like wielding a staff, using a fly whisk to draw a circle in the air, or stepping down from the platform abruptly. However, as previously mentioned, the formal lectures are sometimes quite close to or even overlapping in substance and impact with the unrestricted discursive flair of informal sermons contained in the *Treasury*. The records for both kinds of sermons do not contain any mention of question-and-answer sessions that no doubt took place when the master discussed various ideas with the assembly. Another important kanbun-based text from this period is *Dōgen's Monastic Rules*, a compilation of essays on behavioral regulations for monks. While at Eiheiji, Dōgen composed five of the six sections included in this work, which presents detailed regulations regarding administrative functions as well as practitioners' daily activities.[17]

By grouping fascicles into two main divisions Dōgen made it clear that he did not consider the *Treasury* a fixed or finished textual entity, but rather a fluid amalgamation of themes and outlooks he kept adjusting. Dōgen was ill for well over a year and died before completing a final version, and he did not leave behind a well-defined set of instructions for managing the editing process. After his passing, the process of editing was left entirely in the hands of Ejō, who continued to copy and compile manuscripts with the assistance of Gien (?–1314), a former Daruma sect follower who assisted Ejō in the mid 1250s and a couple of decades later became the Fourth Patriarch of Eiheiji. Also, Giun took part in the editing process in 1279 and was appointed the Fifth Eiheiji Patriarch in 1314, when he succeeded Gien and promulgated the 60-fascicle edition along with verse commentary.

Ejō had served as Dōgen's dependable amanuensis ever since 1234, when he joined the Sōtō founder's fledgling assembly at Kōshōji. In the postscript to "Taking Refuge in the Three Jewels," which is included in the 12-fascicle edition, Ejō expresses the limitations of his role. "During the summer retreat of 1255, I made an edited copy from my late master's draft," he reports. "But it was not a polished version, as Dōgen would have surely made additions and deletions. Since that is no longer possible, I am leaving the draft intact" (Kie buppōsōbō: Dōgen 2.386, Nearman 1018, Tanahashi 850).[18] A minor but important discrepancy between Ejō's results and the master's apparent intentions is that some versions of fascicles only have postscripts written by Dōgen, whereas other editions include colophons about the recording or editing process that were composed by Ejō. Some observers have remarked that Ejō might need to be considered a kind of coauthor, since it is plausible that in many instances the copies of the manuscripts he produced altered fairly significantly the content of Dōgen's writing. In any event, there is no question that Ejō made certain key decisions about the organization of various editions of his teacher's text that have affected all subsequent interpretations.

The main reason we should not overemphasize the *Treasury* as Dōgen's paramount text from his time at Eiheiji is that this view disregards the role played by other important writings produced during this period. Table 3.1 compares the number of informal sermons delivered year by year in order to clarify where the composition of the *Treasury* stands in relation to two major compilations that help define Dōgen's approach to Zen religiosity. The main period of the *Treasury*'s production was remarkably compressed, and this phase of creativity began to fade just as Dōgen was emphasizing the delivery of formal sermons included in the *Extensive Record*, with

TABLE 3.1

YEAR	PLACE	SBGZ	EK	ES	OTHER
1231	Anyō'in	1			
1232	Anyō'in	0			
1233	Kōshōji	2			Fukanzazengi
1234-6	Kōshōji	0			MS, EK-9, GY
1237	Kōshōji	0		1	
1238	Kōshōji	1			SZ
1239	Kōshōji	3			
1240	Kōshōji	8	31		⎤
1241	Kōshōji	11	48		⎥
1242	Kōshōji	16	26	6 yrs. =	⎥
1243[1]	Kōshōji	6	21	74 fasc.	⎥
1243	Echizen	17	=126[2]		⎥
1244	Echizen	11	0[3]	1	⎦
1245	Eiheiji	5	15		
1246	Eiheiji	2	74	3	⎤
1247	Eiheiji	0	35		⎥
1248	Eiheiji	0	52		⎥
1249	Eiheiji	0	58	1	⎥
1250	Eiheiji	0	52	6 yrs. =	⎥
1251	Eiheiji	0	68	390 *jōdō*	⎥
1252	Eiheiji	0	51		⎦
1253	Eiheiji	2	0		
Unkn	Eiheiji	11[4]	0		
Total		**96**[5]	**531**	**6**	

Items included in *Treasury* (*SBGZ*), *Eihei kōroku* (*EK*), and *Eihei shingi* (*ES*); also, *MS* is *Mana Shōbōgenzō*, *EK-9* is *Eihei kōroku* vol. 9, *GY* is *Gakudōyinshū*, and *SZ* is *Shōbōgenzō zuimonki*. [1]the year of Dōgen's transition to Eiheiji, with 6 fascicles written before and 18 after the move; [2]the total number of EK sermons delivered at Kōshōji over several years contained in vol. I; [3]a transitional year when there was no Dharma hall; [4]although not officially dated, these were written at Eiheiji and included in the 12-fascicle edition along with one earlier fascicle from Kōshōji; [5]even though the total number of *SBGZ* fascicles is usually given as 95, an additional fascicle was discovered in 1930.

four-fifths of these presented over six years (1246–1251), in addition to the composition of five of the six essays included in *Dōgen's Monastic Rules*.

BRIEF HISTORY OF TRADITIONAL AND MODERN INTERPRETATIONS

During the Kamakura era there were four main hand-copied editions of the *Treasury* available at Eiheiji and a few other key temples, including the 75-, 12-, 60-, and 28-fascicle versions. According to the analysis of modern scholars, the 75-fascicle and 12-fascicle versions have no overlapping sections and constitute one set of manuscripts that over the past fifty years has come to be considered the most authentic edition, and the 60-fascicle and 28-fascicle versions also have no duplication and represent a second, parallel set. However, the editorial situation is not so clear-cut since additional fascicles and alternate versions are extant. Moreover, the 12-fascicle edition, long rumored but unconfirmed for centuries, was not confirmed as authentic until 1930, when a new fascicle included in this manuscript was found.[19]

The 75-fascicle and 12-fascicle editions were both completed by Ejō and Gien in 1255. Less than a decade after that the monk Senne (n.d.), who attended and heard all the sermons as an early member of Dōgen's assembly and left Eiheiji after the master's death to open Yōkō'an temple in Kyoto, started to create a detailed line-by-line commentary on the 75-fascicle edition. Senne's work began in 1263 and was completed twenty years later. A quarter century after this his main disciple, Kyōgō, finished the composition in 1308 by adding supplementary remarks. The combined effort, known as *Distinguished Annotations* (*Kikigakishō*, also known as *Goshō*), is usually studied as a single text, even though the respective sections by Senne and Kyōgō are sometimes read separately. Lost for several hundred years and rediscovered at the end of the sixteenth century, the *Distinguished Annotations* has remained the single most important traditional *Treasury* commentary that is examined carefully by interpretative specialists today.

Master Giun discovered—or perhaps created, according to a prominent theory—a 60-fascicle version when he returned to become abbot of Eiheiji in 1314 after serving as leader of Hōkyōji temple for fifteen years following the death of his teacher Jakuen.[20] The 60-fascicle edition gathers together 50 fascicles from the 75-fascicle edition and adds 10 more; eight were part of the 12-fascicle edition with the other two available as miscellaneous materials.[21] In 1329 Giun wrote a collection of kanbun poems with

TABLE 3.2

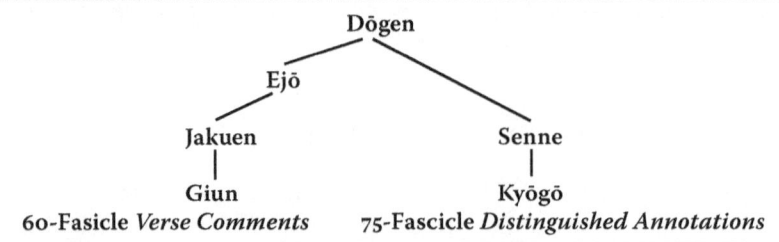

| 60-Fasicle *Verse Comments* | 75-Fascicle *Distinguished Annotations* |

Lineages stemming from Dōgen with two very different commentaries—the only such remarks completed in the early 1300s, before a decline lasting several hundred years and then a boom that occurred beginning in the seventeenth century.

additional capping phrase remarks commenting on each section of the 60-fascicle edition. As shown in table 3.2, there were two major commentaries produced by the end of the Kamakura era: one in prose by Senne-Kyōgō on the 75-fascicle edition, and the other in poetry by Giun on the 60-fascicle edition.[22] Both are among the most influential interpretative materials in the history of the Sōtō tradition, although they have barely been introduced into the world of English-language scholarship on Dōgen.

After the early attention given to the founder's masterwork in these two commentaries, the Sōtō sect continued to spread widely throughout many northern, eastern, and southwestern provinces to become the second largest of the Kamakura Buddhist movements, following the True Pure Land sect. It gained strength primarily by incorporating folk religious elements and converting local temples previously used by the older esoteric sects. It seems, however, that only the most advanced priests residing at or visiting Eiheiji studied the *Treasury* during this phase that lasted for more than two centuries. Although manuscripts were circulated to other temples, no additional commentaries were written until the seventeenth century, when an innovative approach to philological studies of the *Treasury* emerged as part of debates concerning the authenticity of the various versions of the text. In contrast, during the Muromachi era (1336–1573) there was considerable editing activity, and prominent masters such as Daichi cited the *Treasury*'s teachings in poems or other records. Moreover, numerous copies were circulated of a 1419 edition consisting of 84 fascicles that was produced by the monk Taiyō Bonsei (n.d.), who added nine fascicles from the 12-fascicle edition to the 75-fascicle edition. Another edition with 83 fascicles was also popular at the time.

The Bonsei manuscript was prominent until the Edo period, when a new phase of investigating the *Treasury* got under way, driven by several factors. These included increased rivalry with the Rinzai sect under the strict oversight of the Tokugawa shogunate's parish system (*danka seidō*), which required each religious faction to proclaim its self-identity, and the renewed impact of Chinese learning based on the advent of the Ōbaku (Ch. Huangbo) Zen sect, whose leaders arrived from the mainland in the middle of the seventeenth century despite a general ban on immigration. The new conditions led to a vigorous intellectual movement known as the "Restoration of the Sōtō sect" (*shūtō fukko*), spearheaded by the master Gesshū Sōkō (1618–1696), who in his early career had studied monastic rules under Ōbaku teachers. The restoration was primarily based at some of the older temples, including a revived Kōshōji, the long-standing Eiheiji, and nearby Daijōji temple. This site was founded at the end of the thirteenth century by Gikai (1219–1309), a former Daruma school follower who first joined Dōgen's assembly in the early 1240s and almost was chosen as Dōgen's successor before helping establish a new branch headed by Keizan. This initiative sought to rehabilitate and regularize an understanding of the overwhelming importance of the teachings of the founder and to highlight the *Treasury* as his most important work.

However, a related set of interpretative issues led to further controversies. An effort to create an edition containing all the available fascicles was triggered by Manzan Dōhaku (1636–1715), who succeeded Gesshū as abbot of Daijōji and produced a new 89-fascicle edition in 1684. A complete version of the *Treasury*'s informal vernacular writings that took into account all the previous editions was created a decade later, the 95-fascicle edition by Hangyō Kōzen (1627–1693), the thirty-fifth abbot of Eiheiji. Kōzen added six fascicles to Manzan's edition and organized the text based on when the sections were composed. He attempted to compile as many fascicles as possible to come close to the goal of a 100-fascicle edition that Dōgen supposedly planned. The collection included a few compositions that were not part of early editions of the *Treasury*, such as "Discerning the Way," "Conduct in the Novices' Hall," and "Instructions for the Kitchen," among others. Kōzen died before this version was published. It took more than a hundred years until the 95-fascicle edition was released in a still incomplete woodblock printing distributed to members of the sect in the early 1800s. It was another century before the official Main Temple Edition was published in a typeset edition in 1906, albeit with the same number but a different sequence of fascicles than the version from the 1690s.

Meanwhile, in the early eighteenth century Tenkei Denson (1648–1735), backed by some Rinzai skeptics such as Mujaku Dōchū, favored the 60-fascicle edition based on the theory that it deliberately omitted fascicles containing Dōgen's hypercriticism of opposing lineages as well as apparent misuses of Chinese sources. The latter claim derived from the fact that for the first time in centuries Sōtō monks were knowledgeable enough to compare Dōgen's writing with continental texts. Tenkei's view, which led him to rewrite or "correct" numerous passages while eventually producing his own 78-fascicle edition, was emphatically contested by mainstream Sōtō monks from Manzan's lineage led by Banjin Dōtan (1698–1775) and Menzan Zuihō, who collectively wrote six dozen commentaries and labeled Tenkei's faction "worms" eating away at the substance of sectarian doctrine.[23]

When the intention to publish a complete edition of the *Treasury* became clear but was delayed due to various textual controversies, the Sōtō sect institution, with support from the Tokugawa shogunate, outlawed the publication in a ban known as the "Prohibition of the *Treasury*" (*Shōbōgenzō kaiban kinshirei*) that began in 1722 and lasted until 1796. Gentō Sokuchū (1729–1807) became the fiftieth abbot of Eiheiji in 1795 and began publishing the entire collection of the *Treasury* as part of celebrations for Dōgen's 550th death anniversary held in 1803. Gentō died in 1806, a decade before the woodblock edition was finalized, and the project was fulfilled in conjunction with the founder's 650th death anniversary, more than two centuries after Kōzen's initial attempt to construct a 95-fascicle compilation.

Around the turn of the twentieth century, Nishiari Bokusan (1821–1910), who promoted a new approach to *Treasury* studies through holding annual *Genzō-e* retreats, wrote a three-volume set of commentaries on twenty-nine fascicles called *Edifying Investigations of the Treasury* (*Shōbōgenzō keiteki*) that became a tremendously influential. Additional detailed remarks were published by one of Nishiari's leading disciples, Kishizawa Ian (1865–1955), and a first-time paperback edition of the Main Temple Edition was issued in 1939 by Etō Sokuō, then president of Komazawa University. The tide began to turn against the exalted treatment of the 95-fascicle version with groundbreaking studies conducted by various postwar scholars, especially Ōkubo Dōshū (1896–1994), who began to favor the Original Edition containing 75 + 12 in addition to miscellaneous fascicles. This edition is not singular, either, and there are many variations containing different totals. With a base of 87 fascicles, the full number of sections in the Original Edition might be as few as 88 (by adding "Discerning the Way") or 92 (with five miscellaneous fascicles), or as many as 103 by including additional anomalous and alternate versions of various fascicles.

In trying to reconstruct the anomalous editorial process that constructed various versions of the *Treasury*, a major area of scholarly debate pertains to whether Dōgen's attitude may have undergone a "change of heart" (*henka*) from the time he taught in Kyoto, where his community was well versed in Chinese classics and his attitude toward lay or female followers was inclusive, to his tenure in the countryside. The Eiheiji congregation no doubt attracted new members who were less educated in continental literature than monks in the capital and thus required a different way of being introduced to Zen paradoxes. They also probably followed a reclusive lifestyle undistracted by secular pursuits, such as poetry and the arts, featured in urban culture.

Was the move of temple location the main reason for the decline in the production of *Treasury* fascicles and an apparent shift of focus to other kinds of writing emphasizing monastic rules? Moreover, did the lower rate of composition represent a deficiency of ideas during Dōgen's later years, as some researchers argue? Or, conversely, did this reflect a renewal of the master's thinking that sprouted in new directions by emphasizing ethical issues according to another interpretative standpoint? One of the main concerns for current explicators is whether Dōgen intended to express a consistent approach throughout the various sections of the text or purposely changed his theoretical focus and style of writing at crucial turning points of his career. Is the *Treasury* supposed to be read as a single volume, or as a set of variable sub-volumes strung together by later editors?

One view, referred to here as the Decline Theory, which became prominent especially among nonsectarian scholars in the 1970s, suggests that Dōgen lost his creative spark and began to deteriorate at Eiheiji. This opinion can be criticized for failing to appreciate the dynamic relationship between the *Treasury* and other writings from the later stages of Dōgen's life that demonstrate his ongoing productivity despite possible changes of style or thematic focus. Within the Sōtō sect, several significant responses to the Decline Theory have emerged in the past few decades. These include emphasizing that there is a basic continuity throughout Dōgen's entire career; highlighting a sense of rejuvenation or reform that occurred at mid-career stages; and showing that a new focus on social criticism developed near the end of Dōgen's life in reaction to personal and historical circumstances.

The school of thought closely affiliated with the orthodoxy of Sōtō Zen's Traditional Theology (*Dentō Shūgaku*) maintains that a basic steadiness and uniformity of religious vision underlies the various phases of the writing process, so that all the *Treasury* fascicles can be understood in more or less the same way and on a par with Dōgen's other major works. The key factor connecting various periods and genres is an unwavering commitment to the practice of just sitting, which is consistently reflected in both the informal sermons of the *Treasury* and the formal sermons of the *Extensive Record*, as well as the essays of *Dōgen's Monastic Rules*.

An alternative view that, in differing ways, stands at the other end of the spectrum from both the non-Sōtō-oriented Decline Theory and Traditional Theology is Critical Buddhism (*Hihan Bukkyō*). Created within the Sōtō sect by scholars who were concerned with the way Zen attitudes supported policies of discrimination toward outcasts in addition to pre–World War II imperialism, this standpoint argues that Dōgen actually made a significant change on behalf of ethical imperatives primarily expressed in the 12-fascicle edition. That version of the *Treasury*, produced in his final years following what Critical Buddhism claims was a change of heart, emphasizes the inviolability of karmic retribution and the need for repentance to mitigate its effects by all who commit transgressions.

Yet another view that responds to the Decline Theory by defending Dōgen's creativity is Renewal Theology (*Shin Shūgaku*). It offers a compromise position relative to Traditional Theology, which sees Dōgen's approach as unvarying, and Critical Buddhism, which maintains that Dōgen had a major shift in outlook toward the end of his life. The Renewal standpoint sees Dōgen moving back and forth among philosophical positions taken at different career phases. There is no straight line of development leading either horizontally or vertically, but an ongoing crisscross path that nevertheless consistently expresses the master's fundamental belief. Renewal stresses that during the few years just before and during the transition to Echizen from 1242 to 1246, Dōgen began revising or rewriting several fascicles, especially "Buddha Nature," "Great Awakening," and "Going Beyond Enlightenment," which can be seen from preserved manuscripts originally written in his own hand.[24] The manuscripts reveal a process of relatively minor yet nevertheless significant shifts, rather than either a static attitude or a monumental period of conversion.

Table 3.3 highlights the relation among the four major interpretative standpoints based on the issue of whether and to what extent Dōgen may have altered his stance in regard to thematic topics, styles of writing, and attitudes toward metaphysics and ethics, as reflected in what each theory considers to be the primary edition of the *Treasury*. This table shows that, whereas the Decline Theory favors the Main Temple Edition and Critical Buddhism is dedicated to the 12-fascicle edition, the Traditional and

TABLE 3.3 Comparison of different theories of *Treasury* interpretation

	Theme	Style	Attitude	Edition
DECLINE	changing	unvaried	newly inauthentic	Main Temple (95)
TRADITION	unchanging	unvaried	always authentic	Original (75 + 12)
RENEWAL	unchanging	variable	authentic striving	Original (75 + 12)
CRITICAL	changing	variable	newly authentic	12 fascicles only

Renewal theories in respective ways admire the Original Edition covering 75 + 12 fascicles in addition to some alternate versions.

A thoroughgoing analysis of Dōgen's writings in light of these various methodological viewpoints requires a unified scholarly vision to clarify the complicated history and controversial structure along with the doctrinal sophistication and rhetorical elegance of the masterwork. This approach links an examination of Dōgen's biography to thorny text-historical issues regarding multiple versions of the *Treasury*, which encompasses fascicles written in diverse styles and with sometimes seemingly divergent religious goals. Taking into account varying theories is meant to paint a clearer picture of the intentions and implications of Dōgen's viewpoints in relation to his overall oeuvre and career choices that have been reconfigured by so many interpreters over the centuries. Doing so fulfills the hermeneutic task of categorizing the variety of ideas and ideals expressed in different editions.

This volume treats the *Treasury* in terms of a holistic view of its entirety, encompassing all of the fascicles so that subdivisions are seen as contributing to a single work in a way that reflects the inclusive 95-fascicle Main Temple Edition. At the same time, my examination remains sensitive to deviances and divergences from this version that contribute to a more careful understanding of how changes in Dōgen's outlook, especially in the later stages of his career, may have affected the text's structure. Such a nuanced approach is reflected in the Original Edition. A focus on the combination of the 75-fascicle and 12-fascicle versions that is widely accepted in Japan today, though not yet fully disseminated in the West, does not exclude materials included in the Main Temple Edition, since miscellaneous fascicles are also contained in recent publications of the Original Edition. The ensuing chapters refer to fascicles from both the Main Temple and Original editions because, in the final analysis, the basic content is more or less the same even though the organization varies considerably.

PART II

RELIGIOUS TEACHINGS AND PRACTICES

{ 4 }

REALITY AND MENTALITY

ON PERCEIVING THE WORLD OF SENTIENT AND
INSENTIENT BEINGS

OVERVIEW OF PART II

Throughout the *Treasury of the True Dharma Eye*, Dōgen articulates in great depth and detail many of the basic notions for which he is best known in ways that generally complement and reinforce the content and style of his other major writings, especially the formal lectures in the *Extensive Record* and the six essays in his *Monastic Rules*. Dōgen's teachings, which after his death became associated with the main philosophical principles and monastic instructions of Sōtō Zen, are to a large extent compatible with the approaches to theory and practice that were typical of the Chinese Chan and Rinzai Zen movements, as well as various other Japanese sects that emerged in the Kamakura era. However, in many instances his outlook differs significantly and contradicts notions endorsed by various Buddhist schools at the time, including branches of Zen. While striving to explicate the universal foundations of the Dharma, Dōgen clearly sought to distinguish his own ideas appropriated from, but by no means fully reliant on, the views of his mentor Rujing from those of predecessors and rival lineages.

The chapters in the second part of this book critically review five main themes expressed in Dōgen's masterwork: (1) the metaphysical foundations of the fundamental unity of human and natural existence as reflected in the variability of individual perceptions and perspectives; (2) the importance of contingency realized through an awareness of the inevitability of transiency and death for shaping one's religious quest; (3) the question whether language and discourse constitute a creative enhancement to or a duplicitous distraction from the experience of awakening; (4) guidelines for performing just sitting meditation in order to trigger and maintain unceasingly the transcendent state of nonthinking; and (5) regulations for additional kinds of ritual practices involving daily chores and annual ceremonies, as well as the ethical implications of monastic activities.

The main topic discussed in this chapter is speculative musings concerning the relation between perceptivity, or the diversity of human viewpoints, and the indivisibility of true reality. Dōgen maintains that absolute oneness, encompassing the universality and multiplicity of essentially undefiled (*fuzenna*) and undivided manifestations of Buddha nature, is based on the collective rapport of all forms of existence, which consist of disparate sentient and insentient beings. Among the diversity of entities, humans are characterized by endlessly shifting observations and opinions that can be polished and refined through zazen, so as to apprehend uniformity without sacrificing variety. For Dōgen, the process of self-cultivation based on meditative practice involves analyzing distinct ways of understanding the unity of Buddha nature that particular perspectives reflect, yet also distort.

The next area of theoretical reflections, examined in chapter 5, concerns the topics of temporality and mortality, or a focus on mindful awareness of the meaning of death as seen in light of the momentariness and continuity of time. Dōgen emphasizes the evanescent yet enduring quality of temporal existence in his notion of the identity of birth and death (*shōji*), which represent inseparable and intertwined aspects of experience. In order to attain spiritual authenticity, practitioners must come to terms with the inevitability of finitude that is realized not only at the end of life but also in every transient moment of being-time. Dōgen recommends that each practitioner confronting the unavoidability of mortality maintain his or her utmost and steadfast dedication to the path of attaining liberation, instead of withdrawing from a state of concentration out of a sense of hopelessness or, contrariwise, false optimism.

Chapter 6 treats the *Treasury*'s third main conjectural topic, the role of expressivity and duplicity, or the interconnections between various forms of speech and silence in either conveying or concealing the implications of the Dharma for trainees undertaking the strenuous path of seated meditation. Dōgen asserts that religious insight can and must be disclosed through the remarkable efficacy of rhetorical inventiveness (*dōtoku*), including poetic language, which encompasses deceptive tendencies that can be transformed into vehicles for the productive dissemination of Zen truth. For Dōgen, all forms of discourse are eminently useful, including those usually categorized as illusory such as dreams, imaginary ideas, and visions. He applies this principle to interlinear investigations of multifarious kōan dialogues that disclose the process of attaining self-realization in addition to the doctrinal discourses of Mahāyāna sūtras.

The fourth main topic in the *Treasury*, investigated in the seventh chapter, involves practical guidelines for the performance of just sitting. Dōgen links the act of meditation characterized by ongoing reflexivity, or the capacity of the mind to deliberate and try to purify its own functions, with the flexibility of spontaneous insight and the potential to realize great awakening (*daigo*) by being liberated at any moment from conceptual fetters through contemplative awareness that penetrates to the level of unimpeded truth. His analysis represents an innovative approach to understanding the inner workings of training techniques, examining the significance of nonthinking through interpreting several pertinent kōan cases and related Buddhist sayings. For Dōgen, any apparent distinction between the polarities of thought and thoughtlessness, means and end, or dynamism and quietude is overcome by the refutation of deficient views that fail to reflect the unremitting practice of zazen.

The fifth thematic area, discussed in chapter 8, features the significance of rituality and causality based on Dōgen's thought-provoking interpretations of ancient Indian Buddhist precepts and temple procedures in light of guidelines for the etiquette of reclusion promoted by the Chinese Chan school beginning in the twelfth century. Traditional approaches to monastic discipline (*shingi*) are reevaluated in the *Treasury* to undermine the customary bifurcation between actions and ideals, in which following directives for everyday behavior is considered a discrete realm of religious pursuit separable from the effects of meditative exercises. For Dōgen, all aspects of eremitic behavior must be combined with ceremonial observances based on the creative elucidation of subjective factors that motivate intensive Zen training and contribute to each practitioner's continual cultivation of contemplative consciousness. This approach is applied uncompromisingly to all individual and communal situations, including selecting appropriate successors to receive lineal transmission and making critical decisions about moral dilemmas.

Two Fundamental Discursive Standpoints

Two fundamental components of Dōgen's discourse underlying his approach to writing are crucial for understanding various thematic elements expressed in his teachings. One key component is a strong emphasis on realizing the oneness of practice-realization (*shushō ittō*) at all stages of spiritual development and levels of monastic experience. The second component, which I refer to as Dōgen's "basic interpretative standpoint," is his complex hermeneutic method for analyzing both doctrinal and functional issues based on expressing a particularly provocative religious vision. This outlook is characterized by a creative process of interrupting and intruding on diverse textual sources cited in the *Treasury* to uncover deeper layers of philosophical meaning embedded in ordinary speech and action through innovative interpretations of human behavior.

By virtue of these two discursive components, Dōgen continually seeks to break through the illusory boundaries imposed by the devious presuppositions of dualistic thinking in order to clarify the open-ended and adaptable quality of meditative awareness, whereby puzzling and perplexing paradoxes are reconciled and redeemed through inversions, repetitions, or reversals based on wordplay and other resourceful rhetorical devices. Once achieved, the state of unconditional freedom remains liberated from defective assumptions and self-imposed restrictions so as to constantly activate the creative resources of nondual thinking, the realm of nonthinking that lies beyond yet operates in terms of the apparent dichotomy of rational and irrational modes of logic and language. Discussions of being-time, for example, are not a matter of idle speculation about reality but concrete evocations of what it means to realize and embody the true meaning of existence each and every moment. In contrast to many Zen styles of interpretation that tend to deny the efficacy of deliberation and expression because they turn into distractions that hinder the pathway to enlightenment, Dōgen emphasizes that when applied appropriately, reason and speech are very much conducive to reflecting the multiple meanings of realization, and thus should be continually cultivated rather than abandoned.

Oneness of Practice-Realization

Perhaps the single most distinctive aspect of the *Treasury*, seen in the context of Dōgen's lifelong mission to transmit Zen from China to Japan, is an unwavering emphasis on the inseparability of ongoing training and the goal of realizing enlightenment, which is not an end point reached but a process endlessly renewed. Dōgen consistently asserts the unity of practice-realization, or training and attainment, from the time of the earliest *Treasury* writing in the fascicle "Discerning the Way," composed in 1231.

This was just four years after his return from China, where he listened attentively to the sermons of Rujing and wrote poetry alongside his mentor while they also conversed extensively in the otherwise restricted inner chamber of the abbot's quarters. In numerous passages Dōgen maintains that the overcoming of his doubt achieved through the experience of casting off body-mind reflects the oneness of the otherwise divided realms of practice, usually conceived as a means that leads to a final result, and realization, customarily regarded as a destination. Dōgen's stance is not unique, however, as it recalls the emphasis on "postrealization cultivation" (*shōtaichōyō*) advocated by several prominent Rinzai Zen thinkers, especially Daitō (1282–1337) during the medieval era and Hakuin (1686–1768) in early modern Japan.

In conveying this insight, Dōgen's view can be contrasted with the Japanese Tendai sect's notion of original awakening as an innate endowment or potential to be manifested, as well as the contrary but equally deficient idea of acquired enlightenment (*shikaku*), which sees *nirvāṇa* or the cessation of desire and ignorance as a goal to be reached only after, and as the consequence of, a prolonged course of training. Both notions of original and acquired awakening, according to Dōgen, tend to reduce Buddha nature to an abstraction independent from the immediacy of human existence. Instead, Buddha nature should be seen as coterminous with or a provisional verbal designation for an enlightened being's active exertion (*gyōbutsu*) here and now (*nikon*) that is perpetually transforming itself. Dōgen also sought to overcome the anthropocentric tendency to view Buddha nature primarily in terms of human spirituality, rather than as a universal principle encompassing all phenomena yet surpassing the standpoint of any particular person.

In response to a hypothetical question about why a person who has gained enlightenment should bother to keep practicing meditation after the breakthrough of casting off body-mind, Dōgen writes in "Discerning the Way" that such an imperative does apply because "The Dharma is amply present in every person, but unless one continues to practice, it is not manifested; and unless there is ongoing realization, it is not attained" (Bendōwa: Dōgen 2.460, Nearman 1, Tanahashi 3). In that vein, he strongly encouraged his teacher Myōzen to travel to China in 1223 based on the urgency of the spiritual quest, instead of staying home to care for an ill parent. Dōgen furthermore maintains the reciprocity of means and end: "Because the realization of practice is already apparent there is no limit of realization, and because this is the practice of realization there is no beginning of practice" (Bendōwa: Dōgen 2.470, Nearman 12, Tanahashi 12). By

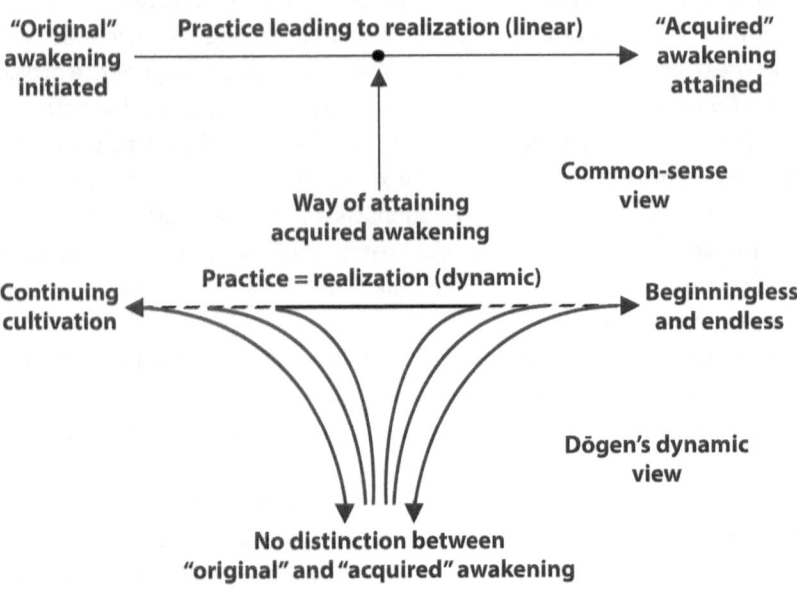

FIGURE 4.1 Dōgen's view of awakening contrasted with the conventional view

Adapted from Masao Abe, *A Study of Dōgen: His Philosophy and Religion*, ed. Steven Heine (Albany: State University of New York Press, 1994), 25–26

abandoning an aim-seeking attitude that objectifies the religious goal, which is thereby rendered inaccessible, the practitioner becomes fully aware of the present moment without needing to rely on a conventional sense of starting or finishing the path.

The illustrations in figure 4.1 contrast the misleadingly dualistic view with the appropriately nondual outlook Dōgen expresses in regard to the relation between realms. According to Dōgen, the relationship between practice and realization is at once linear and sequential, in that practice can be thought to serve as an indispensable ground or basis of a step-by-step or irreversible path toward attaining enlightenment, without beginning or end, because the insubstantial but inexhaustible experiences of practice qua realization are simultaneous and overlapping. Practice and realization represent provisionally reversible accomplishments in terms of the twin possibilities of gaining advancement beyond awakening and undergoing a backsliding away from attainment that is nevertheless still a form of realization.

Dōgen emphasizes that oneness means realization is only maintained so long as the practice of meditation continues. But the converse is also true in that, as soon as one aspires to or arouses the thought of pursuing realization and begins to meditate, enlightenment at that very moment is already being realized, at least in a partial sense, yet with the notable caveat that for Dōgen partiality encompasses entirety. Therefore, four main stages of training—(a) arousing the longing and resolve for enlightenment (*hosshin*), (b) practicing with determination (*shugyō*) to attain nirvāṇa, (c) realizing the awakening of wisdom (*bodai*, Skr. *bodhi*), and (d) cultivating the body-mind after realization (*gyōji*)—are sequential and successive only on the surface level. From a deeper understanding these states become amalgamated indicators of the all-encompassing "ring of the way of continuous effort" (*gyōji dōkan*), a Daoist term for nonduality rejecting distinctions between "this" and "that" also used in Zen by Hongzhi. According to the fascicle "Sustained Exertion," "In the great way of buddhas and ancestors, unremitting effort is supreme since the path is circulating ceaselessly. There is not even the slightest gap between resolution, practice, wisdom, and postrealization awareness because the impact of continuous effort is always distributed everywhere" (Gyōji: Dōgen 1.145, Nearman 374, Tanahashi 332). Therefore, the four modes of training are intertwined and actualized each and every instant.

Although in building creatively on previous Chinese and Japanese interpretative styles Dōgen is greatly admired for exceptional discursive craftsmanship, his emphasis on the oneness of practice-realization makes it abundantly clear that he does not wish to be considered primarily a literary figure. Nor is he a philosopher, despite the profound metaphysical significance and ethical implications of much of the *Treasury*'s contents, because his attitude is that of not an armchair thinker but an avid pioneering proponent of Zen as a complete way of life.[1] In "Discerning the Way" Dōgen writes, "Let us be clear that, for a Buddhist, the main issue is not a matter of debating the superiority or inferiority of one teaching or another, or of establishing arguments in regard to their respective depths. All any adept needs to understand is whether practice is authentic or not" (Bendōwa: Dōgen 2.467, Nearman 9, Tanahashi 9).

Additionally, Dōgen remarks, "As for the truth of Buddha nature: Buddha nature is not incorporated prior to attaining buddhahood; it is incorporated upon the attainment of buddhahood. Buddha nature is always manifested simultaneously with the attainment of buddhahood (*jōbutsu*).

This truth should be very deeply penetrated in dedicated practice based on at least twenty or thirty years of diligent Zen training" (Busshō: Dōgen 1.22, Nearman 254, Tanahashi 241). Moreover, "When they hear the term 'Buddha nature,' a great many students of Buddhism mistake this for the false sense of an eternal self that is expounded by the Senika heresy. This occurs because they have not yet encountered a true person, actualized their real inner self, or met an authentic teacher" (Busshō: Dōgen 1.15–16, Nearman 246, Tanahashi 235–236).

For Dōgen, the search for and realization of Buddha Dharma, as well as speculative disclosures regarding this intricate lifelong process, are uniquely combined by virtue of the oneness of practice-realization. The modern scholar Masao Abe suggests that this notion enables Dōgen's theoretical eloquence: "Dōgen employed a vivid, personal style grounded in his subjective speculations. Even when he used traditional Buddhist phrases, passages, etc., he interpreted them in unusual ways in order to express truth, as he understood it."[2] Furthermore, Abe argues that this inimitable quality catapults Dōgen to the status of one of the greatest exponents of East Asian Buddhism in that "he was endowed with a keen linguistic sensibility and philosophical mind. His main work, the *Treasury*, perhaps unsurpassable in its philosophical speculation, is a monumental document in Japanese intellectual history. In Dōgen, we find a rare combination of religious insight and philosophical ability. In this respect, he may well be compared with Thomas Aquinas, born twenty-five years after him."[3] Despite—or, ironically, because of—not being primarily a philosopher or a writer, Dōgen regularly utilizes those sorts of insights and abilities to his pedagogical advantage.

Dōgen's Basic Interpretative Standpoint

Throughout the *Treasury*, Dōgen applies his speculative skill accompanied by rhetorical savvy to provide inventive elucidations of traditional Zen views of theory and training. The distinctive interpretative approach of the majority of the fascicles is dependent on, but also somewhat divergent from, various kinds of Song Chinese writings Dōgen learned on the mainland. To understand the copious literary connections that helped create the rich and highly allusive texture of his corpus filled with intertextual citations and references, it is necessary to see how Dōgen incorporated materials culled from manifold Chan texts that first appeared in the eleventh century and flourished for a couple hundred years. Major influences on Dōgen included transmission histories of various lineages and the recorded sayings of individual masters, all of which treat the lives of eminent adepts whose intense experiences embody the realization of ineffable Zen truth with universal significance.[4]

Dōgen's discourse also appropriates the evaluative literary style of the *Blue Cliff Record* and other kōan compilations centered on assessing numerous case narratives by analyzing the symbolism of encounter dialogues. The *Blue Cliff Record* adds extensive prose and poetic commentaries to these sources, in addition to hybrid or prose-poetic capping-phrase remarks (*jakugo*) that evoke a host of related anecdotes, parables, and legends about the experience of realization. Unlike the multilayered style of Song compilations that interpret a particular dialogue surrounded by diverse kinds of commentaries, the structure of the *Treasury* focuses first and foremost on doctrinal themes or topics of religious practice. Nearly every fascicle raises a key Zen or Mahāyāna Buddhist notion involving philosophy or monastic behavior. The kōan exchange, which constitutes the core literary unit of a case record, plays a crucial role in Dōgen's novel interpretative framework that I refer to as the "hermeneutics of intrusion," because of the way original sources are interrupted, displaced, and altered by the master's special insights reflecting his genius for reading (or misreading) Chinese sources.[5]

The fluidity and flexibility of Dōgen's informal sermons, originally delivered to a small group of disciples and later edited, collected, and eventually published, make the *Treasury* less conservative in structure than the major kōan collections like the *Blue Cliff Record* that adhere to a fixed pattern for making remarks on each case. Nevertheless, Dōgen's masterwork is consistent with these compilations in allowing for—or even demanding—license to be taken with convention in order to capture the true spirit and intention of the original (supposedly) spontaneous and irreverent utterances of generations of Chan masters representing diverse lineages. In addition to its highly refined literary quality borrowed in part from Japanese rhetorical techniques used to reinterpret Buddhist classics, Dōgen's writing in the *Treasury* shows a considerable degree of influence from early Indian Abhidharma or *śāstra* literature in its use of a line-by-line (or interlinear) style of analysis exploring the conjectural and psychological implications of various teachings.

There are four main rhetorical steps constituting the hermeneutics of intrusion that can be tracked by examining key passages from the *Treasury*: (1) the proposition, or setting up of the main theme and explicating why it is important for the overall endeavor of maintaining meditative awareness; (2) the citation of kōan cases, including passages from collections of remarks about the dialogues proffered by previous Zen teachers, all of which serves as exemplary expressions illustrating the significance of the key topic; (3) the atomization, or zeroing in to interpret innovatively through wordplay and free association the specific wording of the dialogues and various comments cited, so that meaning is not taken for granted but freshly appreciated and appropriated; and (4) the evaluation, or assessing the underlying significance of cases for putting forth Dōgen's overall vision of the unity of practice-realization. This last step usually involves disagreeing with and deconstructing stereotypical standpoints while demanding that the reader take full responsibility for the interpretative process by advancing his or her own approach to contemplative training. At the end of the fascicle "The Nature of Things," for instance, Dōgen challenges a traditional Chan saying and then turns to the audience to demand responses from members of the assembly by saying, "Speak up, now! Speak up, now!" (Hōsshō: Dōgen 2.30, Nearman 652, Tanahashi 562).

In his discussions of kōan cases, Dōgen's method of explanation and evaluation at once builds upon and departs from that of most Zen commentators by constantly challenging and intruding upon the dialogues discussed in order to turn commonplace readings and renderings upside down or inside out. By offering a comprehensive sweep of views regarding the topic and then undertaking an atomized investigation of particular phrasings from the standpoint of multiperspectivism, which fosters the inversion of hackneyed interpretations, Dōgen frequently alters the course of the dialogue in the original case record. He first changes the way the exchange transpires and then makes suggestions and countersuggestions in the spirit of irreverent creativity aimed at capturing the contemporaneous significance of the case for his group of disciples and, by extension, later generations of readers. Moreover, he consistently resists the tendency of previous commentators to identify winners and losers of a contest by questioning the merit of an apparent victor's contribution while also uplifting the remarks of the so-called defeated party.

TRUE REALITY

One of many illustrations of how Dōgen uses the hermeneutics of intrusion to explicate kōans in order to shed light on the true meaning of reality and perceptivity embedded in everyday words is found in the fascicle "Everyday Life." This title refers to the behavior of monks in training, regarded as no more or less valuable than simply "sipping tea and eating rice." These actions signify supreme dedication that makes the most of each and every mundane function. In accord with traditional approaches to the topic, Dōgen writes, "Buddhas and ancestors prepare tea and rice, and tea and rice help sustain and support buddhas and ancestors. Since this is so, for our part we do not need to rely on anything other than the efficacy of sipping from their cup of tea and eating from their bowl of rice" (Kajō: Dōgen 2.124, Nearman 734, Tanahashi 621).

In the second step of the hermeneutic process Dōgen cites various Chan sources, including over half a dozen sayings and poems attributed to Rujing. One of the verses, written when Rujing was once visiting a temple in the remote mountains, suggests that eating rice is coterminous with meditation and thus contributes to one's capacity to trigger an instantaneous self-realization symbolized by a dramatic natural occurrence: "For half a year I ate rice sitting atop a cloud-covered peak, / concentrating on breaking through thousands of layers of dense mist. / All of a sudden, I heard a resounding clap of thunder and saw a bolt of lightning overhead. / The whole area was lit up with springtime colors from apricot blossoms aglow in crimson red" (Kajō: Dōgen 2.127, Nearman 738, Tanahashi 634). Near the end of the fascicle, Dōgen mentions a famous exchange involving Zhaozhou, one of the most popular masters, whose dialogues are cited in numerous kōan collections. Zhaozhou asks a newly arrived novice, "Have you come here before or not?" When the novice replies, "Yes, I have," the master tells him, "Go have some tea." After this, another novice responds to the query that he has not "come here before," and Zhaozhou gives the same instruction. When a more advanced monk stops by to ask why the two opposite responses elicited the identical directive, Zhaozhou gestures to him and says, "Go have some tea" (Kajō: Dōgen 2.128, Nearman 739, Tanahashi 625).

Whereas most interpretations of this kōan deal with the paradoxical relation between contradictory answers in the subexchanges that both culminate in the offering of tea, in the third step of his hermeneutics Dōgen analyzes the seemingly commonplace question posed by Zhaozhou about whether the novices had ever "come here" (*tōshi*), a phrase used six times in the case record. Dōgen argues that this double-edged query should not be understood, as it unfortunately was by Zhaozhou's interlocutors, as a superficial inquiry about a factual matter of where the person is or ever was situated. Instead, Dōgen argues, it represents a probing investigation of the practitioners' spiritual state by asking, in effect, whether or not they had ever been able to realize the moment of being-time that is manifested here and now.

"This term 'come here,'" Dōgen remarks, "is not something said off the top of one's head; nor does it refer to the nostrils [in the sense of monastic discipline], or to the personhood of Zhaozhou" (Kajō: Dōgen 2.129, Nearman 740, Tanahashi 625). The message of the case's instruction is that for failing to seize the opportunity to respond according to the master's deeper level of understanding, all three clerics—including the third monk, who should have known better than to succumb to the same error as two novices—must go back to the starting point of their practice by enacting everyday life in the monastery in an authentic way. According to Dōgen, "By being liberated from 'here' [in the literal sense], Zhaozhou's question asks about the monks 'coming here' or 'not coming here' [in the spiritual sense]. From that lofty standpoint, the authentic question of whether a monk 'has come here' or 'has not come here' [in the sense of attaining self-realization] can be evaluated" (Kajō: Dōgen 2.129, Nearman 740, Tanahashi 625). At this very moment of being-time, drinking tea does not represent either a rejoinder or a lead-in to another activity but, if appropriately realized, the full manifestation of practice-realization.

Finally, in step 4 of the interpretative method, Dōgen cites a comment by Rujing criticizing typical practitioners, whose delusions are so deep-seated and stubbornly held that they are left incapacitated by Zhaozhou's probing query: "Those who abide within the picture of a wine shop [signifying the ordinary world filled with misunderstandings] cannot get to know Zhaozhou well enough to have a chance to sip from his cup of tea" (Kajō: Dōgen 2.129, Nearman 740, Tanahashi 626). Dōgen concludes the fascicle by challenging the reader to come to terms with the full effect of Rujing's expression, asserting, "If you can understand this exclamation, then you will realize that the everyday life of buddhas and ancestors is nothing other than sipping tea and eating rice" (Kajō: Dōgen 2.129, Nearman 740, Tanahashi 625).

One of the main implications of Dōgen's unique reading of Zhaozhou's tea dialogue is to show how a dedicated Zen trainee must be able to abandon conventional views that divide reality into artificial polarities of "this" and "that." Such oppositions are nothing other than self-imposed boundaries to realization that impede a direct experience of the immediate moment, and therefore do not allow a full range of attitudes to unfold in distinctive ways, encompassing various shadings. This recalls comments by Jonathan Z. Smith (1938–2017), a prominent historian of the ancient world who argued that nearly all worldwide religious thinkers in their respective styles have been engaged in the primary task of negotiating polarities by "devising ways to manage the distance between us and them, the proper and the improper, the tame and the wild, the planned and the accidental, or here and there and now and then."[6]

Indivisibility and Multiplicity

Dōgen's rhetorical flourishes based on reversals and inversions highlight and transform, without ignoring or suppressing, contradictions and inconsistencies that are part of contemplative consciousness of the unity of existence. This level of understanding navigates two inseparable extremes by embracing absolute indivisibility, which is unconditionally unified yet filled with endlessly diverse human and nonhuman activities, and limitless multiplicity, which utterly lacks overabundance or random unevenness since its disparate manifestations are based on oneness.[7]

According to the teachings of the *Treasury*, all conceptual dichotomies, such as apparent oppositions between life and death, practice and realization, being and becoming, beginning and end, mind and objects, speech and silence, and Buddha nature and sentient beings are overcome and dissolved into an incomprehensible unity that does not seek to eliminate but rather restores and preserves an emphasis on the variability of specific perspectives. Dōgen recognizes that each and every aspect of reality is perceived differently depending on how one's perception unfolds in a given context. Therefore, the fundamentally paradoxical standpoint highlighting underlying connections between evanescence and stability, spontaneity and duration, equality and hierarchy, and unification and inconsistency continues to intrigue and inspire, yet also challenge and befuddle readers.

To put in historical context the incongruous but, from the Sōtō founder's view, ultimately resolvable relationship between the indivisibility of true reality and the multiplicity of phenomena that compose existence, Dōgen's approach extends an understanding of the traditional Buddhist notion of nirvāṇa. This state is regarded as the realm of nonduality, which harbors no distinctions and represents the intuitive awareness of transcendental wisdom (Skr. *prajñā*, Jp. *hannya*) that cannot be grasped objectively or known through analytical thinking alone. For Dōgen, such a realization is not necessarily the outcome of a lengthy path persistently advancing toward enlightenment; it can happen at any or every time because each instance of apparent duality is inseparable from and rests on a moment of being-time that actualizes nonthinking. The dynamic manifestation of enlightenment here and now (*genjōkōan*), an unmediated yet mysterious unfolding of nirvāṇa within a life of change and decay, constitutes the fundamental contradictoriness of true reality that, in effect, harbors no conflict whatsoever. Dōgen suggests that everyone has the capacity to realize this dynamic state that is "not one, not two" through just sitting, in addition to daily monastic activities conducted by perpetually casting off body-mind.

One extreme embraced without conflict is the holistic standpoint of undivided existence that is complete and unwavering. This sense of absolute identity is often articulated in *Treasury* fascicles in terms of *via negativa*, or a negative approach to defining ultimate reality through the use of terms such as nonduality (*funi*, lit. "not two"), nondiscrimination (*mufunbetsu*), the undefiled (*fuzenna*), the indistinguishable (*fui*), the dissimilar (*fudō*), and the uninterrupted (*mukandan*). At the same time, an understanding of unity is expressed by means of *via positiva*, or positive terminology, including phrasings like oneness (*ichinyo*), one mind (*isshin*), one body (*ittai*), one realm (*ittō*), equality (*byōdō*), or the selfsame substance (*dōtai*).[8]

Furthermore, some positive expressions indicate that ultimate unity is not independent of the relativity of the vibrant phenomenalism of total activity (*zenki*), or complete dissemination (*entsū*) of the circle of the Way (*dōkan*) by actualizing the dharma position (*hōi*) that emerges through the full exertion (*gūjin*) of arising-becoming (*gōjō*) or the manifesting (*genjō*) of each entity. All these terms point to the link between the extreme of oneness and the other extreme, the partiality and variability of discrete momentary elements of existence that give rise to diverse perceptions and manifold perspectives. Additional constructive terms expressing the harmony of true reality in relation to multiplicity include the suchness (*immo*) of the ancient mirror (*kokyō*), the moon (*tsuki*), the one bright pearl (*ikka myōjū*), and the radiant light (*kōmyō*).

The images suggesting brightness, polish, and luster are in the end considered no different than the deepest darkness, in another supreme paradox suggesting that doubt and despair continue during enlightenment, even as the potential for realization permeates the most deceptive delusions. In the fascicle "One Bright Pearl," Dōgen cites Master Xuansha's (835–908) saying, "The whole universe in every direction is one bright pearl." When a disciple merely mimics these words instead of trying to grasp their inner meaning, Xuansha replies, "I see you are still making your living in a demon's cave on some pitch-black mountain" (Ikka myōjū: Dōgen 1.78, Nearman 38, Tanahashi 35). Dōgen adds that the novice's attitude of futility is "nothing other than chasing a thief while riding the horse of the robber"

(Ikka myōjū: Dōgen 1.79, Nearman 39, Tanahashi 36). However, the fascicle concludes with the following observation:

> Why worry about whether or not some specific thing is a bright pearl? Even if you are perplexed and lost in delusion, do not think that this is not the action of a bright pearl. Since there is no deed or thought ever generated that does not reflect the bright pearl, even going back and forth or in and out of a demon's cave on a pitch-black mountain is nothing other than the manifestation of one bright pearl. (Ikka myōjū: Dōgen 1.81, Nearman 41, Tanahashi 38)

A prime example of Dōgen's rhetorical acumen showing the basic unity of the conceptual and tangible realms usually seen as separate categories occurs in the fascicle "The Moon," which reinterprets a saying attributed to Śākyamuni Buddha, "Buddha's true Dharma body, as it is, is empty of form. In response to things, forms appear. Thus it is like (*nyo*) the moon reflected in water" (Tsuki: Dōgen 1.262, Nearman 545, Tanahashi 453).[9] According to his reinterpretation of the simile of lunar light shining on a sea to highlight that true reality is embodied in all phenomena, Dōgen maintains, "The thusness of, 'Thus it is like the moon reflected in water,' is itself the moon in water. It is water as thus, moon as thus, thusness in, and in thusness. The term 'thus' does not mean that it is 'like something,' but that it is the very thing" (Tsuki: Dōgen 1.262, Nearman 545, Tanahashi 453). Therefore, "like" (*nyo*) is not used to indicate conventional "resemblance" (*sōji*). In Dōgen's view, "the thusness of being like something else is instead the thisness of its concrete existence" (*nyo wa ze nari*) (Tsuki: Dōgen 1.262, Nearman 545, Tanahashi 453).

Dōgen reads the term *nyo* in the key phrase "like the moon reflected in water" (*nyosui chūgetsu*) not in the ordinary way but as the word that appears in the important Mahāyāna Buddhist term *shinnyo* (lit. "true likeness"), a Chinese translation of the Sanskrit *tathatā* that is usually rendered into English as "thusness," "suchness," "as-it-is-ness" or "true reality." "Thisness" (*ze*) refers to the "concrete," the "definite," or "that thing." So the truth of all phenomena—the "thusness" of their "thisness" and the "thisness" of their "thusness"—is the moon-in-water reality of the true Dharma body of the Buddha, a vast emptiness embracing each entity without priority or distinction. Beyond the speculative implications of his deliberate misreading of the original source, Dōgen stresses that understanding all concrete particularities in relation to every aspect of existence is worthy of a practitioner's fully engaged training efforts undertaken from the perspective of sitting meditation, which unifies diverse standpoints.

Dynamism and Stability

To avoid any lingering sense of there being a subtle dichotomy that might divide self from other, mind from body, or thought from sensation, Dōgen reinterprets or devises several metaphors to portray the sense of dynamism that characterizes the oneness of indivisibility and multiplicity. An example refers to the rolling action of a pearl in a bowl. In the fascicle "Spring and Autumn," Dōgen cites a verse by Chinese master Yuanwu (1063–1135), one of the premier kōan commentators of the Song dynasty, who authored the commentaries of the *Blue Cliff Record*:

> The bowl spins the pearl, and the pearl spins in the bowl,
> as an example of the ephemeral in the eternal and the eternal in the ephemeral.
> An antelope uses its horns to hang from the branches of a tree, thereby leaving no trace;
> yet hunting dogs, circling the forest, trample a path in vain pursuit.
> (Shunjū: Dōgen 1.412, Nearman 749, Tanahashi 634)

In his prose comments Dōgen says he admires the strikingly unusual phrase, "the bowl spins the pearl," as "an unprecedented and incomparable expression that has rarely been heard in the past or present. Previously, people have only referred to the pearl rolling around in the bowl, as if the container was something constant and unchanging" (Shunjū: Dōgen 1.412, Nearman 750, Tanahashi 634). By presenting the complementary image, Dōgen points out, Yuanwu clearly discloses an appropriately holistic standpoint linking the movement of the pearl with that of the bowl. As part of his creative interpretation, however, Dōgen goes on to question the last two lines of the verse evoking the legend that an antelope representing a savvy adept is able to use its horns to escape the stalking canine. He suggests that Yuanwu should have also said, "the forest is circling the hunting dogs" (Shunjū: Dōgen 1.413, Nearman 750, Tanahashi 634).

In the fascicle "Thusness," Dōgen reinterprets yet another metaphor for dynamic activity by citing a story about the eighteenth Indian ancestral teacher according to Zen lore, Saṃghanandi (Jp., Sōgyanandai), and his successor *Gayāśata (Jp., Kayashata; the Sanskrit is reconstructed from the Japanese). Upon hearing chimes hung in a chamber ring when blown by the wind, the teacher asks Gayāśata, "Would you say the wind is ringing or the chimes are ringing?" Gayāśata replies, "It is not the wind ringing or the chimes ringing; it is the mind that is ringing." Saṃghanandi asks, "What is the mind?" When Gayāśata answers, "It is equivalent to saying that everything is altogether tranquil in its stillness," the teacher approves and transmits the *Treasury of the True Dharma Eye* (Inmo: Dōgen 1.206, Nearman 367, Tanahashi 327).[10]

In this dialogue, neither the notion of sound existing outside the mind nor the notion of the mind existing outside sound is acceptable, since both fail to appreciate that nothing beyond sensory impressions exists and sensations do not have any independence from the mind that perceives them. According to Dōgen, "The underlying principle is that if one thought or thing is truly still, all the myriad thoughts and things are also still along with it. If the wind's blowing is still, then the bell's ringing will be still; hence, Gayāśata spoke of everything being altogether tranquil in its stillness" (Inmo: Dōgen 1.206, Nearman 367, Tanahashi 327). Through his hermeneutics of intrusion, however, Dōgen resists holding to the doctrine of tranquility and brings out a deeper implication by suggesting that "The sound heard in the mind is beyond the sound created by the wind or the sound generated by the bell, and thus the sound that is stirred by the mind is beyond the sound that is heard in the mind" (Inmo: Dōgen 1.207, Nearman 367, Tanahashi 327). Therefore, Dōgen argues, Gayāśata "should also have said that the sound is the ringing of the wind, the ringing of the bell, the ringing of blowing, and the ringing of ringing" (Inmo: Dōgen 1.207, Nearman 368, Tanahashi 328). Since all aspects in their collectivity and connectivity contribute to what the bell produces, the tautological final phrase resembles Edgar Allen Poe's use of "tintinnabulation" in "The Bells" to refer to "the jingling and the tinkling" of chimes.

The wording in Dōgen's comment also recalls a verse enunciated by Rujing on the sound of a wind bell that Dōgen praises highly and cites in the fascicle "The Perfection of Great Wisdom" and elsewhere, including the fascicle "Empty Space":[11] "My whole being is like the mouth of a bell hanging in empty space: / It does not ask whether the wind blows east, west, north, or south. / In unison, it speaks of wisdom for the sake of others: / The ringing and jingling is the tintinnabulation of the bell" (Makahannya haramitsu: Dōgen 1.11, Nearman 28, Tanahashi 27).[12] In Dōgen's reworked version of the poem in the *Extensive Record*, the last line is identical but the first and second lines have minor, though significant, differences (highlighted in italics), subtly indicating an emphasis on activity rather than impartiality. The main distinction from Rujing's verse lies in the third line, where Dōgen stresses the unique quality of each individual sound disclosing its own truth instead of a blending of sounds to convey universality:

> My whole being is a mouth of a bell *differentiating* empty space
> As wind *rises* from east, west, north, or south.
> In unison, *each clear sound speaking its particular expression*:
> The ringing and jingling are the tintinnabulation of the bell.[13]

Another analogy using the image of sailing a boat, evoked in the fascicle "Total Activity," at once emphasizes and overcomes apparent dualities of the universal and particular, human and natural, mental and physical, and internal and external, while allowing for endless diversity and division of subject and object or means and end. This state, achieved without falling into the conceptual trap of either monistic or phenomenal reductionism, was described in a lecture presented to Hatano and his entourage while Dōgen was living in Kyoto. The metaphor is quite similar to a passage about riding a vessel featured in "Realization Here and Now" as a deceptively simple way of conveying the meaning of the true Dharma eye:

> Life is just like sailing in a boat. Although I raise the sails, row with an oar, and steer, the boat is giving me a ride and I could not ride without the boat. But by sailing in the boat I make the boat what it is.... Hence, I make life what it is, and life makes me what I am. When riding in a boat, my body-mind and the relation between self and environment are altogether the dynamic function of the boat (*fune no kikan*), and the whole earth and the entire sky take part.... At this very moment there is nothing other than the world of the boat. The sky, water, and shore are all part of this very moment of boating, which is completely different from occasions when I am not in a boat. Thus, life is what I make it to be and I am what life makes me to be. (Zenki: Dōgen 1.260, Nearman 526, Tanahashi 451)

By expressing indivisibility yet variability in the final sentence, thus recalling the image of the pearl and bowl spinning together, the boat metaphor highlights unceasing activity involving all aspects of existence engaged collectively at each and every instance of being-time. On the other hand, in order to characterize the profound challenges to attaining correct understanding, Dōgen is careful to warn practitioners against forming an attachment to the concept of movement without recognizing that stability is equally relevant. In this vein, he occasionally cites a Zen phrase used in the *Blue Cliff Record* and elsewhere suggesting that human experience is like "a silver mountain or iron wall" (*ginzan teppeki*).[14]

BUDDHA NATURE

Much of Dōgen's hermeneutic outlook is indebted to the approach of the highly influential Chinese Mādhyamika (Middle Way) school thinker, Jizang (549–623, Jp. Kichizō), who maintained that the "refutation of erroneous views is the illumination of right views" (Ch. *boxie xianzheng*) and vice versa. The corrective process is like using water to extinguish a fire without allowing the water to be affected, since there would then not be any means available to douse its flame.[15] In order to overcome any clinging to a misleading notion of movement, in the fascicle "Buddha Nature" Dōgen criticizes countless unreflective people who tend to conflate true reality with the mere motion of the wind blowing or a fire burning. They embrace the vagaries of ordinary consciousness that tends to fancy different sensations without cultivating genuine self-awareness.

Dōgen clarifies that authentic unity is neither "an infinite number of miscellaneous fragments" nor "a single, undifferentiated steel rod" (Busshō: Dōgen 1.16, Nearman 247, Tanahashi 236), seemingly opposite characterizations that both violate the basic Buddhist tenet of interdependent origination (Skr. *pratītya samutpāda*, Jp. *engi*). Identity cannot be understood in terms of an amalgamation of various objects because the world would not be causally linked; nor is it represented by one pole, since that would mean that existence is unchanging and unmoving. Dōgen then suggests that reality is "neither large nor small," a negation that represents a correct view but still falls short of disclosing concrete existence. A living image is evoked by the term "a raised fist" in the next passage to reflect the appropriate action that an adept makes while teaching disciples.[16] Such a characterization is vivid and animated. Yet Dōgen also points out that "Buddha nature cannot be compared to a Buddhist sage and cannot be compared to Buddha nature itself" (Busshō: Dōgen 1.16, Nearman 247, Tanahashi 236). Any saying that seems effective in a certain context is merely an expedient pedagogical device that ultimately falls short of conveying reality, even though failure in its own way constitutes a form of truth.

Whole-Being Buddha Nature

"Buddha Nature" is by far the longest and most complicated fascicle of the *Treasury* from both philosophical and philological standpoints, based on its sustained discussion in multiple sections of various kōan cases and other maxims about the main topic. At the very beginning, Dōgen cites and radically reinterprets a famous passage from the *Nirvāṇa Sūtra*. According to this scripture, a hallmark of Mahāyāna theory that has influenced nearly all Buddhist schools in East Asia, including Japanese Tendai and Pure Land in addition to Zen, "Śākyamuni Buddha said, 'All (*issai* 一切) sentient beings (*shujō* 衆生) without exception (*shitsu* 悉) have (*u* 有) Buddha nature (*busshō* 仏性). The Tathāgata always abides, without any change'" (Bussho: Dōgen 1.14, Nearman 244, Tanahashi 234). The second sentence involving the possible duality of change and changelessness will be discussed in detail in the examination of the topic of time in chapter 5.

In exploring the ramifications of the *Treasury*'s radical reappraisal of the sūtra's opening sentence for understanding Dōgen's view of true reality in relation to authentic human experience, we find the master deliberately intruding on the source by reinterpreting the passage to indicate a single unified phrase, "whole-being-Buddha nature" (*shitsu-u-busshō*) (Busshō: Dōgen 1.14, Nearman 245, Tanahashi 235). This wording means something quite different than a typical understanding of the expression. Dōgen's interpretation indicates the nonduality or oneness of those who realize truth, which encompasses the entire realm of sentient and insentient beings even though only the former are specifically mentioned, and that which is realized, or Buddha nature itself. His view covers the simultaneity of reality (nature) and the experience of enlightenment (Buddha), which reinforces the identity of practice-realization by overcoming the conventional standpoint that sees attainment as a potential to be actualized in the future.

The rhetorical sleight of hand expressed at the beginning of the "Buddha Nature" fascicle epitomizes Dōgen's hermeneutic method by reading—or intentionally misreading—each of the characters in the key sentence to bring out their innermost significance, rather than relying on literal meaning alone. Two main ideas are featured. First, Dōgen manipulates the character 有 (*u*), which is also critical for interpreting the term *uji* (有時) as "being-time" instead of "sometimes." The word *u* can mean "have," as if Buddha nature were something owned as a kind of possession or an embedded attribute. This is like saying humans have a basic goodness that is contained within but not yet realized, which implies a duality between beings and truth or existence and essence. However, *u* can also mean "is," indicating "to be" or "being," so that the term *shitsuu* (悉有) is regarded by Dōgen as a single word that means "whole-being," instead of "without exception have." Furthermore, this interpretation at once modifies and, in effect, deletes the initial term, "all sentient beings" (*issai shujō* 一切衆生), since the upshot is that existing entities, whether living or nonliving, in their entirety must include each and every being that is part and parcel of whole-being, which in turn is coterminous with Buddha nature.

To sum up Dōgen's analysis, the traditional reading indicating that "all sentient beings without exception have Buddha nature" is first transformed into the holistic notion, "whole-being is Buddha nature." Since the copula "is" no longer would be needed because whole-being equals Buddha nature and vice versa, the entire sentence becomes one multihyphenated term, "whole-being-Buddha nature." The matter is by no means settled, however, since Dōgen then makes a concerted effort to warn the reader against various misconceptions of whole-being, which he argues "is not the being of being and nonbeing, emergent being, original being, mysterious being, conditioned being, or illusory being. It has nothing to do with such things as mind and object or substance and form" (Busshō: Dōgen 1.15, Nearman 246, Tanahashi 235).

Whole-being is not original (or timeless) being, because it fills the past right on up through the present; not arising (or becoming) being, because it does not contain even a particle of dust; not an accumulation of separate individual beings, because it is an all-inclusive whole; not beginningless being, because it is here and now; not being that appears at a certain time, because it is the everyday mind. Put in a more positive and concrete way, whole-being "is a buddha's words, a buddha's tongue, the pupils of a buddha's or an ancestor's eyes, the nostrils of a Zen monk.... The entire world is completely free of all objective sensations in that the immediacy of right here and now manifests but there is no second person!" (Busshō: Dōgen 1.15, Nearman 245, Tanahashi 235), evoking a saying of the young Buddha who realized his unique spiritual status on heaven and earth.

In later sections of the "Buddha Nature" fascicle, Dōgen examines from nearly every imaginable angle the seemingly contrary notion of negation (*mu* 無) understood in relation to the truth of Buddha nature that can indicate "does not have," "is not," or simply "no." This term for denial also suggests the metaphysical notions of negation, nonbeing, or nothingness in the sense of the Buddhist notion of "emptiness" (*kū* 空), or the vacuity of all conceptual categories that interfere with spontaneous realization. Similar to the analysis that being Buddha nature is different from a commonplace sense of identity, the notion of nothingness Buddha nature (*mu-busshō*) must not be mistaken for mere absence or lack, or for hopelessness, pessimism, relativism, or nihilism.

While emphasizing the parity of affirmative and negative modes of discourse, Dōgen does not overlook the critical and subversive aspect of language, whose foundation is the insubstantiality of nothingness Buddha nature, a standpoint he much prefers to the mere denial of Buddha nature (*busshō-mu*) or the termination of any productive discussion regarding the implications of doctrine. "You should know," he writes, "that the very act of uttering or hearing nothingness Buddha nature is the direct and immediate path to buddhahood. Because of this, a practitioner is a buddha right at the very instant of manifesting nothingness Buddha nature. Not to have experienced or articulated nothingness Buddha nature is not to have attained buddhahood" (Busshō: Dōgen 1.23, Nearman 255, Tanahashi 242). Yet, whenever Dōgen speaks of the merits of *mu* as a corrective to various false theories of affirmation, he quickly reverses himself and relativizes any conclusion with an emphasis on the fact that in some instances it is preferable to indicate "yes" (*u*) instead of "no."

Below is a partial list of various theories of Buddha nature that Dōgen enumerates; some are complementary while others seem contradictory. Yet each tends to play off and reinforce, while at the same time undermine, all of the other possibilities. Collectively they should be considered part of an inseparable interpretative compendium of ideas rather than discrete doctrinal items:

being Buddha nature	*u-busshō* (有仏性)
whole-being Buddha nature	*shitsuu-busshō* (悉有仏性)
Buddha nature manifest here and now	*busshō-genzen* (仏性現前)
impermanence Buddha nature	*mujō-busshō* (無常仏性)
nothingness Buddha nature	*mu-busshō* (無仏性)
emptiness Buddha nature	*kū-busshō* (空仏性)
denial of Buddha nature	*busshō-mu* (仏性無)

Moreover, to correct delusions tending to either identify truth with the ordinary world or presuppose that it reflects a realm beyond concrete existence, thereby violating the Buddhist middle path, Dōgen seeks in "Buddha Nature" to subvert and surpass various kinds of delusion with positive notions encompassing a unity of opposites. These ideas include: *shitsuu* ("whole-being" 悉有), which overcomes the conflict between anthropocentrism and transcendence; *shingen* ("manifesting body" 真現), which overcomes cosmology versus substantiality; *gyō* ("activity" 行), which overcomes teleology versus potentiality; *setsu* ("disclosure" 説), which overcomes ineffability versus reason; *mujō* ("impermanence" 無常), which overcomes time versus eternity; *i* ("dependence" 衣), which overcomes causation versus liberation; and *gabyō* ("painted rice cake" 画餅), which overcomes reality versus illusion. In a sense, all of these provisional categories are, depending on context and intention, both usefully correct or instructive and uselessly incorrect or hindering of authentic understanding. Their validity depends on the particular instructive setting in which they are evoked, and their utility corresponds to the level of knowledge of those who receive the teachings. Each notion remains susceptible to the deconstructive thrust of a Zen master when it is no longer suited to a particular learning situation.

Nuances of Naturalism

In several prominent *Treasury* fascicles, Dōgen highlights the role of the natural world encompassing innumerable living and nonliving beings as crucial for understanding true reality. His approach to nature is multifaceted. On the level of personal practice, he celebrates the seclusion and serenity of deep mountain forests, such as those where Eiheiji temple was established in Echizen province, as an ideal location for the continuing cultivation of contemplative consciousness far removed from the realm of secular distractions. Dōgen wrote dozens of poems in the *kanbun* and *waka* styles memorializing this reclusive setting as ideal for Zen training. His outlook, which is sometimes summed up by a Sōtō saying that "only in the deep forests can enlightenment be realized," recalls what was said about a retreat held at the massive South Korean Zen complex at Woljeongsa temple based in remote Pyeongchang province, the home of the 2018 Winter Olympics. The natural setting "provides a chance to reset your mind, practice meditation, and soak up the mountain scenery, the monastic lifestyle, Buddhism and *chamseon* (Jp. *zazen*)."[17] According to head monk Tai Woo, "With the peaceful atmosphere of the mountain and the different views and scenery (changing with the seasons), [this] is a very peaceful place that makes every day feel like another new day."[18] Similarly, Dōgen was most content after he fled worldly conflicts occurring in Kyoto for the splendor of the Echizen area, where he experienced a constant state of communion with the deeply forested environment.

On a theoretical level, Dōgen's view of naturalism is influenced by East Asian visual and literary aesthetic traditions that depict the environment as a mirror and model for human behavior in a way that destabilizes anthropocentric attitudes by emphasizing the holistic background of human experience. Dōgen's goal is to embrace extreme positions simultaneously by enhancing the mysterious qualities of nature while maintaining a focus on the Buddhist quest to attain enlightenment as a personal goal. As Hee-Jin Kim explains:

> His approach was neither the humanization of nature, the mechanistic, scientific manipulation of nature, nor the romantic paradisiac absorption into nature. Whether he spoke of humans or nature, Dōgen inevitably (and quite consistently) returned to the non-dualistic soteriology of Buddha nature, radically conceived with the logic of realization rather than the logic of transcendence. Humans and nature, in myriad configurations and forms, while existing and perishing, shared their destinies as the flowers of emptiness.[19]

In the fascicle "Plum Blossoms," delivered when three feet of snow was on the ground during his first autumn in the Echizen mountains, Dōgen cites numerous poems by Rujing admiring the symbolism of spiritual renewal embodied by the earliest spring flowers that bloom and exude an intoxicating fragrance while snowfall still covers the branches of the tree. "The fundamental meaning of what Rujing expressed," Dōgen writes, "is that once the plum flower has blossomed, myriad manifestations of springtime are quick to follow its lead, and these are but one or two of the meritorious functions of the plum tree. As spring transforms multifarious phenomena into events that are fresh and rejuvenated, our variable thoughts about external things are altered in an auspicious, subjective way" (Baika: Dōgen 2.75, Nearman 690, Tanahashi 586).

In the fascicle "Insentient Beings Preaching the Dharma," Dōgen cautions that we should "not explore the matter of insentient beings (*mujō*) preaching the Dharma (*seppō*) as if it were necessarily like that of sentient beings, which generate vocal sounds. To take verbal and nonverbal utterances emerging in the realm of sentient beings out of their context and then liken them to expressiveness manifested in the realm of insentient beings is not the Buddha way" (Mujō seppō: Dōgen 2.4, Nearman 655, Tanahashi 550). However, Dōgen insists that a trainee should remain open to "hearing," both literally and figuratively, though not in a superficial sense, whatever is communicated, which may or may not be spoken with words or any audible sounds, including the ringing of a wind bell, chirping of a bird, rustling of leaves, or murmur of wind blowing.

The theme of a meditative practitioner's intimate, yet somehow separable connection with nature is further indicated in the fascicle "Sounds of Valleys, Colors of Mountains," which cites a famous verse by the eleventh-century poet and statesman Su Shi. Su was one of the premier writers and intellectuals in Northern Song (960–1126) China, who frequently practiced zazen and also wrote poetry along with numerous friends who were Chan monks. One night, while keeping a vigil in a deep forest after being inspired by the abbot's sermon earlier that day on the preaching of inanimate objects, Su Shi composed an elegy that draws from symbolism in the *Lotus Sūtra*:

> The valley stream's sounds are the long tongue [of Buddha],
> The mountain's colors are none other than his pure body.
> With the coming of night, I heard eighty-four thousand songs,
> But with the rising of the sun, how am I ever to explain them to you?
> (Keisei sanshoku: Dōgen 1.274, Nearman 66, Tanahashi 86)[20]

In remarks on this verse reflecting the hermeneutics of intrusion, Dōgen wonders whether the poet was thinking about a famous kōan case attributed to Dongshan, in which insentient beings are said to be preaching the Dharma. Without Su being consciously aware of the inspiration, Dōgen maintains, this recollected content was likely intermingled in his mind with the immediate sound of the stream rippling throughout the night. Dōgen further ponders whether it was the voice embodied by the stream or the sermon's words that actually led to the awakening of the poet. Moreover, he asks ironically, based on the poem's anthropomorphic imagery in highlighting the underlying link between human and nonhuman as well as sentient and insentient beings, "Did layman Su Shi get awakened by viewing the mountains and streams, or were they awakened by viewing him?" (Keisei sanshoku: Dōgen 1.275, Nearman 67, Tanahashi 87). Dōgen concludes by challenging his assembly members to develop their own understanding of the verse, demanding, "Who among you today can clearly see the long tongue and pure body of the Buddha?" (Keisei sanshoku: Dōgen 1.275, Nearman 68, Tanahashi 87).

HUMAN PERCEPTIVITY

The valorization of nature evident in Dōgen's comments relating Su Shi's recorded experience to important implications for understanding true reality is extended and at the same time undermined in the fascicle "Mountains and Rivers Proclaiming the Sūtras." First delivered as a midnight sermon at Kōshōji temple a few weeks after the composition of "Being-Time," this work provocatively suggests that peaks and rivers are both flowing and not flowing or are at once moving and still. The difference between the seemingly opposite states is not fixed or predetermined in an obvious way but depends on various kinds of perceptions of humans and other kinds of beings. Levels of perceptivity should be examined from an all-inclusive standpoint, according to Dōgen, because even advanced practitioners may have trouble reconciling alternative perspectives on reality without succumbing to the cynicism or despair of relativist and nihilist fallacies.

Here and elsewhere in the *Treasury*, Dōgen argues that multiple views about natural phenomena, such as a drop of water, must be taken into account, including sacred and secular or spiritual and scientific standpoints in addition to the views of human or nonhuman as well as actual or mythical beings:

> Not all beings see mountains and rivers in the same way. Some see water as a jeweled ornament, some see water as wondrous blossoms, and hungry ghosts see water as raging fire or pus and blood. Dragons and fish see water as a palace or a pavilion. Some beings see water as seven treasures or a wish-granting jewel and others see water as a forest or a partition. Some see it as the Dharma nature of pure liberation, the true human body, or the form of the body and the essence of mind. (Sansuikyō: Dōgen 1.324, Nearman 148, Tanahashi 158–159)[21]

Dōgen also points out that living in water or imagining the condition of beings that reside there may be tremendously different than (or, more literally, "not the same as," *fudō*) any given human perspective. However, he warns against accepting arbitrary attitudes or conflations by suggesting that the cultivation of the senses through sitting meditation is necessary to avoid being held in the sway of random judgments:

> Although what is seen may differ drastically according to the one perceiving it, we should not be too hasty in accepting this as absolutely so. Are there really many variable ways of seeing any particular single object? Have you committed an error by mistaking for a plethora of images what is actually one entity? At the very utmost of your struggles, you must make an even greater effort to concentrate. (Sansuikyō: Dōgen 1.324, Nearman 149, Tanahashi 159)

The primary point behind these reflections is that Dōgen maintains a Zen adept cannot stand pat with a certain (mis)understanding, since there is always a need to adjust and seize upon new opportunities for gaining self-realization, as each occasion of changing standpoints becomes an opportunity for spiritual growth. According to an aphorism attributed to the Nobel Prize-winning playwright Samuel Beckett, known for his minimalist approach to theatrical dialogue and staging, "Ever tried. Ever failed. No matter. Try again. Fail again. Fail better." This recalls Dōgen saying that enlightenment is an endless process of "disentangling entangled vines by means of entangled vines." Beckett's remark also reminds us of Dōgen's pronouncement, "There is one mistake compounded by another mistake (*shushaku jōshaku*). Because there is mistake after mistake, this slips into the standpoint of non-Buddhists" (Sokushin zebutsu: Dōgen 1.53, Nearman 46, Tanahashi 53); however, the key phrase is often taken to mean recognizing a mistake as a mistake or making the right mistake. In writing, "When one side is illumined, the other side is dark" (Genjōkōan: Dōgen 1.3, Nearman 32, Tanahashi 30), Dōgen suggests that all human comprehension is innately limited by sensations, yet we can use each impression, however seemingly inadequate or faulty, as a window to gain at least a provisional or partial view of wholeness that becomes the basis of further spiritual development.

Concerned that in seeking to overcome deficiencies, trainees will frequently succumb to either a false sense of self-confidence or an overdrawn attitude of self-deprecation, Dōgen points out that "When the Dharma has not yet completely filled someone's body-mind, that person is apt to think their knowledge is already sufficient; but when the Dharma sufficiently fills body-mind, that person feels sure that some aspect is still lacking" (Genjōkōan: Dōgen 1.4, Nearman 33, Tanahashi 31). Therefore, by embracing the outlook of genuine nonthinking, practitioners must learn how to navigate and negotiate between the twin flaws of giving in to restrictions without a struggle and trumpeting artificial flexibility in an arrogant way. In a passage in "Realization Here and Now," Dōgen further compares the state of nonthinking to the life of fish and birds, which are comfortable in their environment and will die if removed from the natural habitat of water or air, respectively. He suggests, however, that unlike those animals, humans must be capable of grasping the shifts and relativity of perspectives by continually adjusting to movements based on their own initiative, sustained through the ongoing exertion of contemplation coupled with monastic discipline.

As an analogy for the way fluctuating circumstances affect human understanding, Dōgen considers the image of a boat drifting out to sea that requires one to make rapid changes in the perception of truth:

"When you go out in a boat to the middle of the ocean beyond the sight of any land or mountain (*yamanaki*) and look around, all you will see is the vast encircling water, and you will soon get used to the idea that the whole universe seems to be just the same" (Genjōkōan: Dōgen 1.4, Nearman 33–34, Tanahashi 31). Dōgen continues, "The vast ocean is neither circular nor angular but has additional inexhaustible qualities, although for some observers it is likened to a dragon's glittering palace or a jeweled necklace" (Genjōkōan: Dōgen 1.4, Nearman 34, Tanahashi 31). Instead of getting overwhelmed by following the path of variability in all possible directions, one should focus on the immediacy of here and now: "We must realize that an inexhaustible storehouse is present not only all around us, but right beneath our feet and within a single drop of water" (Genjōkōan: Dōgen 1.4, Nearman 34, Tanahashi 31).

Despite challenging anthropocentrism in various expressions of doctrine emphasizing the unity of all beings without exception or preference, Dōgen recognizes that the primary aim of Zen teaching is to enable humans to actualize their knowledge of absolute indivisibility in relation to limitless multiplicity as represented in each and every bead of water, grain of sand, flake of snow, or piece of hair. Key to this process is understanding that the mind does not arise suddenly in a vacuum or exist independent from the body, which is entwined with the objects of sense impression. Eyes contribute to producing sights that are the product of continuous interaction, and the nose supports but is not equal to the scents it perceives. Therefore, the human brain cannot be said to contain its own thoughts; nor is the self some sort of thing endowed with an identity considered an eternal or separate existence in a way that is detachable from the entire environment. "Indeed," according to Dōgen, "what is called 'mind' is the great earth with its mountains and rivers, and it is the sun, moon and stars . . . it is the tiles and stones used for walls and fences, and it is the four elements and five aggregates of existence" (Sokushin zebutus: Dōgen 1.57, Nearman 50–51, Tanahashi 40).

{ 5 }

TEMPORALITY AND EPHEMERALITY

ON NEGOTIATING LIVING AND DYING

THE MEANING OF IMPERMANENCE

Perhaps the main feature of Dōgen's distinctive approach to reinterpreting Buddhist theory and practice in the *Treasury of the True Dharma Eye* is the way he emphasizes that religious training must be based on an insightful "contemplation of impermanence" (*mujō-kan*) in its full, unadulterated significance.[1] This level of understanding underlies, and to a large extent undermines, conventional notions of uncertainty about change that fall short of embracing an authentic response to ephemerality experienced in everyday life, which Dōgen argues should be seen as manifesting the fundamental unity of being-time rather than in a sequential view of temporality.

Dōgen's outlook was greatly influenced by the Japanese aesthetic tradition's evocative lyrical expressions of sorrow and grief, understood in terms of the notion of *mono no aware* (poignant sadness at the passing of things). This feeling was reflected in his own tragic family circumstances and unsettled upbringing during a volatile sociohistorical epoch at the dawn of the Kamakura era.[2] Dōgen frequently criticizes Mahāyāna and Zen Buddhist notions of enlightenment by adamantly refuting any standpoint that fails to take into account how the evanescence of existence affects the existential meaning of time and death, which serves as the key to spiritual realization. As Dōgen says in the fascicle "Thusness," "Myself is not 'I,' since all life is propelled by the flow of days and months that cannot be stalled even for an instant. Where is the ruddy complexion of youth? We can try to search, but it leaves no trace" (Inmo: Dōgen 1.204, Nearman 364, Tanahashi 325).

The primary aim of the *Treasury* is not to produce a heartrending expression of melancholy associated with recognizing the fleeting beauty of nature or to show distress about the loss of a personal relationship or other source of emotional attachment. Rather, it is to examine the impact of contingency and finitude on human experience in order to discover a genuine sense of detachment that enables full engagement with all aspects of reality. This paradoxical state is derived from an evenhanded acceptance of and immersion in the inevitability of alteration by redefining the relationship between the present moment and its antecedents or consequences, accentuating the immediacy of Buddha nature manifested here and now. Dōgen enjoins his followers to resist doctrines that conceal the genuine significance of impermanence and exert themselves strenuously through sustained meditative practice, to realize the moral value of being-time that is apprehended each and every transitory instant. An authentic understanding of the incessancy of instability is reflected in an injunction distilled from Dōgen's teaching that is often used in Sōtō Zen temples: "Great is the matter of life and death. All is impermanent, quickly fading away. Do not waste this life. Instead, take each moment as an opportunity to awaken."

Dōgen's view of time and death is rooted in an aloof approach to feelings about the fleetingness of all things that recalls a dictum expressed by the ancient Roman philosopher Lucretius. In the first book of *On the Nature of Things* (*De rerum natura*), Lucretius writes, "Time by itself does not exist; but from things themselves there results a sense of what has already taken place, what is now going on, and what is to ensue. It must not be claimed that anyone can sense time by itself apart from the movement of things." This classical standpoint, which suggests that the constancy of motion triggers an interior response to temporality linking all three tenses, is echoed in modern philosophy by Martin Heidegger's notion of the multidimensional self-unfolding and self-displaying ontological "Event" (*Ereignis*). The Event appropriates and conjoins lofty and mundane realms based on full awareness of the evanescence of time.[3] Heidegger's doctrine, influenced by a medieval Christian mystical poem suggesting, "The flower blooms, without ever asking why," is often associated by comparative philosophers with Dōgen's interpretation of complete dynamism as an ongoing process that overcomes any lingering reliance on a clock or calendar to evaluate time.[4]

Contemplating Ephemerality

Dōgen gained firsthand knowledge of the ephemeral quality of all aspects of human and natural existence through intense personal experiences of sorrow and regret. After mourning his parents, who died during his early childhood, he resolved to abandon secular life and become a monk so as to conquer the apparent duality of life and death. Fifteen years later, he encouraged his senior colleague Myōzen to travel to China with a great sense of urgency in regard to the quest to attain enlightenment, even though his teacher lay ill. In the late 1240s, by virtue of his consistently held religious impulse refusing to compromise with the secular world, Dōgen declined an offer to lead a new temple to be built by the shogun in the temporary capital at Kamakura in order to return to Eiheiji temple and oversee his assembly of monks, who had clearly missed the founder's authentic style of leadership during his absence.[5]

Contemplation of impermanence was furthermore the basis for Dōgen's appreciation of invariably shifting phenomena manifested in the fragile yet robust natural surroundings of the Echizen mountains. The outlook developed at this magnificent location, where each of the four seasons can be appreciated in its splendor, is expressed eloquently in the lyrical discourse of many fascicles of the *Treasury*, in addition to other examples of Dōgen's prose and poetic writings. In one of his waka poems, Dōgen extols the environment at Eiheiji: "The white mountains of Echizen / Are my winter retreat. / A blanket of clouds / Covers the frosted peaks / And fills the snowy slopes."[6] Successive shades and textures of wintry paleness are accentuated by the wordplay on "white mountains" (*shirayama*, another pronunciation for Mount Hakusan, a perpetually snow-covered peak situated near the monastery). This literary technique helps conjure the doctrine of radical impermanence, whereby an infinite variety of fleeting cyclical phenomena reflect a basic unity. That theme is similarly conveyed by a famous Zen saying often cited by Noh playwright Zeami, "A white heron reflected by the moonlight sits on a silver vase in the snow." The Echizen-inspired waka is one of numerous examples showing why Dōgen is admired for the way his literary evocations of evanescence hold universal spiritual significance.

Another interesting example emphasizing the ephemerality of natural beauty appears in the fascicle "Sounds of the Valleys, Colors of the Mountains," in which Dōgen cites a famous verse by Tang-dynasty master Lingyun (n.d.), who after considerable struggle for several decades to attain awakening eventually had a realization one day upon viewing peach blossoms in bloom. Lingyun then wrote, "For thirty years I have been searching; / How many cycles have passed featuring leaves falling and branches budding anew. / But with just one glance at the flowering peach blossoms / Suddenly, I was aware of the termination of every doubt" (Keisei sanshoku: Dōgen 1.277, Nearman 69, Tanahashi 88). Referring to this story after citing a similar account of Master Xiangyan (?–898) gaining instantaneous illumination following much strife by simply hearing a pebble strike a bamboo tree, Dōgen praises Lingyun's expression here and in several other *Treasury* passages.

While praising the approach to awakening often referred to as "seeing forms and hearing sounds" (*kenshiki monsho*), Dōgen also cautions his followers against accepting the idea that external circumstances are the key to triggering realization. Rather, the transformative process must involve reciprocal interaction with one's own deepest understanding of the true meaning of temporality, developed in light of the finitude of all phenomena.[7] Also, in the fascicle "Udambara Blossoms," which refers to the flower the Buddha saw bloom just when he was enlightened, Dōgen cites a Rujing verse, "Lingyun saw peach blossoms opening, / But I see peach blossoms scattering" (Udonge: Dōgen 2.172, Nearman 764, Tanahashi 645). Instead of one-sidedly celebrating the arising of beauty, Rujing suggests that the falling of petals functions as a reminder of the release of human attachments in a way that corresponds to the experience of casting off body-mind as well as nothingness Buddha nature.

Based on the sense that it is crucial to recognize impermanent existence reflecting the unity of being-time, Dōgen's concern is that many of the doctrines and rituals used in the typical Buddhist training of his era betray a subtle clinging to a dualistic view of reality that fails to comprehend the full significance of ephemerality. His mission in various *Treasury* fascicles is to expose and uproot these insidious misconceptions. For example, according to the conventional reading of the second sentence of the passage from the *Nirvāṇa Sūtra* regarding the doctrines of Buddha nature, which Dōgen dissects at the beginning of the fascicle on this topic (as discussed in the previous chapter), "Tathāgata [Thus-Come or Buddha] abides forever, and is without change" (*Nyorai jōjū, mu u henyaku*). Whether it is intended or not, at face value this metaphysical assertion implies a permanent status for absolute reality that stands in stark contrast to the ebb and flow of relative, transient elements of experience characterized by the interconnections of living and dying.

In a revision reflecting the hermeneutics of intrusion, by repositioning or deliberately misplacing the comma in a way that affects the overall meaning (the original Sino-Japanese is not punctuated, so all grammatical markers have been supplied by later editors), this assertion can be radically recast as "Tathāgata (*Nyorai*) does not abide forever (*jōjū mu*), and is always changing (*u henyaku*)."[8] The new phrasing suggests that the negative term *mu* or "not" modifies "abide forever," whereas the positive term *u* or "is" refers to "always changing." This change of syntax indicates that Buddha nature must be found entirely within, rather than by trying to withdraw from, the world of constantly fluctuating temporal conditions (*jisetsu*). Accordingly, Dōgen argues, "There is no Buddha nature that is not manifested here and now (*genzen*)" (Busshō: Dōgen 1.18, Nearman 249, Tanahashi 238). Moreover, "Seeing mountains and rivers is seeing Buddha nature, which is also seeing a donkey's jowls or a horse's mouth" (Busshō: Dōgen 1.19, Nearman 249–250, Tanahashi 238), in the sense that concrete ordinary occurrences, no matter how apparently trivial, constitute displays of true reality.

By clarifying temporality through reconciling the status of Buddha nature with the fragility and contingency of all short-lived things, Dōgen shows that whole-being Buddha nature does not constitute emergent being, which would begin at a certain point in time, because it is coterminous with the ordinary mind right now (*nikon*), to cite a term featured in the "Being-Time" fascicle. Nor is Buddha nature original or timeless being that fills the past right up through and into the present moment. True reality, therefore, is neither a realm that exists before practice nor one attained after performing training exercises. Not a constant essence, whole-being Buddha nature is also not something hidden and awaiting realization or a potential from the past that will inevitably come to fruition in a rapidly approaching future.

In other *Treasury* passages, Dōgen reinforces an emphasis on the immediacy of experience by maintaining that the notions of the "ancient Buddha mind" (*kobusshin*) and "ancient mirror" (*kokyō*), both the topics of fascicles, are actually contemporaneous with the manifesting of being-time at this very moment. He justifies that view by suggesting that the word *ko*, which literally means "old," "former," or "antique," should not be understood as a chronological term because it entails the original state of wisdom realized right now. Conversely, "Mountains and Rivers Proclaiming the Sūtras" opens with the saying, "Mountains and rivers at this very moment are manifesting the way of primordial [or ancient] buddhas (*nikon no sansui wa kobutsu no dō genjō nari)*" (Sansuikyō: Dōgen 1.316, Nearman 142, Tanahashi 154). No matter when phenomena have transpired or will transpire, all are examples of the innumerable appearances of wholebeing Buddha nature. From a similar angle, Dōgen argues in the fascicle "The Nature of Things" that an immeasurable bygone eon is not an endless expanse of time, as in the conventional view, but is "nothing other than what we call the nature of things in that past, present, or future . . . is like water flowing and leaves falling" (Hosshō: Dōgen 2.28–29, Nearman 651, Tanahashi 560–561).

As Dōgen further indicates in scathing criticisms featured in "Buddha Nature" and several other fascicles concerning the so-called Senika heresy—a throwback to pre-Buddhist conceptions of reality that emphasize an everlasting self (*ātman*) situated beyond the world of contingency—the tendency to support a philosophy of eternal truth still lingers among Buddhist theorists and infects various forms of Zen thought. This predisposition becomes the foremost barrier to enlightenment, very difficult to displace and overthrow, because the assumption of duality between this moment and eternity infuses everyday thought in ways that have devastating implications for the attainment of spiritual realization. Although the teachings of Buddhism from its origins consistently stressed the twin doctrines of the insubstantial or selfless (Skr. *anātman*, Jp. *muga*) and impermanent (Skr. *anitya*, Jp. *mujō*) quality of all elements of existence as the true basis of reality, Dōgen feels that this standpoint all too often gets subverted or distorted. He finds authentic Buddhism succumbing frequently to misapprehensions that must be recognized and corrected at their source through a careful analysis of experience expressed with rhetorical savvy. Weeding out the stubborn roots of misguided presuppositions about sequential time leading to false views of awakening is the primary task of Dōgen's examination of temporality.

Delusions concerning temporality vis-à-vis eternity are evident in various articulations of the Mahāyāna doctrines of Buddha nature and original enlightenment thought, especially when they posit a substratum not bound by the strictures of insubstantial existence. Misconceptions about temporality also rear their heads in some well-regarded Zen notions, Dōgen argues, such as "seeing into one's nature" (*kenshō*), attributed to Sixth Patriarch Huineng; the "true man of no rank" (*shinjin mui*) according to the teachings of Linji; and the view of "silent illumination" (*mokushō*) expressed by Caodong school Master Hongzhi. Dōgen greatly admires Hongzhi and often cites his lineal predecessor's recorded sayings in the *Extensive Record* but, based on rethinking the view of time in relation to meditation, he astutely critiques and rewrites the Chan teacher's most famous poem in the fascicle "The Lancet of Zazen," to be discussed in chapter 7. All of the approaches Dōgen critically assesses, either directly or indirectly, rely on a false sense of separation between ordinary and everlasting time. This reveals an attachment to the view that truth is to be found in a realm outside concrete experience, rather than realizing awakening through the particular circumstances of evanescence or in the midst of the process of living and dying on all levels of human and natural existence.

The starting point for Dōgen's investigation of the meaning of temporality, therefore, is not the typical question, "What is time?" as if it were an abstraction to be conjectured. Instead he asks, "What does it mean to be in time?" in terms of continuing contemplative practice and discovers that since temporality and ontology are one and the same, there is no need to think of existing "in" some time frame, as if it were a kind of container holding entities. Human decision making and self-realization must be negotiated in terms of the unity of being-time, which, like all factors of nonduality, is differentiable when appropriately discerned. Being-time is not to be thought of as something independent that exists prior to actuality; nor is it to be considered an idea that humans construct through conceptualization. Buddhist practice is possible only within living reality, understood as change and flux. Enlightenment, which cannot occur outside this incessant flow, involves experiencing inexhaustible sensations based on living a life that is harmonious with mutability. That outlook, Dōgen maintains, does not conflate the realms of enlightenment and nonenlightenment but instead is attuned to their inevitable intertwining.

Despite his frequent criticisms of false views, Dōgen's approach appears to be consistent with that of many previous Zen notions, such as the command to "follow along with the movement of all things or circumstances while staying free [from clinging to a sense of loss]" (Ch. *renyun zizai*, Jp. *ninun jizai*). His approach also recalls a dialogue alluded to in "The Lancet of Zazen" that involves the Tang-dynasty Master Baizhang (749–814) and his teacher Mazu (709–788), who one day while walking together happen to see a flock of wild geese soaring by. When Mazu asks where the birds are going, Baizhang replies in common-sense fashion that they have just flown away. Mazu twists Baizhang's nose until he calls out in pain, and the master remarks, "You say they've flown away, but from the beginning they're right here!"[9] In some versions of this kōan, Baizhang is at first thrown into a cold sweat out of intense anxiety but quickly recovers and undergoes a great realization. This is proven to the master in a spontaneous way the first chance he gets, when Baizhang defies and tries to one-up Mazu during the morning lecture the very next day.

    A key difference between Dōgen's outlook and conventional kōan literature, however, is that in "Being-Time" and several other fascicles he articulates a novel vocabulary to explain the genuine meaning of temporal experience and its implications for gaining enlightenment. This rhetorical innovation helps overcome any assumption about sequential time, which is calculated, and clarifies the apparent contradictions that characterize authentic temporality, including connections between momentariness and duration, mortality and durability, and linearity and reversibility. Dōgen formulates more than a dozen key expressions, such as "coming and going" (*korai*), "right now" (*nikon*), and "holistic passage" (*kyōryaku*), which—like the notion of being-time itself—are revisions of everyday forms of discourse, reconfigured or reinterpreted to characterize unimpeded dynamic movement. Additionally, he uses atypical imperatives including "You must [partake of] being-time!" (*uji subeshi*) and "Make it manifest!" (*genjō suru*), verbal expressions devised through the use of neologisms or distortions of commonplace grammatical constructions, for example, turning a noun (e.g., being-time) into a verb or vice versa (e.g., manifesting).

DISCARDING DELUSIONS

Dōgen's complete identification of being-time with the unremitting realization of Buddha nature can be expressed as an equation indicating that times = beings = whole-being Buddha nature = self-realization = continuing effort. This kind of integrative standpoint is only grasped by those who adhere to authentic Zen practice without giving in to obstructions or hindrances that creep into typical misunderstandings. In the fascicle "Arousing the Aspiration for Enlightenment (or: Awakening the Bodhi-Seeking Mind),"[10] Dōgen argues that the true meaning of the mind, which is neither an individual faculty nor a corporeal object but a level of contemplative awareness that is comprehensive and thus equivalent to Buddha nature, should not be grasped in terms of one of numerous misguided assumptions about temporality:

> Mind is neither something innate nor something that suddenly arises anew at this moment, nor is it singular or plural. It is not spontaneous or planned; it is not situated within our physical body, nor is our body fixed within the mind. Mind does not permeate the entire universe of thoughts and things,

nor is it something of the past or future. It is neither present nor absent; nor is it something intrinsic or produced by an external cause. It is neither a combined quality nor of a causeless nature. (Hotsu bodaishin: Dōgen 2.333, Nearman 969, Tanahashi 656)

Figure 5.1 provides an illustration of the process Dōgen depicts for liberating the meaning of mind from one-sided fabrications based on making misleading distinctions. Understanding being-time manifested as all phenomena is crucial to transforming an unenlightened state into an experience of enlightenment that is, in turn, applied to everyday life. This is achieved by casting off misconceptions and realizing freedom from discrimination by

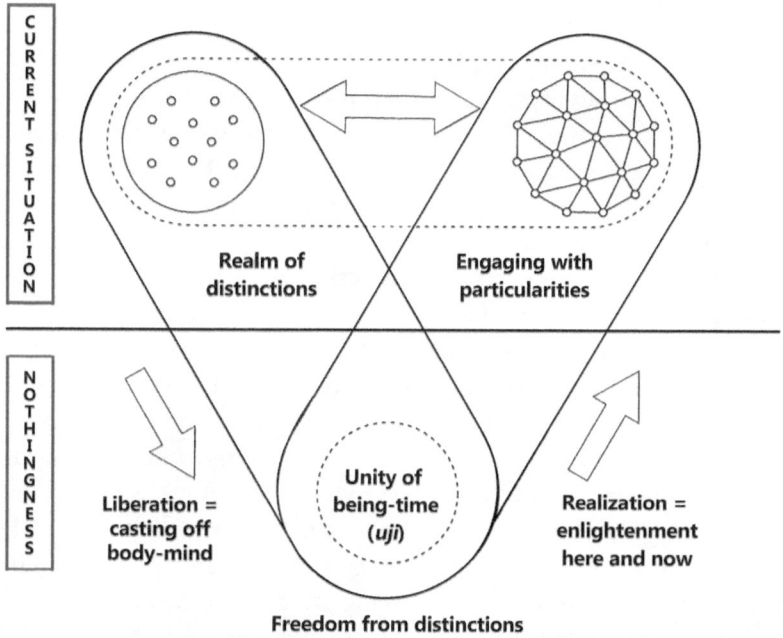

FIGURE 5.1 Dōgen's view of transforming everyday into enlightened reality
Adapted from Yorizumi Mitsuko, *Introduction to the Treasury* [*Shōbōgenzō nyūmon*] (Tokyo: Kadokawa sofia bunko, 2014), 121. See also Yorizumi Mitsuko, *Dōgen's Thought* [*Dōgen no shisō*] (Tokyo: NHK bukkusu, 2011)

virtue of insubstantiality or nothingness, which enables a productive reentry into the differentiated world of intricate particularities.

Why is it, Dōgen probes, that misconceptions regarding temporality play such a devious and duplicitous role in blocking realization? In the fascicle "Being-Time," he suggests that the average person (*bonbu*), who is ignorant of the unity of temporal existence, imagines the passing away of things as if "time were flying like an arrow swiftly moving by" (Uji: Dōgen 1.242, Nearman 111, Tanahashi 106). False thinking believes that we remain stationary while motion surrounds us, as reflected in Baizhang's initial response to Master Mazu pointing out the soaring geese. An unawakened person thinks of motion in deficient fashion: "It is like I have crossed a river and climbed a mountain: the river and mountain may still exist, but I feel I have now left them behind and at the present moment I reside in a splendid vermilion palace located on the mountain peak.... Therefore, mountains and rivers in the natural landscape and in one's own sense of self are as distant as heaven is from earth" (Uji: Dōgen 1.242, Nearman 110, Tanahashi 105–106).

In trying to overcome a defective outlook, Dōgen points out, we must recognize that a static conception of time tends to be so deeply ingrained that ordinary people consider it self-evident and beyond question or doubt. This leads to a preoccupation with the calculation of chronology in terms of hourly, seasonal, and annual sequences, rather than a focus on authentic subjective experience.

In divorcing itself from being-time, as shown in figure 5.2, commonplace thinking tends to disperse temporality into separate slots or entities that are mutually exclusive so that one point (T2) cannot be considered to begin until the first (T1) is finished; once completed, it (T2) has relatively little bearing on the next point (T3). But, Dōgen asks, where in the analogy mentioned above is the true meaning of flux to be found, in movement from the valley (T1) to the river (T2), then to the mountain (T3), and finally to the summit (T4), where there appears to be a magnificent edifice blissfully removed from all the prior turmoil? If time were merely flying past, he suggests, there would be no unifying principle of the present moment and "gaps" (*kenkyaku*) (Uji: Dōgen 1.242, Nearman 111, Tanahashi 106), however minuscule, would mistakenly appear everywhere in the temporal process.

Dōgen argues against that view, "The true state of things is not found in this one direction alone" (Uji: Dōgen 1.242, Nearman 112, Tanahashi 106). Moreover, "At the time the mountain was being climbed and the river was being crossed, I was there [as being-time]. Therefore, the time has to

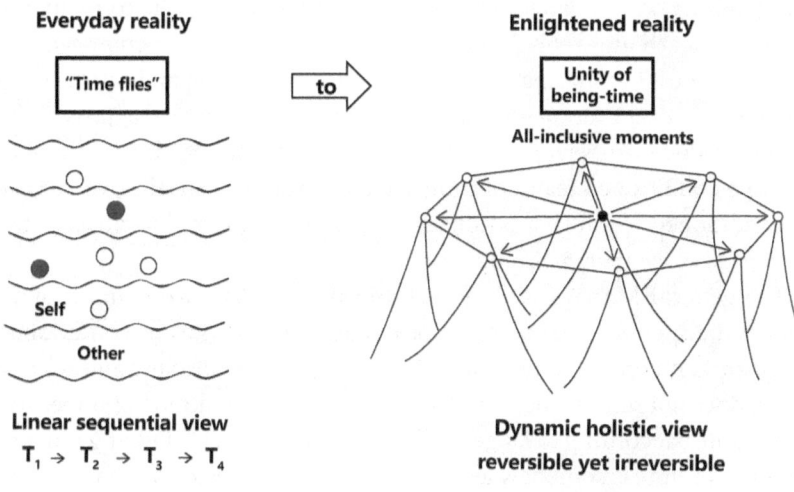

FIGURE 5.2 The conventional linear view of time overcome by Dōgen's dynamic view
Adapted from Yorizumi, *Introduction to the Treasury*, 147

be in me. Inasmuch as I am still here, it cannot be that time passes by since ... the existence of myself in the immediate present is itself being-time" (Uji: Dōgen 1.241, Nearman 110, Tanahashi 106). Dōgen furthermore asks, "Does not the very moment of climbing the mountain and crossing the river swallow up and spit out the time of the splendid vermilion palace?" (Uji: Dōgen 1.241, Nearman 111, Tanahashi 106). The rhetorical question posed in this passage refers to the idea that every activity at once negates ("swallows up") illusions about time and affirms ("spits out") the multifarious capacities of genuine temporality; these become manifest as instantaneous moments of the immediate present that are also continuous, connecting productively the entire course of movement covering past and future.

Based on this, Dōgen is critical of many misleading ways the meaning of time has been portrayed in the history of Buddhist philosophy, especially when the fundamental doctrines of selflessness and impermanence have been altered or distorted. According to basic Buddhist teachings that are in accord with being-time, the elements of experience compose a perpetual, mutually conditioning flux of arising/desistence, appearance/disappearance, or continuity/discontinuity taking place each and every moment that, if rendered static by desire and ignorance, generates suffering (Skr. *dukkha*, Jp. *kūrushii*), resulting in karmic bondage to recurring cycles of death and rebirth. One of the Indian scholastic controversies involving the Abhidharma schools concerned measuring and categorizing the duration of the momentariness of things. This theoretical approach, for Dōgen, reduces impermanence to a speculative issue by dividing reality into the conditioned realm of time, characterized by causality, versus the unconditioned realm that is conceived of as nontemporal and associated with pure space (Skr. *ākāśa*, Jp. *kokū*).

The general Mahāyāna Buddhist approach to the overcoming of all conceptual polarities and the consequent identification of conditioned (*saṃsāra*) and unconditioned (nirvāṇa) realms, or of absolute and relative truth, does not fully account for the deeply existential notion of impermanent reality, according to Dōgen's analysis, because an underlying sequential view of time is somehow left unchallenged. The basic conundrum that must be overcome is the idea that Buddha nature is considered beyond and thus immune to the conditioning of time, yet enlightenment is seen as a linear development of now points leading sequentially to a future goal. Even the Chinese Huayan (Jp. Kegon) school's notion of the simultaneous interpenetration of ten phases of time, a holistic doctrine that Dōgen incorporates indirectly into some of his teachings, is still an abstraction removed from an understanding of how temporal conditions function in everyday life, which is essential for realizing being-time.

Nevertheless, as seen in other examples of his thinking, Dōgen finds truth hidden within delusions in that, "Even a form [of understanding] that makes a blunder is being-time" (Uji: Dōgen 1.243, Nearman 114, Tanahashi 107). He also writes ironically, "Intended meaning and expression that get halfway to the mark are being-time; intended meaning and expression that do not get halfway to the mark are also being-time" (Uji: Dōgen 1.246, Nearman 118, Tanahashi 110). In other words, the unity of temporality and ephemerality is not affected by whether or not this truth is clearly apprehended by any particular person. Moreover, a partial realization discloses in its own way some degree of true reality that becomes a useful stepping-stone on the pathway to enlightenment. For Dōgen, "the times before and after someone instantly displays a blunder are both the dwelling places (*jū-hōi*) of being-time" (Uji: Dōgen 1.243, Nearman 113, Tanahashi 107).

With this penetrating analysis, Dōgen seeks to correct several misconceptions about the temporal dimension of Buddha nature. In the "Buddha Nature" fascicle, he cites a saying attributed to Śākyamuni, "If you wish to know Buddha nature's meaning, you must contemplate temporal conditions. If the time arrives, Buddha nature will manifest itself" (Busshō: Dōgen 1.17, Nearman 248, Tanahashi 237). Dōgen then offers a characteristically intrusive interpretation that rephrases key parts of the passage. "If you wish to know Buddha nature's meaning," for example, is read as, "Right now you know Buddha nature's meaning." Also, "you must contemplate temporal conditions" implies a future dimension but really means, "right now you know temporal conditions" (Busshō: Dōgen 1.17, Nearman 248, Tanahashi 237). Therefore, realizing Buddha nature does not investigate time outside whole-being but instead understands that truth is nothing other than temporality. Furthermore, the utterance "If the time arrives" (*jisetsu nyakushi*) means for Dōgen, "The time is already (*nyakushi*) here at each moment of the twenty-four hours of every day, and there can be no doubt about it. There has never yet been a time 'not arrived' (*mitō*). There can be no Buddha nature that is not Buddha nature manifested right here and now. Hence, being-time already arrived is in itself the immediate manifestation of Buddha nature" (Busshō: Dōgen 1.18, Nearman 249, Tanahashi 238).

The *Treasury*'s creative (mis)reading of various source passages is designed to dismiss three essentialist views that tend to infect misappropriations of the notion of Buddha nature. One view takes Buddha nature to represent an entity that inherently exists in humans or in all sentient beings. Dōgen argues that Buddha nature should not be posited as an attribute that is possessed by anyone, so the alternative reading he proposes can be paraphrased tautologically as, "Whole-being impermanence is nothing other than Buddha nature impermanence!" Another essentialist view posits a substantive Buddha nature as a kind of seed that ripens, and "When it receives the nourishment of Dharma rain, it begins to sprout so that branches and leaves, flowers and fruit, appear and the fruit contain seeds within" (Busshō: Dōgen 1.16, Nearman 247, Tanahashi 236). Dōgen criticizes the seed analogy as dualistic, separating training or cultivation from realization or fruition and thus reducing present practice to a secondary status devoid of value. To correct this, he reads, "seed and flower and fruit are each, individually, the unobstructed [Buddha] mind itself . . . the roots, stem, branches, twigs, and leaves are all equally Buddha nature, living the same life and dying the same death as whole-being" (Busshō: Dōgen 1.17, Nearman 247, Tanahashi 237). A third essentialist outlook sees Buddha nature as the fruit or result that will come naturally in a future time. Those who hold such a view, according to Dōgen's critique, think that "realization of Buddha nature comes about spontaneously, as a matter of natural course" (Busshō: Dōgen 1.19, Nearman 248, Tanahashi 238). This implies that the outcome of awakening does not depend upon the supreme effort of current practice continually carried out, which he rejects as another form of dualism separating present and future by overlooking the need to perpetually undertake training.

ENCOUNTERING DEATH

The unavoidable and undeniable pivot point that transforms deficient and partial understanding into an authentic awareness of the unity of being-time is based on encountering impermanence in terms of personal experiences of sorrow. This leads beyond a focus on individual regret to a recognition of the universal mutability of phenomena. As Dōgen writes in "Arousing the Aspiration for Enlightenment," "The life of a sentient being changes swiftly through birth and death without ceasing" (Hotsu bodaishin: Dōgen 2.337, Nearman 974, Tanahashi 659). In a fleeting instant, like the twinkling of an eye or the snapping of a finger, we are able to realize that the loss and absence caused by inevitable mortality, if appropriately apprehended, reveals the true nature of temporality.

In the final analysis, facing death for Dōgen is not a source of disillusionment, despair, frustration, or futility, but the transformative key to attaining spiritual liberation based on seeing the inseparability of living-dying each and every moment without beginning or end. This approach is expressed paradoxically in the fascicle "Birth and Death":

> To seek Buddha apart from birth-and-death is like pointing the head of a cart northward when you want to go south to the capital or facing south to see the northern Dipper. This only aggravates the conditions of birth-and-death and deprives you all the more of the way of redemption. Just understand that birth-and-death itself is nirvāṇa, and you will neither hate one aspect for representing birth-and-death [in the sense of mortality] nor cherish the other aspect as being nirvāṇa [in transcending transiency]. . . . Only then can you be free from birth-and-death, that is, by not making the mistake of thinking you will pass [in sequential fashion] from life into death. (Shōji: Dōgen 2.528, Nearman 93, Tanahashi 884–885)

This passage shows that Dōgen's overall view of impermanence appears to reflect a productive combination of basic Buddhist philosophy, which examines logically the finite nature of reality in terms of momentariness, with the lyrical sensibility of Japanese religiosity, which recognizes through poetic expressions an aesthetic appreciation of the emotional effects of ephemerality. In "Arousing the Aspiration for Enlightenment," Dōgen advocates that the basic Buddhist analysis of the succession of *setsuna* (Skr. *kṣaṇa*), or instants indicating the smallest possible unit of time measurement, can lead directly to awakening:[11]

> Sixty-five instants (*setsuna*) occur when someone snaps their fingers, during which the five aggregates of human existence come into being and perish. Unawakened people, who are unaware of this, think that moments of time are as uncountable as the sands of the Ganges. But they do not realize that there are actually as many as six billion, four hundred million, ninety-nine thousand, nine hundred and eighty instants transpiring within one day and night, when the five aggregates are continually coming into existence and perishing. (Hotsu bodaishin: Dōgen 2.335, Nearman 973, Tanahashi 658)

Because most people are not cognizant of these basic facts, according to Dōgen, they are unable to arouse the aspiration for enlightenment, but those who comprehend the *Treasury of the True Dharma Eye* and the wondrous mind of nirvāṇa understand deeply the principle of the unity of birth-and-death taking place moment by moment.

Lyrical Evocations

Appreciating the difficulty many people have in trying to comprehend the traditional quantitative analysis of incessant change, Dōgen often takes an alternative approach by giving voice to key elements of the Japanese literary understanding of impermanence expressed through the use of lyrical imagery. The opening paragraph of "Realization Here and Now" (Genjōkōan: Dōgen 1.2, Nearman 31, Tanahashi 29), which serves as the introductory section of the 75- and 60-fascicle editions of the *Treasury*, consists of just four sentences powerfully constructed in dialectical fashion to conclude with an evocation of philosophical lyricism using the images of flowers falling in dismay and weeds spreading amid chagrin.

The first sentence of the paragraph conjures the way enlightened adepts speak to one another by presenting a portrait of undivided activity, whereby the polarities of "delusion and realization, life and death, and buddhas and sentient beings" are affirmed in terms of a holistic view encompassing particularity. From an awakened understanding such paradoxical utterances are articulated without creating confusion because interlocutors understand that what may seem like contradictions on the common-sense level are not really problematic. The second sentence of the opening paragraph addresses the concerns of those still seeking to attain enlightenment. The contradictory quality is taken to another level by controverting the previous sentence in disavowing the set of polarities, so that "there is no delusion or enlightenment, no life or death, no buddhas or sentient beings." This denial reminds readers that negation (*naku* or *nashi*, meaning *mu*) must go alongside affirmation (*ari*, meaning *u*). Encountering incongruity enables an unawakened person to doubt his assumptions and therefore seek to surpass ordinary logic. The third sentence, targeting an audience struggling with the question of whether and why it is significant to pursue enlightenment, reaffirms the existence of polarities, but from the standpoint of unclarity rather than resolution.

The last sentence of the paragraph switches style dramatically to tackle the spiritual needs of those who have not yet consciously begun to consider the meaning of enlightenment. It expresses a deceptively simple yet illuminating challenge designed to stir the uninitiated from their religious slumber and instigate the quest of transcendence. "Nevertheless," Dōgen writes, "flowers wither despite our affection for them, and weeds spring up much to our regret" (Genjōkōan: Dōgen 1.2, Nearman 31, Tanahashi 29). Here, the logical contradictions of the previous three statements are replaced by emotional conflicts regarding the cycles of nature highlighted as an analogy for the perpetual spiritual dilemma, in that humans long to hold on to what they want to possess and disdain what they wish to jettison.

Understanding this conundrum is a crucial initial stage on the route to apprehending the meaning of being-time underlying all experience. Dōgen's lyrical passage is comparable to the opening paragraph of Chōmei's thirteenth-century essay, *An Account of My Hut*, which recounts all the factors that led the author to withdraw from the capital to reside in serene reclusion at a countryside retreat, where the four seasons are experienced directly as emblematic of reaching the Pure Land. According to Chōmei, "Some die in the morning; others are born in the evening. That's the way it is with people of this world, like bubbles floating on the water. Though the river's current never fails, the water passing, moment by moment, is never the same . . . no one expects the dew to last until evening."[12]

Some translators interpret Dōgen's final sentence in the opening paragraph of "Realization Here and Now" as a mere afterthought or an implicit instruction to eliminate all feelings, and their renderings suggest that human attachments are what "cause" the loss of flowers as well as the growth of weeds.[13] My view is in accord with interpreters who maintain that by underlining the pervasiveness of impermanence lyrically, the last sentence undercuts any clinging to a false notion of eternal truth. It motivates concentrated exertion through an immersion in the realm of finitude by accepting uncompromisingly and resigning oneself to the realization that everything is perishable. The fundamental contradiction evident at this level of understanding ephemerality is that even the effort to overcome selfhood must be abandoned and cast aside. Yet, the self can be truly dropped only by gaining an aesthetic attunement to the sorrow that stimulates a person to seek spiritual release in the first place.

In summary, the first three sentences of the fascicle form an intricate paradoxical pattern that seeks to surpass an articulation of the doctrine of time in the conventional sense. By using natural symbolism in a way that appeals to sensations regarding concrete reality, rather than the intellectual abstraction of the first three statements, the fourth sentence radically departs from the previous conceptual arrangement by at once fulfilling and overthrowing its discursive function. The whole passage, though quite short, features incongruities displaced yet completed through poetic symbolism. Dōgen's last sentence could be rewritten as, "Even so, to learn the Dharma is to be sorrowful about transiency. To be sorrowful is to transcend despair (as a source of attachment) and to realize impermanence as the insubstantiality of all phenomena." However, this version sacrifices the cryptic eloquence of Dōgen's sparse yet stirring lyrical imagery.

AUTHENTIC TEMPORALITY

In several fascicles Dōgen makes insightful though perplexing comments about the immediacy of temporality such as, "The boundless spring appears with the earliest plum blossoms" (Baika: Dōgen 2.75, Nearman 690, Tanahashi 586), and "Being-time is fulfilled at the very moment spring arrives because all the manifestations of spring are themselves being-time" (Uji: Dōgen 1.244, Nearman 115, Tanahashi 108). These phrasings are similar to the concluding sentence of the first paragraph of "Realization Here and Now," highlighting that the true meaning of impermanent reality is not a matter of calculation, conceptualization, or logical investigation, as found in scholastic speculations, but constitutes an essential experiential realm wherein human sensations are continually engaged with phenomenal contingency experienced in the natural setting. Dōgen's aim is to empower practitioners to avoid living in the fabricated vermillion palace, supposedly unbound by the contingencies of time and thus epitomizing delusion embedded within delusion by failing to recognize transiency. Instead, he encourages them to commune with instantaneous manifestations of being-time that motivate an adept to continue to overcome a static sense of what it means to become Buddha.

Figure 5.2 illustrates the transition from the linear view of time flying by like an arrow, which causes an observer to be deluded by a false objectification of movement, to the holistic notion of temporality as expressed by the sayings, "The pearl is spinning in the bowl, and the bowl is spinning the pearl," or "I make the boat, and the boat makes me." What constitutes the all-inclusivity of being-time? This is understood when the ordinary view, which sees twenty-four hours of clock time pass quickly as a succession of sequential points coming and going (*korai*) while awaiting what has not yet (*mitō*) transpired, is transformed into complete consciousness of spontaneously arising *setsuna* manifesting the perpetual process of living-dying (*shōmetsu*) or the dynamic actualization (*genjō*) of a season that is already here (*nyakushi*). Put another way, the immediacy of experience right now (*nikon*) realized at this very moment has no duration; "life is a complete manifestation of activity, and death is a complete manifestation of activity (*shōya zenkigen shiya zenkigen*)" (Zenki: Dōgen 1.261, Nearman 526, Tanahashi 451). Each and every discrete appearance of being-time is a moment of arising that emerges and vanishes as well as a moment of dissolving that emerges and vanishes.

Duration and Continuity

Despite all the emphasis placed on the instantaneity of the present expressed in novel ways, Dōgen realizes that the biggest concern in explicating the vitality of being-time is that a convincing interpretation must explicate the difference between what happens before and after any particular occurrence. It cannot simply dismiss the gap apparently separating "now" from "then," whether this refers to what takes place before or after a particular moment. The apparent contradiction between the aspects of immediacy, which manifests here and now, and continuity, which encompasses prior and subsequent experience, needs to be resolved since both aspects are equally embedded in authentic temporality occurring in and through all situations, whether exalted or mundane.

This topic also involves explaining the dynamic quality of spiritual transformations that occur over the course of time, particularly the experience of casting off body-mind that suddenly relinquishes attachments yet is endlessly prolonged. The matter of continuity furthermore must apply to understanding crucial ceremonial transitions, such as the opening and closing of the annual ninety-day summer retreat that begins at the time of the full moon of the fourth month, according to the Chinese lunar calendar. As prescribed in Zen monastic regulations, this is a regularly scheduled event, the occasion for all monks in the assembly to take part in intensive meditation and spiritual renewal. This is achieved through calm, concerted reflection on how to steady the mind, to gain redemption from succumbing to defilements or committing transgressions. In the fascicle "Summer Retreat," Dōgen acknowledges that every year the period starts and ends on a certain date, so that participants prepare accordingly and expect to feel changed by the close of the yearly rite. Yet he also maintains, "The gateway for the summer retreat is beyond being considered new or old and is not characterized by the coming or going of past or present" (Ango: Dōgen 2.218, Nearman 856, Tanahashi 724).

To clarify the apparent inconsistency regarding momentariness and duration, as well as the irreversibility of linear time and the multidimensional reversibility of being-time, Dōgen develops additional terminology regarding the true meaning of temporality. In explaining the complicated relationship between firewood and ash, the following passage from "Realization Here and Now" features the notion that all phenomena are "abiding in a dwelling place [or Dharma position]" (*jū-hōi*) that is "possessed of, yet cut off from, before and after" (*zengo saidan*):

> Firewood turns to ashes and cannot become firewood again. But you should not hold the view that ashes occur after and firewood takes place before. You must realize that firewood abides in the dwelling place of firewood, for which there is before and after. Although there is a difference between before and after, firewood is cut off from before and after. Ashes abide in the dwelling place of ashes, and there is before and after. Just as firewood does not become firewood again after it has become ashes, a human being does not come back to life after death.... This is like winter and spring. One does not say that winter becomes spring or that spring becomes summer. (Genjōkōan: Dōgen 1.3–4, Nearman, 33, Tanahashi 30–31)

Here and elsewhere in the *Treasury*, Dōgen explains that the paradoxical nature of true temporality is experienced in terms of the absolute moment of here and now that is at once vanishing and enduring, discrete and unremitting. The notion of abiding in a dwelling place indicates the unique, unrepeatable stage of a thing's existence at any given moment, which encompasses everything that caused its current status and, in turn, it helps generate. To refer to a "thing," however, is misleading since there is no substantive entity moving along that lasts through time. The moment of now emerges, or is reborn, thousands of times per second because beings are invariably temporal occurrences, and time always manifests as all beings. The delusional human mind tries to connect these inclusive present moments into a series or sequence of before and after by assuming that beings somehow exist outside this very moment and can observe the flow of time from a distance.

For Dōgen, this deception can be corrected by embracing the view that each entity abides independently in its own all-embracing dwelling place, which is conjoined with the seemingly contrary notion that "holistic passage" (*kyōryaku*) or endurance transpires. The concept of passage is derived from a word (pronounced *keireki* in modern Japanese) referring to a person's background, lifetime record, and/or career trajectory that can be encapsulated in a summative résumé indicating the persistence of events manifested at this very moment of thought, speech, or activity. Since movement in the authentic sense occurs without ever being removed from the instantaneous present, it represents an unceasing occurrence of "nows" revealing themselves intermittently as independent stages. Holistic passage is thus a discontinuous continuity of dwelling places, each of which is discrete yet incorporates the before and after of other moments of being-time by including all of these within its own dynamism.

In an intriguing section of the "Being-Time" fascicle, Dōgen offers the main definition of continuity by delineating various aspects of holistic passage:

> Being-time makes passage from today to tomorrow, from today to yesterday, from yesterday to today, from today to today, and from tomorrow to tomorrow as one of the main qualities of being-time. Past time and present time do not overlap or pile up in a row.... Since self and other are being-times, practice and realization are being-times as well. So is entering the mud and water. (Uji: Dōgen 1.242, Nearman 112, Tanahashi 106–107)

This refers to the comprehensive asymmetrical process of a true adept's existential activity and philosophical reflection, taking place right now and moving simultaneously in and through past and future by actively engaging the passenger (self) and passageway (environment), as well as the full context of experiential reality surrounding and permeating movement. Holistic passage extends through all dimensions and gathers the total weight of previous experience as well as future possibility into this present moment.

Of the five aspects of holistic passage listed by Dōgen, "passage from today to yesterday" rings true to linear approaches to time. Also, "passage from today to yesterday" resonates with commonplace occurrences of memory, recollection, reminiscence and nostalgia or remorse, but without falling into the trap of trying to move literally backward, whereas "passage from today to tomorrow" resonates with anticipation, expectation, probability, and hope or suspense, but without attempting to jump over one's shadow. Moreover, "passage from today to today" and "passage from tomorrow to tomorrow" indicate the intensive experiences of moving forward while exerting effort right here and now.

Another important implication is that, by virtue of participating in the historical dimension of holistic passage, the lives of formerly existent Chan masters are not to be represented as a series of names listed retrospectively in the chronological sequence of a lineage symbolized as a family tree. Instead, they are understood as simultaneous (*dōji*) and interpenetrating occasions of the spontaneous manifestations and continuing transmissions of an adept's realization of being-time. This encompasses, but is by no means limited to, communing now with previous prestigious persons or memorable events, because the so-called past continues to transpire each and every moment in the most mundane activities.

IMPERATIVES FOR ACTION

Philosophical reflections on temporality disclosed in several prominent fascicles of the *Treasury* are not intended to be considered a matter of armchair speculation. Indeed, Dōgen's various ideas may seem disorganized without an interpreter's integrative analysis of their underlying texture. Rather, his teachings about time and death serve as an injunction or call to action for practitioners to engage in training in an urgent yet unrelenting manner, so as to attain enlightenment before death by fully accepting their own mortality and exercising compassion toward Zen practitioners and all beings of the past, present, and future. Reinforcing this imperative is the title of a Japanese verse by Dōgen often used as a motto characterizing monastic activities: "Not a moment is to be spent idly in twenty-four hours!" (*juniji jūfukukūka*). While staying at Eiheiji and looking back on his life, Dōgen reveals in this poem, he is startled to realize that "Over forty years have so quickly passed!"[14]

This approach recalls the "seize the day" (*carpe diem*) ideology expressed by Horace in *Odes* I.XI, which emphasizes that, since life is brief and unpredictable, we must not allow precious time to fly away frivolously because we never know if this could be our last moment.[15] However, Dōgen's focus on continuing ascetic training, reflecting a studied indifference not trapped by the extremes of pleasure or pain, stands in sharp contrast to Horace's emphasis on enjoying life's indulgences, like "emptying a wine bottle" before it is too late. The Zen master's view is seemingly closer to the notion of *memento mori* (remembering death) in the medieval Christian practice of contemplation on mortality, a means of considering the vanity of life in light of the transient nature of every earthly pursuit.[16]

The main components of the *Treasury*'s imperative to be eminently active based on the notion that "you must become one with being-time" (*uji subeshi*) include: (1) living life in terms of the unity of birth-and-death; (2) demonstrating an awareness of simultaneous experiences from aesthetic and spiritual perspectives; (3) gaining self-realization by understanding the bounds of perceptual horizons; (4) engaging fully in each particular activity (*ippō gūjin*); (5) prolonging the "sustained exertion" (*gyōji*) of everyday practice; and (6) confronting serenely one's imminent demise, as evident in Dōgen's own experience of death.

First, in facing the inevitability of dying every changing moment, during which current circumstances vanish as each new instant of being-time is revealed, Dōgen instructs that one must not view the multifarious phenomena of existence standing over and against death as if they were diametrically opposed, since that would mean that nirvāṇa is dualistic. From moment to moment, existence is to be apprehended as dying life that partakes of the oneness of living and dying, which transpires in the midst of living life. Moreover, when living the moment of dying, death is not to be regarded merely as demise but as living death. The anticipation of death that comes at the end of life actually constitutes the fulfillment of the mission of living by enabling calm insight into the profound oneness of all aspects of temporal existence experienced each moment.

The second component of Dōgen's urgent call to action involves the simultaneity of experiences in that, "All beings of the entire Dharma realm are time's occurrence at each, every, and any moment" (Uji: Dōgen 1.241, Nearman 109, Tanahashi 105). This takes place without hesitation or limitation, such that "the arousing of aspiration [in different minds] at the selfsame time is the arousing at [different] times of the selfsame mind (*kono yoheni dōji ho[tsu]shin ari, dōshin hotsuji ari*)" (Uji: Dōgen 1.241, Nearman 109, Tanahashi 105). By virtue of that level of collective awareness, the Buddha is not to be considered a separate or higher being but represents the capacity to fulfill his duration within the realm of being-time; although he may appear to be located someplace else, his existence invariably occurs in the immediate present. According to the fascicle "Expressing Mind, Expressing Nature," "a pale yellow silken thread" symbolizing the writings of the sūtras binds buddhas and ancestors together and functions as their pivot or point of transformation (Sesshin sesshō: Dōgen 1.451, Nearman 530, Tanahashi 494). Furthermore, in "Arousing the Aspiration for Awakening," "When we initially establish a reciprocal spiritual communion (*kannō dōkō*) with a master, this gives rise to nonthinking that realizes enlightenment. That level of mentality is not an endowment that buddhas confer upon us; nor is it something that we create for ourselves. Instead, this state of mind arises by means of mutual connectivity and is neither instantaneous nor incomplete" (Hotsu bodaishin: Dōgen 2.333, Nearman 969, Tanahashi 656).

The third component of the imperative indicates that, despite the celebratory tone of the above comments, Dōgen is the first to emphasize the innate limitations of human consciousness, since perceptivity reflecting the constraints of our sensations is restricted by the horizon of awareness as "when one side is illumined, the other remains dark." This saying recalls a typical Song-dynasty Chan putdown of arrogant priests, who are said to "carry a board across their shoulder," which means their vision is blocked and partial. Everyone must realize that even Buddha is subject to this limitation, so that both awakened and unawakened beings are manifested here and now as part of being-time but do not always recognize its significance.

Nonetheless, the fourth component suggests that out of darkness and distress, there emerge light and release in that partiality has the potential to reveal the whole of being-time. In discussing whether or not intended meaning and expression achieve a projected goal, Dōgen observes, "Getting there is obstructed by getting there, but not by not getting there. Not getting there is obstructed by not getting there, but not by getting there.... Obstruction obstructs obstruction and thus realizes obstruction. All of this is itself being-time" (Uji: Dōgen 1.246, Nearman 118, Tanahashi 110). Based on that level of paradox, he develops the notion of the full realization of a single thing or, "When a person practices and verifies the way of buddhas, then doing one thing is penetrating that one thing fully and following one practice is cultivating that one practice fully" (Genjōkōan: Dōgen 1.6, Nearman 35, Tanahashi 32). According to this standpoint, momentary instances of holistic discernment, especially after prolonged periods of doubt, such as when Lingyun saw peach blossoms flowering or

Xiangyan heard the sound of a pebble striking bamboo while sweeping a courtyard, involve complete absorption in the unmediated realm of forms and sounds. As a particular sensation is realized, crossing over the perceptual horizon for even a single instant helps one attain a state of liberation that is ever shifting and thus challenging to uphold.

The fifth aspect of Dōgen's moral imperative indicates that transcendent yet transient realization can and must be perpetuated through "sustained exertion" (*gyōji*), which enables an adept to "continually go beyond Buddha" (*bukkōjōji*); both notions serve as titles for *Treasury* fascicles. The term *gyōji* (行持) can be translated in various ways, but the first character 行 (*gyō*) indicates the discipline of practice or monastic conduct, and the second character 持 (*ji*) suggests keeping or persisting in the resolve to continue unrelenting over an extended period. Practice in this sense is an even broader category of training than zazen in that *gyōji* represents an underlying attitude of supreme dedication driving the commitment to enact ongoing meditation.

In philosophical passages at the beginning of the fascicle "Sustained Exertion," Dōgen depicts *gyōji* as a cosmic power that supports buddhas and beings, life and death, and right and wrong each and every moment. This represents an all-encompassing principle embracing its opposite, "Since all activity is a manifestation of dedicated practice, any attempt to avoid dedicated practice is an impossible evasion because the attempt itself is a form of dedicated practice" (Gyōji: Dōgen 1.146, Nearman 376, Tanahashi 333). The source of Dōgen's notion of the "unbroken ring of the way of practice (*gyōji dōkan* 道環)" (Gyōji: Dōgen 1.145, Nearman 374, Tanahashi 332) expressed in this fascicle is a prominent comment on a kōan case known as "Yangshan's Symbol," in which a rival monk draws a circle around the master's ancient mystic symbol (swastika) traced on the ground and Hongzhi's verse remarks, "The empty circle of the way is never filled."[17] For Dōgen, circularity is occupied and thereby fulfilled by the self-exertion of beings constantly emptying and replenishing their provisional shape or bearing.

By including detailed accounts of more than two dozen Chinese masters in the main portions of this lengthy two-part fascicle, "Sustained Exertion" is much closer than any other work in Dōgen's corpus to the genre of Chan transmission of the lamp, or illumination records that catalogue the life and thought of eminent monks. With the assertion that "a single day of sustained practice is worth more than many lives lasting vast eons" (Gyōji: Dōgen 1.146, Nearman 375, Tanahashi 333), Dōgen's overall *carpe diem*-based reading of the histories of these patriarchs sends a clear message that determination affirmed through continuous practice in the present moment of this fleeting, fragile existence of living-dying is a more superior avenue for attaining enlightenment than conventional virtuous behavior. Dedication to sitting meditation is compatible with, yet takes priority over, following external guidelines for conduct, including monastic institutional regulations, especially if these are seen as authoritative rules rather than interior inspirations.

Dōgen writes, "Calmly consider that a lifetime is not very long.... Do not vainly chase after the humbug of fame and fortune.... I recommend that casting aside the myriad entanglements of this world promotes the sustained exertion that all buddhas and ancestors are practicing ceaselessly" (Gyōji: Dōgen 1.202, Nearman 434, Tanahashi 379). He particularly praises the life of Furong Daokai (1043–1118), a Caodong school master and ancestor of Hongzhi who was trained in both Buddhist and Daoist austerities. He eventually became well known for his fierce spirit of autonomy in declining an offer of the prestigious imperial purple robe, usually considered the highest honor bestowed on a priest by the government, because he had little use for such finery and wished to stay free from secular pressures.

Traditional accounts suggest that Dōgen declined such a gift on two occasions by remarking that even wild monkeys in the mountains would mock his appearance, before he reluctantly accepted the third offer. While appearing to advocate a departure from the path of orthodox conduct, Dōgen seeks to avoid the pitfall of antinomianism by virtue of a firm commitment to spiritual integrity, which is further evidenced by the legacy of Zen teachers living in thatched huts on remote peaks in order to abandon worldly temptations, yet returning to regular monastic life in ways that promote strict adherence to prescribed principles and procedures, understood as manifestations of inner discipline.

The final component of the call pertains to Dōgen's active outlook during the last couple of years of his life when he became ill and drastically cut back on many temple functions, selecting Ejō to succeed to the abbacy of Eiheiji. In these ways he prepared to face imminent death, which transpired in the eighth month of 1253 as, according to tradition, he was sitting in the upright zazen posture after returning to Kyoto to seek medical treatment. During this phase, Dōgen stopped delivering formal sermons in the Dharma hall, which had become his main method of preaching during his late career phase. However, he continued to write and edit fascicles, especially those included in the New Draft edition.

During his last trip to Kyoto, Dōgen wrote a waka about anticipating death that plays off the traditional Japanese poetic theme of travel and the imagery of ephemerality to convey his dual sense of exhilaration and anxiety, and expectation and frailty:

Kusa no ha ni	Like a blade of grass,
Kadodeseru mi no	My frail body
Kinobe yama	Treading the path to Kyoto
Kumo ni oka aru	Seeming to wander
Kokochi koso sure.	Amid the cloudy mist on Kinobe Pass.[18]

Kusa no ha (a blade of grass), an intricate symbol that indicates the fragility and vulnerability pervading yet undercutting the existence of each and every being, also recalls several passages in the *Treasury* in which Dōgen equates "the radiance of a hundred blades of grass" (Muchū setsumu: Dōgen 1.295, Nearman 502, Tanahashi 432) with the true nature of reality or maintains that "a single blade of grass and a single tree are both the body-mind of all buddhas" (Hotsu mujōshin: Dōgen 2.163, Nearman 773, Tanahashi 649). The opening line thereby expresses a convergence of departure and return, or feeling and detachment, with universal nonsubstantiality.

A final important image in the poem involves the word *oka* used in line 4, which means "hill" and makes an association with "Kinobe Pass," a steep precipice Dōgen crossed midway between Eiheiji and Kyoto. The syllable *ka* (questioning) also conveys his deep uncertainty about his current medical condition as his spirit seems to float and feels lost or lofty among the clouds. He at once transcends his physical problems and realizes he can never be free from the travails of impermanence. The alliteration of the *k* sound at the beginning of each line adds a solemn or reverent undertone, while the word *kokochi* (a synonym for *kokoro* or heart/mind) softens the sentiment by transmuting it into an expression of subjective realization. The mind appears to be released, although the "body" (*mi* in line 2) is bound by suffering. The image of clouds recalls the traditional Zen notion that trainees are considered to be "floating like the clouds, flowing like the water" (*unsui*). Thus, the poem represents a transformation of a personal sentiment and aesthetic perception into a holistic experience of liberation that is also conveyed through literary skills evident throughout the *Treasury*.

{ 6 }

EXPRESSIVITY AND DECEPTIVITY

TO SPEAK OR NOT TO SPEAK

SPEECH AND SILENCE

The degree of creativity that is consistently evident in the *Treasury of the True Dharma Eye*, in addition to his other prose and poetic works produced in both *kana* (vernacular) and *kanbun* (Sino-Japanese) styles, clearly demonstrates why Dōgen is considered a major literary figure, praised by the prominent scholar Hee-Jin Kim as "a magician or alchemist ... a superb master of language, appreciating it not for its rhetorical use-value, but rather for its appeal to reason and rationality."[1] In a detailed analysis of how inventive rhetorical methods are utilized effectively throughout the *Treasury* to reveal a distinctive spiritual vision, Kim further notes that for Dōgen, "The interior and exterior of language are the very fabric of existence," in the sense that he is "constantly experimenting with [words] and challenging the ordinary locution."[2] This tirelessly innovative oratorical approach enables Dōgen to articulate religious insights that otherwise would not be readily conveyed. His high-minded goal of radically refashioning Buddhist theory and practice is dependent on and facilitated through diverse discursive devices that express his unique understanding of authentic Zen experience in ways particularly relevant to his audience.

In support of Kim's argument, the *Treasury* is regularly included in lists of exceptional traditional Japanese literature that generally refer to just a small handful of Buddhist works like *An Account of My Hut* or *Essays in*

Idleness.³ Also, there have been several important scholarly investigations in which a Buddhist studies scholar with expertise in Dōgen's allusions to various Chinese sources was joined or aided by a specialist in Japanese and comparative literature, primarily to track the native rhetorical qualities in Dōgen's writing, including allusions, punning, and other kinds of wordplay. This kind of collaboration contributed to the editing of one of the most prestigious editions of the masterwork, published in the early 1970s by the leading academic press in Japan, Iwanami shoten, and is also key to two more recent book-length examinations of the fascicle "Sustained Exertion."⁴ Moreover, a couple of the most influential works on the topic of the *Treasury*'s remarkable literary elegance were produced not by Buddhist studies scholars but by literary experts. These include *Dōgen's Universe of Language* (*Dōgen no gengo uchū*), written by a researcher of classical Japanese poetry, Terada Tōru, who also coedited the *Treasury* edition mentioned above, and *Dōgen and Zeami* (*Dōgen to Zeami*), by the noted historian of Noh theater Nishio Minoru.⁵

On Nonspeaking

Whereas Dōgen's manner of comprehension is referred to as "nonthinking" (*hishiryō*), which functions beyond the distinction between the rational and irrational, his mode of expression can similarly be characterized as "nonspeaking" (*higogen*). This notion refers to the capacity to disclose the Dharma in a way that is unlimited by the usual distinction between speech and verbosity or silence and reticence, since both modes of communication are ultimately avenues for conveying genuine awareness. Dōgen reveals his inclusive discursive outlook, encompassing creative uses of language in addition to the occasional dismissal of words and phrases, in a short poem included as the opening passage of the fascicle on "A King Asks for Saindhava":

> Whether using words or not using words,
> Expression is vines entangling a tree.
> It is feeding a donkey or feeding a horse,
> Diving deep into water, or flying high amid the clouds. (Ōsaku sendaba:
>   Dōgen 2.253, Nearman 889, Tanahashi 755)

According to this verse, using or refraining from using verbal expressions is a choice that depends on whether a teacher instructs a novice ("donkey"), who ceases doing evil and begins to train ("diving deep into water") by cutting through conceptual fetters as an obstacle to awakening, or an advanced practitioner ("horse"), who does good deeds ("flying high amid the clouds") by transmitting the Dharma so that others will be able to realize truth.[6] In either case the pedagogical situation resembles creepers wrapping around a tree in that these organisms represent the symbiotic relationship of teacher and disciple, whose existences are interdependent and reliant on each other, rather than seeing vines as something that stifles their host. For Dōgen, the image of entangling wisteria (*kattō*) evokes a student constructively learning from and contributing to the knowledge of his master. The exchange partners continually conduct dialogues in order to develop and polish their mutual understanding of whatever topic is being considered that promotes the perpetual pathway to actualizing self-realization. The teacher's skill is conditioned by the disciple's reactions and challenges, and vice versa.

The *Treasury* thus serves the dual function of being a caretaker or guardian of tradition, introducing and propagating Chinese approaches in the Japanese context, and a disrupter or reformer of this legacy, producing a substantial body of work that—in irreverent, tables-turning fashion characteristic of Zen discourse—is continually undermining and revising traditional standpoints. Dōgen's insightfully critical handling of Chan literary materials that often originated in the oral delivery of lectures or sermons constitutes an approach to nonspeaking designed to stymie the stereotypical views of disciples and reorient their minds toward a state of nonthinking that explores all possible perspectives without being fixated on any specific option. Like resourceful continental predecessors he considered role models to be emulated and surpassed, Dōgen uses a wide range of rhetorical methods, such as parables and paradoxes, images and analogies, and allegories and metaphors, to explicate the significance of nonthinking in provocative nonspeaking ways. In contrast to conjectural formulations preferred by some schools of Buddhism that emphasize a systematic approach to doctrine over the capacity of nonthinking, Dōgen's outlook is more illustrative than argumentative, more concrete than abstract, and more vivid than obscure in demonstrating how enlightenment is manifested through all the particularities of everyday life.

With an even greater focus than many of his peers, most of whom also wrote extensive poetry and prose collections yet also stressed the innate limits of language and logic in trying to capture and convey inexpressible truth, Dōgen staunchly argues that all types of verbal as well as nonverbal communication function as essential teaching tools. In "Expressing the Way" he suggests:

> Buddhas and ancestors have all expressed what they personally realized.... When trying to determine whether a practitioner has achieved the status of being considered an adept they invariably ask, "Can that person explain his or her realization effectively, or not?" They raise this question in regard to the practitioner's mind and body or walking staff and ceremonial fly whisk, and about whether he embodies a pillar or stone lantern that stands on the temple grounds. (Dōtoku: Dōgen 1.374, Nearman 510, Tanahashi 439)

While highlighting actual objects rather than ideas in this passage, Dōgen clarifies that "For those who are not truly buddhas or ancestors, the question of expressivity does not even arise," because it is taken for granted that only a genuine master knows how to utilize this facility. Therefore, "Expressing whatever one has realized is an ability that is not gained by keeping in lockstep with others, nor is it some kind of innate talent" (Dōtoku: Dōgen 1.374, Nearman 510, Tanahashi 439). This ability must be refined and renewed each and every moment by self-discipline and intense involvement with the learning process in ways that accord with the unity of being-time.

Expressivity is, therefore, a crucial component of Dōgen's ongoing religious quest to realize enlightenment and accomplish the accompanying pedagogical mission of transmitting the Dharma to a new generation of followers studying Zen in a remote country. His view of authentic discourse includes original elucidations of kōan cases in addition to sūtra passages that twist or upend the sources and culminate in challenges proffered to readers, who are encouraged to discern and proclaim their own evaluation of those literary materials. Dōgen's thoughtful articulations furthermore encompass various forms of disclosure, such as dreams, imaginary ideas, pictures, visions, or visualizations, that seem deceptive or unreal in that they are separate from and opposed to the standpoint of practical knowledge. However, in their respective ways, all of these modes contribute to gaining authentic insight when properly appreciated and appropriated as revelatory.

Whatever the subject matter under consideration, in nearly every fascicle of the *Treasury*, Dōgen's distinct rhetorical style features many kinds of flourishes, such as inversions and puns in both Chinese and Japanese, so as to confound common views by uncovering the deeper levels of significance of enlightened experience. This understanding, he points out, undergirds ordinary speech but remains generally unrecognized due to conceptual hindrances and emotional fetters that obstruct a correct view of multidimensional reality, unbound by a preoccupation with polarized or this-versus-that conceptualizations. Dōgen's reinterpretation of previous Buddhist works is designed to retrieve and reinvigorate the true spirit of Zen in support of nonthinking by emphasizing full awareness of the pervasive dynamism that defies categorization in all forms of existence.

Through his creative uses of language, Dōgen's views and methods are woven together in the *Treasury* to form a cohesive approach to achieving realization: making unrelenting efforts toward self-realization while engaging reflectively with each and every aspect of everyday life, understood as concrete manifestations of the dignified activities of Buddha nature. According to Dōgen, typical views that see "transcendence" as a static and aloof state somehow standing outside this world must be constantly contested in order to depict all moments of experience as the basis of reality, embracing a constant interplay between delusion and enlightenment.

Therefore, Dōgen's hermeneutic method for transforming an everyday utterance into an unexpected yet illuminative expression is applied in various techniques that "change word order, shift syntax, indicate alternate meanings, create new expressions, and revive forgotten symbols."[7] Another tactic is to suggest the permutation of a central concept, as in discussions of ambiguous but weighty terms like "this mind" or "dream within a dream," into many possible combinations, most of which deliberately defy common sense but nevertheless uncover hidden connotations.

As translator Kazuaki Tanahashi points out, "In exploring the deeper meanings of Zen stories, poetry, teachings, and Buddhist sūtras, Dōgen expands, twists, and manipulates the meanings of the words from the texts he quotes. By presenting unique and at times outrageous interpretations, he unleashes a great variety of descriptions on the state of meditation."[8] For example, Dōgen reworks the significance of words like "yes" and "no" as a way to interpret the fleeting quality of the moment or the universality of Buddha nature. He maintains, for example, "The nothingness (*mu*) of all the various nothings (*shomu*) must be learned in terms of understanding the nothingness of no Buddha nature (*mu-busshō*)" (Busshō: Dōgen 1.24, Nearman 256, Tanahashi 243).

A partial list of simple, yet transformative utterances analyzed by Dōgen includes "this" and "that," "like" and "such," "what" and "where," along with many other examples that are more obscure or specialized, such as "moon," "water," "rice cakes," and "flowers." In addition, as seen in the previous chapter, he intentionally conflates the conditional phrase, "if the time arrives," with the recast, "it has already arrived," so as to emphasize the priority of present practice. He furthermore speculates about a boat floating away from the shoreline until all evidence of land disappears in order to highlight the relativity of movement vis-à-vis types of perception, and he subverts the accepted meaning of time's coming and going to posit the nondual notion of holistic passage or discontinuous continuity (*kyōryaku*) that encompasses actor and activity as well as circumstantial elements influencing their interactions. Moreover, Dōgen seeks to show that what seems abstract and ethereal is concrete and material and vice versa, as when he says in "Ancient Buddha Mind, "the ancient mind is nothing other than walls, tiles, and stone" (Kobusshin: Dōgen 1.90, Nearman 569, Tanahashi 471) or in "Mountains and Rivers Proclaiming the Sūtras," "mountains are walking over rivers ... while the water stands still" (Sansuikyō: Dōgen 1.318, Nearman 144, Tanahashi 155–156). He furthermore maintains in that fascicle that this paradoxical outlook "liberates us from getting bogged down with inferior words and phrases" (Sansukyō: Dōgen 1.318, Nearman 145, Tanahashi 156).

Another feature of Dōgen's intricate discursive style is the turning of inquisitive expressions into declarative statements such as (mis)reading, "What do you think about?" as "What you do think?" (Zazenshin: Dōgen 1.104, Nearman 336, Tanahashi 303), or "What do you understand?" as "This is what you understand" (Ikka myōjū: Dōgen 1.79, Nearman 39, Tanahashi 36), an approach to language demonstrating that the word "what" can indicate at once an unassuming inquiry about an occurrence or a more profound evaluation of the quiddity (distinctive features or "what-ness") of that phenomenon. In these and related ways, the audience is led to an understanding of enlightenment as a here-and-now experience occurring without limitation, delay, or division, or to an affirmation of reality just as it is (*arinomama*). This is further suggested by a variety of terms that are used as titles of fascicles, such as "realization here and now" (*genjōkōan*), "total dynamic activity" (*zenki*), and "expressing the Way" (*dōtoku*).

Dōgen's rhetorical methods must be seen to have two-sided functions in accord with, yet modifying or extending, a famous motto that characterizes the Zen tradition as a "special transmission outside the teachings, without reliance on words and letters." Borrowing from the ideas of Chinese Chan predecessors, Dōgen consistently argues that all types of expression are appropriate to particular pedagogical situations and therefore should never be taken at face value or as perpetually valid, because they always need to be thought anew and adjusted or cast aside to suit to the occasion. The master Linji mentions that the aim of his discourse is not to teach doctrine but to cure illness by untying the knots or releasing the bonds of misunderstanding, and Master Mazu similarly refers to his method as a way to stop a baby from crying. In that vein, Watsuji Tetsurō points out that while Dōgen never rejects verbal expressions and does "allow that linguistic expressions could be used independently," he also maintains, "It is not the real truth if it is not expressed in accordance with the face-to-face transmission between buddhas."[9] Language is therefore used as a remedy to treat the ailment of ignorance, recalling the Buddha's "parable of the raft" in that specific approaches can and should be discarded when no longer useful.

Dōgen provides a philosophy that stresses the necessity and efficacy of employing language at every single stage of the transmission process without ever dismissing its utility. In contrast to numerous Zen thinkers for whom language tends to conceal by representing "clothing that hides truth," for Dōgen literary discourse operates as a window that divulges reality by providing an opportunity to convey authentically any circumstance, while recognizing that delusion invariably pervades any expression of realization. He writes in the fascicle "Entangling Vines":

> Although all Buddhist sages in their training study how to cut off entanglements (*kattō*) at the root, they do not study how to cut off entanglements by using entanglements. They do not realize that entanglements entangle entanglements. How little do they know what it is to transmit entanglements in terms of entanglements! How rarely do they realize that the transmission of the Dharma is itself an ongoing entanglement. (Kattō: Dōgen 1.416–417, Nearman 57, Tanahashi 478–479)

Even if all expressions are considered partial and misleading, in seeking realization language provides an unlimited resource for revealing the Dharma. Existential awareness is articulated through each and every form of discourse, because truth is revealed in routine words when they are plumbed for hidden depths of meaning.

The next two sections of this chapter examine Dōgen's approach to the main forms of Buddhist discourse he inherited yet revised: Zen kōan cases and passages in Mahāyāna sūtras.

INTERPRETING KŌAN CASES

When Dōgen studied in China in the 1220s, the cultural milieu of the Chan movement encompassed a veritable explosion of various kinds of literary texts that supplemented or replaced sūtra commentary by treating creatively biographical materials regarding eminent masters and philosophical debates about the meaning of enlightenment in ways that proved instrumental for the transplantation of Zen to Japan. The fundamental question about the role of discourse raised by many masters was: Does the use of elaborate imagery and rhetorical flourishes serve as an effective vehicle for expressing an understanding of the true nature of reality, surpassing conventional doctrine in order to convey genuine insight? Or is involvement in such forms of writing a distraction that inevitably detracts from authentic realization? Put another way, can linguistic elegance provide an aesthetic aid that enhances enlightenment, or is it one more example of the futility of "adding frost to snow" or "putting flowers on a gold brocade"? These phrases are traditional Zen putdowns for those who suffer from an attachment to words, but Dōgen suggests that in the appropriate context even those sayings indicate in a very positive sense productive augmentations of mindfulness.

The controversy about using words preoccupied Chinese thinkers who were part of a highly competitive Song-dynasty religious context dominated by the social class of well-educated and erudite literati known as scholar-officials (*shidafu*). The literati often trained under or collaborated with Buddhist teachers in order to polish their mental capacities for the process of creative writing. The issue ultimately resulted in a conflict. One view emphasized the notion of Nonliterary or Antiliterary (*muji*, Ch. *wuzi*) Zen, which preferred silence to speech and avoided involvement in the secular world of literary pastimes by giving up pen and paper along the path of renunciation. The opposing view stressed the role of literary (*monji*, Ch. *wenzi*) Zen that persisted in writing about the spiritual quest, especially in voluminous kōan commentaries, in order to instructively evoke feelings of aspiration and longing for attaining the Dharma through the use of language.[10]

This debate was dramatically played out in terms of the fate of the *Blue Cliff Record*, an elegant collection of complicated commentaries on kōan cases published by Yuanwu in 1128, but apparently destroyed about a dozen years later by his primary disciple, Dahui, who objected to the text's supposed excessive verbosity. According to a preface written for a reconstructed edition that was published in the early 1300s:

> The intentions of both elders were right. Yuanwu was concerned for students of later generations, so he commented on kōan cases. Dahui was

interested in saving people from burning or drowning, so he destroyed the *Blue Cliff Record*. Śākyamuni Buddha expressed the whole great canon of scriptures but in the end said that he had never uttered a single word. Was he fooling us? Yuanwu's intention was like that of Śākyamuni speaking the scriptures, and Dahui's intention was like that of Śākyamuni denying that he had ever spoken.[11]

The *Treasury* contributed to the transmission of Chinese kōan collections by presenting and interpreting dozens of case narratives. It is clear that Dōgen created the *300-Case Treasury* without commentary in 1235 as a way of recording his favorite kōans learned abroad, many of which are cited in various fascicles of the vernacular or kana text. The *Treasury* is by no means a rehash of the writings of continental precursors who represented literary Zen because it features two highly original elements, one structural, the other rhetorical. The primary structural difference from kōan collections like the *Blue Cliff Record* and the *Gateless Gate* is that, instead of focusing on cases presented as discrete literary units, Dōgen's masterwork is organized around thematic topics and evokes dialogues or related sayings only when these sources exemplify a broader subject matter. In terms of the style of delivery, rather than remarks written in advance, for the most part Dōgen's fascicles began as informal sermons (*jishu*), a free-form style of Zen oratory that could take place at whatever time was convened by the teacher and at almost any location in the temple compound, including the monks' hall or abbot's quarters. The Chinese kōan commentaries, in contrast, were usually derived from formal sermons (*jōdō*) that incorporated carefully rhymed poetic schemes in addition to flowery prose remarks enunciated in the ceremonial setting of the Dharma hall.

The main rhetorical difference from previous Chinese kōan collection commentaries involves conflicting views of the function of interpretation. In "Mountains and Rivers Proclaiming the Sūtras," Dōgen is quite critical of conventional Zen standpoints that in Japan became associated with the Rinzai sect, whereby masters would routinely shout and slap or strike disciples with a staff as a way of shocking and prodding them to go beyond rational understanding by abandoning the use of intellect. In contrast to that approach, Dōgen maintains, "Just because some teachers say that such stories are not subject to rational understanding, you should not fail to learn through your training the intellectually comprehensible pathways of buddhas and ancestors" (Sansuikyō: Dōgen 1.320, Nearman 147,

Tanahashi 158). Another discursive discrepancy is that, by transferring and thereby translating kōan cases into Japanese syntax, Dōgen frequently takes license to alter the dialogues, recasting the original wording to reflect his view that reality is dynamic rather than static. The immediacy of enlightenment is experienced in the words of the master's interpretations, instead of as an occurrence recalled from the past or anticipated in the future.

Dōgen did learn from and in many ways sought to emulate the interpretative style used in numerous Chinese kōan collections. To give one of manifold examples that seem to have influenced his approach, Master Chengtian Zong (n.d.) says to his assembly, "According to one dictum, 'The ocean is calm, and the rivers are clear,' but in another dictum, 'The wind is high, and the moon is cold.' One of these two sayings is like riding a robber's horse while chasing the robber [symbolic of ignorance], so try to understand the difference between them. Should a disciple in the assembly step forward to argue, 'That's not the right way,' I will simply dismiss this reply by saying he sees with just one eye."[12] Here, Chengtian seems to have decided that, of two strikingly similar alternatives highlighting serenity and detachment through evoking natural imagery, one is correct while the other reflects an exercise in futility. Chengtian does not explain which one represents the correct standpoint or how he makes an evaluation that others may consider arbitrary. The implication is that Chengtian's view is based on assessing, on the spur of the moment, the mystical quality of spiritual authenticity embodied by a practitioner that at once stands beyond and is conveyed through particular words.

A similar dialogue demonstrating a creative interpretation through deceptively simple wordplay that reflects the style of discourse evoked in the *Treasury* pertains to the legend of Japanese pilgrim Kakushin (1207–1298). Kakushin studied with Dōgen for a spell before traveling in the 1240s to China, where he visited the famous teacher Wumen (1183–1260), author of the *Gateless Gate*. During their initial meeting Wumen says, "My place has 'no gate' [the literal meaning of his name 無門 (*mumon*, Ch. *wumen*)]; so tell me, how did you get in?" and Kakushin answers that he was able to enter because he already has an "enlightened mind" [the literal meaning of his name 覺心 (*kakushin*, Ch. *juexin*)].[13] Although this dialogue took place about two decades after Dōgen's journey to the continent, it is mentioned here to highlight the way a disciple one-ups his teacher and is admired for this apparent putdown. The exchange reveals the flexibility of Zen pedagogy that transpires through an intimate form of communication endorsed by Dōgen's creative expressivity.

Turning Topsy-Turvy

One of dozens of examples of Dōgen's innovative approach to the role of language appears in the fascicle "Extensive Studies" and involves the term *henzan*, which usually refers to the custom of a novice traveling around the country at specified times of the year, especially after the summer retreat, in search of new teachers before eventually settling with one mentor, who would be able to guide him to enlightenment. Dōgen's interpretation reverses the typical meaning by eliminating the literal implication of wide-ranging wandering, based on his view that subjective communion between master and disciple is all that is needed to fulfill practice. He argues that the authentic meaning of *henzan* thus refers to thoroughly exploring Zen by training intensively with one's own mentor in a way that does not require leaving the temple.

Dōgen opens the fascicle by citing an exchange in which the conventional meaning of the key term is upended. According to this dialogue, the trainee Xuansha (835–908) insists that there is no need to venture forth, much to the approval of his teacher Xuefeng (822–908). When Xuansha is asked, "Why haven't you gone out on for extensive studies by seeking another teacher to train with?" he replies, "Bodhidharma did not come east to China, nor did the second ancestor go west to India." Dōgen remarks, "In this case, the typical use of 'extensive studies' has been turned completely upside down! Since what Xuansha said is not to be found in the Buddhist canon, there is no way to try to categorize or measure the depths of his awakening" (Henzan: Dōgen 2.112, Nearman 718, Tanahashi 609). This emphasis recalls T. S. Eliot saying that the end of all exploring is to arrive where one started and truly know this place for the first time.

Another key example in which Dōgen drastically alters the typical view of a kōan is his analysis of the famous phrase, "skin, flesh, bones, marrow," which is radically reinterpreted in "Entangling Vines" and also evoked in several other fascicles. The source narrative involving the selection of a successor by First Patriarch Bodhidharma is recorded in different versions that include varying numbers of participants and sequences of events.[14] In the best-known account referenced by Dōgen, Bodhidharma interviews four prospects: the first disciple neither affirms nor rejects words and is said to realize the teacher's "skin"; the second (a nun, quite unusual for the literature of this era) explains a quickly vanishing utopian vision and realizes the "flesh"; the next declares universal emptiness and realizes the "bones"; and the final disciple, Huike (487–593), maintains a noble silence and realizes the "marrow." Huike is awarded transmission to become the second patriarch, and for most commentators the message is quite clear that his reticence has prevailed in the competition.

According to Dōgen's interpretation, however, we should not think there is a hierarchy whereby the "skin" representing words is considered the most superficial level of understanding and the "marrow" of silence the most profound, along with two intermediary levels. Instead of reifying Huike's absence of speech, he writes, "You need to recognize that the skin, flesh, bones, and marrow of which Bodhidharma spoke are beyond being characterized as shallow or deep. . . . All his disciples, in their respective ways, conveyed their profound learning. What each realized represents the skin, flesh, bones, and marrow that springs forth from their body-mind. Every response encompasses the skin, flesh, bones, and marrow of casting off body-mind" (Kattō: Dōgen 1.418, Nearman 579, Tanahashi 480). Dōgen goes further in relativizing the various responses by suggesting that if Bodhidharma had had five, six, or many more followers, additional exchanges would have been needed. Indeed, there might be dozens, hundreds, or even thousands of possible replies that are each in their own way expressions of realization. Therefore, Bodhidharma's evaluation of the superior or interior versus inferior or exterior capabilities of interlocutors would be adjusted accordingly.

At once typical of and diverging from interpretations Dōgen studied in China, the rhetorical outlook of the *Treasury* is open-ended and invitational, appealing to members of the audience to reach their own conclusion based on subjective experience rather than taking the words of any speaker to be sacrosanct, no matter how exalted by tradition. According to the verse comment on case 20 in the *Gateless Gate*, which features exaggerated images of the capacity of an adept to express truth, "He lifts his leg to stir the seas; / And lowers his head to gaze down upon the highest state of meditation. / There is no space vast enough to contain his body— / Let someone else complete this verse."[15] The last line indicates not so much that there is nothing left to say, but that it is up to the reader to extend the train of thought expressed in the poetic remarks in any interpretative direction seen fit.

Following this outlook, Dōgen frequently suggests in the *Treasury* that an ancient master may have expressed an idea one way, but later teachers came along to interrupt and further interpret the original saying according to their own approach. What really counts in reviewing citations of prior sayings is to put forth a novel form of expression that prompts one to think (or nonthink) the matter through for himself. In the fascicle "Turning the Wheel of Dharma,"[16] Dōgen begins by explaining how a lecture by Rujing once referenced a saying attributed to Śākyamuni, "When one person opens up reality and returns to the source, all of space in ten directions vanishes" (Tenbōrin: Dōgen 2.182, Nearman 807, Tanahashi 692).[17]

In his remarks Rujing indicates that any utterance of a buddha or ancestor "must be an extraordinary expression" because it illumines ignorant disciples, and he recounts briefly several well-known interpretations of the saying (Tenbōrin: Dōgen 2.182, Nearman 807, Tanahashi 692): Wuzu says, "Pounding and crackling resounds throughout space in ten directions," making the abstraction seem concrete; Foxing says, "The space in ten directions is just the space in ten directions," providing an insightful tautology; and Yuanwu says, "In space throughout the ten directions flowers are added on brocade," suggesting that understanding the true meaning of space is at once enhanced and delimited by commentaries. These remarks indicate concrete particularity, universality, and naturalism, and encompass attitudes of ironic praise and disingenuous blasphemy. Each comment is valid in its own way, but none by itself—or as part of a group—should be considered authoritative. Rujing responds by distancing himself from the predecessors while proffering an alternative view, "When one person opens up reality and returns to the source, some mendicant smashes his rice bowl" (Tenbōrin: Dōgen 2.182, Nearman 807, Tanahashi 692), which indicates that there is no longer any need for a trainee who has completed the path to enlightenment to plead like a beggar for instruction from his teacher.

In the fascicle, Dōgen concludes this part of the discussion not by endorsing or disputing any of the previous stances but by suggesting his own approach: "Others have put it in their own words, but I say, 'The space throughout ten directions opens up reality and returns to the source'" (Tenbōrin: Dōgen 2.183, Nearman 807, Tanahashi 692–693), thus affirming space itself in an altogether impersonal way. Is Dōgen's own saying really any different than or superior to the others? Perhaps, as a modern interpreter suggests, it "expresses a deeper appreciation for the vitality of the spatial environment and for the actual spiritual potency and capacity of the world to manifest awakening."[18] In any event, Dōgen's seemingly inscrutable discussion reinforces that all Zen teachers, including Rujing, are noteworthy for insights conveyed but are not necessarily to be revered, since their words can be critiqued for what is left out, seems misleading, or is otherwise correctible.

Playing Games with Words

Dōgen's view of the relation between expressivity and awakening can be summarized in a paraphrase of some *Treasury* passages, "There is satori (sudden illumination) in the midst of delusion, and there is delusion in the midst of satori." Even the state of enlightenment has its partiality and blind spots, whereas the state of delusion harbors glimmers of insight. The pedagogical aim of Zen, therefore, is not to insist on any given standpoint or expression but to assist the reader in surveying various modes of understanding before reaching an evaluative perspective and becoming capable of asserting their own mark.

In the fascicle "Empty Space," which can also be rendered "Unbounded Space," Dōgen's interpretation of the concept of the term *kokū*, which usually indicates the unmoving vacuum that is contrasted with objects populating the world that are affected by the flux of time, derives from a wordplay on the double meaning of *kū* 空 as both space and emptiness. Whereas space implies something physical, emptiness conveys the nondual sense of true reality beyond distinctions. According to Dōgen, space should not be understood as the mere absence of forms; nor is it the void between things. Rather, space is things themselves or, as suggested in "Discerning the Way" and several other fascicles, it represents "grasses and trees, walls and fences, tiles and pebbles, for all things in every direction constitute the plenitude of space" (Bendōwa: Dōgen 2.463, Nearman 5, Tanahashi 6). For Dōgen space is itself form, the nostrils breathing and the nose around it, or "one ball that bounces here and there."[19]

Dōgen begins this fascicle with a case about two Chinese masters, Shigong (n.d.) and his younger Dharma brother, Zhizang (735–814). When Shigong asks Zhizang to grab on to space and in response, the junior colleague waves his hand in the air as if grabbing something, Shigong then grasps his nose and yanks hard. Zhizang yells in pain, "You're killing me! You just tried to pull my nose off!" and Shigong declares, "Now you know what it means to grab on to space!" (Kokū: Dōgen 2.208–209, Nearman 846–847, Tanahashi 718). Before his nose was tugged, Zhizang thought that space was just empty air, so the elder's query seemed nonsensical and he gave a similar reply. With the immediacy of his own unexpectedly painful and embarrassing experience, he could finally understand the true meaning of space. From the standpoint of nonthinking, it is no longer seen as an abstraction, but as concretely physical yet fully integrated with and inseparable from the dynamic activities of everyday life.

However, in his typically intrusive way Dōgen shows that he is not entirely satisfied with the mentor's approach. On Shigong saying, "Now you know what it means to grab on to space," Dōgen suggests that had he been there, he would have remarked, "At the time you yanked Zhizang's nose, if you had wanted to really show him how to grab on to space, you should have yanked your own nose. And you should have also demonstrated what it means to grab hold of your fingertips with your own fingertips" (Kokū: Dōgen 2.210, Nearman 848, Tanahashi 718–719). Following these comments on the source dialogue, Dōgen briefly mentions a line from Rujing's verse that he cites and praises elsewhere in the *Treasury*, "My whole being is like the mouth of a wind bell hanging in empty space" (Kokū: Dōgen 2.211, Nearman 849, Tanahashi 719). This time Dōgen remarks, with an apparent revision of his mentor that recalls "Turning the Dharma Wheel," "Clearly you should realize that the whole body of space is hanging in space" (Kokū: Dōgen 2.211, Nearman 849, Tanahashi 719).

In the fascicle "The Ungraspable Mind," Dōgen demonstrates an elaborate version of the hermeneutics of intrusion by providing a creative interpretation of a kōan case dealing with Master Deshan's comeuppance suffered at the hands of an elderly laywoman. This is one of several prominent examples in Zen lore in which a female, either a cleric or not, outsmarts a male teacher. Dōgen recasts and extends the narrative content by questioning its assumptions through an atomization and interruption of the rhetorical structure of the source dialogue.[20] Well known for his expertise in the *Diamond Sūtra* (Ch. *Jingang jing*, Jp. *Kongōkyō*) but realizing subconsciously that he is overly attached to studying doctrinal discourse, Deshan is traveling in search of the Dharma to the southern part of China in Jiangxi province, where the Zen movement was flourishing during the Tang dynasty.[21] He comes across a woman selling rice cakes by the side of the road. She asks the priest why he wants to purchase one, and Deshan replies in a straightforward way, "I am hungry and need some refreshments." The word for refreshments 點心 (*tenshin*, Ch. *dianxin*, also pronounced *dimsum* in Cantonese), indicates tasty treats to eat but literally means, "pointing to the mind," based on the idea that traditionally each village had its own special way of preparing a favorite delicacy.

When Deshan impatiently proclaims himself to be "King of the *Diamond Sūtra*," who carries his voluminous notes and commentaries in his backpack, the woman evokes an ingenious wordplay that involves an irony concerning one of the scripture's best-known teachings:

> I have heard it said that, according to the *Diamond Sūtra*, "past mind is ungraspable (*shinfukatoku*, Ch. *xinbukede*), present mind is ungraspable, and future mind is ungraspable." So where is the "mind" 心 (*shin/xin*) that you wish to "refresh" 點 (*ten/dian*) with rice cakes (*tenshin/dianxin*)? Venerable priest, if you can answer, I will sell you a rice cake. But if you cannot answer, I will not sell you any rice cakes today. (Shinfukatoku: Dōgen 1.83, Nearman 190, Tanahashi 192)

Deshan is struck speechless by this putdown, and the old woman gets up abruptly and leaves without giving him a single treat. Dōgen's commentary tries to reverse the conventional understanding that privileges the seller and dismisses the buyer by criticizing the woman and those interpreters who eagerly praise her handling of Deshan's inability to make a comeback. Dōgen agrees with other commentators that while Deshan thought he was about to investigate the old woman, she turned the tables and found him wanting, but innovatively he challenges Deshan for not asking in response to her query, "I cannot answer your question, so let me ask what you would say about the matter" (Shinfukatoku: Dōgen 1.86, Nearman 191, Tanahashi 194). Dōgen then suggests that the woman should not have simply let the dialogue end in silence but instead could have said, "Venerable priest, if you cannot answer my question, try challenging me with a question to see if I can answer you" (Shinfukatoku: Dōgen 1.85, Nearman 192, Tanahashi 193). Instead, as Dōgen points out, she ruffles her sleeves and walks away "as if there was a bee in her garment." According to his interpretation, it is not clear that the woman is awakened, since she is a marginal figure who might be able to casually challenge a deluded monk lacking full understanding; she should not be considered of equal status to a genuinely enlightened adept.

Dōgen argues further that Deshan should have replied, "If you say so, then don't bother to sell me any rice cakes" (Shinfukatoku: Dōgen 1.85, Nearman 191, Tanahashi 193). Or, to be even more effective, he could have upset the woman by inquiring, "As past mind is ungraspable, present mind is ungraspable, and future mind is ungraspable, where is the mind (*shin/xin*) that now makes the rice cakes used for refreshment (*ten/dian*)?" (Shinfukatoku: Dōgen 1.85, Nearman 192, Tanahashi 193). Then the woman would confront Deshan by saying paradoxically, "You know only that one cannot refresh the mind with a rice cake. But you do not realize that the mind refreshes the rice cake or that the mind refreshes [or liberates] the mind" (Shinfukatoku: Dōgen 1.85, Nearman 192, Tanahashi 193). And just as Deshan is feeling overwhelmed and bewildered, she would continue with feigned kindness, "Here is one rice cake each for the past ungraspable mind, the present ungraspable mind, and the future ungraspable mind" (Shinfukatoku: Dōgen 1.85, Nearman 192, Tanahashi 193). But, should he fail to reach out his hand to take these, she would slap him with one of the treats and say, "You ignorant fool, don't be so absentminded" (Shinfukatoku: Dōgen 1.86, Nearman 192, Tanhashi 194). Dōgen concludes by arguing, "Therefore, neither the old woman nor Deshan was able to hear or express adequately the past ungraspable mind, present ungraspable mind, or future ungraspable mind" (Shinfukatoku: Dōgen 1.86, Nearman 192, Tanahashi 194). Based on Dōgen's playful critique of the old woman and his contention that neither party was capable of "truly savoring the rice cake" (Shinfukatoku: Dōgen 1.86, Nearman 193, Tanahashi 194), it is no longer clear that she has prevailed over the monk with one of the most intriguing puns in the history of Zen discourse.

READING AND RECITING SŪTRAS

Dōgen's approach to interpreting the role of the vast corpus of Mahāyāna sūtra literature, which is supposed to convey the spoken words of the Buddha but no doubt was written in later periods, is quite complicated and characteristically contradictory. Prior to the formation of the Zen school, Chinese and Japanese Buddhist teachings were mainly disseminated through a variety of sūtras that were originally composed in Sanskrit, which gave them prestige, and were translated into Chinese by Xuanzang (602–664) and numerous other Tang-dynasty priests, many of whom either traveled to India or in some cases came to China from there. The two main Buddhist factions of the Tang dynasty that were developed on Chinese soil and spread to Japan, the Huayan (Jp. Kegon) and Tiantai (Jp. Tendai) schools, were each associated with a main scripture, the *Avataṃsaka Sūtra* and the *Lotus Sūtra*, respectively, which was examined extensively in voluminous commentarial literature.

Based on his lengthy analysis of the case involving Deshan, who in another set of legends is said to have seen the error of his ways after being bested by the old woman and burned the massive set of materials about the *Diamond Sūtra* he had collected before having a spontaneous realization, it might appear that this represents the emblematic iconoclastic view of rejecting sūtra literature as unnecessary and counterproductive. That approach is supported by the image of Sixth Patriarch Huineng ripping up sūtra scrolls, in addition to Rujing's injunction to Dōgen that the technique of just sitting vitiates the need for other kinds of practices, including reading, reciting, memorizing, and writing copies of sūtras.

As a product of the Japanese Tendai monastic training regimen, Dōgen studied the entire Buddhist canon consisting of diverse Mahāyāna sūtras along with additional scriptural resources before traveling to the continent to undertake the practice of seated meditation. He cites many of these works extensively, while also revising or refuting them in innovative fashion. In contrast to the typical Zen view, Dōgen claims in the earliest *Treasury* fascicle, "Discerning the Way," to support all of the sūtras as a meaningful form of discourse that is compatible with the method of just sitting. He acknowledges that a skeptic of zazen practice might ask him, "Both the Tendai (school based on the *Lotus Sūtra*) and the Kegon (school based on the *Avataṃsaka Sūtra*) are considered to be the fundamental traditions of Mahāyāna Buddhism.... What is so superior about the training technique of seated meditation that causes you to insist on disregarding traditional teachings in exclusive pursuit of a new approach to Buddhist practice?" (Bendōwa: Dōgen 2.467, Nearman 9, Tanahashi 9).

Dōgen responds to this hypothetical query by maintaining, "You should understand that within the Buddha's family there can be no arguing over 'superior' or 'inferior' teachings, and no singling out of some expression as being more shallow or profound than others" (Bendōwa: Dōgen 2.467, Nearman 9, Tanahashi 9). He adds, "All the myriad images that fill the universe are surpassed by the far-reaching, remarkably rich words of Buddha" (Bendōwa: Dōgen 2.467, Nearman 9, Tanahashi 9). His main point is that sūtras are considered invaluable tools that are ultimately equal in status to zazen and kōans. Their words can be seen as equivalent to the innumerable grains of sand or specks of dust that populate the universe. This implies that sūtras, in the sense of doctrinal writings contained in scrolls, should not be elevated to an elite level over and above the method of just sitting.

Dōgen's approach to sūtra practice can be examined from two standpoints: theoretical, which concerns his comments on the true meaning of the sources in relation to the overall role of expressing the Way; and practical, which involves his understanding of prescriptions for temple rituals dealing with scrolls as venerated sacred objects. In both cases, Dōgen is at once respectful and irreverent. In the fascicle "Empty Space," for example, he at once relativizes and expands the role of sūtras by analyzing a dialogue involving an eminent scholar of Buddhist scriptures known as lecturer Liang (n.d.) from the Hongzhou region of Jiangxi province, a center for thriving Chan temples during the Tang dynasty. One day Liang visits Master Mazu, who is known for his strong emphasis on irreverent, sūtra-denying Chan rhetoric. Mazu inquires, "Which scripture do you lecture on?" and Liang replies, "The *Heart Sūtra* (Ch. *Xin jing*, Jp. *Shingyō*)." Mazu then asks, "On what basis do you speak about it?" and Liang answers, "It is based on my mind" (Kokū: Dōgen 2.211, Nearman 849, Tanahashi 719).

Mazu next says, "The mind is like the lead actor of a play, our will is its supporting performer, and the six senses play the accompanying cast. How can any of these interdependent entities possibly know how to lecture on a scripture?," since this effort requires independent thought. Liang responds, "If the mind is unable to give a lecture, surely empty space could hardly do so!" but Mazu retorts, "On the contrary, it is precisely space [in its true meaning as the emptiness of all conceptual categories] that is able to give lectures" (Kokū: Dōgen 2.211, Nearman 849, Tanahashi 719). After this Liang is enlightened and becomes a recluse, never to be heard from again. Dōgen remarks, "Accordingly, buddhas and ancestors alike are persons who expound the sūtras, and they invariably make use of empty space in doing so. Were it not for space, they would not be able to expound even one sūtra. Whether they explicate the mind or the body as sūtras, the elucidation is carried out by means of space" (Kokū: Dōgen 2.211, Nearman 849, Tanahashi 719).

Dōgen's View of the *Lotus Sūtra*

Despite this apparent criticism of conventional sūtra learning as something lesser than, and thus exceeded by, true reality, there are several hundred instances in the *Treasury* in which Dōgen quotes or alludes to passages culled from the *Lotus Sūtra*.[22] This scripture was the mainstay of Japanese Buddhism in the Heian era, particularly prized for its creative use of parables illustrating how to attain enlightenment through the path of One Vehicle, and also for its self-referential commands that followers must chant and copy the contents of the scripture in order to gain direct access to salvation.[23] Dōgen's citation process is executed with a mixture of enthusiastic veneration and determined revisionism. In the fascicle "Taking Refuge in the Three Jewels," he refers to the *Lotus Sūtra* as "the great king and the grand master of all the various sūtras that Śākyamuni Buddha ever taught, with all the others serving as its loyal subjects" (Kie buppōsōbō: Dōgen 2.374, Nearman 1008–1009, Tanahashi 842). Yet he also makes clear that the symbolic quality of any scripture is rooted not so much in words written on scrolls but in terms of whether and how these writings are understood by a trainee from the standpoint of nonspeaking, beyond the distinction of words and no words.[24]

In that vein, in a couple of fascicles Dōgen cites at length a prominent passage from the *Platform Sūtra* in which Sixth Patriarch Huineng, much like his second-generation successor Mazu in the dialogue with Liang mentioned above, tells the monk Fada (n.d), a specialist in *Lotus Sūtra* recitation, that no sūtras should be taken literally, so chanting thousands of times does not lead to genuine realization. Fada admits that he has simply been memorizing the text mindlessly. The sixth patriarch tells him that the basic point of a sūtra is to motivate the practitioner to read between the lines of the Buddha's preaching so that when the mind is deluded, it is turned or transformed by the *Lotus Sūtra* and when the mind is awakened, it turns or transforms the sūtra (Hokke ten hokke: Dōgen 2.489, Nearman 176, Tanahashi 182). Furthermore, Dōgen emphasizes, when the mind goes beyond the duality of delusion and awakening, that holistic state represents the *Lotus Sūtra* turning the *Lotus Sūtra* without regard for intercession.

The final phrase of Huineng's remark serves as the title of a *Treasury* fascicle, "The Lotus Turning Lotus," which could also be rendered as "Dharma Flowers Turning Dharma Flowers" ("Hokke ten hokke") based on the literal meaning of the Sino-Japanese term 法華 (*hokke*, Ch. *fahua*) used to render "lotus blossoms." This essay, originally included in the 60-fascicle edition, is one of more than two dozen fascicles that are significantly informed by the sayings and symbols of the *Lotus Sūtra*, with about half of those passages representing extended commentaries on key sections of the scripture. Overall, the *Lotus Sūtra* contributes significantly to the vocabulary Dōgen uses in discussing the multiple dimensions of true reality and authentic realization, including such key terms (which also serve as titles of fascicles) as "suchness" (*immo*), the "true form of all dharmas" (*shohō jissō*), "the moon" (*tsuki*), "empty space" (*kokū*), "ten directions" (*jippō*), and "the nature of things" (*hosshō*), among other examples. Another fascicle founded on a *Lotus Sūtra* doctrine that appears in the 95-fascicle edition (but is not included in either the 75- or the 60-fascicle edition because it was edited after Dōgen's death) is "Only Between a Buddha and a Buddha," which teaches that "Each buddha on his own, together with all buddhas, is directly able to realize fully [the true form of all thoughts and things]" (Yuibutsu yobustu: Dōgen 2.519, Nearman 1091, Tanahashi 876).

In several prominent instances, Dōgen cites concepts from the scripture that convey in their original textual setting a level of otherworldly significance by implying that a spiritual goal can be reached sometime in the future. He then provides a demythologizing interpretation, emphasizing that the true meaning of the key term pertains to here-and-now realization. For example, the fascicle "Confirmation" drastically revises the notion known as *juki* (Skr. *vyakarana*), which in the *Lotus Sūtra* refers to a prediction or assurance by Buddha in regard to someone's forthcoming attainment of enlightenment based on the idea that all sentient beings are capable of realizing Buddha nature at this very moment.

In typical Japanese Buddhist practice, this technical term could refer to predicting buddhahood, the act of a master making such a forecast, or confirming someone's realization. Toward the end of the fascicle Dōgen writes the word *juki* (授記) using a different first character for the compound so that it becomes 受記 (pronounced *jūki*), which conveys the meaning of receiving, accepting, or acknowledging confirmation, and he also refers to the notion of proactively "expressing confirmation" 得記 (*tokuki*). According to Dōgen's view:

> Witnessing someone being given the prediction of supremely perfected enlightenment is nothing other than the Buddha's wish being fulfilled right now. Experience this through painstaking effort in harmony with the sūtra and you will be "someone who gains awakening by listening to a single line or verse." There is no time to spare in placing a head above a head or realizing the skin, flesh, bones, and marrow. (Juki: Dōgen 1.255, Nearman 455, Tanahashi 394)

The reference to "listening to a single line" of scriptural commentary indicates that enlightenment can be attained inadvertently at any time and in every place.

Similarly, the fascicle "Whole Body of Tathāgata" is a short discourse based on passages from the *Lotus Sūtra* regarding the eponymous concept of *nyorai zenshin* (whole body of Tathāgata). Here Dōgen discusses the identity of individual awakening, or whole body, with the Tathāgata, or Buddha who "thus comes," by virtue of casting off a false notion of self. Neither term refers to an abstract or ethereal entity, but rather an actual person who has attained liberation from conceptual fetters and embodies the essential meaning of Buddhist teachings. Therefore, the whole body of one who is a Tathāgata is not supernal, for it embraces all aspects of the universe. Universal form further incorporates whatever elements historical buddhas leave behind, such as relics, mummies, or other artifacts. The *Lotus Sūtra* is not understood as a textual entity appearing in written scrolls that are venerated, for it constitutes a manner of expressing the Dharma at once through and beyond language that represents the true realization of all beings at all times.

The Paradox of Ritual Activities

Moreover, Dōgen deals extensively with the role of rituals involving the practice known as "reading sūtras" (*kankin*), a term broadly referencing a variety of methods that celebrate sacred scrolls by reading, remembering, rotating, or raising the scriptures, or writing them by hand. The rules for conducting these activities are carefully spelled out in instructional manuals. According to traditional Buddhist practices absorbed into Zen monastic rites, reciting sūtras means viewing the scrolls, turning the repository in which these are held, recalling certain or in some cases all the passages by heart, and copying the titles or even the full contents of chapters, sometimes in blood, as a means of repentance for transgression.

In the fascicle "Reciting Sūtras," Dōgen deliberately creates a paradoxical discursive setting for this set of practices by citing lengthy monastic regulations that detail the way to perform the ceremony of recitation for the benefit of donors or a similar obligation. He inventively surrounds this instructional passage with a dozen irreverent and seemingly blasphemous Zen dialogues that debunk and disregard, or disorient and recast, the practice that is endorsed in the regulations. These kōan cases turn the matter of recitation on its head by emphasizing interior symbolism instead of sacramentalism. According to one of the main examples, in response to an elderly female benefactor's request that he read and rotate the entire collection of sūtras, Master Zhaozhou steps off the meditation platform, walks around it, and says casually to a messenger, "The canon has been rotated." The messenger then reports this to the old woman, who declares ironically, "I asked the master to rotate the entire canon, but he only rotated half of it" (Kankin: Dōgen 1.333, Nearman 234–235, Tanahashi 226).

Although it is not clear whether, in this apparent contest of wills, the donor has bested the master or vice versa, the point for Dōgen is that both parties understand implicitly that authentic practice must occur without ulterior motive or the seeking of any reward in order to reflect a state of harmony with ongoing realization. He furthermore proclaims in the fascicle "Buddhist Sūtras," "The notion of procuring [or getting hold of the essence of] a sūtra really refers to being able to see whatever appears right now before your very eyes as the whole universe manifesting in all directions" (Bukkyō: Dōgen 2.15, Nearman 611, Tanahashi 538). According to this view, reading and reciting words written on a scroll is not the most relevant activity because "Appropriating the meaning expressed between the lines of the sūtra, or from what lies behind the scenes and is conveyed outside of the words, is surely an opportunity to transform scattered flowers into a garland of blossoms" (Bukkyō: Dōgen 2.16, Nearman 611, Tanahashi 539). This fascicle also suggests that there are two types of reading. One is a misguided sūtra recitation based on literal sequential performances that only serves to mire a practitioner further in delusion, but the second, more meaningful activity involves the "casting off of sūtra recitation" (*datsuraku no kankin*) or "sūtra recitation for which one has no practical use" (*fuyō no kankin*) (Bukkyō: Dōgen 2.18, Nearman 614, Tanahashi 540), in that it is free from any attachment to gaining a direct result. The implication is that the genuine act of reciting sūtras represents the act of "just reciting" or could be termed the "nonreciting" of scriptures.

In a related discussion of sacred language as part of the fascicle "Spells," the title of the essay refers to the incantations or magical formulae (Skr. *dhāraṇī*, Jp. *darani*) evoked throughout the Buddhist world, especially in the practice of esoteric schools (*mikkyō*) that were particularly popular in medieval Japan, including in key factions of the Sōtō sect after Dōgen's death. Dōgen's approach disregards the usual concern with utilizing these utterances to reach a desired goal or ward off evil and instead interprets the term as a call to enact the etiquette of ceremonialism, especially when meeting, greeting, paying obeisance, and making offerings to one's teacher. In contrast to esotericism, this fascicle is dedicated to instructing the proper procedure for exchanging salutations with a master, since the practice of *darani* "reflects a mutual encounter with the correct transmission of the essential teachings of buddhas and ancestors, who continually and uninterruptedly realize and preach the Dharma" (Darani: Dōgen 2.32, Nearman 538, Tanahashi 563–564).

DEALING WITH DECEPTIONS

The *Treasury* provides a straightforward but complex rationale for understanding the crucial role played by apparently deceptive or illusory forms of communication in conveying the Dharma, an approach that is contrary to typical Buddhist efforts to eradicate attachments to delusion. Dōgen is particularly influenced by Huineng's dictum suggesting that the awakened mind turns the *Lotus Sūtra*, whereas the deluded mind is turned by it. In addition, Huineng points to a level of understanding that goes beyond conventional distinctions between illusion and reality by recognizing that the "*Lotus* is turning the *Lotus*," in that the sūtra constantly divulges its content since it is continually being thought or recited day and night, so there is no time when it is out of a practitioner's mind. This recalls Yuanwu's saying that a pearl spinning in a bowl is also being spun by the container.

From this nondual standpoint, all delusions can be seen as examples of the true meaning of the Dharma, since authentic reality is perpetually causing our minds to be stirred in pursuit of self-realization. This occurs even when someone appears lost while wandering in the realm of deception, for delusions are manifestations of the Dharma's flowering that enable truth to reveal itself within one's thoughts. Therefore, at the time a practitioner is being led astray, he is also on the verge of discovering authenticity.

Dōgen repudiates the falsity of misrepresentations that are designed to defy or violate the pursuit of truth through deceit and distortion, fabrication and fallacy, or hyperbole and hypocrisy. Those modes of discourse go against the grain of the Confucian emphasis on the rectification of names (Ch. *zhengming*, Jp. *shōmyō*), or the proper and correct use of terminology. Yet Dōgen does seek to justify the function of several phenomena that usually indicate the antithesis of reality because they seem to involve illusoriness and duplicity, or fantasy and phantasm. These notions, including dreams, visions, and figments imagined, are to be seen as the vines of metaphorical expressions that are powerful paradoxical examples of the flowering of the Dharma turning or setting in motion the Dharma blooming within. Dōgen's strategy is not to dismiss deceptions but to refute any bifurcation or gap between realms by arguing for the ultimate identity of whatever is portrayed in conventional approaches as false, misleading, or imaginary with the reality of insubstantiality or nothingness.

The *Treasury* maintains, for example, "If there is no disclosing a dream (*muchū setsumu*), there are no buddhas. If there is no being within a dream, buddhas do not transmit the wondrous Dharma" (Muchū setsumu: Dōgen 1.297, Nearman 504, Tanahashi 433). In addition, Dōgen suggests that "only the painting of rice cake (*gabyō*) satisfies hunger" (Gabyō: Dōgen 1.273, Nearman 524, Tanahashi 449), and "flowers in the sky (*kūge*) blossom forth as manifestations of universal emptiness or unbounded space [the literal meaning of *kū*] that do not necessarily cloud our vision" (Kūge: Dōgen 1.129, Nearman 555, Tanahashi 460). Dōgen also points out, as previously discussed, "the moon is not like, but is enlightenment" and "the entanglement of vines is a necessary means for disentangling vines." These expressions should not be taken as an analogy that represents the truth from a distance yet remains metaphorical (*hiyu*). Rather, the sayings convey the "true form of reality" (*shohō jissō*) just as it is.

Dōgen justifies such provocative interpretations as a matter of "making the right mistake" (*shoshaku jushaku*) by arguing that, although various kinds of speech acts stemming from delusion may seem inadequate, so long as they are not purposely misrepresentative, they reflect insightful and illuminative elucidations of the genuine nature of existence normally concealed by ignorance and attachment. In the fascicle "Bodhisattva Kannon," for instance, he comments extensively on the phrase "a head sits atop a head." This expression, referring to the multiheaded (and multilimbed) iconography of the goddess, is generally used in Zen as a putdown implying a useless or secondary level of discussion that fails to contribute to genuine discourse. "In hearing this phrase," Dōgen argues, "foolish people think that it cautions against adding unnecessary verbiage about any given topic. Usually they evoke the saying to suggest something that should not occur, as in, 'How can you possibly place a head on top of another head?' But that way of talking is erroneous" (Muchū setsumu: Dōgen 1.297–298, Nearman 504, Tanahashi 433–434). He similarly suggests that the phrase "putting frost on snow" implies unique creativity, rather than mere repetition that would normally be considered delusory.

In the fascicle "Flowers in the Sky," Dōgen reinterprets a sūtra passage in which Śākyamuni Buddha says, "[Ignorance] is like a person who has clouded eyes seeing flowers appearing in the sky. If the sickness of having clouded eyes is cured, then flowers vanish from the sky" (Kūge: Dōgen 1.129–130, Nearman 556, Tanahashi 461). The conventional Buddhist understanding of this statement is that average people's eyes are deceived by karmic obstructions, so they are unable to see things vividly. Instead they perceive flowers floating in thin air, which was also a common idiom in Chinese locution for suffering from the then-incurable eye disease of having cataracts. The notion of flowers appearing in space—or, put more positively, the flowering of emptiness—is interpreted by Dōgen to refer to the Dharma revealing itself to our senses, because it appears vague or unclear and is not recognized at first, but eventually discloses its true significance. Throughout this fascicle, Dōgen's comments characteristically turn the main topic upside down by understanding that illusory blossoms are manifesting what buddhas teach or are "the vehicle upon which the buddhas ride," in appearing for the sake of awakening beings from the afflictions of the mundane world.

Another main example of transforming delusory discourse into confirmation of awakening is found in the fascicle "Disclosing a Dream Within a Dream." The title is taken from a phrase used in the *Large Perfection of Wisdom* (Ch. *Da Mohebore jing*, Jp. *Dai Makahannyakyō*, no. 596), but Dōgen's examination of dream (*mu* or *yume*) also draws on imagery in various aspects of Asian thought, ranging from Hindu and early Buddhist philosophy and mythology in India to the writings of Zhuangzi in China, in addition to numerous examples in classical Japanese religion and poetry. Mahāyāna "Perfection of Wisdom" literature often evokes reverie or fantasy as a prime symbol of the untrue and unreal that is generated by "discrimination and false intellection... like a cloud, a ring produced by a firebrand, a castle of the Gandharvas (gods), a vision, a mirage, the moon as reflected in the ocean and a dream."[25] A famous verse (Skr. *gāthā*, Jp. *ge*) in the *Diamond Sūtra* further emphasizes, "All things phenomenal / are like dreams, *māyā* (illusion), bubbles; / like dew and lightning flashes, / this is how one should regard them."

For numerous East Asian thinkers, however, it is the very contingency and ephemerality of dreams, illustrating the world of falsity, that makes this a key metaphor for the insubstantial and ultimately void or empty nature of true reality. As Kuang-ming Wu suggests, "Dream is the activity that most powerfully convinces us that we ourselves are part and parcel of the process of interchange among things.... We are one among things that mutually change, influence, co-arise, and co-cause one another."[26] Therefore, "perfection is like a dream... because one cannot apprehend the one who sees the dream."[27]

Dōgen argues that disclosing a dream within a dream is not like "delusion mounted on top of delusion" (*madoi ni madoi o kasaneru*). Although in some sense delusion is always being compounded, he suggests that even for the enlightened the path to attaining the Dharma is only realized through "delusion that is surpassing delusion" (*madoi no ue no madoi*) (Muchū setsumu: Dōgen 1.296, Nearman 502, Tanahashi 432). Therefore, "A tree without roots, a land without sun or shade, and a valley without an echo are themselves the realization of disclosing a dream within a dream; this is 'the mystery within mystery,' 'the wondrous within the wondrous,' 'the confirmation within confirmation,' and 'a head atop a head'" (Muchū setsumu: Dōgen 1.297, Nearman 503–504, Tanahashi 433). By rearranging the juxtaposition of lexical components of the key phrase, Dōgen further writes, "Because supreme enlightenment is supreme enlightenment, a dream is called a dream. It is a dream disclosing a dream within (*chūmu ari mu setsu ari*), or it is within a dream disclosing a dream (*setsumu ari muchū ari*)" (Muchū setsumu: Dōgen 1.297, Nearman 504, Tanahashi 433). Although dream can indicate two opposite states, the ideal beyond the mundane and the illusory separated from truth, in Dōgen's interpretation, disclosing a dream within a dream represents a single unified view of reality because there is essentially one dream, simultaneously delusory and awakened.

FOUR LEVELS OF AWARENESS

In the various kinds of discourse in the *Treasury*, Dōgen recognizes that most people are not able to appreciate the underlying inseparability and interdependence of the polarities of dream and awakening or illusion and reality, in addition to human and natural existence, living and dying, now and eternity, mind and body, and speech and silence. His analysis of temporality and expressivity shows that various levels of awareness can be evaluated in terms of their degree of understanding, or misunderstanding, the foundations of truth that is unbound by discrepancies or divisions yet allows for endless differences and distinctions to be revealed. In "Realization Here and Now," Dōgen sums up the ranking by stating in chiasmic form, "Those who have great realization about delusion are buddhas, and those who have great delusion about realization are sentient beings. There are those who continue to attain realization beyond realization, and those who remain in delusion in the midst of delusion" (Genjōkōan: Dōgen 1.3, Nearman 32, Tanahashi 29). From this brief passage seen in connection to "Disclosing a Dream Within a Dream," which distinguishes between dream as relative (illusion about form) and as absolute (realization of the formless), it is possible to discern four main stages of awareness articulated in the masterwork, ranked in descending order in terms of reaching or falling short of genuine contemplation of impermanence:[28]

(1) The highest state of awareness, which fully expresses authentic reality based on genuinely contemplating impermanence, is "realization that continually goes beyond realization," or "continuous enlightenment beyond Buddha" (*bukkōjōji*). This refers to actualizing the absolute truth of the unity of being-time within the realm of the relativity of phenomena by means of a spiritual understanding that continues to surpass itself, not pausing at an artificial conclusion or endpoint, so that an authentic adept no longer even seeks or needs to be classified as a buddha. According to Dōgen, "When buddhas are truly buddhas, they do not think of themselves as buddhas. By not thinking of this, they are realized buddhas who

continually manifest Buddha nature" (Genjōkōan: Dōgen 1.3, Nearman 32, Tanahashi 29). They thereby reflect unremittingly the self-surpassing circumstances of disentangling vines by means of entangling vines or finding the correct mistake through appreciating the indivisibility of time and death in terms of their separateness.

(2) The second state of awareness is "great realization about delusion," which is not yet capable of truly surpassing the level of being aware of one's own Buddha nature because the holistic truths of temporality and expressivity remain artificially differentiated. This consciousness haunted by a subtle duality fails to overcome some deficiency that defeats efforts to apply an authentic understanding of reality to all pedagogical situations. If the practitioner concentrates solely on achieving the aim of meditation, conceived as a final destination, Dōgen argues that enlightenment is concealed and left unrealized, but forgetting or abandoning the pursuit of an end point allows Buddha nature to be manifest right here and now, and this spiritual condition can eventually ascend to the highest level of awareness that is endlessly perpetuated.

(3) The next state of (mis)understanding is "holding to delusion about realization." This level of awareness (or lack thereof) is unable to overcome a state of being bound by the viewpoint of a typical sentient being because, even though the relative is seen as incomplete and needing to be surpassed, the practitioner remains deluded about temporality and speech, and thus his forms of expression remain within the realm of deficiency. To overcome a sequential view of time and realize true reality, trainees must go beyond the condition of harboring stubborn delusions. Falsity can and must be transformed through the rigors of meditative exercises that open consciousness to the realm of nonthinking and use language without any lingering attachment, in order to achieve a final goal based on apprehending transiency.

(4) The lowest state or the dimmest level of awareness is "delusion in the midst of (or compounded within) delusion" or "great illusion about enlightenment" (Genjōkōan: Dōgen 1.2, Nearman 32, Tanahashi 29) that perpetuates and compounds ignorance as part of a vicious cycle, failing to overcome defective thoughts and words. This level is not conscious of its own shortcomings or the need to continue striving to go beyond ordinary knowledge, so it cannot even glimpse enlightenment as a remote and unattainable goal. Yet even the hopelessly deluded, who are living in the darkest cave on a pitch-black mountain or picking up the pieces of a shattered mirror, know on some unconscious level that at the right moment they too are capable of breaking through to genuine realization by seeing

that awakening is not a potential to be reached in the future, but is always already functioning without obstruction right now within the realm of impermanence. Dōgen writes paradoxically in the fascicle "Great Awakening," "A truly awakened person continually becomes awakened, but a greatly deluded person or someone who gains awakening yet reverts for a time to delusion is still considered greatly awakened" (Daigo: Dōgen 1.95, Nearman 331, Tanahashi 299). Therefore, "delusion surpassing delusion" reflects an ability to see beyond deception through the deception itself so that delusion is self-surpassing, as in the notion of dream-as-deception becoming an awareness of nonsubstantiality or realizing that flowers in the sky disclose true emptiness.

This analysis of four levels of awareness, whereby full unimpeded enlightenment is never cut off from the fetters of delusion and vice versa, suggests that the basic aim of meditative practice is to use an understanding of delusion as a means of coming to terms with and correcting one's mistakes. This development overcomes a false sense of impermanence and expression and thereby attains awareness of Buddha nature. Once the conventional view of sequential time and speech is surpassed, the state of genuine understanding can be reliably prolonged. Dōgen contrasts his radically here-and-now approach to monastic training with what he feels is the future-based outlook of various Zen views that utilize meditation in an instrumental rather than a realization-based fashion.

The meaning of the process-oriented standpoint is captured by both of the original commentaries from the early fourteenth century on "Realization Here and Now." According to the prose remarks in *Distinguished Comments* by Senne and Kyōgō from 1308, "It is commonly thought that realization and delusion are associated in the same way as good and evil, but we must go beyond while at the same time preserving this dichotomy."[29] Also, Giun's verse commentary from 1329, which includes an introductory remark or capping phrase, indicates:

> Capping Phrase: What is it? [Or: It is what; This is it]
> Do not overlook that which is right in front of you;
> The boundless spring appears with the youngest plum blossoms.
> Using a single word, you can enter the open gate;
> Nine oxen pulling with all their might cannot lead you astray.[30]

The content of the capping phrase is usually read as a question implying that ordinarily, we do not know where to find true reality. However, as indicated in numerous passages reflecting Dōgen's hermeneutics of intrusion, the same saying can be seen as a declarative sentence pointing out that truth is nothing other than what appears right before our eyes. Spontaneous manifestations of reality are symbolized by the emergence of spring flowers that seem to last forever at the moment of their opening and are expressed through barrier-smashing verbal exchanges and other cryptic sayings that defy conventional language and logic. For those who reach the authentic stage of realization, beyond a problematic view of enlightenment as a destination, no external force is strong enough to daunt determined and sustained efforts to actualize the immediacy of being-time through the continuing practice of just sitting, which is examined in the next chapter.

{ 7 }

REFLEXIVITY AND ADAPTABILITY

THE FUNCTIONS AND DYSFUNCTIONS OF MEDITATION

THE ROLE OF JUST SITTING

The primary aim of numerous fascicles in the *Treasury of the True Dharma Eye* is to highlight the importance of different kinds of Zen training techniques, in addition to articulating theoretical standpoints that illumine such diverse yet integrated topics as the unity of human and natural existence, the intimate relation between time and death, and the productive role of language vis-à-vis illusion. Dōgen explicates key aspects of monastic practice that are based on ongoing seated meditation while carrying out other kinds of activities and responsibilities. An emphasis on practice is also featured in many of the formal sermons contained in Dōgen's *Extensive Record* and the six essays included in his *Monastic Rules* text.

The overall message of the *Treasury* and related works suggests that just sitting (*shikan taza*) is the principal vehicle used to cast off body-mind and attain unbounded awareness that can be applied to different pedagogical circumstances and ethical situations. It is not considered a panacea for every conceivable concern or conflict, but if utilized appropriately it serves as the main method for clarifying and refining contemplative consciousness that overcomes in dynamic ways the roots of various disturbances diverging from the true Buddhist path.

This chapter examines Dōgen's instructions regarding the human capacity to realize nonthinking, which is either attained and perpetuated or suppressed and denied based on the quality of the performance of zazen exercises in relation to the fundamental purposelessness of meditation.

Underlying Dōgen's view of practice is an unwavering emphasis on meditation that continually actualizes nonthinking in the present moment of being-time. In "Discerning the Way," for example, Dōgen comments on a kōan based on the adage, "Here comes the hearth god looking for fire" (Bendōwa: Dōgen 2.478, Nearman 21, Tanahashi 19).[1] The term "hearth god" is an informal designation for a novice, whose main task is to light the monastery lamps. The full saying indicates the futility of a practitioner seeking to discover what he already possesses. Or, put more positively, it affirms the fundamental capacity everyone has to actualize awakening through seated meditation, whereby distinctions of self and other, means and end, and passivity and quietude instantly dissolve or drop away.

To highlight the need for aimlessness while avoiding yet another set of misimpressions about zazen indicating that meditation represents the supreme passivity of reclusion, Dōgen makes clear that just sitting is not to be considered a withdrawn or irrational function that conceals ulterior motives of yearning for progress and advancement. In "Discerning the Way" he refers to the outlook of effortless zazen as "self-fulfilling samādhi (*jijiyū zanmai*)" (Bendōwa: Dōgen 2.460, Nearman 1, Tanahashi 3), during which an individual's effort spontaneously manifests universality in that each and every instant of being-time encompasses past and future in the present moment. "This is why," Dōgen writes, "even the meditating of just one person at one instant penetrates and is identical with all forms of being by thoroughly permeating all times. As part of the inexhaustible phenomenal world ranging across past, present, and future, the meditator makes an unceasing effort to guide others in the way of the Buddha" (Bendōwa: Dōgen 2.464, Nearman 6, Tanahashi 7). According to this teaching, anyone's meditative training demonstrates in the twinkling of an eye the same degree of enlightenment, confirmed by all sentient and insentient beings, generated when zazen is genuinely exerted by a person or element of existence.

Unity of Theory and Training

From the standpoint of the oneness of practice-realization, theory and training form an indivisible harmony without regard for a sense of order or progression other than what is suggested provisionally for the sake of promoting a novice practitioner's understanding of the Zen path. Yet Dōgen consistently suggests that unity allows for—or even demands—a calculated reckoning of differentiated sequences and methods that are defined consecutively in order to track a trainee's progress. Therefore, in assessing his view of undivided reality, it can be asked if one aspect, either theory or training, takes priority even if understood in a tentative fashion.

It might seem that theoretical reflections expressed in the *Treasury* on the theme of Buddha nature seen in relation to all beings, as well as the human experience of temporality and capacity for discourse, serve as a prelude to Dōgen's discussions of various aspects of training. In that way, practice would represent not a belated consequence or afterthought of theory, but rather a culmination of the master's ideas about enlightenment, an approach that is implied by the arrangement of this book's chapters examining philosophical themes before aspects of training. From another perspective, however, practice becomes the basis for speculation by serving as the necessary groundwork preceding the realization of nonthinking, considered an outcome of meditation. This outlook might indicate a reason to reverse the order of chapters, so that meditation and ritual would be covered before theoretical issues.

In support of the priority of practice, it seems that Dōgen's attitude recalls that of Pope Francis, who teaches that human actualities invariably supersede scholarly abstractions because "Reality is more important than ideas (*La realidad es superior a la idea*)." This is the pontiff's signature phrase highlighting the function of genuine pastors, who should act "like shepherds living with the smell of the sheep."[2] Francis consistently cautions against clerical leaders falling into the conceptual traps of "rigidity" and "empty rhetoric," or getting "stuck in pure speculation." Similarly, a prominent recent study contends that Dōgen "never was concerned with producing a new, dogmatically consistent philosophical doctrine along the lines of Western philosophical theories. Rather, his philosophy was always at the service of his main purpose: that of religious practitioner and spiritual guide."[3] This assessment is supported by a passage in "Discerning the Way" that maintains, "Religious teachings should be evaluated not in terms of the consistency of doctrinal formulations but by the authenticity of one's own practice" (Bendōwa: Dōgen 2.467, Nearman 9, Tanahashi 9). According to an old Chinese saying, "One who learns but does not practice has not really learned (*zhier buxing feizhiye*)." In a similar vein, Gandhi once said, "The best way to find yourself is to lose yourself in the service of others."

With a few prominent exceptions, Dōgen does not spend much time in *Treasury* fascicles discussing in detail how the practice of zazen should be conducted or answering concerns about obstructions to perpetuating the meditative process. Terada Tōru, a prominent scholar of traditional Japanese literature who in the early 1970s coedited one of the most respected editions of the *Treasury* and also published an important analysis of

Dōgen's inventive use of rhetoric, observes, "The overall impression we get from the *Treasury* is less of Dōgen the meticulous meditator than Dōgen the creative thinker. Consequently, the Dōgen who single-mindedly engaged in zazen is virtually invisible."[4] Other scholars have commented that, whether or not Dōgen wishes to be considered first and foremost a philosopher, he certainly writes like someone who aspires to reach such a goal. Following up Terada's comment, Hee-Jin Kim wonders how researchers should reconcile an apparent "discrepancy" in Dōgen's approach to philosophy and practice, and whether the situation is "self-contradictory," or a "rupture between Dōgen the meditator and Dōgen the thinker."[5]

Other scholars argue that the sheer volume of theoretical reflections by no means overwhelms an emphasis on religious practice. The main factor dissuading us from prioritizing theory over practice is that references to zazen appear in well over a dozen *Treasury* fascicles in addition to his other writings, as shown in table 7.1's list of references to meditation.

To explain the significance of this list, it is necessary to clarify what qualifies as an emphasis on meditation in contrast to philosophy. Dōgen's approach to the technique of just sitting is usually associated with a relatively small group of works, especially the *Universal Recommendation of the Principles of Zazen*, a short essay first composed in 1227 as the initial text Dōgen wrote after returning from China and revised in 1233.[6] Several works composed in the 1230s, including *Essentials of Learning the Way* from 1234 and *Treasury of Miscellaneous Talks* completed in 1238, also treat the topic of just sitting. Moreover, the treatise on *Methods for Discerning the Way (Bendōhō)* from 1246, included in *Dōgen's Monastic Rules*, provides additional details on meditative practice.

In the contents of the *Treasury*, there may appear to be just a couple of fascicles with a primary focus on meditation. One is "The Principles of Zazen" from 1243, sometimes referred to as the "*Fukanzazengi (Universal Recommendation)* Lite Version" because it reiterates some of the practical guidelines contained in the earlier work. Another fascicle dealing primarily with meditation is "The Lancet of Zazen," whose title refers to an acupuncture needle inserted into the area of the body requiring a remedy so as to unblock the flow of vital energy. First composed in 1242 and delivered orally to the assembly a year later, this essay provides a much more extensive conceptual analysis than other writings in regard to the value of just sitting in relation to nonthinking. Because it interprets various kōan cases and poems rather than providing clear guidelines for practice, this fascicle is sometimes misleadingly placed in the category of theory instead of practice.

TABLE 7.1 Dōgen's continuing focus on zazen in *Treasury* and other writings

Yr./Mo./Day	As found in	Main contents
1227	*Fukanzazengi* original	Significance and conduct of zazen
1231	*Treasury* "Bendōwa"	Various questions and answers regarding zazen
1233.7.15	*Fukanzazengi* revised	Additional significance and conduct of zazen
1233.8	SBGZ "Genjōkōan"	Analogies for state of mind produced by zazen
1234.3.9	*Gakudōyōjinshū*	"The direct realization of the Way is attained through training with a Zen master."
1236–1238	*Shōbōgenzō zuimonki*	"The path of Buddha is realized by just sitting."
1239.10.23	*Treasury* "Senmen"	Practice of zazen appears in various passages
1241.1.27	*Treasury* "Daigo"	Discusses results of zazen practice
1241.9.9	*Treasury* "Kokyō"	Mazu's "polishing a brick into a mirror" kōan
1242.3.18	*Treasury* "Zazenshin"	Mazu's "polishing a brick into a mirror" kōan
1242.4.5	*Treasury* "Gyōji"	Praise of buddhas practicing zazen, esp. Rujing
1242.4.20	*Treasury* "Kaiin zanmai"	Discussions of several kōans about zazen
1242.5.21	*Treasury* "Hakujushi"	Zhaozhou: "Discerning the way via zazen is the Buddha path, seated reflection on natural law."
1243.9	*Treasury* "Shohō jissō"	Rujing on Damei (752–839), "The spring, not hot or cold, is the preferable season for zazen."
1243.10.20	*Treasury* "Senmen" rev.	Practice of zazen appears in various passages
1243.11	*Treasury* "Zazenshin" rev.	Mazu's "polishing a brick into a mirror" kōan
1243.11	*Treasury* "Zazengi"	Instructions for the conduct of zazen
1243.11.27	*Treasury* "Henzan"	"Zen is just sitting by casting off body-mind."
1244.2.4	*Treasury* "Soshi seiraii"	Emphasis on state of nonthinking
1244.2.12	*Treasury* "Udonge"	"Twirling the flower is Buddha discerning delusion by just sitting, body-mind is cast off."
1244.2.14	*Treasury* "Hotsumujoshin"	Practicing zazen opens the mind of Buddha
1244.2.15	*Treasury* "Zanmai ō zanmai"	Zazen in the cross-legged (lotus) seated position
1244.2.19	*Treasury* "Jishō zanmai"	Merit of samādhi of buddhas and ancestors
1246	"Bendōhō" (*Eihei shingi*)	Rules for practicing zazen in the monks' hall
1250.1.11	*Treasury* "Senmen" rev.	Practice of zazen appears in various passages

Adapted from Tsunoda Tairyū, ed., *Various Issues in Dōgen's Thought: Based on Contemporary Religious Interpretations* [Dōgen Zenji ni okeru no shomondai: Kindai no shūgaku ronsō wo chūshin toshite] (Tokyo: Shunjūsha, 2017), 75. Also, according to one scholar, Dōgen demonstrates greater concern for the notion of zazen, which is mentioned nearly two hundred times in about sixteen fascicles, than the notion of *shikan taza*, which is mentioned in eleven fascicles, usually very briefly. Other key terms are *zanmai* and *kekka fuza*; see Zuzana Kubovčáková, "Believe It or Not: Dōgen on the Question of Faith," *Studia Orientalia Slovaca* 12/1 (2018): 201–202.

Nevertheless, these two fascicles are by no means the only sections of the *Treasury* emphasizing practice; as shown in table 7.1, there are more than twenty passages referring to the significance of seated meditation. Especially important are three fascicles that deal with the meaning of the highest state of concentration (Skr. *samādhi*, Jp. *zanmai*) attained by means of zazen, "Ocean Seal Samādhi," "The King of All Samādhis," and "Samādhi of Self-Realization." Additional fascicles particularly relevant for an overall understanding of Dōgen's approach to meditation include "Great Awakening," which treats the experience of spontaneous realization, and "Sustained Exertion," a two-part essay highlighting the value of ascetic practice undertaken by many leading Chinese patriarchs from diverse lineages.

CHINESE INFLUENCES ON ZAZEN

The hermeneutic procedures used for Dōgen's explications of rules and directives concerning various aspects of Zen training represent more or less the same set of interpretative methods that are applied in his speculative reflections. The process for articulating philosophy and practice involves citing extensively, yet revising innovatively, diverse Buddhist texts. These include voluminous Chan records plus selected Indian sources and Mahāyāna sūtras, in addition to Chinese or Japanese legends and allegories. In commenting on the topic of practice, although he does refer to kōan narratives, Dōgen is particularly reliant on the regulations known as the *Rules for Purity in Zen Monasteries* (Ch. *Chanyuan qinggui*, Jp. *Zen'en shingi*). This text, published in 1103 by the monk Changlu Zongze (d. 1107, Jp. Chōrō Shūjaku), was widely used in Song-dynasty temples as a guide for the decorum of monks.

Rules for Purity was created during a period in which Chan was becoming a prominent religious movement in China and its leaders urgently needed to demonstrate to government authorities that it was a dignified, self-governing social institution, not an irreverent or disruptive movement. This process of legitimation transpired on the mainland about a century before Dōgen and other pilgrims imported Zen to Kamakura-era Japan. According to the analysis of the scholar Yifa, who published a translation of major portions of Zongze's text, Dōgen exhibited a "great dependence" on the *Rules for Purity*, so that it and "Dōgen's writings complement each other." The work was a "major influence on his subsequent thinking," Yifa maintains, and Dōgen "freely adopted large sections of [the *Rules for Purity]* in his own monastic codes as well as in his largest work, *Shōbōgenzō*."[7]

In various writings on the theme of just sitting, Dōgen borrows heavily from a short tract in Zongze's lengthy *Principles of Seated Meditation* (Ch. *Zuochan yi*, Jp. *Zazengi*), which is the same title as a *Treasury* fascicle. Over a third of Dōgen's *Universal Recommendation*, in addition to the fascicle "The Principles of Zazen," seems based on or almost copied from his predecessor's composition. These passages highlight instructions for how monks should wear their robes when entering the hall to make *gasshō* bows of greeting before circumambulating the room, and then cross their legs and place their hands and palms properly to achieve a state of concentration by focusing the body-mind in an appropriate fashion. Also discussed are the way to rise from sitting, visit the washroom for cleaning, and go to sleep at the end of the day, along with the functions of the abbot's chair as well as the meditation hall manager's actions, which include burning incense and using the sounding board to call the assembly to order. An additional topic involves the directive that a practitioner should swing his body from side to side seven or eight times while gradually reducing the length of the arc, an opening exercise still widely followed in Sōtō Zen meditative practice.

It is clear, however, that Dōgen disagrees in several ways with Zongze's treatise. On a minor point, whereas Zongze prescribes about eight hours a day of sitting, with four two-hour-long sessions taking place at sunrise, after breakfast, following the midday meal, and in the evening, Dōgen increases this amount somewhat, as indicated in table 7.2 with the daily schedule of activities at Eiheiji temple. It is not possible to know for sure

TABLE 7.2 Dōgen's daily meditation schedule

Waking zazen	5:30~6:10
Chores before breakfast	7:00~11:00
Morning zazen	11:10~11:50
Chores before lunch	13:10~15:50
Studying sūtras	16:00~17:00
Chores in late afternoon	17:00~18:00
Evening activities	18:00~20:00
Nighttime zazen	20:00~2:00
Sleep [lying down zazen]	2:00~5:00

Dōgen 5.26–45; see Leighton and Okumura, *Dōgen's Pure Standards for the Zen Community* (Albany: State University of New York Press, 1996), 63–81.

how long zazen was actually performed there, since this timetable does not include any mention of such crucial daily activities as the delivery of sermons, the chanting of sūtras, or the completion of cleaning.

Another difference between the approaches of Dōgen and Zongze pertains to the liberal use of kōan interpretations that focus on practice in *Treasury* fascicles and *Dōgen's Monastic Rules*. This aspect of discourse is entirely lacking in the *Rules for Purity* and similar manuals on temple conduct. Dōgen's view is unique among Zen annals for citing cases that highlight in dramatic fashion the value of unconventional behavior. His examinations of these dialogues help achieve a balance between maintaining order or decorum, enforced by punishments when regulations are broken, and enabling expressions of creativity, which are key to the path of spiritual freedom, continuously applied to everyday affairs and teaching situations. For example, a true master may be excessively strict and harsh or overly kind and indulgent depending on his assessment of the strengths or deficiencies in the learning process of a disciple who may have committed a transgression or given evidence of suffering a setback in training.[8]

Another significant area of discrepancy concerns Dōgen's direct criticisms of Zongze, whose approach to Chan was influenced by detailed Tiantai school writings on the topic of meditation and also by the newly emergent Pure Land practice of continuously reciting the name of Amida Buddha (*nembutsu*, Ch. *nianfo*). Pure Land recitation was understood by its advocates as a contemplative discipline more or less on a par with zazen, especially for lay disciples who lacked the time or expertise required for effective seated meditation. Dōgen accepts some of the techniques endorsed by Zongze, but he noticeably alters or enhances all those methods in various rhetorical and practical ways by returning to the outlook of early Chinese masters, who he feels embodied the pure spirit of Buddhist teaching. These teachers include First Patriarch Bodhidharma, who meditated facing the wall of a cave for nine years until his limbs withered and fell off; Sixth Patriarch Huineng, an illiterate cleric from an outcaste southern region of the country who outsmarted more elite rival monks based on his contemplative prowess; and Baizhang (749–814, Jp. Hyakujō), the first monk to form ideas about Zen monastic rules reflecting zazen as the core practice, without explaining in great detail how the practice should be conducted. Based on these models, Dōgen highlights the fact that all schools of Buddhism throughout history used meditation in some important fashion. He consistently argues that "Just sitting is the proper and most straightforward entryway into what the Buddha taught" (Bendōwa: Dōgen 2.460, Nearman 1, Tanahashi 3).

When Dōgen first studied Zen after leaving the Japanese Tendai sect on Mount Hiei, he learned that the writings of Eisai mentioned zazen only very briefly. The training advocated at Kenninji temple was eclectic in incorporating the threefold Japanese Tendai practice combining complete understanding (*en*), esoteric rites (*mitsu*) and precepts (*kai*), and seated meditation (*zen*), which was seen as an option but not essential in an approach that most major monasteries in Japan had been using for several centuries. Dōgen's emphasis on zazen-only should be seen in light of the way he competed with New Kamakura Buddhist movements, which encouraged followers to select a single technique as the centerpiece of their training.

Dōgen's view of meditation is also frequently understood in terms of how he responded to schismatic controversies that dominated the intellectual landscape of the Chan school during the twelfth century. A couple of generations prior to his pilgrimage to the mainland, Chan was characterized by contentious factionalism. During the mid-1100s, the Linji branch led by Dahui promoted the practice of kōan investigation (Ch. *kanhua chan*, Jp. *kanna zen*), or meditating intensively in order to solve the meaning of puzzling kōans assigned by the teacher. Although they were friends who admired each other's pedagogical prowess, Dahui severely criticized Caodong school patriarch Hongzhi, who advocated the path of silent illumination (*mokushō zen*, Ch. *mozhao chan*), whereby a meditator seeks to maintain a quiet mind that resembles "dead wood" or "dry ashes" in remaining free of any trace of deliberation or engagement with external phenomena.

It is misleading to link Dōgen too closely to either of those views, because he supports some aspects and refutes many key elements of the approaches of both Dahui and Hongzhi. As a critique of the kōan investigation method, he interprets a wide variety of cases with a genuinely creative flair instead of conforming to formulaic responses contained in guidebooks and memorized by sometimes faux practitioners. Yet, to distance himself from silent illumination, which was not endorsed by Rujing, who stressed the notion of dynamic activity, Dōgen emphasizes extending and applying the contemplative state to all endeavors while refraining from withdrawal to a condition of blank consciousness or passivity. Among all his continental predecessors, it seems that Dōgen was particularly influenced by Yuanwu, who inventively advocated the notions of vitality and spontaneity in his interpretations of kōan cases.

DŌGEN'S EARLY AND LATE WRITINGS ON ZAZEN

Dōgen's two earliest writings, completed within a few years after he returned from China but before he established Kōshōji temple in Kyoto—*Universal Recommendation for the Principles of Zazen*, from 1227 and revised in 1233, and "Discerning the Way" from 1231—are theological manifestos that proclaim in quite different though complementary ways the incomparable merits of performing zazen exercises. Dōgen opens the *Universal Recommendation* by evoking the sense of doubt about the relationship between original enlightenment and sustained practice that he experienced while training at Mount Hiei and Kenninji temple, then fully resolved in 1225 through the experience of casting off body-mind:

> The Way is perfect and all pervasive. How could it be contingent upon practice and realization? The Dharma vehicle is free and untrammeled. What need is there for concentrated effort?... And yet, if there is the slightest discrepancy [between practice and realization], the Way is as distant as heaven from earth. If the least bit of liking or disliking phenomena arises, the mind becomes hopelessly lost in confusion. (Dōgen 5.4)

Following this provocative passage, Dōgen answers the rhetorical question, "What is the use of going off hither and thither to practice?" by referring to the act of taking a "backward step" to attain "self-illumination" through realizing one's "original face" that lies beyond, but also incorporates, the use of intellect and words. Attaining this purposeless state vitiates any design to transform oneself into a buddha, for there should be no need to seek what one possesses from the beginning. Here and in the fascicles "The Principles of Zazen" and "The Lancet of Zazen," Dōgen maintains, "Studying Zen (*sanzen*) has nothing whatsoever to do with sitting or lying down." Instead, meditation is epitomized in a cryptic kōan dialogue, "Think of not thinking. How do you think of not thinking? Nonthinking! This in itself is the essential art of zazen" (Zazengi: Dōgen 1.101, Nearman 682, Tanahashi 580).

In contrast to the *Universal Recommendation*, "Discerning the Way" does not include specific instructions for meditation. It starts by enthusiastically embracing the value of zazen in the first few paragraphs and then includes an extended discussion highlighting Dōgen's personal story of venturing to China in pursuit of a genuine teacher. After his initial disappointments on the mainland were erased by meeting Rujing, he returned to transplant the Zen tradition to his native country. The main aim of these passages, designed to persuade converts in Japan to embrace seated meditation, is to situate the transmission Dōgen received from Rujing in the larger Zen institutional context. The tradition begins with Śākyamuni Buddha's communicating insight to Mahākāśyapa by holding up a flower and continues with Bodhidharma selecting Huike as the second patriarch of China based on a competition held with three other disciples. In the second half of "Discerning the Way," Dōgen responds to a series of eighteen hypothetical questions about the virtues of zazen by arguing that sitting meditation is compatible with, yet more fundamental than, carrying out precepts or reciting sūtras. It also has the virtue of being accessible to female and lay practitioners, a point Dōgen apparently disavowed in his later years at Eiheiji temple.

Moreover, while sitting is recognized as the most meritorious physical position, Dōgen asserts that the real aim of zazen is to trigger an instantaneous experience of illumination, as when Lingyun admired the hue of peach blossoms and Xiangyan heard the sound of a pebble striking bamboo. He maintained an emphasis on gaining enlightenment by perceiving "colors and sounds" throughout his career. He argues that this type of sensation is not a matter of affirming physicality over intellect or highlighting the body more than the mind. Rather, it shows that great awakening (*daigo*) is characterized by the unity of enlightenment and delusion, as well as the beginning and end of phenomenal experiences.

In a variant version of the fascicle on this topic Dōgen argues cryptically, "Great awakening never shatters the person and the person never defiles great awakening. Great awakening is surely not something that obstructs great awakening" (Dōgen 2.607).[9] In that context he cites a saying attributed to Master Yunmen (862–949), who delineates three types of practitioners reacting to a kōan case raised by their teacher: one attains awakening by hearing a lecture about the case; another attains awakening by responding to a few choice words evoked in the master's sermon; and the third immediately gains insight as soon as the theme is brought up for discussion (Dōgen 2.606). The three options indicate that the path to great awakening is dependent on the particular capacity and level of awareness of the trainee.

Dōgen stays focused on the value of seated meditation as the main gateway to the Dharma that was invariably practiced by all buddhas throughout the *Treasury*. The topic of zazen is also discussed extensively in both the *Record of the Hōkyō Era*, which is based on his talks with Rujing, and the sermons of the *Treasury of Miscellaneous Talks* culled from lectures presented in the mid-1230s. In addition, a leading Japanese scholar of Dōgen studies, Tsunoda Tairyū, documents more than three dozen tributes to the practice of just sitting that appear in the final set of passages included in Dōgen's *Extensive Record*, containing formal sermons delivered from 1248.[10] This was still Dōgen's focus even after he returned to Eiheiji following his six-month visit to Kamakura, and it lasted until he fell ill four years later.

In various writings Dōgen refers extensively to the contemplative state of just sitting in both literal and figurative senses. The literal meaning refers to a practitioner being seated on a cushion with legs crossed in the lotus position and hands held in place, with head and torso firmly aligned, for sustained periods of time on a daily basis. This technique must be carried out according to carefully delineated guidelines by priests in the monks' hall, the primary place for meditation on the temple grounds, or in a solitary hermitage or retreat in the forest. Dōgen sometimes speaks of the power of seated meditation to cure ailments, such as reversing the effects of hemorrhoids that may stem from excessive sitting, by enabling a practitioner to forget and thus overcome the psychic roots of illness. Since "sickness worsens depending upon one's frame of mind," Dōgen suggests that he conquered severe diarrhea through contemplation after he remained on board the ship for a few months after first landing in China. "Considering this," he says, "I think if we devote ourselves to the practice of the way and disregard everything else, no illness will ever arise."[11] That applies even to uninformed practitioners who meditate, so long as they sustain just sitting single-mindedly, without aim or purpose.

Zazen evoked in the figurative sense of gaining intuitive insight into the true nature of reality at any time and place, regardless of which actual activity is undertaken, is suggested by Dōgen's use of two key terms that appear in several fascicles, especially "The Lancet of Zazen" and "The King of All Samādhis." The first term refers to the act of "sitting upright and steadfast" (*gotsugotsuchi* or *gotsuza*), with the Chinese character 兀 (Ch. *wu*, Jp. *gotsu*) appearing at first glance to resemble an upside-down peak 山 (Ch. *shan*, Jp. *san* or *yama*), so that one translator renders the process of unwavering concentration as "sitting upright and firm like a mountain."[12] The idiom 兀兀 (Ch. *wuwu*, Jp. *gotsugotsu*) indicates whatever is massive and immovable or indifferently towering above everything else in sight. This term is generally used in a twofold way implying either a positive state of concentrated awareness unimpeded by the outside world, which Dōgen emphasizes, or a negative condition of being unmindful or oblivious to external influences, as suggested by critics of unresponsive quietude.

The second term is *kekkafuza*, a standard Buddhist phrase for the cross-legged meditation posture (Skr. *paryaṅka*) that is sometimes called the "lotus position" (Skr. *padmāsana*), which Dōgen indicates in "King of All Samādhis" can be understood for its symbolic rather than literal qualities:

> At the moment of sitting we should investigate whether this occurs while the universe is vertical or horizontal. . . . Does sitting overturn the whole world or move vigorously toward engaging with it? Is it a matter of thinking or not thinking? Is it transforming [into Buddha] or not transforming [into Buddha]? Is it sitting with body-mind or with having cast off body-mind? We must investigate this matter from thousands and tens of thousands of perspectives. We should maintain cross-legged sitting of the body, cross-legged sitting of the mind, and cross-legged sitting of casting off body-mind. (Zanmai ō zanmai: Dōgen 2.177, Nearman 779, Tanahashi 667)

All conceptual categories for describing meditation are thereby thrown aside. Moreover, in the fascicle "Buddha Nature," Dōgen identifies zazen with the true nature of reality that encompasses yet lies beyond the realm of human behavior by suggesting, "'Skin, flesh, bones, and marrow' and the 'treasury of the true Dharma eye' are nothing other than sitting upright and steadfast, which conveys the face [of Mahākāśyapa] at the time of his breaking into a smile" (Busshō: Dōgen 1.31, Nearman 263–264, Tanahashi 248).

According to Dōgen's nonliteral understanding of the power of zazen, meditation encompassing every aspect of human behavior is not just a matter of solving kōan cases or sitting still without thoughts:

> Different kinds of concentration belong to the king of all *samādhi*s. Sitting with legs crossed means keeping your body straight, keeping your mind straight, and keeping your body-mind straight. It is keeping the buddhas and ancestors straight, keeping your practice and realization straight, keeping the crown of your head straight, and keeping the very pulse of your lifeblood straight. (Zanmai ō zanmai: Dōgen 2.180, Nearman 781, Tanahashi 667)

Therefore, meditation remains eminently engaged with all aspects of reality at every occasion, based on enacting zazen in the broader sense of realizing nonthinking as the essence of past, present, and future existence.

THINKING, NOT THINKING, AND NONTHINKING

In "The Lancet of Zazen," the primary *Treasury* fascicle that articulates a theoretical framework in support of the inner dynamics of meditative practice, various topics concerning the method of just sitting are discussed in relation to achieving and maintaining the fundamental condition of nonthinking. This state transcends the ordinary dichotomy of rationality and irrationality through continual practice that is applied to each aspect of everyday life. As Dōgen explains, nonthinking does not indicate a deficiency of thought but is a matter of keeping free from the coveting and grasping that tends to accompany ordinary cogitation, while staying fully involved in creative modes of deliberation and discourse.

In "King of All Samādhis," Dōgen delineates six aspects from among "the hundreds of thousands of kinds of intellectual activity" (Zanmai ō zanmai: Dōgen 2.177, Nearman 779, Tanahashi) that are encompassed by nonthinking:

> There is just sitting of the mind, which is not the same as just sitting of the body. There is just sitting of the body, which is not the same as just sitting of the mind. There is just sitting of casting off body-mind, which is not the same as just sitting 'in order to' cast off body-mind.... We should uphold (1) thoughts (*nen*), (2) ideas (*sō*), and (3) perceptions (*kan*), and investigate (4) mind (*shin*), (5) intention (*i*), and (6) consciousness (*shiki*). (Zanmai ō zanmai: Dōgen 2.179, Nearman 780, Tanahashi 668; numbers added)

Sometimes referred to as an ability to carefully discern distinctions while recognizing the basic unity underlying all apparent differences or a paradoxical nondiscriminative discrimination, the state of nonthinking, or thinking-as-not thinking, reflects the continuing circulation of constructive reflections. This is achieved without lapsing into an attachment to any particular standpoint since all ideas are innately relative and constantly shifting.

One way Dōgen clarifies his view of the significance of nonthinking for understanding seated meditation involves considering the notion of reflexivity, which refers to the way the human intellect seeks to polish and perfect itself through constantly turning back to try to correct and uplift, and ultimately liberate, its own activity. This represents the effort to illumine self-awareness by means of the self that ordinarily exists in a darkened or disguised state, but nevertheless harbors the ability to transform that condition. The function of reflexive thought has either productive or counterproductive features, depending on whether and to what extent the mind is cultivated by developing sustained self-control and self-discipline.

The crucial conundrum that is continually faced by human thinking is summed up by a couple of traditional Buddhist sayings that sometimes appear on plaques at Japanese temples. The first suggests, "A troubled self can only be remedied by means of reliance on the self." The attitude of self-reliance taken by itself is not necessarily decisive, however; it needs to be coordinated with another dictum, "Resolution is not found in terms of self alone, but only through engaging with all phenomena." Therefore, self-reflection implies self-regulation by recognizing that, as part of the interconnected universe, human thoughts and activities are linked to all other beings, whether living or nonliving and natural or supernatural (including ghosts, spirits, ethereal buddhas, and mythical bodhisattvas). Dōgen captures with chiasmic wording the crux of the dilemma of perfecting reflexivity in "Realization Here and Now": "Bringing the self forward to practice and confirm multifarious things represents delusion, but allowing multifarious things to practice and confirm the self represents awakening (*satori*)" (Genjōkōan: Dōgen 1.2, Nearman 32, Tanahashi 29). In other words, the self must overcome the self in terms of itself, but this cannot be accomplished without the self at some point negating itself so as to surpass ordinary awareness through adjusting to all phenomena.

To give a humorous contemporary example of how this situation can affect ordinary human behavior, in *I Love You, Alice B. Toklas*, a romantic comedy from 1968 starring the great comedian Peter Sellers, the actor's awkward lead character is so troubled by some recent events that his easygoing girlfriend grows impatient. She advises him to stop worrying and relax by disregarding or forgetting about the problems with which he is obsessed. "All right," he responds dutifully, "I will try to remember to forget." The implication is that reflexivity involves either a vicious circle of self-deception, resulting in endless frustration and hopeless futility, or a productive cycle leading out of despair and duplicity toward gaining realization through exercising restraint. In highlighting the counterproductive side of reflexivity, Dōgen gives an analysis of ignorance in the fascicle "Dignified Demeanor of Practicing Buddha" by saying, "It is just like losing one's head by accepting its image [in a mirror] as real" (Gyōbutsu iigi: Dōgen 1.67, Nearman 290, Tanahashi 268), that is, mistaking an appearance or likeness for true existence. This is comparable to "forgetting to make your next move" (Gyōbutsu iigi: Dōgen 1.68, Nearman 291, Tanahashi 269; literally, "Concealing one's body but showing your horns"), which refers to inattentiveness while playing a game of chess, leading to unforced errors that hand the advantage to the opponent. The reverse, productive reflexivity, Dōgen points out, requires "making your move one piece at a time," which means that using fewer words expresses a greater and more strategic meaning, thereby recovering the upper hand of an exchange.

One of many intriguing examples demonstrating Dōgen's discursive prowess in highlighting productive reflexivity involves his unique interpretation in "The Lancet of Zazen" of a brief yet highly suggestive encounter dialogue involving Master Yaoshan (751–834) and an anonymous monk in regard to the value of contemplation.[13] According to the case that is also mentioned in a couple of other writings but without analysis, a novice asks Yaoshan, who is deep in meditation, "What do you think about while sitting upright and steadfast (*gotsugotsuchi* 兀兀地)?" The master replies, "I think about not thinking." When the monk probes further, "How do you think about not thinking?" Yaoshan answers enigmatically, "By nonthinking," which can also be rendered as "without or beyond or transcends thinking" (Zazenshin: Dōgen 1.103, Nearman 335, Tanahashi 303). The kōan suggests that the state of nonthinking (*hishiryō* 非思量) must be understood in relation to thinking (*shiryō* 思量) and not thinking (*fushiryō* 不思量). But how do these connections play out? Or, as Edo-period commentator Katsudō Honkō put it, how do we understand the state of thinking-nonthinking (*shiryō-hishiryō* 思量非思量), whereby there is no need to deliberate on the meaning of deliberation in that the vicious cycle of ordinary cogitation is cut off or cast away?

Most commentators highlight a progression of stages, from (a) thought as thesis to (b) its antithesis as no thought, and finally to (c) the culminative synthesis that is beyond thought.[14] Therefore, the typical explanation of the Yaoshan dialogue emphasizes that the master has cleverly outsmarted the inquirer by leading him on a progression from ordinary thinking (*shiryō*) to the stoppage of conceptualization (*fushiryō*), and finally to a transcendent state involving absolute negation (*hishiryō*) that lies outside the conventional boundaries of thought and thoughtlessness. At that point the monk is struck speechless, much like Deshan in his conversation with the old lady selling refreshments.

Dōgen points out that the Yaoshan exchange demarcates a subtle but crucial distinction between two terms indicating negation, "not" (*fu* 不) and "non" (*hi* 非), which are used as modifiers for the noun "thinking." Since these prefixes can appear in other contexts to be almost interchangeable in meaning in a way that is different from the function of this dialogue, it is important to clarify Dōgen's view by keeping in mind his complex discussions in "Buddha Nature" and other fascicles of the significance of nullification involving several kōans that evoke another word for negation, "no" (*mu* 無). This term indicates various aspects of "nothingness" or nonsubstantiality that surpass the ordinary sense of absence, loss, lack, or vacuity, which can also apply to the meaning of *fu* and *hi*, especially when the word "what" is understood as quiddity or whatness rather than as indicating a simple query.

As illustrated in figure 7.1, Dōgen's extended commentary disputes the conventional interpretative position in several ways typical of the hermeneutics of intrusion. According to Dōgen's view, the monk's query about not thinking does not suggest a naïve sense of doubt but contributes to the master's ability to utter a more constructive expression of the meaning of reflexivity than he ordinarily musters. Dōgen asserts that both parties in the exchange, the superior master and the uninformed monk, are actually speaking from the standpoint of enlightenment and are working together to bring each other to an enhanced understanding without the usual sense of competition involving winner and loser.

This contradicts interpretations indicating the one-sided defeat of a benighted disciple by an enlightened master. The monk's final silence suggests understanding rather than a state of being dumbstruck. For Dōgen, the goal is not necessarily to reach satori as a one-time breakthrough experience, but to realize the ongoing process of self-reflection and self-reliance based on the power of nonthinking. Dōgen's reversal of the typical view of the exchange as a three-stage progression is based on his creative (mis)reading of the interrogatory sentences to represent declarative statements. He thereby argues that not thinking is actually a form of thinking that incorporates nonthinking:

> The monk asks, "How do you think about not thinking?" Although not thinking [in the sense of an absence] may represent a long-held view, in probing this sentence further the phrasing suggests, "Not thinking is how you do think." It is not the case that there is no thinking whatsoever while sitting upright and steadfast, or that thinking somehow lies outside the activity of sitting upright and steadfast. (Zazenshin: Dōgen 1.103–104, Nearman 336, Tanahashi 303)

By extending the implications of the founder's approach, various leaders of the Sōtō sect's extensive Edo-era tradition of commentaries on the *Treasury*

Dōgen's View of Kōans in Relation to Satori
Conventional Method Based on Two Kinds of Negation

Dōgen's Interpretative Method Based on Mutually Reciprocal Awakening

According to Dōgen, rather than an unenlightened monk asking an enlightened teacher a question and getting baffled by the answer, both parties are always "already" enlightened and, therefore, leading each other to an expression of ongoing realization (*genjōkōan*), encompassing but not limited to instantaneous illuminations.

FIGURE 7.1 Contrasting Dōgen's view of the Yaoshan *kōan* with conventional approaches
Adapted from Nakao Ryōshin, *Zen* (Tokyo: Natsumesha, 2005), 159, and drawn by Maria Sol Echarren

have shown that the whole case can be read not as a set of questions and answers but as a series of statements, with each remark in the dialogue conveying, instead of concealing, some aspect of the overall profundity of the notion that just sitting equals nonthinking. This interpretation understands the dialogue to mean:

1. Monk: "Thinking while sitting upright and steadfast is 'what.'" (兀兀地思量什麼).
2. Yaoshan: "[Such] thinking is not (*fu*) thinking." (思量箇不思量底).
3. Monk: "Not thinking is how you do think." (不思量底如何思量).
4. Yaoshan: "It is thinking of no particular thing (*hi*)." (非思量).
5. Silence: [Indicates nothing more needs to be said, rather than a failure to speak].

A key aspect of the *Treasury*'s hermeneutics is to suggest that there is no advancement of consciousness toward a culminative state of transcendence because three different standpoints referred to in the dialogue—thinking, not thinking, and nonthinking—actually represent a single mode of awareness, that is, several possible ways of considering its differentiable but underlying unified significance. Therefore, for Dōgen, nonthinking is not separable from the realm of thought, but is fully embedded within it while enabling the interactions of thinking and not thinking:

> Regarding Yaoshan's answer, "Nonthinking," although this term may seem crystal clear, when we are thinking of not thinking we are always already in the process of nonthinking.... Although sitting upright and steadfast functions as sitting upright and steadfast, how could sitting upright and steadfast not be engaged in thinking about sitting upright and steadfast? (Zazenshin: Dōgen 1.104, Nearman 336, Tanahashi 303–304)

For Dōgen, whether referred to as thinking, not thinking, or nonthinking, once the underlying meaning of self-reflection and self-reliance is fully realized, the state is understood as remaining free from grasping and cannot be categorized as conscious or unconscious. Nonthinking represents the dynamic condition of absolute liberation based on perpetually casting off any subtle clinging to a distinction between thinking and not thinking, while remaining unconfined by either side or their apparent contradiction. According to the remarks of eighteenth-century commentator Menzan (1683–1769), "When we actually sit on a cushion in *hishiryō* (non-thinking), the root of the discriminating mind is cut off, intellectual understanding is exhausted, body-mind are dropped off, and delusion and enlightenment are thrown away. You will know it naturally if you are the person sitting."[15]

Another traditional commentary on the *Treasury* suggests, "The moment of zazen is thinking-not-thinking," and also points out that "Zazen is total sitting, for which there is no measure."[16] Dōgen further suggests in "The Lancet of Zazen," "Sitting upright and steadfast does not delimit [literally, "measure"] the significance of Buddha, delimit the Dharma, delimit awakening, or delimit understanding" (Zazenshin: Dōgen 1.104, Nearman 336, Tanahashi 304). Furthermore, "In the realization that was correctly transmitted [from Śākyamuni Buddha all the way down to Yaoshan thirty-six generations later], there was always already thinking about not thinking" (Zazenshin: Dōgen 1.104, Nearman 336, Tanahashi 304). In each and every generation, Dōgen argues, the true meaning of Zen transmission is put forth in a distinctive way according to the standpoint of nonduality embracing multiplicity and particularity. This level of insight is fundamentally the same as every other way of appropriating Buddhist Dharma.

ONENESS OF MEANS AND END

In addition to the innovative examination of the Yaoshan dialogue on nonthinking, the fascicle "The Lancet of Zazen" contains two more lengthy sections that offer complementary interpretations of the fundamental purposelessness of just sitting. One section analyzes inventively a kōan narrative involving Tang-dynasty Master Mazu, and the other reinterprets and rewrites a famous verse on zazen by Song-dynasty Master Hongzhi. Both discussions highlight the oneness of means and end, which, when properly enacted, enables the ongoing practice of zazen without expectation or aim in the positive sense that the exercise is performed for its own sake, minus any ulterior motive of reaching a destination, including even—or especially—the aim of awakening that is at once a by-product of and extraneous to just doing meditation.

The theme of purposeless meditation without an anticipated goal is featured in numerous other writings as well. In the *Treasury of Miscellaneous Talks*, Dōgen remarks, "The Way of buddhas and ancestors is nothing but zazen. Do not pursue anything else."[17] Throughout this work he emphasizes that one should learn the Buddha Dharma to gain a reward but should practice the Buddha Dharma for the sake of the Buddha Dharma. Further reinforcing the notion of unity is a key passage in the variant version of the *Treasury* fascicle "Great Awakening" in which Dōgen cites a saying attributed to Rujing, "Studying Zen is casting off body-mind. It is a matter of 'not letting the awaiting of awakening become standard'" (Daigo variant: Dōgen 2.600).[18] Dōgen points out that his mentor's dictum was regularly delivered in the Dharma hall at formal assemblies attended by many monks from various temples and also spoken day and night in the abbot's quarters during small meetings sometimes joined by visiting clerics.

Regularly bursting forth with the force of "thunder sounding from the blows of Rujing's fists," this saying "was heard by those asleep and by those not asleep. . . . Nevertheless, those who truly listened to his voice were few, although no one ever questioned its veracity" (Daigo variant: Dōgen 2.600). Dōgen comments, "Casting off body-mind is body-mind cast off. Because of the casting off of casting off, there is the casting off of body-mind. Unbound by the scale of large or small and broad or narrow, this experience means nothing other than 'not letting awaiting awakening become the standard'" (Daigo variant: Dōgen 2.609). Dōgen also remarks that "not awaiting awakening" indicates studying assiduously without even entertaining the prospect of great awakening, since expectations defeat attainment of the anticipated goal. After great awakening has occurred, it is necessary to continue to study the way as "the pivot at the head of buddhas" (Daigo variant: Dōgen 2.610) by abandoning any lingering presumption of finality.

Perhaps the main example of zazen as a unity of means and end is found in Dōgen's novel interpretation of a dialogue in which Mazu discusses the role of meditation with his teacher Nanyue (677–744). The teacher asks his disciple who is seated contemplatively in a hermitage, "What are you figuring to do by sitting there in meditation?" When Mazu responds, "I'm figuring to make [or transform myself into] a buddha," Nanyue takes a tile and begins to rub it on a stone in front of Mazu, who inquires, "Master, what are you doing?" Nanyue says, "I'm polishing this to make [or transform it into] a mirror," and Mazu asks, "How can you make a mirror by polishing a tile?" Nanyue's retort is, "How can you make a buddha by sitting in meditation?" (Zazenshin: Dōgen 1.105–106, Nearman 339–340, Tanahashi 306).

The source dialogue and Dōgen's commentary revolve around the reference to a mirror used as a metaphor for the enlightened mind, but they seek to subvert and overthrow this image when it is taken too literally. This is done for different purposes and with nearly opposite conclusions. In the case record, Nanyue evokes the analogy of polishing a tile to create a mirror in order to show the futility in Mazu's enactment of zazen to become a buddha. The dialogue highlights the contradiction between practice and realization through suggesting implicitly that zazen is unnecessary once one is enlightened. Nanyue's rhetorical strategy plays off the image of the mirror by displacing it with the irony of a tile that can never achieve the goal of reflecting objects. This shifting of metaphors highlights Nanyue's view that religious practice is based primarily on instantaneous insight. Just as a tile is not likely to yield a mirror, no matter how much effort one applies, zazen will not result in transforming into a buddha, because original awakening does not depend on cultivation or training to realize it.

In his commentaries on the dialogue in the fascicles "The Lancet of Zazen," "Ocean Water Samādhi," and "The Ancient Mirror," Dōgen upends the subversion proffered by Nanyue in order to affirm emphatically the role of zazen, utilizing the hermeneutics of intrusion that atomizes and redefines the essential function of some of the small verbal units used in the exchange. First, in the *Treasury* versions, Mazu is described as an adept rather than a student trying to advance his standing, which greatly shifts the overall meaning of the case. Furthermore, Dōgen's argument is based on the assertion that polishing a tile in fact does produce a mirror precisely by not seeking to accomplish this. This interpretation may be considered either a realistic application of the mirror metaphor, in that some tiles can attain a reflective surface after being rubbed enough, or a playfully nonsensical twist on Nanyue's ironic remark that further decenters an analogy introduced into the discourse for disruptive purposes.

Dōgen also reconsiders the seemingly simple compound *sabutsu* (作仏), which he shows can be read not as the future-oriented "to make a buddha" but instead as the present-oriented "a made [already realized] buddha," just as the term *zabutsu* (坐仏) means either "to sit [to become] buddha" or "a seated [realized] buddha." He also creates a rhetorical displacement of the image of the mirror by building up a series of tautological and paradoxical expressions, including "a buddha becomes a buddha" and "becoming a buddha does not depend on but is realized by seated meditation" (Zazenshin: Dōgen 1.107, Nearman 340, Tanahashi 306). These sayings contribute to interpreting the core dialogue in a way that legitimates Dōgen's view of just sitting as the true method of practice in realization (*shojō no shu*) that neither advances nor detracts from, but simply manifests, what a buddha is. This is designed to refute any standpoint that might discredit the act of zazen as either something extraneous or a preliminary stage leading eventually to enlightenment.

In the final section of the fascicle, Dōgen comments line by line on, then offers a revised version of, Hongzhi's famous verse known by the name "The Lancet of Zazen" (Ch. "Zuochan zhen," Jp. "Zazenshin"), which promotes the path of silent illumination as key to understanding the function of seated meditation. In these passages Dōgen makes clear that his view of just sitting represents a different, significantly more dynamic approach to contemplative theory and practice than that of his Caodong school predecessor, which he feels prioritizes passivity and quietude in a subtle but nevertheless debilitating way.[19] Dōgen acknowledges that while other Chan masters of the era wrote similar works dealing with zazen, "Hongzhi's is the best of several versions available," because it reflects "the manifestation of the great Zen function through deportment that is beyond sight and sound based on realizing the original state of mind before your parents were born" (Zazenshin: Dōgen 1.113, Nearman 346, Tanahashi 310). Dōgen notes that when Rujing presented sermons, he often referred to Hongzhi (also known from imperial designation as Zhengjue or Capacious Wisdom) using a term of veneration and endearment, "Ancient Buddha" (*kobutsu*, Ch. *gufo*), that he never applied to any other person. Rujing felt that Hongzhi was intimate with truth (or, literally, "knew the music" of the Dharma), and conveyed the same insight transmitted by Dongshan and other lineal ancestors (Zazenshin: Dōgen 1.116–117, Nearman 350, Tanahashi 313).

Despite Rujing's adulation, in reflecting on Hongzhi's verse during the year 1242, about eighty-five years after its composition in the late 1150s, Dōgen is critical of some of its basic implications, and he rewrites the poem accordingly. The opening lines of the original read:

> The essential activity (*yōki*) of every buddha and active essence (*kiyō*) of every ancestor
> Knows (*shi*) without touching things and illumines (*shō*) without facing objects. (Zazenshin: Dōgen 1.113, Nearman 346, Tanahashi 310–311)

By zeroing in on some of the key terms, Dōgen's commentary argues that "knows" should not be conflated with ordinary perception or self-knowledge, and "illumines" refers neither to brilliant comprehension nor to spiritual illumination in the typical sense.

Nevertheless, feeling that those interpretative remarks are insufficient to the critical task, Dōgen offers his own version of the poem: "It is not that

'The Lancet of Zazen' by Hongzhi has not stated the 'one great matter' of seated meditation correctly, but we can go about explaining it in yet another way" (Zazenshin: Dōgen 1.117, Nearman 351, Tanahashi 314). The first line of Dōgen's revision is identical to the original, but a major shift occurs in the next line when he substitutes for the key verbs two words that are associated with the first compound in one of his favorite notions, *genjōkōan*, so that "the essential activity "manifests here and now (*gen*) without thinking and becomes complete (*jō*) without interacting" (Zazenshin: Dōgen 1.117, Nearman 350, Tanahashi 311).

Dōgen's phrasing is intended to highlight the concrete practicality of meditative experience, rather than a sense of withdrawal from the world. Later in the poem he replaces Hongzhi's designations of "subtle" and "mysterious" with "intimate" and "confirmed" to further emphasize that zazen is characterized by expansion instead of an escape from everyday awareness. Dōgen also rewrites the final lines of Hongzhi's poem that read:

The water is clear right through to the bottom, as fish swim lazily along;
The sky is vast without horizon, as birds fly off in the distance.
(Zazenshin: Dōgen 1.113, Nearman 347, Tanahashi 311)

In his revision, Dōgen restores a sense of natural boundaries that are dismissed by his forerunner, making the expression more tangible by depicting the functions of fish and birds realistically without embellishment.

The water is clear right through to the earth, with fish swimming as fish;
The sky is vast straight into the heavens, as birds fly just like birds.
(Zazenshin: Dōgen 1.117, Nearman 351, Tanahashi 314)

Dōgen's view of just sitting, which repudiates any lingering goal-seeking outlook, has been adopted and adapted in the twentieth century by several leading Sōtō Zen teachers, especially Sawaki Kōdō (1880–1965), who is known for the deliberately provocative utterance, "What is zazen good for? Nothing! We should be made to hear this good-for-nothingness so often that we get calluses on our ears and practice good-for-nothing zazen without any expectation. Otherwise, our practice really is good for nothing."[20] Among the sect's clerical and lay leaders, Sawaki is known for almost singlehandedly reviving in a modern context an exclusive focus on the technique of *shikan taza*, which he feels represents the heart of the *Treasury*'s message, readily available to all practitioners interested in Zen training.

Sawaki has often been referred to with affection as "Homeless Kōdō" because of the way he traveled extensively throughout Japan to spread his view of seated meditation without settling at a particular temple, thus highlighting that just sitting can take place anywhere. In that vein, Ishii Seijun and Tsunoda Tairyū, eminent contemporary scholars of Dōgen linked with Sawaki's lineage, point out similarities between Dōgen's view and the inspiring contemporary expression, "The journey is the reward," which was used in a book title by Apple entrepreneur Steve Jobs sometime before he became famous and evoked again in a 2005 commencement speech given at Stanford University.[21] For a number of years Jobs studied Sōtō-style meditation while living in Silicon Valley under the tutelage of Otagawa Kobun (a.k.a. Kobun Chino), a Japanese disciple of Sawaki who emigrated in 1967 to become a teacher at the San Francisco Zen Center led by Suzuki Shunryū.[22] Jobs often made clear that just sitting was very helpful in his career development, especially at times when he needed to overcome feelings of uncertainty while enduring a personal or professional crisis.[23]

An emphasis on the aimlessness of zazen, as propagated by Sawaki and his many followers, has been particularly important because modern Sōtō practice for laypeople was greatly influenced by two key factors that contributed to restricting a focus on traditional meditation, to the extent that the sect was sometimes labeled derisively as representing "Zazenless Zen."[24] One factor is the prevalence of thousands of Sōtō Zen "prayer temples" (*kitō jiin*) located all over the country. Of the nearly 14,000 Sōtō temples, only a couple of dozen are dedicated to seated meditation as monastic training centers (*senmon dōjō*). Prayer temples cater to the desire of ambitious devotees to pursue, through making ritual offerings, the gain of this-worldly pragmatic benefits (*genze riyaku*) such as success and prosperity, rather than a state of awakening as sought by dedicated monks.

The second factor was the 1891 publication of *Principles of Practice and Realization* (*Shushōgi*) by a powerful lay organization. This very short but highly influential text is a drastically abbreviated version of the *Treasury* consisting of just five divisions containing thirty-one sentences with a total of about four thousand characters (*kanji*). *Principles* does not mention the term "zazen" a single time. Instead, drawing primarily from passages included in the 12-fascicle edition of Dōgen's masterwork, it serves as a reminder of the need for repentance in order to gain release from any transgressions committed. As one of its main section headers, the text uses the phrase, "The Eradication of Sins Through Repentance" (*zange metsuzai*).[25] This work was designed to be memorized and recited by all members of the sect, and it remains a mainstay of Sōtō ritual life that is chanted during many kinds of ceremonial occasions, especially funerals and memorials. Nevertheless, it is criticized because it may not genuinely reflect the profound teachings about seated meditation expressed in the *Treasury*.

{ 8 }

RITUALITY AND CAUSALITY

ON MONASTIC DISCIPLINE AND MOTIVATION

THE VALUE OF DIGNIFIED DEMEANOR

In addition to promoting the priority of zazen practice, Dōgen's *Treasury of the True Dharma Eye* is known for its emphasis on many other kinds of religious training methods. These involve following strict disciplinary codes and adhering to traditional clerical precepts as well as strengthening dedication and exertion in light of the significance of the basic Buddhist notions of karmic retribution and repentance for negotiating the effects of moral causality. Dōgen's detailed instructions for cloistered behavior are based on Chinese Mahāyāna writings plus the rites and ceremonies he personally observed and experienced during his four-year pilgrimage to the mainland at a time when Zen was first getting established in Japan and its monks needed to learn from the source of the tradition. These guidelines deal with very specific matters of hygiene, such as washing, wiping, brushing, and trimming, supplemented by more general daily, seasonal, and annual ritual activities as well as lofty ethical injunctions designed to develop and cultivate a gracious, dignified manner carried out in all activities, secular or sacred, monumental or commonplace, by applying the truth of Dharma in relation to the effects of karma.

In speaking about regulating the monks' hall (literally, "cloud hall," or *undō*, which refers to the transient circumstances of many novices), Dōgen preaches that there must be no attention given to fame and fortune or participation in transgressions committed by others. On a more practical level, there is to be no leaving the premises unless necessary, no reading of Zen books or letters from family, no quarreling or speaking loudly with other monks, no blowing one's nose noisily or laughing out loud, no circumambulation of the hall or reading of sūtras (except one time for donors), no wearing patterned garments, no entering the hall drunk, and especially, no dropping one's bowl (which leads to a fine) and no disregard for listening to the teachings (which leads to expulsion).[1]

Instead, all monks must seek to blend together harmoniously like milk and water and show an indebtedness to one another that is greater than to their own father or mother by reporting all comings and goings and matters large and small to the hall chief, while practicing zazen with unremitting diligence and remembering to attend morning and evening consultations with the abbot. Dōgen advocates an old Chinese proverb on paying attention to each and every detail: "A sage does not favor a one-foot-tall jewel while neglecting any speck of time [literally, an inch of shadow]" (Tajinzū: Dōgen 247, Nearman 883, Tanahashi 749), although there are also several passages in the *Treasury* that criticize those whose attention only lasts for a moment. "Overall," he says, "the regulations of the buddhas and ancestors must be strictly observed. We should carve the rules of the purity of the monastery on our bones and seal them in our minds. We must seek a life of peace and tranquility by pursuing the way effortlessly [that is, without forethought or preparation]" (Jūundōshiki: Dōgen 486, Nearman 485, Tanahashi 42).

What, according to Dōgen's teaching, is the connection between the performance of zazen and following rules for behavior that show a trainee's expanding level of self-control but may appear secondary to the function of sitting meditation? Is zazen the primary, if not necessarily exclusive, pathway for the realization of awakening? Do additional forms of practice have equal status, or should they be regarded as spiritual stepping-stones or examples of an outcome of meditation that are of lesser value because they are designed for neophytes, as suggested by many Sōtō commentators? Or, as some contemporary interpreters suggest, particularly those associated with the movement known as Critical Buddhism (Hihan Bukkyō), should zazen and various other Zen practices be understood as religious exercises related to Dōgen's primary focus on overarching ethical rather than strictly ritual concerns, a topic discussed at length in some of the late *Treasury* writings mainly included in the 12-fascicle edition?

Extensive clerical activities endorsed and explained by Dōgen cover the daily customs of reciting chants, cooking meals, cleaning and washing, and temple chores while utilizing implements such as bells, bowls, robes, and scrolls. These practices also include the annual intensive summer retreat as well as intricate long-term procedures for selecting the most promising successors to receive the sect's transmission from the current abbot. Therefore, one scholar characterizes the *Treasury*'s approach as genuinely moralistic in that:

> It illustrate[s] Dōgen's own belief in Buddhas and tathāgatas, in the power of merit transcending the relative and absolute worlds, as well as in the reality of karma of the past, present, and future, and its functioning within all of these worlds. Dōgen frequently writes about past Buddhas and ancestors, and the performance of repentance rituals in front of them, he makes numerous mentions of the importance of a sincere heart, a deep and honest devotion, as well as places emphasis on the enactment of rituals with one's sincere mind and body of faith. To Dōgen, there is no distinction between any of these practices, as they equally lead to Buddhahood."[2]

Based on a Sōtō axiom frequently cited by practitioners trying to steady their coordination of mental awareness and bodily comportment that was formulated in the medieval period as derived from ideas originally expressed in the *Treasury*, "dignified demeanor is the Buddha Dharma (*iigi soku buppō*) and ritual etiquette (literally, transacting the Dharma) is our sect's teaching (*sahō kore shūshi*)." The fascicle "Washing the Face" proclaims, for example, "Ritual etiquette (*sahō*) is itself the sect's teaching (*shūshi*), and attaining the way is itself ritual etiquette" (Senjō: Dōgen 81, Nearman 54, Tanahashi 49).

A prime illustration of this principle, as shown in figure 8.1, occurs regularly today at Eiheiji temple, where novice monks polish the floors of corridors by rushing ahead on their hands and knees while holding a cloth as an exercise that establishes external cleaning as a direct reflection of internal cleansing. The wood becomes so smooth that visitors walking along wearing socks are likely to slip and fall unless they are very careful. In that highly refined setting, everyone involved, including the clerics and visitors, takes part in an enriched and honorable setting. According to Kaoru Nonomura, who wrote a best-selling account, *Eat Sleep Sit*, about spending a year at age thirty fully immersed in Sōtō Zen practice as a respite from humdrum life in Tokyo, the interfusion of meditation and housekeeping is complete each and every day of the year. "At Eiheiji," he writes, "along with sitting, which is done morning and night, collective manual labor is done twice daily . . . [by] cleaning the Monks' hall, the washroom, the walking corridor, the common quarters, the work area, and

FIGURE 8.1 The relation between *zazen* and *samu* (chores) performed daily in the Zen temple.

its washroom and toilet." Furthermore, he reports, "it isn't done on special days or in special places, but takes place every single day, whether or not there is any dirt to speak of."[3]

DOES ZAZEN-ONLY MEAN ONLY ZAZEN?

Because Dōgen's lectures on Zen practice topics are so diverse and sometimes indicate shifts in his thinking from the time of their initial presentation to later revisions, certain passages in the *Treasury* may seem disconnected or incongruous. There are numerous examples of Dōgen altering his perspective and authorial voice in fascicles presented for a specific cloistral occasion that were recorded but sometimes significantly edited by the master or his scribe, Ejō. According to many commentators, Dōgen's apparently contradictory discourse, which admonishes monks to use various training methods in the world of form or objectivity yet overshadows this instruction through an emphasis on formlessness or subjectivity, is meant to transform a practitioner's preoccupation with fixed or static positions into an appreciation for standpoints that are eminently fluid and dynamic. The diversity of views, it is said, helps convert a trainee's focus on either the prologue to or the aftermath following an experience of realization into a level of authentic awareness of the all-encompassing moment incorporating past and future.

An important example of apparent inconsistency that is ultimately resolved involves Dōgen's understanding of Rujing's famous injunction that all training methods other than zazen are to be avoided and abandoned because these techniques do not lead all the way to genuine awakening. Dōgen nevertheless wholeheartedly supports the same list of practices in key passages throughout the *Treasury*. Rujing first presented the edict to his foremost foreign disciple while conversing in 1226 in the abbot's quarters at Mount Tiantong. Dōgen cites this command, with slight variations, a total of nine times in his writings, including in five *Treasury* fascicles.[4] In the version of the pronouncement that appears in "Discerning the Way," where it is presented in Japanese syntax (and, unlike all but one of the other examples, does not attribute the saying to Rujing), five ritual practices are disclaimed that were typical of the Chan monastic routine followed at the time of Dōgen's journey:

> From the start of your studies of Zen (*sanzen*) with a wise teacher, take no recourse whatsoever in the acts of (1) burning incense (*shōkō*) [for purification], (2) making prostrations (*raihai*) [as veneration], (3) reciting the name of Buddha (*nembutsu*) [in devotion], (4) performing repentance ceremonies *(shusan)* [for confession], or (5) reciting sūtras (*kankin*) [by memorization]. Just (*tadashii*) sit (*taza*) and attain the casting off of body-mind (*shinjin datsuraku*). (Bendōwa: Dōgen 2.462, Nearman 4, Tanahashi 5; with numbers inserted)

Despite Rujing's instruction, which indicates that the five non-zazen methods inevitably fail to result in thought and action fully liberated from self-imposed barriers, careful readers of the *Treasury* cannot, according to Griffith Foulk's analysis, "ignore the extensive body of writings in which [Dōgen] not only endorses a wide range of conventional Buddhist practices, but explains in detail exactly how they are to be performed in the daily life of a monastery."[5] In fact, burning incense to purify the circulation of air in a temple hall and making prostrations to demonstrate reverence for elders, icons, and scriptures are so commonly mentioned in the *Treasury*, especially in the fascicle "Summer Retreat," that it hardly seems worth discussing whether or not Dōgen may have disdained those techniques.

The same can certainly be said for reciting the sūtras, which is highlighted in several fascicles. "In point of fact," Foulk argues, "all of the particular practices that [are] dismissed in [Rujing's] passage . . . are explicitly and enthusiastically promoted by Dōgen in a number of [the fascicles] and other works."[6]

Even though Rujing taught that just sitting vitiates the need for other kinds of training, Dōgen found creative ways to justify the methods his mentor disparaged by orchestrating the performance of ritual activities regarded not as conflicting or contradictory forms of practice, but as profoundly disciplined and eminently consistent manifestations of the core spiritual experience of seated meditation. He severely admonishes monks in both China and Japan who have not followed various cloistral regulations, such as shaving the head and keeping fingernails short or wearing and washing the robe properly. This occurs when rules are enforced as authoritarian or externally driven demands unsupported by an authentic internal attitude cultivated through just sitting, a technique that inspires an individual's utmost dedication to the principles of Zen practice.

The basic question of apparent inconsistency between ideal and practical realms is by no means unique to Dōgen's teaching. According to Pei-Ying Lin, throughout the entire history of Zen, which portrays itself as a special dissemination of truth positioned outside typical Buddhist teachings, there is a "paradoxical relationship between the transmission of 'enlightenment' [taking place] 'from mind to mind' and the persistent role of precepts, lineage lines, and various institutional perceptions."[7] Many Zen leaders, Lin notes, have pondered an incompatibility between an emphasis on illumination, defined as the spontaneous sense of freedom from all fetters based on realizing the indivisibility of reality, and the perpetuation of monastic administration, which supports practices rooted in hierarchical rankings based on the implementation of sequential rubrics. Since most prominent masters were engrossed in trying to regulate expanding temple communities, coming to terms with the conundrum of juggling two levels of truth, one united and the other divided, is crucial for explaining "the approach of Chan to the acquisition and assertion of authority."[8]

Foulk shows that this challenge is particularly heightened by readings of the *Treasury* because, "Dōgen has often been cast by modern scholars as the leading proponent of a 'pure' form of Zen practice in which various conventional Buddhist ceremonies and rituals are eschewed, no 'syncretistic' borrowing of elements from the Pure Land or Esoteric Buddhist traditions is tolerated, and no concessions are made to the demands of the laity for funerals, memorials, and offering services for the spirits of their ancestors."[9] Surely, Foulk maintains, the implication that Dōgen only cared about zazen as the vehicle for enlightenment at the expense of almost all other religious practices is at odds with much of the content of the *Treasury*, as well as the regular activities of Sōtō Zen monasteries that are largely based on propagating its teachings. Foulk also disagrees with commentators who claim that the discrepancy between zazen and supplementary types of practice is due to the desire of Dōgen, functioning as a Zen abbot, to accommodate the didactic needs of uninformed initiates with straightforward instructions about rites, since those followers could not be expected to understand the deeper meaning of nonthinking.

The reason behind Rujing's disavowals, according to Dōgen, is that the five practices mentioned are not pivotal to self-realization when carried out in a perfunctory or instrumental way with the assumption that they will result automatically in a benefit accrued, because awakening lies beyond, yet remains inseparable from, conditioned reality. Just sitting helps overcome those deficient tendencies by refining authentic intentionality. In a passage celebrating his mentor in the fascicle "Sustained Exertion," Dōgen writes, "I never heard of anyone other than Rujing who encouraged sitting simply for the sake of sitting. Throughout the world and all over China, only my late master did this. Monks from various regions were alike in praising Rujing, yet he had little admiration for monks far and wide. Unfortunately, there were heads of many large temples who were not even aware of his masterful skills" (Gyōji: Dōgen 1.198, Nearman 430, Tanahashi 376).

Even though eight of nine references to Rujing's dictum, including all five passages in the *Treasury*, were composed prior to the flourishing of Eiheiji temple, where Dōgen developed a new emphasis on ritual training and crafted the main portions of his *Monastic Rules* text (the final compilation of which was completed in the Edo period), it is clear that his aim is never to interpret Rujing's saying as a blanket rejection of observances in favor of zazen as the only practice method. However, to highlight that subjectivity should underlie all training techniques, including zazen, Dōgen concludes a lengthy discussion of Rujing's injunction in a formal sermon delivered in 1251 by suggesting that meditation means nothing other than seeing reality just as it is without embellishment. "During the summer, the lotus blossom opens toward the sun," he remarks, and after a pause, "The nose is aligned vertically with the navel, while ears are level horizontally with the shoulders."[10]

A crucial implication of Dōgen's teaching is that if meditation becomes mechanical, then it too must be spurned; contrariwise, if other practices are performed in a genuinely purposeless way, they should be considered exceptionally valuable techniques fully compatible with just sitting. The key to understanding Dōgen's outlook is that neither zazen nor alternative practices constitute a direct route to awakening conceived as a final destination in a way that is derived from a linear view of temporality. Instead, from the holistic standpoint of the inseparability of practice-realization, each approach to training represents but one of the multitudes of ongoing manifestations of the awakened awareness of nonthinking that transpires each and every moment.

Therefore, Dōgen's view of true practice overcomes the notion of training in the sense of doing something "in order to" attain merit or transfer it to others by emphasizing that commendable behavior is fully embodied in activities for which there is no ulterior motive. Merit is reaped precisely when people act without concern or by casting off any preoccupation about whether or not a reward will ensue. That outlook is to be applied to every kind of comportment, regardless of whether it is considered religious by usual standards or takes place either within or outside the gates of the temple compound.

Like Dōgen's discussions of zazen that rely heavily on citations from the *Rules for Purity in Zen Monasteries*, various *Treasury* fascicles dealing with monastic discipline cite Zongze's twelfth-century Chinese work extensively in order to evoke a sense of authority and precedent.[11] The *Rules for Purity* directly influences the content of at least eleven fascicles covering different training techniques, including "Washing the Face," "Cleaning," "Reciting Sūtras," "Transmitting the Robe," "Summer Retreat," and "Home Departure," which are contained in the 75-fasicle edition; "Merits of Home Departure," "Receiving the Precepts," "Awakening the Bodhi-Seeking Mind," and "Taking Refuge in the Three Jewels," all from the 12-fascicle edition; plus "Instructions on Kitchen Work," which appears only in the 95-fascicle edition. Moreover, several *Treasury* fascicles highlighting the function of kindhearted behavior by superior trainees also reflect Zongze's impact, especially "The Four Exemplary Acts of a Bodhisattva" from the 60-fascicle edition and "Birth and Death" included in the 95-fascicle edition.

According to the analysis of Buddhist monasticism by Ann Heirman and Mattieu Torck in *A Pure Mind in a Clean Body*, Dōgen's masterwork should be seen in light of the fact that he "belongs to a generation of monks who were very keen to preserve the Chan tradition as outlined in [Zongze's] 'rules for purity.' "[12] In several *Treasury* fascicles, "achieving purity—of both body and mind—is the principal motivation for any washing activity.

So, it is unsurprising that [Dōgen] also insists a monk's feet should be spotless when he meditates."[13] Indeed, Edo-period commentator Katsudō Honkō (1710–1773) succinctly sums up the contents of "The Principles of Zazen" fascicle, "Sitting still with clean feet," which could also be rendered, "Washing your feet is a form of meditation." The unity of theory and practice encompassing a broad diversity of training techniques is embodied in all a practitioner's activities.

Once again, Dōgen is by no means unconditionally dedicated to Zongze's approach; he interprets the *Rules for Purity* liberally by shifting to an overall emphasis on the purification of intentionality or motivation. This is based on an adept's genuine religious mindfulness that demonstrates constant steadiness and persistence combined with supreme flexibility and agility, rather than strict obedience to regulation seen as an end in itself. *Treasury* writings consistently demonstrate Dōgen's ingenuity in interpreting kōan cases and other examples of Buddhist lore that challenge conventional views of institutional authority, highlighting dramatic instances of individual authenticity that reflect a Zen adept's knack for knowing intuitively when to bend or break the established rules. According to Dōgen, the main influence on behavioral decisions and their consequences is the impact of the consciousness of the actor on the action and its results.

The *Treasury*'s approach to Zen practice, therefore, resembles that of the Yuan-dynasty (1279–1368) Chan master Zhongfeng Mingben (1263–1323), who after the Mongol takeover of China set up self-sustaining cloisters of monks in the relatively remote area of Mount Tianmu because practice at temples in the major cities of Hangzhou and Ningbo was being suppressed.[14] Like Dōgen helping to initiate the transplantation of Zen in Japan, Mingben was a pioneer exporting the tradition to the wilderness in China. By providing an institutional framework for each individual's purification of the mind, his description of monastic life emphasizes interiority in order to support and sustain the external official regulations. For both leaders, the outer trappings of etiquette and rituals enacted by monks are behavioral and material components of monastic life that fully complement, and in no way conflict with, the ongoing cultivation of subjectivity through the practice of meditation.

PRECEPTS AND PURIFICATION

Dōgen's approach to Zen practice makes a significant contribution to the history of East Asian Buddhism by propagating a distinctive view regarding a complex debate about the function of clerical precepts that was taking place at the dawn of the Kamakura era in Japan. Dōgen steered these discussions toward an emphasis on subjectivity underlying reclusive activities. By emphasizing the purification of consciousness, the fascicle "Receiving the Precepts," included in the 12-fascicle edition of the *Treasury*, drastically streamlines the specific number of rules required for practitioners to a short list of sixteen core precepts.

At the time of the inception of Zen in the thirteenth century, nearly all Japanese monks being trained in the Tendai sacraments performed at Mount Hiei, which generally included some form of meditation along with other ritual techniques, were administered 58 precepts covering general principles of compassionate conduct according to the *Brahma's Net Sūtra* (Ch. *Fanwang jing*, Jp. *Bonmōkyō*), a key Mahāyāna Buddhist text. However, the Tendai school did not carry out the set of 250 Hīnayāna precepts focusing on more specific aspects of behavioral guidelines, known as the *Prātimokṣa*, as explained in early Buddhist Vinaya texts long followed by monastics in India and China. When Eisai went to the mainland, he found that both sets of precepts were strictly obeyed at all Chan temples. On returning to Japan in the early 1190s, more than three decades before Dōgen's pilgrimage began, the Rinzai founder declared in his main work, *The Promotion of Zen for the Protection of the Country* (*Kōzen gokokuron*), the value of combining the Hīnayāna and Mahāyāna precepts in a custom that has been perpetuated by his sect. What impressed Eisai most about continental practice was its firm commitment to the full array of Buddhist rules as a means of developing self-restraint among trainees.

Dōgen was more significantly influenced by the nearly opposite notion that he learned in China about the formless precepts, which stresses the activities of monks not in terms of particular deeds (or misdeeds), although this is by no means excluded, but rather as extensions of Buddha mind continually cultivated through seated meditation. In the opening passage of the fascicle "Way-Seeking Mind," mentioned at the beginning of the first chapter, Dōgen writes, "If you want to pursue the way of buddhas (*butsudō*), you must first of all develop the way-seeking mind (*dōshin*)" (Dōshin: Dōgen 2.530, Nearman 1088, Tanahashi 886). This passage shows that enlightenment is based on inner motivation supporting the authenticity of contemplative awareness and the integrity of unwavering impartiality gained by conducting zazen on a continuing basis.

The *Treasury* considers all activities that are part of collective life in the monastery, including cooking and cleaning or reading and praying, to be displays of interior refinement based on the power of just sitting. Even though many passages give an extraordinary level of attention to the finest details of various priestly rituals, Dōgen's vision of practice encompasses the inseparability of individual and communal actions by virtue of subjectivity that is linked to external circumstances. He frequently uses the term *ehō shōhō* 依報正報, which refers to the connection underlying primary causes and secondary conditions or the unity of self and world.[15]

In this vein Dōgen shifts the monastic focus from the question of the number of precepts to be followed, an emphasis advocated by Eisai, to purifying the mind as the basis for all modes of behavior. Various passages of the *Treasury* concerning discipline are based on how intentionality, rather than external rules, guides the enactment of deeds. The fascicle "Thirty-Seven Methods of Training to Realize Enlightenment" cites a saying attributed in the *Heap of Jewels Sūtra* (Ch. *Baoji jing*, Jp. *Hōsekikyō*) to Śākyamuni, who tells his disciple Upāli—known for strict adherence to the precepts according to the vehicle of the *śrāvaka*, a less advanced practitioner who is required to follow strict regulations—"The *śrāvaka* keeps the precepts, but the bodhisattva [a fully accomplished buddha] breaks the precepts" (Sanjūshichihon bodaibunpō: Dōgen 2.149, Nearman 804, Tanahashi 690).[16] Also, based on a passage from the *Rules for Purity*, the fascicle "Washing the Face" maintains that the central point of the precepts is "knowing what it is to uphold or to break them by understanding what is permitted and what is forbidden. Rely only on the holy words of Buddha and do not heed the words of ordinary people" (Senmen: Dōgen 2.48, Nearman 676, Tanahashi 66). The level of insight that is able to bend or break the rules as deemed appropriate, Dōgen suggests, reflects the essence of Dharma that has been transmitted by all buddhas and ancestors.

Therefore, the *Treasury* bypasses almost entirely the debate about monks receiving 58 Mahāyāna vis-à-vis 250 Hīnayāna precepts by showing that a more limited set is sufficient if practiced with wholehearted concentration. The fascicle "Receiving the Precepts" provides instructions, still followed during ordination ceremonies held as a crucial part of Sōtō ritual life today, for administering three refuges, three pure precepts, and ten grave precepts.[17] Modern scholars sometimes refer to Dōgen's standpoint as the "precepts of One Mind (*isshin*)," in that there are no meaningful regulations aside from the self-awakening and self-realization of authenticated Buddha nature permeating all sentient and insentient beings. An implication of the radical reduction in the number of rules is that Dōgen assumed most practitioners of his era had already memorized and probably mastered longer lists that helped them understand and appropriate the essential principles captured in the sixteen precepts.

In other fascicles Dōgen discusses the role of various ceremonial activities not specified in the precepts that are required of enlightened monks as part of the reclusive regimen. This includes a list provided in the "Thirty-Seven Methods of Training to Realize Enlightenment," which covers four types of mindfulness, four kinds of correct effort, four modes of supranormal powers, five faculties, five powers, and seven branches of awakening, in addition to the traditional Buddhist eightfold path. To ensure that followers do not take the quantitative aspect of practice too seriously, Dōgen points out that these methods are the same as "Riding an ox backward right into the Buddha hall, then doing one lap around the hall, two laps, three, four, or five laps, so that nine times nine equals eighty-two" (*Sanjūshichihon bodaibunpō*: Dōgen 2.149, Nearman 804, Tanahashi 690), thus deliberately defying common sense. He concludes the fascicle by referring to the realization (*genjō*) of a grand total 1,369 kōans in order to show that ritual practice is no different from the contemplation of case narratives. Also, this seemingly arbitrary amount represents an accurate squaring of the original number, 37, based on the view that each item contains all the others.

This is also the case in the *Treasury*'s discussion of the Mahāyāna practice of the six "perfections" (Skr. *pāramitā*, Jp. *haramitsu*), or the moral deeds of an awakened person including charity, caring, patience, commitment, contemplation, and wisdom. Dōgen explains that all these modes of behavior are of identical value in that each reflects the continuing process of self-realization. Therefore, the six perfections do not represent a prelude to enlightenment in a way usually symbolized by the image of crossing a river on a raft in order to arrive at the "other shore" (*higan*) representing the goal of nirvāṇa, at which point the vehicle can be tossed aside. By incorporating the philosophy of being-time into his analysis of Zen practice, Dōgen significantly recasts the analogy:

> Arriving at the other shore is realization occurring right here and now (*genjōkōan*). Do not think that practice (*shugyō*) will lead you to reach the other shore, because the other shore is realized whenever genuine training takes place. As soon as we begin to practice, that is already an arrival at the other shore, since cultivation is unmistakably bestowed with the capacity to manifest in all realms of the universe. (Bukkyō: Dōgen 1.387, Nearman 308, Tanahashi 282)

Dōgen also disparages those who conceive of the exercise of the six perfections in sequential fashion. He argues that any of the stages could come first, middle, or last, depending on the level of development of a particular practitioner.[18] He thus maintains, "There are really thirty-six perfections in that every single one contains all of the others" (Bukkyō: Dōgen 1.386, Nearman 308, Tanahashi 282). In a typical instance of Zen irony, Dōgen then says that realizing one perfection "is getting hold of snares (literally, 'nets and cages') by using those very snares" (Bukkyō: Dōgen 1.386, Nearman 308, Tanahashi 282). In other words, the process of advancing from perfection to perfection without interference or delay is expressed by an image that typically implies a decline from proficiency to deficiency. This is comparable to an emphasis in the *Treasury* on the struggle to disentangle tangled vines by virtue of entanglements.

Another fascicle featuring a list of moral activities is "The Four Exemplary Acts of a Bodhisattva," delineating essential items of practice including: (1) giving to others through material offerings to relieve ordinary stress and Dharma offerings to engage spiritual awareness; (2) providing kind or loving words to arouse a trainee's mind to seek and accept the way of Buddha; (3) making beneficial actions that create a sense of love and trust between master and disciples in a communal context; and (4) exercising empathy based on the teacher's profound insight that sees clearly the true nature of each being on its own terms in order to act accordingly to facilitate their path to enlightenment. Using the same principle of squaring as in previous passages, Dōgen says that in the final analysis there are really sixteen bodhisattva practices. Additional lists of enlightened accomplishments are provided in two fascicles contained in the 12-fascicle edition that were written in the final stage of Dōgen's life, when he knew his end was near. These include "One Hundred and Eight Gates to Awakening" and "The Eight Realizations of a Great Person," both of which borrow heavily from standard Indian Buddhist texts about how an adept faces imminent death.

Dōgen's primary aim in all of these discussions is to move away from the paradigm of keeping a scorecard of guidelines involving moral rectitude in order to show that the practice of just sitting, whether or not actually cross-legged, experiences reality unfettered and without ulterior purpose and thereby actualizes awakening at each moment and in every action. This holds true whether the deed is sublime, such as viewing autumn foliage on a distant mountain peak and following the vows of compassion, or mundane, like enacting menial daily tasks such as sweeping a dusty floor or repairing a torn garment. In the fascicle "Dharma Nature," a title that can also be read to mean "The Nature of Things" because the term "dharma" (*hō*) can indicate either Buddhist truth or particular phenomena, Dōgen suggests that everyday activity is just as much the fulfillment of awakened experience as any lofty occurrence. "This very experience here and now is none other than Dharma nature, and Dharma nature is none other than experience here and now," he writes, alluding to a passage by Master Mazu. Therefore, "Wearing clothes or eating meals is the fulfilled concentration of Dharma nature that wears clothes or eats meals. Realization is Dharma nature as clothes, it is Dharma nature as meals, it is Dharma nature as the act of eating, and it is Dharma nature as the act of wearing" (Hosshō: Dōgen 2.28, Nearman 650, Tanahashi 560).

The approach to morality evident in the *Treasury* was particularly influenced by the notion of "formless" (Skr. *ārūpya*, Ch. *wuxiang*, Jp. *musō*) precepts, which is accompanied by the corollary function of formless repentance, as first expressed in the *Platform Sūtra* attributed to Sixth Patriarch Huineng and interpreted in numerous subsequent Zen works.[19] The term "formless" (or "signless") refers to the ultimately empty or insubstantial quality of all deeds when seen from the perspective of absolute truth that relativizes and surpasses incomplete perspectives. Seated meditation is the primary tool used to polish and cultivate motivations by enabling a person to think (or nonthink) in a fundamentally impersonal way without purpose or goal, so as to manifest purity in all activities transpiring unobstructed in the present moment. While Dōgen recommends zazen as the foremost training method, he is aware that, from the outlook of formlessness, there are neither specific practices nor aims of practice. Even the basic terms "just sitting" and "casting off body-mind" represent skillful yet, in the final analysis, provisional means of communicating enlightenment realized here and now.

Dōgen's discussions of monastic training in the *Treasury* suggest that the wholesomeness of motivation is revealed in unfettered deeds that demonstrate a merging of exterior and interior levels of interaction based on the paradox of purposeless intentionality.[20] Therefore, washing one's body and cleaning one's garments are no longer considered merely physical exercises, but constitute a process of cleansing or represent cathartic experiences that heighten spiritual awareness. In the fascicle "Transmission of the Robe," Dōgen speaks of the hallowed garb (Skr. *kāṣāya*, Jp. *kesa*) as a "vestment of liberation" by citing a verse from the *Rules for Purity* that is recited three times after placing the garment on one's head, a custom Dōgen saw for the first time in China: "How great the vestment of liberation; / the robe is a formless field of merit. / Wrapping ourselves in formless precepts, / we extensively deliver all living beings" (Den'e: Dōgen 1.373, Nearman 140, Tanahashi 151). Nevertheless, Dōgen is also known as a strict disciplinarian who, though "kindhearted like a grandmother," would not hesitate to castigate disciples who disobeyed the rules of the monastery or his own directives.[21]

OBSERVANCES AND CEREMONIES

The primary link between Dōgen's promotion of just sitting and his meticulous instructions for ceremonial practice is the view that, while carrying out any and all monastic activities, a practitioner should not think of various assignments and responsibilities in a mechanical or instrumental sense that detracts from authentic contemplative awareness of the holistic moment of being-time. Rather than causing deterioration into mindless preoccupation with mundane tasks, ritual functions are designed to enhance the mindful state of nonthinking. The overall approach to various monastic practices proposed by the *Treasury* reveals much of the same rhetorical strategy used in fascicles that deal with philosophical topics by encompassing two extreme standpoints simultaneously. In the fascicle "Lotus Turning the Lotus," for example, Dōgen maintains that the most minute particularity contains the entire cosmos and, conversely, the universe is revealed in each mote of dust: "When we are looking at a particular dust particle it does not mean that we do not see the whole realm of the universe, and our affirming the whole realm of the universe does not mean that we deny any dust particle" (Hokke ten hokke: Dōgen 2.493, Nearman 181, Tanahashi 186). Based on this theoretical outlook, the Sōtō founder emphasizes that the quality of each specific action, such as cooking, eating food, bathing, or wiping oneself, creates an opening that allows one to view symbolically the entirety of the cosmic process of cleansing or purification.

Therefore, the formless precepts reflecting One Mind are paradoxically reflected in a multitude of precise procedures that are given a great deal of consideration. Dōgen explains exactly how to brush one's teeth and scrub one's face; sew a robe, whether made of fine silk or of coarse and tattered cloth; and wash private parts with two fingers after relieving oneself so that food can be prepared and eaten using the three fingers left unsoiled. The significance of the purification of intentionality is expressed in the fascicle "Washing the Face," which was delivered to his assembly on three different occasions. Dōgen writes, "When we are about to chew the willow twig," a device he felt was not being used enough in China, where monks often had bad breath, "we should recite the following verse from the *Flower Garland Sūtra*: 'Chewing the willow twig this morning, /

I pray that all sentient beings / will obtain the teeth for overcoming evil, / so that they may chew up their defiling passions'" (Senmen: Dōgen 2.44, Nearman 672, Tanahashi 63).²²

Dōgen also comments that in India and China, all people from royalty to commoners wash their face every morning, a custom that was not generally carried out adequately in his native country but that he hoped to promote by introducing it through Zen practice that would be taken up more widely. On the other hand, he notes that in Japan the use of the willow twig was commonly followed in a way far superior to that in China. Nevertheless, in "Cleaning," to guarantee that sanitation is fully served, he carefully explains how to defecate in the forest by "taking three balls of earth mixed with clean water to wash and purify the area of excretion" (Senjō: Dōgen 83, Nearman 57, Tanahashi 51).

A focus on the formless quality underlying all forms of practice is further featured in the deceptively simple saying cited in the fascicle "Radiant Light," "The chief cook has entered the kitchen," which Dōgen says is "an expression representing the life of all buddhas" (Kōmyō: Dōgen 1.144, Nearman 490, Tanahashi 421). This suggests that the key to the chore of making food for the assembly is not a specific style of preparation but the attitude and demeanor of the chef, an assignment rotated among the members of the community so that every monk must take their turn and master this skill. Also, in "Instructions for Kitchen Work," Dōgen emphasizes the use of honorific and polite rather than crude or casual forms of speech. A dignified monk should refer to rice or other cooking ingredients as "esteemed." While this kind of exchange is undertaken, Buddhist scriptures should be recited silently, in one's thoughts, even though the words are not actually uttered. Similarly, in discussing the use of vestments, Dōgen refers to the task of washing the robe as "a matter of realizing the kōan (*genjōkōan*) of robe cleaning," which is more significant than, and serves as the basis for, the action.

Another main possession of a Buddhist mendicant that is emblematic of his renunciant status is the alms bowl (*ho'u* or *hatsu'u*), which Dōgen discusses in a fascicle so named. The Chinese term combines the transliteration of a Sanskrit word for "vessel" (*pātra*) with the character for "basin." In the Chan tradition the legend developed that, along with the robe, the bowl was bequeathed to a disciple at the time of succession; this was most famously carried out in the case of sacred objects handed down all the way from First Patriarch Bodhidharma to Sixth Patriarch Huineng.²³ Dōgen focuses his comments not so much on the physical object given to novices at the time of ordination as on the significance of the formless or spiritual dimension of the receptacle that represents a monk's willingness to accept graciously whatever is offered, including sometimes uncomfortable duties and strict obligations required of every member of the assembly. According to the capping phrase commentary on the fascicle composed by Giun, this implement is "perfectly round and all-embracing, consisting of neither metal nor stone." Giun's verse remarks read, "Encompassing all of space and completely bottomless, / it can be used time and again but is never diminished. / By carrying it effortlessly without limit, / a patched-robe monk fulfills his lifelong mission."[24]

In considering the above examples, the modern biographer Takeuchi Michio refers to Dōgen's emphasis on explaining the minutiae of deeds in light of formlessness as the principle of "everyday realism" (*genjitsu shugi*), which suggests a sense of fastidious care and full responsiveness involving each phenomenon in its particularity. This is done without any concern for results, since genuine effectiveness prevails the less a goal is consciously sought because in that way self-control is more profoundly cultivated.[25] Dōgen's view was probably greatly influenced by the Daoist notion of the "utility of the useless" (Ch. *wuyong shiyong*, Jp. *muyō jiyō*). It also recalls a Jewish mystical anecdote indicating that a pupil learns more from watching the rabbi tie his shoes than from reading scripture, and the counsel of a contemporary inspirational basketball coach stressing the importance of every task that affects preparations for a game by telling his team the key to winning is, "Keeping those socks pulled up!"[26]

Furthermore, in the *Treasury* the view of the inseparability of formlessness and form is applied to several important ritual procedures that delineate special boundaries for ceremonial behavior involving specific times and places, although these occasions also reflect the momentariness of being-time that embodies empty space unrestricted by externally imposed limits. A crucial rite in the life of every Zen temple is the annual summer retreat (*ango*), a period for intensive training and reflection, including confession and penitence, that has been held since the earliest days of Buddhist monasticism for a ninety-day cycle beginning on the full moon of the fourth lunar month (in modern times this is regularized as April 15, according to the solar calendar).

The fascicle "Summer Retreat" provides detailed guidelines that Dōgen extracts from the *Rules for Purity*, especially instructions for opening and closing this sacramental phase of activity. In his remarks Dōgen also makes numerous comments indicating that ultimately there is no difference whatsoever in the status of purified intentionality that occurs before, during, or after the prescribed period. Therefore, "The summer retreat from beginning to end (literally, "head to tail") is what a buddha or ancestor is; beyond this, there is not a single additional inch of ground, nor is there anything other than the great earth" (Ango: Dōgen 2.217, Nearman 855, Tanahashi 724). In other words, the true sanctuary transpires every single day of the year, even though monastic rules seem to set apart three special summer months.

Another ritual necessary for the perpetuation of the Zen lineage involves the selection and transmission of the Dharma to worthy successors in a process often symbolized by the transfer of the teacher's implements and other iconic objects, such as robe, bowl, and ceremonial portraiture, all items Dōgen received from Rujing prior to his departure from China in 1227. A small cluster of fascicles focus on the role of dissemination by paying attention to the specifics of the process, and another group features the notion of formlessness as crucial to the fulfillment of transmission.

The first set of fascicles includes "Inheritance Certificates," which provides descriptions of Dōgen's deeply personal feelings of awe and joy when, in the early days of his travels to China, despite being a foreign novice he had the privilege of viewing five rare inheritance documents representing the customs of various Chan lineages that "attested to the truth of the inheritance of the Dharma by buddha after buddha and ancestor after ancestor" (Shisho: Dōgen 1.423, Nearman 159, Tanahashi 168). For Dōgen, the documents are at once superfluous, because the true meaning does not require physical verification, and crucial, since the external manifestation fully objectifies and thus confirms subjective truth. The first group also includes "Buddhas and Ancestors," which recounts the list of Indian and Chinese patriarchs in the Caodong lineage that Dōgen was taught by Rujing; and "Sustained Exertion," in which the Sōtō founder examines key features of the life stories of a couple of dozen Chan leaders who were particularly known for their commitment to strict ascetic practice. Many of the figures who are lavishly praised represent rival schools, yet Rujing's excellence is celebrated in the final extended section of the fascicle as a culmination of the tradition.[27]

A second group of *Treasury* fascicles is designed to highlight the interior quality of succession, which is about not only an individual's sequential attainment of lineal leadership but also the holistic process of uninterrupted transmission moving backward and sideways as much as forward. Each instance of selection is considered identical to the primal moment when the Buddha's eyes were twinkling during his breakthrough to enlightenment, the time he held up a flower while giving a lecture and only one disciple smiled, or the occasion when Bodhidharma extended his skin, flesh, bones, and marrow to four followers when choosing the second patriarch. All of these are examples of disentangling entangled vines, with teacher and student assisting each other in "springing from delusion." To show that buddha after buddha is realized in the present moment of being-time, Dōgen cites two well-known sayings attributed to Bodhidharma, "A flower blooms and the world arises" and "One blossom opens, and five petals appear" (Kūge: Dōgen 1.127, Nearman 552, Tanahashi 458).[28]

In other passages Dōgen refers to the special rapport or "spiritual communion" (*kannō dōkō*) involving the "unity of master-disciple" (*shitei funi*), who recognize each other immediately when they meet "face to face" (*menjū*) for the first time and realize that their communication "occurs only between a buddha and another buddha" (*yuibutsu yobutsu*). In two fascicles Dōgen cites ancient Indian parables demonstrating the intuitive interaction that takes place during this exchange. In "A King Asks for Saindhava," the Sanskrit term *saindhava* (Jp. *sendaba*), which means "something from Sindh," refers to four products from the Indus River area that were held in great esteem throughout ancient India. Asking for an item from Sindh, including salt, a goblet, water, and a horse, is considered equivalent to requesting the very best that can be offered appropriate to any given situation (Ōsaku sendaba: Dōgen 2.253, Nearman 889–890, Tanahashi 755). These goods are alike in having one and the same term of reference. Dōgen views the acts of one person asking for *saindhava* and another presenting the requested item as a model for pedagogical relationships. He also suggests that the ideal student would know when to bring a different product than the one requested, should he intuitively understand that this is better suited to the circumstances.

Similarly, the fascicle "Four Horses" is based on a tale cited in early sūtras where the Buddha once told his monks about several kinds of stallions. The first kind is startled into following the wishes of the rider upon seeing the shadow of the whip; the second does not react until the whip touches its hair. The third kind is stunned only after its flesh feels the lash, and the fourth is stimulated to race when the pain inflicted by the rider reaches its bones. The message of the parable is that a genuine disciple must elevate the status of his rapport to the level of the attentive and anticipatory first stallion, who responds immediately and without hesitation, thus relieving the rider from enduring the kinds of delays and obstructions that plague the other three horses.

KARMIC RETRIBUTION AND REPENTANCE

One of the five practices in Rujing's injunction is repentance, which Critical Buddhist scholars point out is particularly emphasized in the 12-fascicle edition of the *Treasury*. These scholars argue that near the end of his life, after returning from an unsuccessful visit with the shogun in the garrison town of Kamakura, for the first time in his teaching career Dōgen expressed a genuine commitment to the act of atonement that requires concrete confessional behavior as part of acknowledging and remedying one's wrongdoings in light of the inviolability of karmic retribution. An important passage from the first formal sermon he delivered after going back to Eiheiji, which is included in the *Extensive Record*, signals a change of heart that influenced all his late *Treasury* writings. Dōgen said to his assembly, which had felt anxious about the master's absence, "I am afraid that up until now I have been unable to explain the significance of cause and effect (*inga*). So many mistakes have been made in trying to cultivate the way; it is a shame that I have come to resemble an [untamed] ox."[29] This straightforward focus on causality is supported by the 12-fascicle edition's consistent attention to the topics of gaining merit (*kudoku*), demonstrating reverence (*kuyō*), adhering to preceptual rules (*shingi*), and maintaining a penitent state of mind (*zange*), all monastic practices that mitigate the effects of retribution.

The main argument that captures the essence of the Critical Buddhists' view concerns Dōgen's new approach to karmic causality and its relevance for overcoming deficient ethical views in the contemporary world, including discrimination against the Burakumin community and unequal treatment of female practitioners. Individuals belonging to these groups were long regarded by Buddhist institutions as "innately impure" for the inappropriate reason that they "must have gotten the fate they deserved" (*jigō jitoku*) as a consequence of past behavior. They were therefore removed from the assembly of monks without an opportunity to express their own genuine intention to realize enlightenment. In the name of supporting the ultimate equality of all forms of existence based on the Mahāyāna theory that Buddha nature is universal and all inclusive, these groups were denied access to avenues of spiritual practice made available to elite members of the Zen community.

The debate involves a basic discrepancy evident in two key fascicles that are both dedicated to discussing a kōan case dealing with cause and effect. The first is "Great Cultivation," which is included in the 75-fascicle edition, and the other is "Deep Faith in Causality," which is one of five sections in the 12-fascicle edition that represent rewritten or modified versions of previous compositions. "Great Cultivation" and "Deep Faith in Causality" provide nearly opposite interpretations of the so-called Fox Kōan, an anecdote originally included in Master Baizhang's (749–814, Jp. Hyakujō) recorded sayings that is cited in a wide variety of Zen records and commentaries.[30]

According to the complex case narrative, filled with mythical symbolism, an ancient monk was transfigured for five hundred lifetimes into a "wild fox" (*yako*), a supernatural entity known for its capacity for deception and betrayal, as punishment for expressing a misunderstanding of karma. One time, in response to a disciple's inquiry, he maintained that even a person of great cultivation (*daishugyō*) does "not fall into causality" (*furaku inga*). The monk is released from this fate through the transformative "turning word" (*ittengo*) offered by Baizhang, who maintains the virtue of "not ignoring [or being benighted by] causality" (*fumai inga*). The fundamental paradox is that, by verbally denying causality, the monk is victimized by karma, yet from Baizhang's affirming its impact, he gains release. The fox corpse is then buried on the temple grounds with full Buddhist rites, which triggers a fierce debate among members of Baizhang's assembly about why a nonhuman (*hinin*) would be allowed to have a sacred burial.[31]

The Fox Kōan's message about the principle of karma, as indicated by the phrase "not ignoring causality," seems quite clear. However, the commentary by Dōgen in the early fascicle "Great Cultivation" highlights the provisional quality, and ultimately the indistinguishability, of the "not falling" and "not ignoring" responses. In the New Draft, Dōgen supports the conventional reading of the case by emphasizing that the power of karmic retribution is delusory. This is also suggested by the verse remark in the *Gateless Gate* collection: "Not falling, not ignoring, / two faces of the same die. / Not ignoring, not falling, / hundreds and thousands of mistakes."[32]

In "Great Cultivation" Dōgen raises several interesting interpretative issues not found in most other traditional commentaries, including asking whether the reference to five hundred lives indicates the typical duration of a person or an animal and wondering about the destiny of the fox-monk: does he continue to transmigrate, or can he escape this fate by attaining full enlightenment free from the cycle of rebirth? Dōgen also ponders the idea that the vulpine shape-shifter might have deceived Baizhang into believing it was really a priest, in which case its corpse should not have received a proper Buddhist burial according to the *Rules for Purity*. Nevertheless, in this fascicle Dōgen echoes the conventional view: "Because causality necessarily means full cause and complete effect, there is no reason for a discussion concerning the relation between falling into or not falling into and ignoring or not ignoring causality. If not falling into causality is incorrect, then not ignoring causality is also incorrect" (Daishugyō: Dōgen 2.187, Nearman 825, Tanahashi 707).[33]

Both fascicles dealing with the Baizhang dialogue are critical of the Senika heresy, which advocates a false sense of return to an original nature or primal source and sees the release from the fox body as a symbol of the monk resuming his true essence. Yet, whereas "Great Cultivation" refuses to criticize in a thoroughgoing way the old man's view of not falling, "Deep Faith in Causality," written near the end of Dōgen's life, repudiates the position of formlessness that he supported a decade before when he equated causality with the transcendence of karma. In the later fascicle he asserts quite emphatically that only the form-based practice of repentance based on the notion "not ignoring causality" is acceptable, and that "not falling" amounts to the counterproductive denial of causality (*hotsumu inga*) that is mistaken and must be rejected. "The single greatest limitation of the monks of Song China today," he writes, "is that [more than thirty commentators on the case] do not realize that not falling into causality is a false teaching. It is a pity that, even though they encounter the true Dharma of the Tathāgata correctly transmitted from patriarch to patriarch, they accept the views of those who would deny causality" (Jinshin inga: Dōgen 2.390, Nearman 1022, Tanahashi 853). Dōgen severely criticizes the standpoints of both Dahui, a prominent lineal rival belonging to the Linji school, and Hongzhi, an important Caodong predecessor, for failing to recognize the flawed thinking evident in their respective verse comments that advocate the nonduality, rather than clear separation, of causality and noncausality.[34]

The crucial implication for Critical Buddhism is that, as part of a new emphasis following his change of heart after returning to Eiheiji from Kamakura, Dōgen requires the clear recognition of causality and the performance of repentance to mitigate retribution for transgressions. This topic is discussed at length in several sections of the 12-fascicle edition. In the 75-fascicle edition, there is only one scant reference to repentance, in the fascicle "Sounds of Valleys, Colors of Mountains." In the context of examining what is involved in the realization of sudden awakening, Dōgen explores the need for atonement as one of several important steps taken in the process of gaining wisdom. For Critical Buddhism, the Old Draft does not articulate well-defined ethical guidelines, and therefore its vagueness can all too easily lead to antinomianism. This term refers to an all-too-common trend affecting many mystical traditions worldwide that foster equanimity by vitiating unwittingly the need for moral principles, which are not considered applicable for someone who has attained a level of comprehension beyond the conventional dichotomy of right and wrong.[35] An unfortunate by-product of antinomian implications is that overt examples of misconduct can easily get exacerbated yet remain hidden from scrutiny beneath a cloak of purity and perfection provided by the formlessness of rules.

Critical Buddhism argues that Dōgen's frequent references in the 75-fascicle edition to knowing when to break the precepts exemplify the problematic tendencies of antinomianism, even though the early *Treasury* writings also clearly indicate his eagerness to spurn possible unethical implications of the Senika heresy that characterized the approach of the Daruma school, which was banned by the government. The Daruma leaders advocated abandoning a commitment to objective behavioral guidelines based on the belief that any natural, uncultivated action, such as simply raising an arm or lifting a bowl, in and of itself constitutes an expression of the Dharma without the need for refinement through practice.[36]

The 75-fascicle text, Critical Buddhism claims, puts too much emphasis on refining intentionality without sufficient regard for evaluating the concrete effects of actions on worldly affairs. For example, in the fascicle "Refrain from Committing Evil" that is part of the Old Draft, Dōgen analyzes a verse extracted from the early Buddhist text originally written in Pali known as the *Path of Dharma* (*Dhammapada*): "Refrain from committing any evil whatsoever, / uphold and practice all that is good, / thereby purifying your own intentions (Jp. *jijō kii*. Ch. *zijing qiyi*); / That is the teaching of every buddha" (Shoaku makusa: Dōgen 1.343, Nearman 78, Tanahashi 95). This passage, highlighting in the third line the role of purification as the basis for avoiding evil, is frequently evoked in Zen writings, including the works of Eisai that Dōgen studied when he resided at Kenninji temple in Kyoto before traveling to China in 1223. The outlook so expressed suggests that if intentions are untainted, then wholesome deeds will invariably result, an implication flatly rejected by Critical Buddhism.

Therefore, Critical Buddhist scholars claim the 12-fascicle edition provides a useful model for overcoming social discrimination in society today due to its renewed emphasis on form repentance. Dōgen's outlook in this version of the *Treasury* is reinforced by formal sermons from his late period, included in the *Extensive Record*, also emphasizing the inviolability of karmic causality.[37] If properly enacted, the form-based approach could enable the modern Sōtō sect to evoke a compelling intellectual vehicle rooted in Dōgen's original thought to redeem its wrongdoings toward an aggrieved local community, in addition to expressing remorse for instances of pre-World War support of Japanese imperialism. However, some skeptics of Critical Buddhism point out that the 12-fascicle edition passages do not sufficiently caution practitioners against another ethical conundrum, that is, the unfortunate effects of confession performed in a perfunctory way with a fixed expectation of results. Expressing contrition in that manner may end up endorsing the misleading notion of the "eradication of evil through repentance." This term was coined in the *Principles of Practice-Realization*, a short text mainly recited during ceremonies for contemporary lay followers. It could suggest, falsely, that mouthing the empty words of a repetitive ritual will eliminate the severe penalties for misdeeds committed.

In considering whether there is a fundamental change in Dōgen's thinking from the time of the 75-fascicle to the composition of the 12-fascicle edition of the *Treasury*, some challengers argue that such shifts are by no means as unidirectional or clear cut as Critical Buddhism suggests. For example, the Sōtō founder's views regarding the role of female and lay practitioners, among other social concerns, probably did alter over the course of his twenty-year career serving as abbot in two very different temple environments. One was Kōshōji, located in the capital, where Dōgen for the most part encouraged an inclusionary model in accord with other Kamakura-era Buddhist reform movements; the other was Eiheiji, situated in the provinces, where he emphasized the priority of male renunciants, even though women and lay followers no doubt attended many of his sermons.

The distinction between early and late standpoints is not well defined, however, since in "The Ungraspable Mind" from the 1230s Dōgen indicates a reluctance to sanction the authority of a legendary nonclerical female interlocutor in a dialogue with Master Deshan, despite her apparent wisdom. Yet his comments just a couple of years later in the fascicle "Obtaining the Marrow Through Veneration" offer great praise for a witty Chan nun and attack those men who deny the capabilities of legitimately ordained women. A recently retrieved alternative version of this fascicle originally included in the 28-fascicle edition of the *Treasury* offers an even more positive view and thus makes interpreting the role of women in Dōgen's thought quite complicated. Nevertheless, it seems clear that at Eiheiji temple, Dōgen preserved the traditional Buddhist hierarchy of 1) monks, 2) nuns, 3) lay male followers, and 4) lay female followers.[38]

Ethical controversies based on interpreting different versions of the *Treasury* have triggered wide-ranging ideological debates not confined to basic disagreements between Traditional and Critical Buddhist commentators, since many other interpretative standpoints are continually being put forth. An interesting compromise approach is found in a book by Nakano Tōzen, a prominent Sōtō priest who was part of the original task force convened more than thirty-five years ago that spawned the analysis of the 12-fascicle edition by Critical Buddhism, in reaction to a then-urgent social crisis about discrimination. The title of Nakano's more recent work, which literally means *Sunday Treasury* (*Nichiyōbi Shōbōgenzō*), suggests that Dōgen's teachings are applicable to the everyday lives of nonclerical followers.[39] Nakano seeks to balance fairness and equitability toward others as key to the process of self-realization by understanding that the relativity and interdependence of all dichotomies, including good and evil, is not simply reducible to a view that opposites reflect "two sides of the same coin."

Moreover, Nakano links an engagement with social affairs to a deep sense of appreciating the consequences of one's action or inaction. His standpoint is encapsulated in a string of chapters that start with the fundamental query, "Who am I?," and cover such timely topics as "Living on the borderline of having a defiled mind while seeking the realm of purity," "Surpassing conventional selfhood by encountering nonthinking," and "Discovering ways of communing with nature" by probing "What would it mean to live in hell?" Nakano's approach to developing self-discipline as a key to moral decision making can be summed up by a cryptic saying extracted from the fascicle "Empty Space" that highlights evenhandedness and proportionality: "Whether you are being controlled by the twenty-four hours of a day or are in control of the twenty-four hours of a day, you should know that when a stone is large it is large just as it is and when a stone is small it is small just as it is" (Kokū: Dōgen 2.212, Nearman 850, Tanahashi 720).[40]

Appendix 1

TITLES OF *TREASURY* FASCICLES

This list reflects the Original Edition consisting of 75 fascicles in addition to 12 fascicles, plus various appended or alternative fascicles that add up to 16 entries for a grand total of 103 fascicles, as in the first two volumes of the seven-volume *Dōgen Zenji zenzhū* (Tokyo: Shunjūsha, 1989–1993). This list is also being used in the forthcoming translation by the Sōtō Zen Translation Project. Most of these fascicles are included in the 95-fascicle or Main Temple Edition that is used by Nearman, Tanahashi, and most other translators. As discussed in the preface, these translations have a different sequence of fascicles and also use renderings that are sometimes quite different from mine. However, the pronunciations of the titles and the characters for them are the same.

THE 75-FASCICLE EDITION

1. Genjōkōan 現成公案 — Realization Here and Now
2. Makahannya haramitsu 摩訶般若波羅蜜 — The Perfection of Great Wisdom
3. Busshō 仏性 — Buddha Nature
4. Shinjingakudō 身心學道 — Learning the Way with Body-Mind
5. Sokushin zebutsu 即心是仏 — The Mind Itself Is Buddha
6. Gyōbutsu iigi 行仏威儀 — Dignified Demeanor of Practicing Buddhas
7. Ikka myōju 一顆明珠 — One Bright Pearl
8. Shinfukatoku 心不可得 — The Ungraspable Mind

9. Kobusshin 古仏心 — The Ancient Buddha Mind
10. Daigo 大悟 — Great Awakening
11. Zazengi 坐禪儀 — The Principles of Zazen
12. Zazenshin 坐禪箴 — The Lancet of Zazen
13. Kaiin zanmai 海印三昧 — Ocean Seal Samādhi
14. Kūge 空華 — Flowers in the Sky
15. Kōmyō 光明 — Radiant Light
16. Gyōji 行持 — Sustained Exertion
17. Inmo 恁麼 — Thusness
18. Kannon 觀音 — Bodhisattva Kannon
19. Kokyō 古鏡 — The Ancient Mirror
20. Uji 有時 — Being-Time
21. Juki 授記 — Confirmation
22. Zenki 全機 — Complete Activity
23. Tsuki 都機 — The Moon
24. Gabyō 畫餅 — Painted Rice Cakes
25. Keisei sanshoku 谿聲山色 — Sounds of Valleys, Colors of Mountains
26. Bukkōjōji 佛向上事 — Going Beyond Buddha
27. Muchū setsumu 夢中説夢 — Disclosing a Dream Within a Dream
28. Raihai tokuzui 禮拜得髓 — Attaining the Marrow Through Veneration
29. Sansuikyō 山水經 — Mountains and Rivers Proclaiming the Sūtras
30. Kankin 看經 — Reciting Sūtras
31. Shoaku makusa 諸悪莫作 — Refrain from Any Evil
32. Den'e 傳衣 — Transmission of Robes
33. Dōtoku 道得 — Expressing the Way
34. Bukkyō 佛教 — Buddhist Teachings
35. Jinzū 神通 — Spiritual Powers
36. Arakan 阿羅漢 — Arhat
37. Shunjū 春秋 — Spring and Autumn
38. Kattō 葛藤 — Entangling Vines
39. Shisho 嗣書 — Transmission Documents
40. Hakujushi 柏樹子 — Cypress Tree
41. Sangai yuishin 三界唯心 — Triple World Is Mind Only
42. Sesshin sesshō 説心説性 — Disclosing Mind, Disclosing Nature
43. Shohō jissō 諸法實相 — True Form of All Things
44. Butsudō 仏道 — Way of Buddha
45. Mitsugo 密語 — Intimate Language
46. Mujō seppō 無情説法 — Insentient Beings Preaching the Dharma

APPENDIX 1 {229}

47. Bukkyō 仏經	Buddhist Sūtras
48. Hosshō 法性	The Nature of Things
49. Darani 陀羅尼	Spells (*Dhāraṇī*)
50. Senmen 洗面	Washing the Face
51. Menju 面授	Face-to-Face Transmission
52. Busso 仏祖	Buddhas and Ancestors
53. Baika 梅華	Plum Blossoms
54. Senjō 洗淨	Cleaning
55. Jippō 十方	Ten Directions
56. Kenbutsu 見仏	Seeing Buddha
57. Henzan 徧參	Extensive Study
58. Ganzei 眼睛	The Eyeball
59. Kajō 家常	Everyday Life
60. Sanjūshichihon bodaibunpō 三十七品菩提分法	Thirty-Seven Methods of Training to Realize Awakening
61. Ryūgin 龍吟	The Howl of Dragons
62. Soshi seirai i 祖師西来意	The First Patriarch Coming from the West
63. Hotsu mujōshin 發無上心	Arousing the Supreme Mind
64. Udonge 優曇華	Udambara Blossoms
65. Nyorai zenshin 如來全身	The Complete Body of Tathāgata
66. Zanmai ō zanmai 三昧王三昧	The King of All Samādhis
67. Tenbōrin 轉法輪	Turning the Dharma Wheel
68. Daishugyō 大修行	Great Cultivation
69. Jishō zanmai 自證三昧	The Samādhi of Self-Realization
70. Kokū 虛空	Empty Space
71. Ho'u 鉢盂	The Bowl
72. Ango 安居	Summer Retreat
73. Tajinzū 佗心通	Reading Other Minds
74. Ōsaku sendaba 王索仙陀婆	The King Asks for Saindhava
75. Shukke 出家	Home Departure

THE 12-FASCICLE EDITION

1. Shukke kudoku 出家功徳	The Merits of Home Departure
2. Jukai 受戒	Taking the Precepts
3. Kesa kudoku 袈裟功徳	The Power of Robes
4. Hotsu bodaishin 發心菩提	Arousing the Aspiration for Enlightenment
5. Kuyō shobutsu 供養諸仏	Veneration for All Buddhas

6. Kie buppōsōbō 歸依佛法僧寶 — Taking Refuge in the Three Jewels
7. Jinshin inga 深信因果 — Deep Faith in Causality
8. Sanjigō 三時業 — Karmic Effects in Three Times
9. Shime 四馬 — Four Horses
10. Shizen biku 四禪比丘 — The Four Stages of a Monk
11. Ippyakuhachi hōmyōmon 一百八法明門 — One Hundred and Eight Gates to Awakening
12. Hachidainingaku 八大人覺 — The Eight Realizations of a Great Person

FASCICLES NOT ORIGINALLY INCLUDED

1. Bendōwa 辨道話 — Discerning the Way
2. Jūundōshiki 重雲堂式 — Conduct for the Cloud Hall
3. Hokke ten hokke 法華轉法華 — The Lotus Turning the Lotus
4. Shin fukatoku 心不可得 (Part B) — The Ungraspable Mind
5. Bodaisatta shishōbō 菩提薩埵四攝法 — The Four Activities of a Bodhisattva
6. Jikuinmon 示庫院文 — Instructions for Monks in the Kitchen
7. Yuibutsu yobutsu 唯仏與仏 — Only Between Buddha and Buddha
8. Shōji 生死 — Birth and Death
9. Dōshin 道心 (also: Butsudō 仏道) — The Way-Seeking Mind

ALTERNATE VERSIONS OF FASCICLES

1. Bendōwa 辨道話 — Discerning the Way
2. Shisho 嗣書 — Transmission Documents
3. Bukkōjōji 佛向上事 — Going Beyond Buddha
4. Senmen 洗面 — Washing the Face
5. Henzan 徧參 — Extensive Study
6. Daigo 大悟 — Great Awakening
7. Sanjigō 三時業 — Karmic Effects in Three Times

Appendix 2

COMPARISON OF VERSIONS OF THE *TREASURY*

95	75	60	12	28*	Date	Place
1. Bendōwa					1231.8/15	Anyō'in
2. Makahannya haramitsu	2	2			1233.4-7	Kannon'in
3. Genjōkōan	1	1			1233.8	Kannon'in
4. Ikka Myōju	7	7			1238.4/18	Kōshōji
5. Jūundōshiki					1239.4/25	Kōshōji
6. Sokushin zebutsu	5	5			1239.4/25	Kōshōji
7. Senjō	54	54			1239.10/23	Kōshōji
8. Senmen	50	50			1239.10/23	Kōshōji
9. Raihai tokuzui	28			b	1240.3/7	Kōshōji
10. Keisei sanshoku	25	25			1240.4/20	Kōshōji
11. Shoaku makusa	31	31			1240.8/15	Kōshōji
12. Uji	20	20			1240.10/1	Kōshōji
13. Kesa kudoku		41	3		1240.10/1	Kōshōji
14. Den'e	32			m/32	1240.10/1	Kōshōji
15. Sansuikyō	29			m/29	1240.10/18	Kōshōji
16. Busso	52			e/52	1241.1/3	Kōshōji
17. Shisho	39			m	1241.3/27	Kōshōji
18. Hokke ten hokke	12				1241.4-7	Kōshōji
19. Shinfukatoku	8	8		b/8	1241.4-7	Kōshōji
20. Shinfukatoku Part B				b/8	1241.4-7	Kōshōji
21. Kokyō	19	19			1241.9/9	Kōshōji
22. Kankin	30	30			1241.8/15	Kōshōji
23. Busshō	3	3			1241.10/14	Kōshōji
24. Gyōbutsu igi	6	6			1241.10/15	Kōshōji
25. Bukkyō (Teachings)	34			m/34	1241.11/14	Kōshōji
26. Jinzū	35	35			1241.11/16	Kōshōji
27. Daigo	10	10			1242.1/28	Kōshōji

(continued)

95		75	60	12	28*	Date	Place
28. Zazenshin	12					1242.3/18	Kōshōji
29. Bukkōjōji	26	26			b	1242.3/22	Kōshōji
30. Immo	17	29				1242.3/20	Kōshōji
31A. Gyōji 1	16	16				1243.1/18	Kōshōji
31B. Gyōji 2	16	17				1242.4/5	Kōshōji
32. Kaiin zanmai	13	13				1242.4/20	Kōshōji
33. Juki	21	21				1242.4.25	Kōshōji
34. Kannon	18	18				1242.4/26	Kōshōji
35. Arakan	36	36				1242.5/15	Kōshōji
36. Hakujushi	40	40				1242.5.21	Kōshōji
37. Kōmyō	15	15				1242.6/2	Kōshōji
38. Shinjingakudō	4	4		1242.9/9	Kōshōji		Kōshōji
39. Muchū setsumu	27	27		1242.9/21	Kōshōji		Kōshōji
40. Dōtoku	33	33				1242.10/5	Kōshōji
41. Gabyō	24	24				1242.11/5	Kōshōji
42. Zenki	22	22				1242.12/17	Hatano Y.
43. Tsuki	23	23				1243.1/6	Kōshōji
44. Kūge	14	14				1243.3/10	Kōshōji
45. Kobusshin	9	9				1243.4/29	Rokuhara
46. Bodaisatta shishōbō		28				1243.5/5	Kōshōji
47. Kattō	38	38				1243.7/7	Kōshōji
48. Sangai yuishan	41	32				1243.7/1*	Kippōji
49. Sesshin sesshō	42			e/42		1243	Kippōji
50. Butsudō	42	44		b/44		1243.9/16	Kippōji
51. Shohō jissō	43	43		b/42		1243.9	Kippōji
52. Mitsugo	45			m/45		1243.9/20	Kippōji
53. Bukkyō (Sūtras)	47	34		m/47		1243.9	Kippōji
54. Mujō seppō	46	46				1243.10/2	Kippōji
55. Hōsshō	48	48				1243.10	Kippōji
56. Darani	49	49				1243	Kippōji
57. Menju	51			e/51		1243.10/20	Kippōji
58. Zazengi	11	11				1243.11	Kippōji
59. Baika	53					1243.11/6	Kippōji
60. Jippō	55	45				1243.11/13	Kippōji
61. Kenbutsu	56	47				1243.11/19	Yamashibu
62. Henzan	57	37				1243.11/26	Yamashibu
63. Ganzei	58	44				1243.12/17	Yamashibu
64. Kajō	59	43				1243.12/17	Yamashibu
65. Ryūgin	61	51				1243.12/25	Yamashibu
66. Shunjū	37					1244	retreat
67. Soshi seiraii	62	52				1244.2/4	retreat
68. Udonge	64	54				1244.2/12	Kippōji
69. Hotsu mujōshin	63	53				1244.2/14	Kippōji
70. Hotsu bodaishin		34	4			1244.2/14	Kippōji
71. Nyorai zenshin	65	55				1244.2/15	Kippōji
72. Zanmai ō zanmai	66			b/66		1244.2/15	Kippōji
73. Sanjūshichi bodaibunpō	60			b/60		1244.2/14	Kippōji
74. Tenbōrin	67			m/67		1244.2/27	Kippōji

APPENDIX 2 [233]

95		75	60	12	28*	Date	Place
75. Jishō zanmai		69			m/69	1244.2/19	Kippōji
76. Daishugyō		68			m/66	1244.3/9	Kippōji
77. Kokū		70	56			1245.3/6	Daibutsuji
78. Hatsu'u		71	42			1245.3/12	Daibutsuji
79. Ango		72	57			1245.6/13	Daibutsuji
80. Tajinzū		73				1245.7/4	Daibutsuji
81. Osaku sendaba		74				1245.10/22	Daibutsuji
82. Jikuinmon						1246.8/6	Eiheiji
83. Shukke		75			e/75	1246.9/15	Eiheiji
84. Hachidainingaku				12	m/12	1253.1.6	Eiheiji
85. Sanjigō			8	8		1253.3/9	Eiheiji
86. Shime			39	9		(1255.4-7)	Eiheiji
87. Shukke kudoku			58	1		(1255.4-7)	Eiheiji
88. Kuyō shobutsu			59	5		(1255.4-7)	Eiheiji
89. Kie buppōsō			60	6		(1255.4-7)	Eiheiji
90. Jinshin inga				7	b/87	(1255.4-7)	Eiheiji
91. Shizen biku				10	e/10	(1255.4-7)	Eiheiji
92. Yuibutsu yobutsu					e/38	unknown	Eiheiji
93. Shōji					b	unknown	Eiheiji
94. Bustudō (Dōshin)					b	unknown	Eiheiji
95. Jukai				2	m/2	unknown	Eiheiji
96. Ippyakuhachi hōmyōmon					11	unknown	Eiheiji

*the ordering in the traditional text
**1a243 was an intercalary year

VARIETY OF EDITIONS

103 = 75 + 12 plus miscellaneous

100 = Ejō says this was Dōgen's goal

95 = Main Temple Edition

89 = edition by Menzan Dōhaku

88 = 75 + 12 plus "Bendōwa"

87 = 75 + 12

84 = edition by Taiyō Bonsei

83 = another medieval edition

75 = Old Draft

60 = edition by Giun in 1329

28 = also known as Himitsu edition

12 = found in 1930

VARIOUS *TREASURY* COMPILATIONS

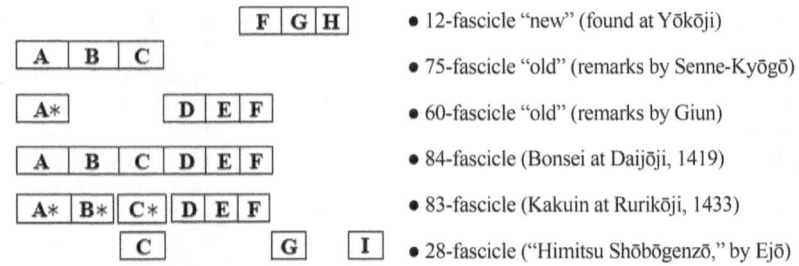

- 12-fascicle "new" (found at Yōkōji)
- 75-fascicle "old" (remarks by Senne-Kyōgō)
- 60-fascicle "old" (remarks by Giun)
- 84-fascicle (Bonsei at Daijōji, 1419)
- 83-fascicle (Kakuin at Rurikōji, 1433)
- 28-fascicle ("Himitsu Shōbōgenzō," by Ejō)

Note: 75- and 12-fascicle versions linked together, and 60- and 28-fascicle versions form another grouping

A (50 fascicles ∗ The 60 and 83-fascicle texts include Gyōji 1 and 2 as separate, for 51 fascicles)

Genjōkōan · Makahannyaharamitsu · Busshō · Shinjingakudō · Sokushinzebutsu · Gyōbutsu iigi · Ikkya myōju · Kobusshin · Daigo · Zazengi · Kaiin zanmai · Kūge · Kōmyō · Gyōji (1—2) · Immo · Kannon · Kokyō · Uji · Juki · Zenki · Tsuki · Gabyō · Keisei sanshoku · Bukkōjōji · Muchū setsumu · Kankin · Shoaku makusa · Dōtoku · Jinzū · Arakan · Kattō · Hakujushi · Sangai yushin · Mujō seppō · Hosshō · Darani · Senmen · Jippō · Kenbutsu · Henzan · Ganzei · Kajō · Ryūgin · Soshiseiraii · Hotsumujōshin · Udonge · Nyorai zenshin · Kokū · Ho-u · Ango

B (6 fascicles ∗ The 83-fascicle text does not include Shunjū)

Zazenshin · Shunjū · Baika · Senjō · Tashinzū · Ōsakusendaba

C (19 fascicles ∗ The 83-fascicle text does not include Shisho)

Shinfukatoku · Raihaitokuzui · Sansuikyō · Den'e · Bukkyō (Teaching) · Shisho · Sesshin sesshō · Shohō jissō · Butsudō · Mitsugo · Bukkyō (Sutras) · Menju · Busso · Sanjūshichibon bodaibunpō · Zanmai ō zanmai · Tenbōrin · Daishugyō · Jishō zanmai · Shukke

D (1 fascicle) Hokke-ten-hokke

E (1 fascicle) Bodaisatta-shishōbō

F (7 fascicles) Sanjigo · Shime · Hotsubodaishin · Kesa kudoku · Shukke kudoku · Kuyō shobutsu · Kie buppōsōbō

G (4 fascicles) Jukai · Jinshin inga · Shizen biku · Hachidainingaku

H (1 fascicle) Ippyakuhachihōmyōmon (considered the 96th fascicle, after its discovery)

I (5 fascicles (Beppon) Shinfukatoku · (Beppon) Butsukōjōji · (Beppon) Butsudō (Dōshin · Shōji · Yuibutsu yobutsu

Others (2 fascicles included in 95-fascicle or 96-fascicle editions): Jūundoshiki, Jikuinmon

Additional Beppon: Bendōwa · Shisho · Senmen · Hensan · Daigo · Sanjigo

Question: Did Dōgen hope to complete 100 fascicles, as mentioned by Ejō?

Appendix 3

TIMELINE FOR DŌGEN AND THE *TREASURY*

1200 Born in Kyoto
1202 Father dies
1204 Reads Japanese classics
1206 Reads Chinese poetry
1207 Mother dies; has powerful sense of impermanence
1208 Studies Buddhist Abhidharma texts
1209 Consults family about career options
1211 Declines offer to serve in court
1212 Makes Buddhist home departure (*shukke*)
1213 Becomes ordained and enters Mount Hiei
1214 Experiences "Great Doubt"
1215 Meets Eisai at Kenninji temple and is first exposed to Zen kōan literature
1217 Visits the Tendai temple, Onjōji, and reads the Tripitaka
1218 Enters formally practice at Kenninji
1221 Receives transmission from Myōzen, Eisai's disciple
1223 In fourth month goes to China with Myōzen, is detained on ship for three months, and in summer visits Tiantong and Ayuwang temples
1224 Stays at Tiantong, then travels to various Five Mountains temples
1225 Visits temples at Jingshan and elsewhere; Myōzen dies and Dōgen returns to Tiantong; meets Rujing in fifth month and experiences *shinjin datsuraku* two months later
1226 Ongoing conversations with Rujing recorded in *Hōkyōki*

1227	Returns to Japan "empty-handed," but with materials from Rujing; writes *Fukanzazengi*
1228	Rujing dies (sometimes listed as 1227)
1229	Returns to Kenninji
1230	Stays at Anyō'in retreat in Fukakusa outside Kyoto
1231	"Bendōwa" (1 fascicle)
1233	Makahannya haramitsu and Genjōkōan (2 fascicles); Kōshōji opens; revises *Fukanzazengi*
1234	*Gakudōyōjinshū*; Ejō arrives at Kōshōji
1235	*Busso shōden bosatsu kaihō*, *Mana Shōbōgenzō*
1236	Kōshōji Dharma hall opens; first formal sermons; *Eihei Kōroku* volume 9
1237	*Tenzokyōkun*
1238	*Shōbōgenzō zuimonki* completed by Ejō; "Ikka myōjū" (1 fascicle)
1239	"Jūundōshiki," "Sokushinzebutsu," "Senjō," "Senmen" (4 fascicles)
1240	"Raihaitokuzui," "Keiseisanshoku," "Shoaku makusa," "Sansuikyō," "Uji," "Kesa kudoku," "Den'e" (7 fascicles)
1241	"Busso," "Shisho," "Hōkke ten hōkke," "Shinfukatoku" (plus B), "Kokyō," "Kankin," "Gyōbutsu igi," "Bukkyō" (Teachings), "Jinzū" (10 fascicles); Daruma school followers join Dōgen, who writes supplement to Rujing's record
1242	"Daigo," "Zazenshin," "Bukkōjōji," "Immo," "Gyōji," "Kaiin zanmai," "Juki," "Kannon," "Arakan," "Hakujushi," "Kōmyō," "Shinjingakudō," "Muchū setsumu," "Dōtoku," "Gabyō," "Zenki" (16 fascicles); receives Rujing's recorded sayings from China, writes supplement
1243	"Tsuki," "Kūge," "Kobusshin," "Bodaisatta shishibō," "Kattō" (5 fascicles before moving); moves to Echizen 7/18 in intercalary year; "Sangai yuishin," "Sesshin sesshō," "Butsudō," "Shohō jissō," "Mitsugo," "Bukkyō (Sūtras), "Mujō seppō," "Hōsshō," "Darani," "Menju," "Zazengi," "Baika," "Jippō," "Kenbutsu," "Henzan," "Ganzei," "Kajō," "Ryūgin" (18 fascicles after move, total of 23)
1244	"Shunjū," "Soshi seiraii," "Undonge," "Hotsu mujōshin," "Hotsu bodaishin," "Nyorai zenshin," "Zanmai ō zanmai," "Sanjūshichihon bodaibunpō," "Tenbōrin," "Jishō zanmai," "Daishugyō" (10 fascicles); Daibutsuji opens in fourth month
1245	"Kokū," "Hō'u," "Ango," "Tajinzū," "Ōsaku sendaba" (5 fascicles); *Bendōhō*
1246	"Jikuinmon," "Shukke" (2 fascicles); *Risshun*, *Chiji shingi*
1247	Leaves for Kamakura in fall to preach to Hōjō Tokiyori

1248 Returns to Eiheiji in spring
1249 *Shūryō shingi*
1250 "Senmen" delivered for third time; receives new version of Tripitaka as gift from Hatano
1251 Flowers said to fall from sky over Eiheiji and other auspicious signs
1252 "Genjōkōan" edited; becomes ill in late fall
1253 "Hachidainingaku," "Sanjigō" (2 fascicles, plus 11 undated are from late phase); dies in Kyoto in eighth month

1255 Additional posthumous editing of various versions of the *Treasury* by Ejō and other disciples

Appendix 4

COMPLETE TRANSLATIONS OF THE *TREASURY*

THE SENSE of intricacy involved in discerning the complicated discourse of the *Treasury of the True Dharma Eye* compels translators to try to align the goal of maintaining accuracy and faithfulness to the original with the complementary aim of creating a readable and accessible version for an expanding contemporary audience generally unschooled in East Asian Buddhist textual models, yet open and receptive to learning Dōgen's captivating spiritual message. Leaning too far in either direction can result in a stilted or misleading rendition. The most reliable translations follow carefully the text's line-by-line wording, but at times must make an intuitive leap to capture levels of significance expressed between the lines of the source material.

Translators must also make an important decision about which of several different editions of the Japanese text to follow, a choice that reflects varying views regarding Dōgen's literary methods used for religious purposes. As discussed in chapters 3 and 8, the primary versions available are the Main Temple (Honzan) Edition containing 95 fascicles and the Original (Kohon) Edition containing 75 + 12 plus miscellaneous fascicles. While most translations use the Main Temple edition, the merits of adhering to the Original Edition, much preferred by leading Japanese scholars across interpretative standpoints, are increasingly recognized.

The translations cited below are arranged alphabetically by translator. A list of partial translations is included in the bibliography, and additional complete translations into French, German, Italian, Polish, Portuguese, and Spanish are being developed.

Ferreras, Pedro Piquero, trans. *Shōbōgenzō: Tesoro del verdadero ojo del Dharma*. 4 vols. Málaga, SP: Sirio, 2013–2016. A translation into Spanish that is based on the first of two English translations by Nishijima and Cross. It follows the Main Edition and includes the valuable supplementary materials contained in Nishijima's work.

He Yansheng 何燕生, trans. *Zhengfayanzang* 正法眼蔵 (Jp. *Shōbōgenzō*). Beijing: Zongjiao wenhua chubanshe, 2003. Produced by a Chinese monk who was sent to Japan in the early 1980s; he became a professor who published an award-winning book on Dōgen and Chinese Chan thought. This translation gives insight into Dōgen's idiosyncratic Japanese interpretations of traditional Chinese sources by re-creating the discourse in modern Chinese. It follows the Original Edition.

Kristkeitz, Werner, trans. *Shōbogenzo. Die Schatzkammer des wahren Dharma-Auges*. 8 vols. Heidelberg: Werner Kristkeitz Verlag, 2008–2012. A German translation based in part on Nishijima's rendering and in part on reading the original Japanese sources.

Nearman, Hubert, trans. *Shōbōgenzō: The Treasure House of the Eye of the True Teaching, A Trainee's Translation of Great Master Dōgen's Spiritual Masterpiece*. Mount Shasta, CA: Shasta Abbey Press, 2007. The Nearman translation, chosen for use in this book to complement my renderings, is an accurate version that is available in a single, easily accessible and searchable PDF. It contains 96 fascicles (the Main Edition and one additional fascicle) and includes insightful introductory comments for each fascicle, as well as a useful glossary of key terms as an appendix. There are a couple of somewhat eccentric features. First, Nearman uses initial capitalization for a very broad assortment of terms he feels suggest spiritual significance. Second, his translations of fascicle titles tend to be wordy; instead of "Being-Time" for "Uji," for instance, he uses "On 'Just for the Time Being, Just for a While, For the Whole of Time is the Whole of Existence.'" Third, he inserts plum blossom asterisks where he considers that there is a thematic break in the flow that are not part of the original text.

Nishijima, Gudō Wafu 西嶋愚道和夫, and Chodo Cross, trans. *Master Dogen's Shōbōgenzō*. 4 vols. Woods Hole, MA: Windbell Publications, 1994–1999; and Nishijima, Gudō Wafu, and Chodo Cross, trans. *Shōbōgenzō: The True Dharma-Eye Treasury*. 4 vols. Berkeley: Numata Center for Buddhist Translation and Research, 2007–2009. These are two different but largely overlapping renditions in terms of content produced by the same translators, featuring the insights of Nishijima, a Sōtō Zen priest who was known for his modern Japanese translations of Dōgen and other Buddhist works. Both translations follow the Main Edition and include valuable resources, such as a comprehensive list of Dōgen's references to the *Lotus Sūtra* that are also featured in Nishijima's Japanese publication of the *Treasury*. Both translations are reliable and reflect a great deal of research into the various Buddhist sources that influenced Dōgen, as is particularly evident in the extensive footnotes of the earlier publication. However, the editing of the English was never really completed for either version.

Nishiyama, Kōsen 西山廣宣, and John Stevens, trans. *Shōbōgenzō: The Eye and Treasury of the True Law*. 4 vols. Tokyo: Nakayama shobō, 1975–1983. This was the first attempt at a complete translation into English and was issued before a great deal of scholarship on Dōgen had been published in English. Following the Main Edition, this version changes drastically the sequence of fascicles without providing any explanation. Also, it appears to be based primarily on consulting various modern Japanese translations rather than the source text, which results in paraphrases, deletions, and other divergences from the original material.

Orimo, Yoko, trans. *Shōbōgenzō: la vraie Loi, Trésor de l'Oeil*. 8 vols. Vannes, FR: Sully, 2007–2016. A French translation based in part on the original Japanese and in part on consulting various English translations. It follows the Main Edition.

Sōtō Zen Translation Project, trans. *Shōbōgenzō* 正法眼藏, *Treasury of the True Dharma Eye by Dōgen* 道元: *An annotated translation by the Soto Zen Text Project*. Tokyo: Sōtōshū Shūmuchō, forthcoming. Over two decades in the making by an international team led by the Sōtō Sect Office in Japan and headed on the Western side by eminent Dōgen scholars, including Carl Bielefeldt, William Bodiford, and Griffith Foulk, the result will be an eight- or nine-volume bilingual version with extensive annotations and at least one whole volume dedicated to introductory and supplementary materials. The project adheres to the Original Edition contained in *Dōgen's Collected Works* (*Dōgen Zenji zenshū*), which includes a total of 103 fascicles. With its emphasis on accuracy and thoroughness as well as the inclusion of explanations of major and minor themes and ideas in terms of their roots in Zen and Buddhist literature, this promises to be recognized as the definitive English translation. But Dōgen's writing is so complex that any given sentence or passage could be rendered differently, so other interpretations will remain of value.

Tanahashi, Kazuaki 棚橋一晃, ed. and trans. *Treasury of the True Dharma Eye: Zen Master Dogen's Shobo Genzo*. Boston: Shambhala, 2010. This translation cited here is the result of an immense collaboration involving Tanahashi, an authority and longtime translator of Dōgen's writings; associate editor Peter Leavitt, a noted poet; and nearly three dozen practitioners from the San Francisco Zen Center who have long been immersed in the theory and practice of the *Treasury*. The publication, which follows the Main Edition but with some minor changes in the sequence of fascicles, also includes outstanding supplementary materials, including explanations of the origin of all the fascicles and a detailed 120-page glossary of names and terms with characters provided. Originally published as two volumes, this work was soon reissued as a single volume and it is also available in a searchable Kindle edition. One qualification is that, since so many co-translators labored over the renderings during the course of many years, there tend to be some inconsistencies in phrasing and interpretation of key ideas.

Villalba, Dokushō, trans. *Shōbōgenzō: La preciosa visión del verdadero*. Barcelona: Editorial Kairós, 2016. A Spanish translation produced over twenty-five years by a team of translators, mainly practitioners, who consulted French as well as English and Spanish renditions, this follows the Main Edition.

Yokoi, Yūho 横井雄峯, trans. *Shōbō-genzō*. Tokyo: Sankibō Buddhist Bookstore, 1986; and Yokoi, Yūhō, with Daizen Victoria, trans. *Zen Master Dōgen: An Introduction with Selected Writings*. Tokyo: Weatherhill, 1976. Although the two translations came out separately a decade apart and were not intended as a single offering, they are linked here because both involved the work of Yokoi Yūho. Since the earlier publication contains the 12-fascicle edition and the later publication covers the 75-fascicle edition, combining the volumes in effect creates the first English translation of the Original Edition. However, there is a drastic difference in quality. *Zen Master Dōgen*, coedited by Daizen (Brian) Victoria, is a through and excellent publication, one of the best Dōgen translations ever produced. The *Shōbō-genzō*, which was done only by the non-native speaker Yokoi, is rather poor in readability yet can still be recommended for some passages.

CHARACTER GLOSSARY

This list is sorted into the categories of names, titles, terms, temples/places, and eras. See appendix 1 for a list of *Treasury of the True Dharma Eye* fascicle titles with characters and translations.

NAMES

Abe Masao 阿部正雄
Bai Juyi 白居易
Baizhang 百丈
Banjin Dōtan 萬仭道坦
Bashō 芭蕉
Bodaidaruma 菩提達磨
Changlu Zongze 長蘆宗賾
Chengtian Zong 承天宗
Dahui 大慧
Daichi 大智
Daitō 大燈
Damei 大梅
Daolin 道林
Dayu Shouzhi 大愚守芝
Deshan 德山
Dōgen 道元
Dongshan 洞山
Eisai 榮西

Ejō 懷奘
Enni 圓爾
Etō Sokuō 衛藤即応
Fada 法達
Foxing 佛性
Furong Daokai 芙蓉道楷
Gemmyō 玄明
Gentō Sokuchū 玄透即中
Gesshū Sōkō 月舟宗胡
Gien 義演
Gikai 義介
Giun 義雲
Hakamaya Noriaki 袴谷憲昭
Hakuin 白隠
Hangyō Kōzen 版撓晃全
Hatano Yoshishige 波多野義重
He Yansheng 何燕生
Hōjō 北条
Hōjō Tokiyori 北条時頼
Hōnen 法然
Hongzhi 宏智
Huayan/Jp. Kegon 華嚴
Huike 慧可
Huineng 惠能
Ippen 一遍
Ishii Seijun 石井清純
Jakuen 寂円
Jien 慈円
Jizang 吉藏
Kagamishima Genryū 鏡島元隆
Kakushin/Jueshin 覺心
Kamo no Chōmei 鴨長の明
Katsudō Honkō 活動本興
Keizan 瑩山
Kishizawa Ian 岸沢惟安
Kōbun Chino Otagawa
Kōshō Chidō 光紹智堂
Kurebayashi Kōdō 榑林皓堂
Kyōgō 經豪
Liang 亮

Lingyun 靈雲
Linji/Rinzai 臨済
Manzan Dōhaku 卍山道白
Matsumoto Shirō 松本史朗
Mazu 馬祖
Meihō 明峰
Menzan Zuihō 面山瑞方
Mizuno Yaoko 水野弥穗子
Morimoto Kazuo 森本和夫
Mujaku Dōchū 無著蒩忠
Musō 夢窓
Myōzen 明全
Nakao Tōzen 中野東禅
Nanyang Huizhong 南陽慧忠
Nanyue 南嶽
Nichiren 日蓮
Nishiari Bokusan 西有穆山
Nishitani Keiji 西谷啓治
Niutou Fayong 牛頭法融
Nōnin 能忍
Ōkubo Dōshū 大久保道舟
Otagawa Kōbun Chino 乙川弘文
Rankei Dōryū 蘭溪道隆
Rujing 如淨
Ryōkan 良寬
Sawaki Kōdō 澤木興道
Senne 詮慧
Shigetsu Ein 指月慧印
Shigong 石鞏
Shinran 親鸞
Su Shi 蘇軾
Suzuki Daisetsu 鈴木大拙
Suzuki Shunryū 鈴木俊隆
Taiyō Bonsei 太容梵清
Tanabe Hajime 田辺元
Tatematsu Wahei 立松和平
Tenkei Denson 天桂傳尊
Tsunoda Tairyū 角田泰隆
Wansong 萬松
Watsuji Tetsurō 和辻哲郎

Wumen/Mumon 無門
Wuzu 五祖
Xiangyan 香嚴
Xuansha 玄沙
Xuanzang 玄奘
Xuefeng 雪峰
Yaoshan 藥山
Yoshida Kenkō 吉田兼好
Yuanwu 圜悟
Yunmen 雲門
Zeami 世阿弥
Zhanran 湛然
Zhaozhou 趙州
Zhengjue 正覺
Zhiyi 智顗
Zhizang 智藏
Zhongfeng Mingben 中峰明本

TITLES

Baoji jing 寶積經
Bendōhō 辨道法
Biyanlu/Jp. *Hekiganroku* 碧巖錄
Butsu hongyō jikkyō 仏本行集経
Chanyuan qinggui 禅苑清規
Chiji shingi 知事清規
Da Mohebore jing 大般若波羅蜜多經
Derrida kara Dōgen e: datsu-kochiku to shinjin datsuraku デリダから道元へ——脱構築と身心脱落
Dōgen no gengo uchū 道元の言語宇宙
Dōgen no tsuki 道元の月
Dōgen to Zeami 道元と世阿弥
Dōgen Zenji no in'yo kyōten-goroku no kenkyū 道元禅師の引用経典・語録の研究
Eihei kōroku 永平廣錄
Eihei shingi 永平清規
Eihei Shōbōgenzō shūsho taisei 永平正法眼藏蒐書大成
Fahuajing 蓮華經
Fanwang jing 梵網經
Fukanzazeng 普勧坐禅儀

Fushuku hanpō 赴粥飯法
Gakudōyōjinshū 学道用心集
Goshō 御抄
Gukanshō 愚管抄
Himitsu Shōbōgenzō 秘密正法眼蔵
Hōjōki 方丈記
Hōkyōki 宝慶記
Huayan jing 華嚴經
Ichiya *Hekiganroku* 一夜碧巖
Jingang jing 金剛經
Kana Shōbōgenzō 仮字正法眼蔵
Kenzeiki 建撕記
Kikigakishō 聞書抄
Kissa yōjōki 喫茶養生記
Kōzen gokokuron 興禪護國論
Kyōgyōshinshō 教行信証
Mana Shōbōgenzō 真字正法眼蔵
Nichiyōbi Shōbōgenzō 日曜日正法眼蔵
Niepan jing 涅槃經
Oku no hosomichi 奥の細道
Rujing 如淨語錄
Shamon Dōgen 沙門道元
Shinkokinwakashū 新古今和歌集
Shōbōgenzō/Zhengfayanzang 正法眼蔵
Shōbōgenzō-Eihei kōroku yōgo jiten 正法眼蔵―永平広録用語辞典
Shōbōgenzō hinmokuju 正法眼蔵品目頌
Shōbōgenzō keiteki 正法眼蔵啓迪
Shōbōgenzō no tetsugaku shikan 正法眼蔵の哲学私観
Shōbōgenzō sanbyakusoku 正法眼蔵三百則
Shōbōgenzō zuimonki 正法眼蔵隨聞記
Shoulenyan jing 首楞嚴經
Shōyōroku 從容錄
Shuryō shingi 衆寮箴規
Shushōgi 修證義
Shūso toshite no Dōgen Zenji 宗祖としての道元禅師
Sŏnmun yŏmsongjip 禅門拈頌集
Taishō shinshū daizōkyō 大正新脩大藏經
Taitaiko gogejarihō 対大己五夏闍梨法
Tan jing 壇經
Teiho Kenzeiki zue 訂補建撕記圖會

Tenzokyōkun 典座教訓
Tsurezuregusa 徒然草
Weimojie jing 佛説維摩詰經
Wumenguan 無門關
Xin jing/Shinkyō 心經
Zazengi/Zuochan yi 坐禅儀
Zazenshin/Zuochan zhen 坐禅箴
Zazenyōjinki 坐禅用心記

TERMS

ango 安居
ari 有り
arinomama 有りのまま
bansan 晩参
beppon 別本
bodai 菩提
bonbu 凡夫
boxie xianzheng 破邪顯正
bukkōjōji 仏向上事
Burakumin 部落民
busshō 仏性
busshō-genzen 仏性現前
busshō-mu 仏性無
butsu 仏 (佛)
butsudō 仏道
butsu-soku-ze-shin 仏即是心
byōdō 平等
chi'in 智音
chūmu ari mu setsu ari 中夢有り夢説有り
daichi 大地
daigo 大悟
daishugyō 大修行
Daizōkyō 大藏經
danka seido 壇家制度
darani 陀羅尼
Daruma-shū 達磨宗
datsu-kōchiku 脱構築
datsuraku 脱落
datsuraku datsuraku 脱落脱落

datsuraku no kankin 脱落の看經
datsuraku shinjin 脱落身心
Dentō Shūgaku 伝統宗学
dō/dao 道
dōji 同時
dōkan 道環
dōri 道理
dōshin 道心
dōtai 同体
dōtoku 道得
ehō shōhō 依報正報
en 縁
engi 縁起
fu 不
fudō 不同
fui 不違
fumai inga 不昧因果
fune no kikan 舟の機関
funi 不二
furaku inga 不落因果
furyū monji 不立文字
fushiryō 要思量
fusui/Ch. *fengshui* 風水
fuyō no kankin 不要の看經
fuzenna 不染汚
fuzenna no shushō 不染汚の修證
ga 我
gabyō 画餅
ganzei 眼睛
gasshō 合掌
ge 偈
gen 現
gendaiyaku 現代訳
genjitsu shugi 現実主義
genjō 現成
genjōkōan 現成公案
genjō suru 現成する
genzen 現前
genze riyaku 現世利益
Genzō-e 眼蔵会

Genzō-ka 眼蔵家
ginzan teppeki 銀山鉄壁
godoku tensai 誤読天才
gōjō 合成
goroku 語録
gotsu 兀
gotsugotsu 兀兀
gotsugotsuchi 兀兀地
Gozan/Ch. Wushan 五山
gūjin 究盡
gyō 行
gyōbutsu 行仏
gyōji 行持
gyōji dōkan 行持道環
gyōjū zaga 行住坐臥
Hakusan Gongen 白山権現
hannya 般若
haramitsu 波羅蜜
henka 変化
henzan 徧參
hi 非
higan 彼岸
higogen 非語言
Hihan Bukkyō 批判仏教
hinin 非人
hishiryō 非思量
hiyu 比喩
hō 法
hōgo 法語
hōi 法位
hokke 法華
hongaku 本覺
hongaku shisō 本覺思想
Honzan 本山
hosshin 発心
hosshō 法性
hossu 拂子
hotsumu inga 撥無因果
ho'u 鉢盂
i 意

ichinyo 一如
iigi soku buppō 威儀即仏法
ikka myōju 一顆明珠
immo 恁麼
inga 因果
ippō gūjin 一法究盡
issai 一切
issai shujō 一切衆生
isshin 一心
ittai 一体
ittengo 一転語
ittō 一等
jakugo 着語
ji 時
jigō jitoku 自業自得
jijiyū zanmai 自受用三昧
jijō kii 自淨其意
jinen gedō 自然外道
jippō 十方
jiriki 自力
jisetsu 時節
jisetsu nyakushi 時節若至
jishu 示衆
jōbutsu 成仏
jōdō 上堂
jōjū 常住
jōjū mu 常住無
jū-hōi 住法位
juki 授記
jūki 受記
juniji jūfukukūka 十二時中不虛過
junsui 純粋
ka か
kan (contemplation) 觀
kan (feeling) 感
kan (perception) 勘
kana 仮名
kanbun 漢文
kanji 漢字
kankin 看經

kanna zen/Ch. *kanhua chan* 看話禅
kannō dōkō 感應道交
Kannon/Ch. Guanyin 觀音
kanshi 漢詩
kattō 葛藤
kekkafuza 半跏趺坐
kenkyaku 間隙
kenshiki monsho 見色聞聲
kenshō 見性
kesa 袈裟
kimon 鬼門
kirin/Ch. *qilin* 麒麟
kitō jiin 祈祷寺院
kiyō 機要
ko 古
kōan 公案
kobusshin 古仏心
kobutsu 古仏
kōchiku 構築
Kohon 古本
kokochi 心地
kokoro 心
kokū 虚空
kokyō 古鏡
Komazawa Daigaku 駒沢大學
kōmyō 光明
kono yueni dōji ho[tsu]shin ari, dōshin hotsuji ari このゆえに同時發心あり同心發時あり
korai 去来
kū 空
kū-busshō 空仏性
kudoku 功徳
kurushii 苦しい
kūge 空華
kusa no ha 草の葉
kūshu genkyō 空手還郷
kuyō 供養
kyōge betsuden 教外別傳
kyōryaku (keireki) 経歴
kyusō 旧草

madoi ni madoi o kasaneru 惑いに惑いを重ねる
madoi no ue no madoi 惑いの上の惑い
maki (kan) 巻
manga 漫画
mappō 末法
menjū 面授
mi 未
mikkyō 密教
mitō 未到
mitsu 密
mokushō 默照禅
mokushō zen/Ch. *mozhao chan* 默照禅
monji Zen 文字禅
monogatari 物語
mono no aware 物の哀れ
mu 無
mu-busshō 無仏性
muchū setsumu 夢中説中
mufunbetsu 無分別
muga 無我
muji 無字
mujō 無常
mujō-busshō 無常仏性
mujō-kan 無常観
mujō no keijijōgaku 無常の形而上学
mukandan 無間断
musō 無相
mu u henyaku 無有變易
nashi 無し
nehan myōshin 涅槃妙心
nembutsu 念仏
nen 念
nikon 而今
nikon no sansui wa kobutsu no dō genjō nari 而今の山水は古仏の同現成なり
Noh 能
nyakushi 若至
nyo 如
Nyorai 如來
Nyorai *jōjū mu u henyaku* 如來常住無有變易
nyorai zenshin 如來全身

nyosui chūgetsu 如水中月
nyo wa ze nari 如は是なり
nyūshitsu 入室
Ōbaku 黄檗
oka 丘
ōsaku sendaba 王索仙陀婆
raihai 禮拜
renyun zizai 任運自在
Rinzai/Ch. Linji 臨濟
sabutsu 作仏
sahō 作法
sahō kore shūshi 作法是宗旨
samu 作務
sanzen 参禅
sasshi 冊子
satori 悟り
sendaba 仙陀婆
senjaku 選択
senmon dōjō 専門道場
Senni gedō 先尼外道
seppō 説法
setsu 説
setsumu ari muchū ari 説夢有り夢中有り
setsuna 刹那
shakujō 錫杖
shi 知
shidafu 士大夫
shikaku 始覺
shikan taza 只管打坐
shiki 識
shin 心
Shin Kamakura Bukkyō 新鎌倉仏教
shinfukatoku 心不可得
shingen 真現
shingi 清規
shinjin/Ch. *shenxin* 身心
shinjin datsuraku 身心脱落
shinjin dokudatsu 身心獨脱
shinjin mui 真人無位
shinjin ui 真人有位

shinnyo 真如
Shin Shūgaku 新宗学
shinsō 新草
shin-soku-butsu-ze 心即仏是
shirayama 白山
shiryō 思量
shiryō-hishiryō 思量非思量
shitsu 悉
shitsuu 悉有
shitsu-u-busshō 悉有仏性
shō 證
shōbō 正法
Shōbōgenzō kaiban kinshirei 正法眼蔵開版禁止令
shohō jissō 諸法實相
shōji 生死
shojō no shu 衆生修
shōkō 燒香
shōmetsu 生滅
shomu 諸無
shoshaku jushaku 將錯就錯
shōshi 松枝
shōtaichōyō 聖胎長養
shōya zenkigen shiya zenkigen 生也全機現死也全機現
shugyō 修行
shujō 衆生
shusan 修参
shushaku jōshaku 將錯就錯
shūshi 宗旨
shushō ittō 修證一等
shūtō fukko 宗統復古
sō 想
sōdō 僧堂
sōji 相似
soku-shin-butsu-ze 即心仏是
soku-shin-ze butsu 即心是仏
Sōtō/Ch. Caodong 曹洞
Sōtōshū Daigaku 曹洞大学
suteru 捨てる
tadashii 只しい
tada suware 只座れ

taigi 大疑
tariki 他力
taza 打坐
ten 點
tenbōrin 轉法輪
Tendai/Ch. Tiantai 天台
tenshin 點心
tenzo 典座
tokuki 得記
toriaezu 取敢えず
tōshi 曾到
tsuki 都機
u 有
u-busshō 有仏性
u henyaku 有變易
udonge 優曇華
ui shinnin 有位真人
uji 有時
uji subeshi 有時すべし
undō 雲堂
unsui 雲水
waka 和歌
wuyong shiyong 無用之用
xinchen 心塵
yako 野狐
yama 山
yamanaki 山なき
yōki 要機
yomikae 読替え
yuibutsu yobutsu 唯仏與仏
yuige 遺偈
yume 夢
zabutsu 坐仏
zanmai 三昧
zange 懺悔
zange metsuzai 懺悔滅罪
zazen/Ch. *zuochan*/Kr. *chamseon* 坐禅
ze 是
ze-butsu-shin-soku 是仏心即
Zen/Ch. Chan/Kr. Sŏn 禅 (禪)

zengo saidan 前後際斷
zenki 全機
zhengming 正名
zhier buxing feizhiye 知而不行非知也
zuihitsu 随筆

TEMPLES/PLACES

Anyō'in 夏安院
Daibutsji 大仏寺
Daijōji 大乗寺
Echizen 越前
Eiheiji 永平寺
Enryakuji 延暦寺
Entsūji 圓通寺
Fukakusa 深草
Fukui 福井
Fukushima 福島
Hajakuji 波着寺
Hakusan 白山
Hangzhou 杭州
Heisenji 平泉寺
Hieizan 比叡山
Hōkyōji 宝慶寺
Hongzhou 洪州
Kenchōji 建長寺
Kenkon'in 乾坤院
Kenninji 建仁寺
Kippōji 吉峰寺
Kōshōji 興聖寺
Kyoto 京都
Kyushu 九州
Ningbo 宁波
Onjōji 園城寺
Rokuhara 六波羅
Sengakuji 泉岳寺
Sōjiji 總持寺
Tianmu shan 天目山
Tiantong shan 天童山
Tōfukuji 東福寺

Tōunji 洞雲寺
Yamashibu-dera 禪師峰寺
Yōkō'an 永興庵
Yōkōji 永光寺
Yoshimine-dera 吉峰寺
Zhejiang 浙江

ERAS

Bei (Northern) Song 北宋
Edo 江戸
Heian 平安
Kamakura 鎌倉
Meiji 明治
Muromachi 室町
Nan (Southern) Song 南宋
Song 宋
Tang 唐
Yuan 元

NOTES

1. CREATIVITY AND ORIGINALITY

1. This passage is from "The Way-Seeking Mind," which is also known as "The Buddhist Way," but since that is also the title of a different fascicle the alternative is generally used.
2. Other renderings of the title include: *Treasury of Insights Into the True Dharma*, or *Eye and Treasury of the True Dharma*; the term "eye" (*gen*) or "eyeball" (*ganzei*) refers to the inner source of insight and wisdom, whereas "treasury" indicates a storehouse or repository, usually an actual construction of a hall or library used to collect scrolls and other sacred objects.
3. Robert E. Buswell and Donald S. Lopez, eds., *The Princeton Dictionary of Buddhism* (Princeton, NJ: Princeton University Press, 2013), 1940–1941.
4. *Record of the Transmission of Illumination by the Great Ancestor, Zen Master Keizan* 太祖瑩山禪師撰述傳光録 *Taiso Keizan Zenji senjutsu Denkōroku, Volume Two: Introduction, Front Matter, Glossary, and Bibliography*, ed. T. Griffith Foulk (Tokyo: Sōtōshū Shūmuchō, 2017), 91.
5. The title was first used for a collection of commentaries in China by Dahui (1089–1163), who was from a different lineage and was considered a rival by Dōgen; in Japan, the title was attributed to a short kōan collection by Keizan (1268–1325), one of the foremost Sōtō ancestors.
6. The main modern collection of the Buddhist canon (*seiten*) is the *Taishō shinshū daizōkyo*, which includes an important edition of the *Treasury* in vol. 82, no. 2582, with 95 fascicles; however, as will be explained, this is no longer considered to be the most accurate edition.
7. Citations for these sayings are: a) Genjōkōan: Dōgen 1.3, Nearman 32, Tanahashi 30; b) Sokushin zebutsu: Dōgen 1.53, Nearman 46, Tanahashi 43; c) Sansuikyō: Dōgen 1.328, Nearman 155, Tanahashi 164; d) Gabyō: Dōgen 1.273, Nearman 523, Tanahashi 449; e) Kūge: Dōgen 1.130, Nearman 566, Tanahashi 461; f) Zazenshin: Dōgen 1.104, Nearman 336, Tanahashi 303; g) Kattō: Dōgen 1.416, Nearman 577, Tanahashi

478–479; h) Busshō: Dōgen 1.17, Nearman 248, Tanahashi 238; i) Uji: Dōgen 1.243, Nearman 139, Tanahashi 107; and j) Muchū setsumu: Dōgen 1.297, Nearman 504, Tanahashi 433–434.
8. Gudo Wafu Nishijima, *Understanding the Shobogenzo* (Woods Hole, MA: Windbell, 1992), 2–5.
9. Before Dōgen's era, Japanese Buddhist monk-scholars universally read and wrote in Chinese, that is, with only characters used in continental syntax pronounced in a Japanese approximation of Chinese pronunciation. The Japanese writing system Dōgen used in the *Treasury* combines Chinese ideographs with Japanese phonetic letters. Its grammar has inflections and parts of speech, so the sentence structure is usually more explicit than Chinese syntax.
10. Puqun Li, *A Guide to Asian Philosophy Classics* (New York: Broadway Press, 2012), 328.
11. Heinrich Dumoulin, *Zen Buddhism: A History, Japan.* 2 vols. (New York: Macmillan, 1988), 2:51.
12. Heinrich Dumoulin, *Zen Enlightenment: Origins and Meaning* (New York: Weatherhill, 1979), 90.
13. Dumoulin, *Zen Buddhism*, 73.
14. Pedro Piquero Ferreras, trans., *Shōbōgenzō: Tesoro del verdadero ojo del Dharma*, 4 vols. (Málaga, SP: Sirio, 2013–2016). This Spanish translation is based on the four-volume English translation with notes and appendices by Gudo Nishijima and Chodo Cross, *Master Dogen's Shobogenzo* (Woods Hole, MA: Windbell, 1994). Also, a German translation is based in part on Nishijima and Cross and in part on the original Japanese: Werner Kristkeitz, trans., *Shōbōgenzō: Die Schatzkammer des wahren Dharma-Auges*, 4 vols. (Heidelberg: Werner Kristkeitz Verlag, 2008–2012). Note also an important translation into Mandarin: He Yansheng, trans., *Zhengfayanzang* (Beijing: Zongjiao wenhua chubanshe, 2003). See appendix 4.
15. Giun, *Verse Comments on the Treasury* [*Shōbōgenzō hinmokuju*], in *Taishō shinshū daizōkyō*, vol. 82:476; this commentary examines a particular version of the *Treasury* containing 60 fascicles that was, due to Giun's strong influence, considered the standard edition during the late medieval period.
16. David E. Riggs, "The Life of Menzan Zuihō, Founder of Dōgen Zen," *Japan Review* 16 (2004): 92 (67–100).
17. There are at least five books in English available on "Realization Here and Now," and two on "Mountains and Rivers Proclaiming the Sūtras"; thematic studies of the *Treasury* tend to focus on the topics of time, meditation, aesthetics, nature, and ethics.
18. For the first two years Eiheiji temple—*ji* means temple—was known as Daibutsuji; Dōgen changed its name in 1246.
19. Pierre Souyri, *The World Turned Upside Down: Medieval Japanese Society* (New York: Columbia University Press, 2003); for a brief discussion of Dōgen's role, see 77–78.
20. Eisai made two trips abroad. The first lasted for just six months in 1167, when he went to study Tiantai Buddhism but discovered that the Chan school had been dominant in China for a couple of centuries during a prolonged lull in Japanese travels to the continent. His second journey was from 1187 to 1191; during this trip he attained enlightenment at Mount Jingshan temple near Mount Tiantong, a site Dōgen visited in 1225, and received lineal transmission in the Linji Chan school before returning home to introduce and implement these teachings.

21. The main traditional biographical source is the *Record of Kenzei* (*Kenzeiki*), which was first published in 1472, then revised with extensive annotations by Edo period monk-scholar Menzan Zuihō in the *Teiho Kenzeiki* published in 1752, and finally given over sixty illustrations in the *Teiho Kenzeiki zue* produced in 1803; see Nara Yasuaki, et al., eds., *Your Principles of Practice and Realization* [*Anata dake no Shushōgi*] (Tokyo: Shōgakukan, 2001).
22. The designation "Five Mountains" was later used in Japan for the main Rinzai Zen temples located in both Kyoto and Kamakura.
23. *Rujing's Recorded Sayings* [*Rujing yulu*, Jp. *Nyojō goroku*], in *Taishō shinshū daizōkyō*, no. 2002A.
24. However, the Caodong predecessor Hongzhi (1091–1157) did one time use the expression, "Body and mind spontaneously drop off (身心獨脱, pronounced *shinjin dokudatsu*), and movement and stillness are both forgotten"; *Taishō shinshū daizōkyō*, vol. 48:40c. In other contexts Hongzhi used the term *datsuraku* for casting or dropping off.
25. As examined in chapter 8, the practice methods cited by Rujing are supported by Dōgen, except for the *nembutsu* chant, which is compared in "Discerning the Way" to the pointless "croaking of a frog without producing any benefit" (Bendōway: Dōgen 2.466, Nearman 8, Tanahashi 8); however, if the term *nembutsu* (lit. "thinking of Buddha") is interpreted more broadly to represent a state of mindfulness, then it too applies to Dōgen's practice.
26. Hee-Jin Kim, *Dōgen Kigen—Mystical Realist* (Tucson: University of Arizona Press, 1975), 46.
27. Dōgen 3.34; see Taigen Dan Leighton and Shohaku Okumura, trans., *Dōgen's Extensive Record* (Boston: Wisdom, 2010), 111.
28. See Steven Heine, *Chan Rhetoric of Uncertainty in the Blue Cliff Record: Sharpening a Sword at the Dragon Gate* (New York: Oxford University Press, 2016).
29. Frédéric Girard, *The Stanza of the Bell in the Wind: Zen and Nenbutsu in the Early Kamakura Period* (Tokyo: The International Institute for Buddhist Studies of The International College for Postgraduate Buddhist Studies, 2007), 30 (modified).
30. Girard, *The Stanza of the Bell in the Wind*, 30.
31. He Yansheng, *Dōgen and Chinese Chan Thought* [*Dōgen to Chūgoku Zen no shisō*] (Kyoto: Hōzōkan, 2001), viii, xii.
32. Etō Sokuō, *Zen Master Dogen as Founding Patriarch*, trans. Ichiumura Shohei (Washington: North American Institute of Zen and Buddhist Studies, 2001), 455 (modified); the comment is attributed to Shigetsu Ein (1689–1764).
33. The phrase "existential moment" is proposed by Rein Raud, "The Existential Moment: Rereading Dōgen's Theory of Time," *Philosophy East and West* 62, no. 2 (2012): 153–173.
34. St. Augustine, *On Genesis*, ed. John E. Rotelle (Hyde Park, NY: New City Press, 2006), 389; and *The Confessions*, ed. Michael P. Foley (Indianapolis: Hackett, 2002), 242.
35. See, for example, the discussion in appendix B of the novel based largely on Dōgen's teachings about time evoked in a contemporary setting by Ruth Ozeki, *A Tale for the Time Being* (New York: Penguin, 2013), 409.
36. Hubert Nearman, O.B.C., trans., *Shōbōgenzō: The Treasure House of the Eye of the True Teaching, A Trainee's Translation of Great Master Dogen's Spiritual Masterpiece* (Mount Shasta, CA: Shasta Abbey Press, 2007), 160 (modified).
37. Nearman, *Shōbōgenzō*, 161; Japanese terms are added.

[262]   1. CREATIVITY AND ORIGINALITY

38. Thomas Cleary and J. C. Cleary, trans., *The Blue Cliff Record* (Boston: Shambhala, 2005), 129 (modified).
39. Steve Bein, trans., *Purifying Zen: Watsuji Tetsurō's Shamon Dōgen* (Honolulu: University of Hawaii Press, 2011).
40. See Etō Sokuō, *Zen Master Dogen as Founding Patriarch*.
41. Tanabe Hajime, *My Philosophical View of Dōgen's Treasury* [*Shōbōgenzō no tetsugaku shikan*] (Tokyo: Iwanami shoten, 1939), 11.
42. Like most other Buddhist-affiliated institutions of higher education in Japan, Komazawa University began in the 1880s as a kind of advanced seminary housed at a couple of temples in Tokyo. The name was changed once it became a secular institution in the early 1900s, and after education reforms during the American Occupation it became a full-fledged university. But it has always maintained a large Buddhist studies department teaching Zen and many other topics.
43. *The Zen Master Dōgen and the Moon* [*Dōgen no tsuki*] by Tatematsu Wahei was performed at the Kabuki-za Theater in Tokyo. According to "Zazen and the art of playwriting: A new kabuki drama shows the path to enlightenment," a review by Rei Sasaguichi, "In this refreshing modern kabuki play, Tatematsu truly conveys Dogen's message: Wherever we live, we can make it a place of spiritual discipline"; in *The Japan Times* (March 20, 2002), n.p.
44. The main critics were Mujaku Dōchu (1653–1744) of the Rinzai sect and Tenkei Denson (1648–1735), along with his numerous followers, from the Sōtō sect.
45. An example of a detailed discussion of various kinds of revisions made in the *Treasury* compares two versions of the fascicle on "Washing the Face" based on two different late medieval manuscripts in Ishii Seijun, "On 'Washing the Face' in the Kenbon'in and Tōunji Temple Versions" ["Kenkon'in bon 'Senmen' to Tōunji bon 'Senmen' ni tsuite"], *Komazawa Daigaku Bukkyōgakubu kenkyū kiyō*, part 1 (of 3), 48 (1991): 76–90.
46. The 60-fascicle edition of the *Treasury* leaves out over a dozen fascicles, apparently for the reason that they criticize various Chinese Chan luminaries.
47. Thomas P. Kasulis, "The Incomparable Philosopher: Dōgen on How to Read the *Shōbōgenzō*," in *Dōgen Studies*, ed. William R. LaFleur (Honolulu: University of Hawaii Press, 1985), 90.
48. Kasulis, "The Incomparable Philosopher," 90.
49. Li, *A Guide to Asian Philosophy Classics*, 305.
50. Professor Ishii Shūdō, in a conversation in his Komazawa University office on October 22, 2018.
51. Kasulis, "The Incomparable Philosopher," 90.

2. RECEPTIVITY AND RELIABILITY

1. Kagamishima Genryū, *Dōgen's Citations of Recorded Sayings and Sūtras* [*Dōgen Zenji no in'yō kyōten-goroku*] (Tokyo: Mokujisha, 1965). In carrying out this kind of examination of the text, researchers often disagree on some of the fine points that seem unclear or ambiguous since sources are sometimes incidentally or implicitly cited by Dōgen. The following is a list of the frequency of patriarchs cited, according to Kagamishima's textual analysis:

   Śākyamuni   69
   Huineng   35

Rujing	35*
Mahākāśyapa	26
Linji	26
Bodhidharma	25
Nanquan	22
Eka	21
Mazu	19
Dongshan	19*
Qingyuan	17
Baizhang	16
Zhaozhou	16
Yunmen	16
Yuanwu	14
Nanyang	12
Shitou	12
Xuansha	12
Huangbo	11
Guishan	11
Yaoshan	10
Hongzhi	8*
Furong	7*
Dahui	5

*Caodong lineage ancestors

2. Some examples of Rujing citations are not included in the official version of his record, so it appears that Dōgen improvised based on his recollections.
3. Hakuin, *Poison Blossoms from a Thicket of Thorn*, trans. Norman Waddell (Berkeley, CA: Counterpoint, 2014), 42–44. Hakuin praises Dōgen's commitment to continuing practice (*gyōji*), but the high regard in which Hakuin holds Dōgen contrasts sharply with the vigorous attacks he makes on contemporary Sōtō teachers for their "do-nothing" attitude toward training.
4. The warrior class was generally disposed to endorsing the Zen path, as shogun Hōjō Tokiyori and his successors favored Rinzai priests at temples in Kamakura, whereas the subsequent group of Ashikaga shoguns patronized monks in Kyoto, including Daitō (1282–1337) at Daitokuji temple and Musō (1275–1351) at Tenryūji temple.
5. William M. Bodiford, "The Rhetoric of Chinese Language in Japanese Zen," in *Zen Buddhist Rhetoric in China, Korea, and Japan*, ed. Christoph Anderl (Leiden: Brill, 2012), 285–314.
6. See Charlotte Eubanks, "Performing Mind, Writing Meditation: Dōgen's *Fukanzazengi* as Zen Calligraphy," *Ars Orientalia* 46 (2016): 173–197.
7. Rujing's lecture style is also discussed as "very rare and excellent" (Dōgen 2.72); Taigen Dan Leighton and Shohaku Okumura, trans., *Dōgen's Extensive Record* (Boston: Wisdom, 2010), 153–154.
8. Robert Aitken, trans., *The Gateless Barrier: The Wu-Men Kuan (Mumonkan)* (New York: North Point Press, 1991), 46.
9. In the fascicle on "Radiant Light," Dōgen criticizes a minister's silent response to the emperor's misleading question that is usually praised in Zen commentaries (Kōmyō: Dōgen 1.141, Nearman 486, Tanahashi 417–418).

10. The Sōtō Zen Fourth Patriarch Keizan also compiled a special kōan collection containing ten cases with prose commentary that is known as the *Private* (*Himitsu*, lit. "Secret") *Shōbōgenzō*.
11. Hee-Jin Kim, "The Reason of Words and Letters: Dōgen and Kōan Language," in *Dōgen Studies*, ed. William R. La Fleur (Honolulu: University of Hawaii Press, 1985), 54–82.
12. Kim, "The Reason of Words and Letters," 62.
13. Dōgen also says in "This Mind Itself Is Buddha" that the process occurs "without any need for mortar or water to bind these elements together" (Sokushin zebutsu: Dōgen 1.57, Nearman 51, Tanahashi 46).
14. Dōgen 4.276; Leighton and Okumura, *Dōgen's Extensive Record*, 627.
15. He Yansheng, trans., *Zhengfayanzang* (Jp. *Shōbōgenzō*) (Beijing: Zongjiao wenhua chubanshe, 2003).
16. Jundo Cohen, "Dogen: A Love Supreme"; http://www.treeleaf.org/forums/showthread.php?9332-SIT-A-LONG-with-JUNDO-Dogen-A-Love-Supreme (accessed April 20, 2018); see also a series of books by Brad Warner beginning with *Don't Be a Jerk: And Other Practical Advice from Dogen, Japan's Greatest Zen Master* (San Francisco: New World Library, 2016).
17. See Keiji Nishitani, *Religion and Nothingness*, trans. Jan van Bragt (Berkeley: University of California Press, 1982).
18. Martin Heidegger, *Being and Time*, trans. John Macquarrie and Edward Robinson (Oxford: Blackwell, 1962), 401.
19. T. S. Eliot, *The Four Quartets* (Orlando, FL: Harcourt, 1971), 13.
20. Ruth Ozeki, *A Tale for the Time Being* (New York: Penguin, 2013), 409.
21. Morimoto Kazuo, *From Derrida to Dōgen: Deconstruction and Casting off Body-Mind* [*Derrida kara Dōgen e: datsu-kochiku to shinjin datsuraku*] (Tokyo: Fukutake Books, 1989); the term *kōchiku* (construction) suggests theories of architectural design rather than the act of building.
22. Jan Hokenson, *Japan, France, and East-West Aesthetics: French Literature, 1867–2000* (Teaneck, NJ: Fairleigh Dickenson University Press, 2004), 370.
23. On the role of women see Miriam L. Levering, "'Raihaitokuzui' and Dōgen's Views of Gender and Women: A Reconsideration," in *Dōgen and Sōtō Zen*, ed. Steven Heine (New York: Oxford University Press, 2015), 46–73; see also Michiko Yusa, "Dōgen and the Feminine Presence: Taking a Fresh Look Into His Sermons and Other Writings," *Religions* 9 (2018): 1–22.
24. There is a contrast between the approaches in "Attaining the Marrow Through Veneration," which supports women in the 75-fascicle edition, and "The Merits of Becoming a Monk," which is the first fascicle in the 12-fascicle edition; differences between these editions of the *Shōbōgenzō* are discussed in chapters 3 and 8.
25. For some writings by the leading thinkers of the movement, Hakamaya Noriaki and Matsumoto Shirō, in addition to various responses by Japanese and Western scholars, see Jamie Hubbard and Paul L. Swanson, eds., *Pruning the Bodhi Tree: The Storm Over Critical Buddhism* (Honolulu: University of Hawaii Press, 1997).
26. See Brian Victoria, *Zen at War*, 2nd ed. (Lanham, MD: Rowman and Littlefield, 2006).
27. Jason M. Wirth, *Mountains, Rivers, and the Great Earth: Reading Gary Snyder and Dōgen in an Age of Ecological Crisis* (Albany: State University of New York Press, 2017), back cover.

3. MULTIPLICITY AND VARIABILITY

1. Mizuno Yaoko, ed., *Daichi: Geju, Jūni hōgo, kana hōgo* (Tokyo: Kōdansha, 1994), 113.
2. There is a debate about whether Ejō intended to imply the single twelfth fascicle ("Eight Realizations of a Great Person") or the entire 12-fascicle edition of the *Treasury*.
3. The early modern Sōtō poet Ryōkan (1758–1831) wrote a prominent poem about his first reading of Dōgen's *Extensive Record*; see Taigen Dan Leighton and Shohaku Okumura, trans., *Dōgen's Extensive Record* (Boston: Wisdom, 2010), 69–71.
4. Examples of these fascicles include "Washing the Face," "Inheritance Certificates," "Merits of the Robe," "Bodhisattva Kannon," "Face-to-Face Transmission," "Plum Blossoms," and "Realizing the Marrow Through Veneration."
5. Kim Hee-Jin, *Dōgen Kigen—Mystical Realist* (Tucson: University of Arizona Press, 1975), 4.
6. Additionally, new buildings were constructed at Eiheiji and revised biographies of Dōgen were produced, including novels, Kabuki plays, TV shows, and issues of *manga* (comics).
7. William M. Bodiford, "Textual Genealogies of Dōgen," in *Dōgen: Textual and Historical Studies*, ed. Steven Heine (New York: Oxford University Press, 2012), 24; the revising process began in late 1242 and probably continued to the end of Dōgen's life.
8. Not all editions containing 95 (or sometimes 96) fascicles are identical to the Main Temple Edition because the order and exact content may vary.
9. Tsunoda Tairyū, *Intellectual Studies of Zen Master Dōgen* [*Dōgen zenji no shisōteki kenkyū*] (Tokyo: Shunjūsha, 2015), v.
10. There is a theory that this text, discovered posthumously, was actually created by Dōgen late in his life.
11. Nishiari Bokusan, a famous commentator on the *Treasury* at the beginning of the twentieth century, has suggested that the three main fascicles are the "Ben-Gen-Bu," that is, "Discerning the Way" ("Bendōwa"), "Realization Here and Now" ("Genjōkōan"), and "Buddha Nature" ("Busshō").
12. Various fascicles in which indirect criticism of the Daruma school is mentioned include "Discerning the Way," "Buddha Nature," "This Mind Itself Is Buddha," "Sustained Exertion," "The Samādhi of Self-Realization," "Transmission Documents," "Flowers in the Sky," and "The Moon"; see Vincent Michaël Nicolaas Breugem, "From Prominence to Obscurity: A Study of the Darumashū: Japan's First Zen School," Ph.D. diss., Leiden University, 2012, 192–202. Also, some of Dōgen's harsh criticisms of Dahui were probably a veiled way of attacking the Daruma school because a member of Dahui's lineage was said to have given transmission to the disciples of Nōnin, founder of the Daruma school who sent them to China in his stead.
13. Examples include the topics of "Total Activity" (*zenki*) in sermon 52, "Realization Here and Now" (*genjōkōan*) in sermon 60, "Suchness" (*inmo*) in sermon 38, "Entangled Vines" (*kattō*) in sermon 46, "Great Awakening" (*daigo*) in sermon 62, "One Bright Pearl" (*ikkya myōjū*) in sermon 107, "Flowers in the Sky" (*kūge*) in sermon 162, "A King Asks for Saindhava" (*ōsaku sendaba*) in sermon 254, and "Udumbara Blossoms" (*udonge*) in sermon 308, among many other instances. Moreover, the central components of the fascicle on "Turning the Dharma Wheel" (*tenbōrin*) are nearly identical to sermon 179.

14. A primary example is included in "The Lancet of Zazen," to be discussed in chapter 7.
15. Bashō, *Narrow Road to the Far North and Other Travel Sketches*, trans. Nobuyuki Yuasa (London: Penguin, 1966), 138–139.
16. Kenchōji temple was awarded to an émigré monk from China, Rankei Dōryū (1213–1278, Ch. Lanqi Daolong).
17. This text compiled by Eiheiji abbot Kōshō Chidō in 1667 contains: *Tenzokyōkun* on rules for the chief cook with an emphasis on Dōgen's experiences in China, written in 1237; *Taitaiko gogejarihō* on how junior monks are respectful of their seniors, written in 1244; "*Bendōhō*" on daily conduct including meditation, written in 1246; *Fushuku hanpō* on serving and eating food, written in 1246; *Chiji shingi* on six senior administrative officers, written in 1246; and *Shuryō shingi* on the interactions of fellow monks, written in 1249; see Taigen Dan Leighton and Shohaku Okumura, trans., *Dōgen's Pure Standards for the Zen Community* (Albany: State University of New York Press, 1996).
18. This is also the case for "Deep Faith in Causality."
19. This is the fascicle "One Hundred and Eight Gates to Enlightenment."
20. Jakuen, who arrived from Mount Tiantong to join Dōgen's assembly in the 1230s, founded Hōkyōji in the 1260s and was followed there by Giun in the 1280s.
21. This edition actually contains 59 fascicles because "Sustained Exertion," which has two parts that are separated in other editions, is counted as one fascicle.
22. Senne also edited the first volume of Dōgen's 10-volume *Extensive Record*, which includes kanbun sermons given at Kōshōji, as well as the ninth and tenth volumes that cover Dōgen's kanbun poetry with over 250 examples. Giun, with Gien and others, assisted Ejō in transcribing and editing some of the *Treasury* fascicles in 1279, when he worked on "Empty Space," "Summer Retreat," and "Taking Refuge in the Three Jewels."
23. Etō Sokuō, *Zen Master Dōgen as Founding Patriarch*, trans. Ichiumura Shohei (Washington, DC: North American Institute of Zen and Buddhist Studies, 2001), 451.
24. See Ishii Shūdō, "On the Origins of *Kana Shōbōgenzō*" / *Kana Shōbōgenzō* wa itsu seiritsu shitta ka," *Komazawa Daigaku kenkyūsho nenpō* 28 (2016): 234–280.

4. REALITY AND MENTALITY

1. According to Kazuaki Tanahashi, "Nowadays many people including those in the Western world regard him as one of the greatest thinkers of East Asia. But regarding Dogen as a thinker, writer, poet, or even a mystic or religious figure may not represent him fully. He was all these combined. And above all he was a master of nonthinking." In "Dogen: A Thirteenth-Century Post-Existentialist," *Dharma Eye* 9 (2001), n.p.
2. Masao Abe, *A Study of Dōgen: His Philosophy and Religion*, ed. Steven Heine (Albany: State University of New York Press, 1994), 19.
3. Abe, *A Study of Dōgen*, 18.
4. See John R. McRae, *The Northern School and the Formation of Early Ch'an Buddhism* (Honolulu: University of Hawaii Press, 1986), 73–100.
5. This interpretative style is also used in the Sino-Japanese (*kanbun*) sermons in Dōgen's *Extensive Record*.
6. Russell T. McCutcheon, "In Memoriam: Jonathan Z. Smith (1938–2017)," *Religious Studies News* (January 5, 2018). Similar to a characterization of Smith's

interpretative method by one of his colleagues, Dōgen realizes that genuine answers to the matter of here and now vis-à-vis there and then, as one of countless examples of typically counterproductive oppositions, are to be found "in that playful, *but always consequential*, middle space, somewhere between the strange and the familiar... often [grasped] with a wink, sometimes a laugh or maybe even a scowl... and plenty of gestures, shrugs, and expressions." McCutcheon indicates that an interpreter's personality and proclivities, including idiosyncratic or eclectic reactions to particular topics of discussion, contribute to our understanding of their overall interpretative approach.

7. See Eitan Bolokan, "Dimensions of Nonduality in Dōgen's Zen: A Study in the Terminology of the *Shōbōgenzō* and the *Eihei-Kōroku*," Ph.D. diss., Tel Aviv University, 2017.
8. Bolokan, "Dimensions of Nonduality in Dōgen's Zen."
9. The image of the moon is used elsewhere, including in two seemingly contradictory ways in "Realization Here and Now."
10. This recalls a similar but better-known anecdote often used as a kōan case involving Huineng's interaction with a couple of novices about the waving of a flag in the breeze, which is included as case 29 in the *Gateless Gate* collection.
11. "The Perfection of Great Wisdom" was the first sermon presented at Kōshōji temple, and a decade later, "Empty Space" was the first presented at Eiheiji temple, showing the importance of Rujing's imagery for interpreting the sacred space of these monastic settings.
12. It also appears in Dōgen's *Extensive Record* and the *Record of the Hōkyō Era*.
13. Dōgen 4.220; Taigen Dan Leighton and Shohaku Okumura, trans., *Dōgen's Extensive Record* (Boston: Wisdom, 2010), 575.
14. Dōgen 4.256; Leighton and Okumura, *Dōgen's Extensive Record*, 611.
15. David Rogacz, "Knowledge and Truth in the Thought of Jizang (549–623)," *The Polish Journal of the Arts and Culture* 16 (2015): 125–138.
16. Elsewhere Dōgen refers to other examples that cannot be fully comprehended by ordinary discernment, including a banner, a needle, or a mallet; a fly whisk, a staff, or a shout.
17. Kate Springer, "Woljeongsa Temple: Spend the night in a South Korean landmark," CNN Travel (February 19, 2018), n.p.; this account refers to experiences promoting spiritual well-being through drinking tea with a monk, attending a workshop on crafting traditional prayer beads, or taking a walk through the dense fir pine forest. The atmosphere recalls Rujing's injunction that, on returning to Japan, Dōgen should steer clear of worldly distractions that affect urban life, and also resembles Yunmen's inspirational Zen saying, "Every day is a good day."
18. Springer, "Woljeongsa Temple."
19. Hee-Jin Kim, *Dōgen Kigen—Mystical Realist* (Tucson: University of Arizona Press, 1975), 262.
20. Dōgen also wrote a Japanese *waka* verse in five lines with thirty-one syllables about this topic: "Colors of the mountains, / Streams in the valleys, / All in one, one in all / The voice and body / Of our Sakyamuni Buddha" (Dōgen 7.153); see Steven Heine, *The Zen Poetry of Dōgen: Verses from the Mountain of Eternal Peace* (Mt. Tremper, NY: Dharma Communications, 2005), 109. Waka translations generally do not try to capture the number of syllables in the original poem.
21. In the same fascicle, Dōgen makes a similar point regarding perspectives about mountains, which are natural phenomena perceived in various ways by different

[268]   4. REALITY AND MENTALITY

beings, yet are adorned with spiritual treasures that manifest buddhas. Therefore, "some see a grove of tropical trees and everything as earth and sand, grass, and rocks; others see the immaculate splendor of gold, silver, and seven treasures; others see a place for the practice of all buddhas in the three times; still others see it the inconceivable realm of true Dharma" (Sansuikyō: Dōgen 1.318, Nearman 144–145, Tanahashi 156). Dōgen further cautions against limited views adhering to only one outlook while disregarding a holistic standpoint that embraces the diversity of particular circumstances.

5. TEMPORALITY AND EPHEMERALITY

1. Dōgen's view is sometimes referred to as a "metaphysics of impermanence" (*mujō no keijijōgaku*); also, the term "contemplation" (*kan* 観) is a homophone for another character associated with reacting to impermanence that means "sensing" or "feeling" (感) the significance of impermanence (*mujō* 無常), which implies an emotional response that does not attain enlightenment.
2. See Steven Heine, trans., *The Zen Poetry of Dōgen: Verses from the Mountain of Eternal Peace* (Mt. Tremper, NY: Dharma Communications, 2005).
3. See Martin Heidegger, *The Event*, trans. Richard Rojcewicz (Bloomington: Indiana University Press, 2012).
4. See Joan Stambaugh, *Impermanence Is Buddha-Nature: Dōgen's Understanding of Temporality* (Honolulu: University of Hawaii Press, 1990).
5. Dōgen 3.166–168; see Taigen Dan Leighton and Shohaku Okumura, trans., *Dōgen's Extensive Record* (Boston: Wisdom, 2010), 246.
6. Dōgen 7.170; see Heine, *The Zen Poetry of Dōgen*, 122.
7. Dōgen wrote the following waka: "Petals of the peach blossom / Unfolding in the spring breeze, / Sweeping aside all doubts / Amid the distractions of / Leaves and branches"; Dōgen 7.156, Heine, *The Zen Poetry of Dōgen*, 113.
8. This reading is suggested by Masao Abe, *A Study of Dōgen: His Philosophy and Religion*, ed. Steven Heine (Albany: State University of New York Press, 1994), 35, from the original, "The Tathāgata (*nyorai* 如來) always abides (*jōjū* 常住), without any change (*muuheni* 無有變易)." In the original compound, *muu* or *mu-u* signifies negation, but once the *u* is separated and independent it indicates affirmation.
9. Dōgen 5:218 (case 182); Kazuaki Tanahashi and John Daido Loori, trans., *The True Dharma Eye: Zen Master Dōgen's Three Hundred Kōans* (Boston: Shambhala, 2005), 244–246.
10. *Treasury* fascicles with the term "mind" (*shin* 心) in the title include "This Mind Itself Is Buddha [Sokushin zebutsu]," "The Ungraspable Mind [Shinfukatoku]," "Learning the Way Through Body-Mind [Shinjingakudo]," "Explaining Mind, Explaining Nature [Sesshin sesshō]," "The Ancient Buddha Mind [Kobusshin]," "Triple World Is Mind Only [Sangai yuishin]," "Arousing the Supreme Mind [Hotsumujōshin]," "Arousing the Aspiration for Awakening [Hotsubodaishin]," plus "The Way-Seeking Mind [Dōshin]."
11. A *setsuna* refers to the smallest possible unit of time. Within the context of how time is measured, it is approximately one seventy-fifth of a second; within one *setsuna*, there are 900 instances of arising and ceasing. One human reflection or moment of thought takes up 90 *setsuna*; snapping one's fingers takes up 63 setsuna, and 32,820,000 *setsuna* occur in one day.

12. Kenkō and Chōmei, *Essays in Idleness and Hōjōki*, trans. Meredith McKinney (New York: Penguin Classics, 2014).
13. See also Dōgen 3.36; Leighton and Okumura, *Dōgen's Extensive Record*, 113.
14. Dōgen 7.157; see Heine, *The Zen Poetry of Dōgen*, 113.
15. According to the original passage, "Ask not—we cannot know—what end the gods have set for you, for me.... How much better to endure whatever comes.... Be wise, strain the wine; and since life is brief, prune back far-reaching hopes! Even while we speak, envious time has passed: pluck the day, putting as little trust as possible in tomorrow!" Also recalled is *Ecclesiastes'* deliberation on the "vanity of vanities."
16. See Tanabe Hajime, "Memento Mori," trans. V. H. Viglielmo, *Philosophical Studies of Japan* (1959): 1–12.
17. Thomas Cleary, trans., *Book of Serenity: One Hundred Zen Dialogues* (Shambhala: Publications, 2005) case 77, 324–331; see also *Taishō shinshū daizōkyō* 48.204c.
18. Dōgen 7.175; Heine, *The Zen Poetry of Dōgen*, 106. Also, Dōgen's death verse (*yuige*), written in kanbun style, reads: "For fifty-three years following the way of heaven, / Now leaping beyond and shattering every barrier. / Amazing to cast off all attachments while still alive, / Plunging into the depths of the Yellow Springs." In Dōgen 7.306; Heine, *The Zen Poetry of Dōgen*, 97.

6. EXPRESSIVITY AND DECEPTIVITY

1. Hee-Jin Kim, "The Reason of Words and Letters: Dōgen and Kōan Language," in *Dōgen Studies*, ed. William R. La Fleur (Honolulu: University of Hawaii Press, 1985), 63.
2. Kim, "The Reason of Words and Letters," 79.
3. The *Treasury* is one of about sixty literary works included in *Japanese Classics* [*Nihon no koten*], ed. Ogawa Yoshio (Tokyo: Sekai bunkasha, 2007); the only other work by a medieval sectarian founder on the list is by Dōgen's contemporary, Shinran.
4. See Terada Tōru and Mizuno Yaoko, eds., *Dōgen*, 2 vols., Nihon shisō taikei (Tokyo: Iwanami shoten, 1970–1971). The authors who analyzed "Sustained Exertion" were the literary historian Yasuraoka Kōsaku and the Zen scholar Ishii Shūdō. In addition, Takasaki Jikidō, a Buddhist studies researcher, collaborated with cultural/literary studies expert Umehara Takeshi on a prominent commentary on Dōgen, *Learning from the Master (Dōgen)* [*Kobutsu no manebi (Dōgen)*] (Tokyo: Kadokawa shoten, 1969).
5. See Terada Tōru, *Dōgen's Universe of Language* [*Dōgen no gengo uchū*] (Tokyo: Iwanami shoten, 1974); Nishio Minoru, *Dōgen and Zeami* [*Dōgen to Zeami*] (Tokyo: Iwanami shoten, 1965).
6. According to one outlook, the efforts of both donkeys and horses reflect negative tendencies in that the donkey is stubborn in his ignorance yet enters the water even if he cannot swim, whereas the horse breaks free from attachments but also tries to float aimlessly above the fray in an unrealistic way.
7. Kim, "The Reason of Words and Letters," 79.
8. Kazuaki Tanahashi, ed., *Treasury of the True Dharma Eye: Zen Master Dogen's Shobo Genzo* (Boston: Shambhala, 2010), xxx.
9. Steve Bein, trans., *Purifying Zen: Watsuji Tetsurō's Shamon Dōgen* (Honolulu: University of Hawaii Press, 2011), 106.

10. Of course, one should avoid setting up an overly binary characterization, since almost all Zen masters of the era were on both sides of the matter, with critics of literary pursuits almost always writing a great deal of poetry because that was considered a *de rigeur* activity for all teachers.
11. Thomas Cleary, trans., *The Blue Cliff Record* (Berkeley, CA: Bukkyo Dendo Kyokai, 1998), 9 (modified).
12. Thomas Cleary, trans., *Book of Serenity: One Hundred Zen Dialogues* (Boulder, CO: Shambhala, 2005), 422–424 (case 98).
13. Isshu Miura and Ruth Fuller Sasaki, *Zen Dust: The History of the Koan and Koan Study in Rinzai (Linji) Zen* (Quirin Press, rpt. 2015), 180.
14. See Steven Heine, *Zen Skin, Zen Marrow: Will the Real Zen Buddhism Please Stand Up?* (New York: Oxford University Press, 2008).
15. Robert Aitken, trans., *The Gateless Barrier: The Wu-Men Kuan (Mumonkan)* (New York: North Point Press, 1991), 132; this version gives a different translation. Also, the poem's ending is similar to the verse comment in the *Blue Cliff Record*, case 54.
16. Some of this content is also contained in sermon 179 in Dōgen's *Extensive Record* (Dōgen 3.118); see also Taigen Dan Leighton and Shohaku Okumura, trans., *Dōgen's Extensive Record* (Boston: Wisdom, 2010), 198–199.
17. As Dōgen points out, this saying is derived from a passage in the *Heroic March Sūtra* (Ch. *Shoulenyan jing*, Jp. *Shūryōgenkyō*).
18. Taigen Daniel Leighton, *Visions of Awakening Space and Time: Dōgen and the Lotus Sūtra* (New York: Oxford University Press, 2008), 11.
19. Leighton, *Visions of Awakening Space and Time*, 119.
20. Yuko Wakayama shows that Dōgen's interpretation of the Deshan dialogue was evolving in different versions during the early 1240s in "The Formation of *Kana Shōbōgenzō*: Tracing Back Beppon (Draft Edition) 'Shinfukatoku' / *Kana Shōbōgenzō wa dono yōni seiritsu shitta ka*," *Komazawa Daigaku kenkyūsho nenpō* 28 (2016): 281–312.
21. In the alternative (*beppon*) version of the fascicle included in the 95-fascicle edition, Dōgen rather significantly recasts some of the basic elements of the case narrative.
22. See Gudo Nishijima and Chodo Cross, *Master Dogen's Shobogenzo*, 4 vols. (Woods Hole, MA: Windbell Press, 1994), I:293–321.
23. According to traditional accounts, Dōgen recited and wrote on the wall in his inner chambers near the end of his life a *Lotus Sūtra* passage from chapter 21 on "The Divine Powers of Tathāgata": "Those who receive, uphold, read, recite, explain, write out, and cultivate the sūtra through speaking about it, in whatever land they may be, are in a place where the sūtra is kept: whether in a garden, in a forest, or beneath a tree; in a monastic dwelling or the abode of white-robed monks; in a palace or hall; or in the mountains, valleys, or wilderness. In all of these places they should build a shrine and make offerings. Why? Because these sacred places are where all buddhas gain supreme enlightenment, turn the Dharma wheel, and enter nirvāṇa."
24. A prominent early Chan figure who appreciated the *Lotus Sūtra* was the founder of the Oxhead school in northern China, Niutou Fayong (594–657; Jp. Gozu Hōyū). It is said that Niutou once lectured for seven days in midwinter on the sūtra while two stalks of golden hibiscus flowers emerged from the snow-covered ground, blooming only until his lectures ended. The various stories of Niutou's magical powers are commonly mentioned in the later Chan tradition, but usually in order to criticize his lack of true understanding in venerating scriptures.

25. Anthony C. Yu, "The Quest for Brother Amor: Buddhist Intimations in *The Story of Stone*," *Harvard Journal of Asiatic Studies* 49, no. 1 (1989): 83; citing the *Laṅkāvatāra Sūtra*, trans. D. T. Suzuki (London: George Routledge and Sons, 1932), 37–38.
26. Kuang-ming Wu, *The Butterfly as Companion* (Albany: State University of New York Press, 1990), 225.
27. Wu, *The Butterfly as Companion*, 225.
28. These four levels can be characterized as: ongoing practice after realization; practice before and thus aspiring for the experience of realization; uncertainty about whether and how to practice; and indifference to practice, yet with an underlying awareness of its importance.
29. In *Shōbōgenzō chūkai zensho*, 11 vols., ed. Jinbo Nyoten and Andō Bun'ei (Tokyo: Nihon bussho kankōkai, 1956–1957), 1:192.
30. Giun, *Verse Comments on the Treasury* [*Shōbōgenzō hinmokuju*], in *Taishō shinshū daizōkyō*, vol. 82:476.

7. REFLEXIVITY AND ADAPTABILITY

1. This represents Dōgen's first citation of a kōan case in the 1231 composition.
2. Mary Eberstadt, "The Prophetic Power of Humanae Vitae: Documenting the realities of the sexual revolution," *First Things* (April 1, 2018), n.p.; other affinities include the idea that time is as powerful as space, unity prevails over the conflict, and the whole is superior to the part.
3. Taigen Daniel Leighton and Shohaku Okumura, trans., *Dōgen's Pure Standards for the Zen Community: A Translation of Eihei Shingi* (Albany: State University of New York Press), 17.
4. Cited in Hee-Jin Kim, *Dōgen on Meditation and Thinking: A Reflection on His View of Zen* (Albany: State University of New York Press, 2007), 97.
5. Kim, *Dōgen on Meditation and Thinking*, 97.
6. Unlike the earlier text carefully crafted in elegant Chinese, the later work is written in the vernacular language used in that era for informal Buddhist homiletic literature.
7. Yifa, *The Origins of Buddhist Monastic Codes in China: An Annotated Translation and Study of the Chanyuan Qinggui* (Honolulu: University of Hawaii Press, 2002), 41–45.
8. Leighton and Okumura, *Dōgen's Pure Standards for the Zen Community*, 13–14.
9. This alternative (*beppon*) version is not included in the Nearman translation.
10. Tsunoda Tairyū, *Various Issues in Dōgen's Thought: Based on Contemporary Religious Interpretations* [Dōgen Zenji ni okeru no shomondai: Kindai no shūgaku ronsō wo chūshin toshite] (Tokyo: Shunjūsha, 2017), 6.
11. Shohaku Okumura and Tom Wright, trans., *Shōbōgenzō Zuimonki: Sayings of Eihei Dōgen Zenji Recorded by Koun Ejō* (Tokyo: Soto-shu Shumucho, 2004), section 187; Dōgen 7.144.
12. Gudō Wafu Nishijima and Chodo Cross, *Master Dogen's Shōbōgenzō*, 4 vols. (Woods Hole, MA: Windbell Publications, 1994–1999), II:115.
13. This case is cited but without any explanation or commentary in both *Universal Recommendation* and "Principles of Zazen."
14. See Thomas P. Kasulis, *Zen Action, Zen Person* (Honolulu: University of Hawaii Press, 1981).

15. Shohaku Okumura, trans., *The Heart of Zen: Practice Without Gaining-Mind* (Tokyo: Soto-shu Shumucho, 1988), 33.
16. Eitan Bolokan, "Dimensions of Nonduality in Dōgen's Zen: A Study in the Terminology of the *Shōbōgenzō* and the *Eihei-Kōroku*," Ph.D. diss., Tel Aviv University, 2017, 170.
17. Dōgen 7.149; Okumura and Wright, *Shōbōgenzō Zuimonki*, 198.
18. This fascicle does not appear in the Nearman or Tanahashi translations.
19. Even though Dōgen is quite critical of Chan Master Dahui, in his assessment of weaknesses in the approach of silent illumination associated with the Caodong school he seems to agree with the Linji school adversary.
20. Uchiyama Kōshō, *Zen Teaching of Homeless Kodo* (Boston: Wisdom, 2014), section 49.
21. Ishii Seijun and Tsunoda Tairyū, eds., *Zen and Apple: Steve Jobs on How to Live* [*Zen to Ringo: Suteebu Jobuzu to iu ikikata*] (Tokyo: MP, 2012).
22. See Suzuki Shunryu, *Zen Mind, Beginner's Mind* (Boulder, CO: Shambhala, 2011).
23. See Kobun Chino Otogawa, *Embracing Mind: The Zen Talks of Kobun Chino Otogawa*, ed. Judy Cosgrove (Los Gatos, CA: Jikoji Zen Center, 2016). In the 2005 commencement speech delivered about a year after being diagnosed with pancreatic cancer, Jobs did not mention the practice of zazen specifically but referred to a Dōgen-like saying, "If you live each day as if it was your last, someday you'll most certainly be right."
24. See Ian Reader, "Zazenless Zen? The Position of Zazen in Institutional Zen Buddhism," *Japanese Religions* 14, no. 3 (1986): 7–27.
25. See Jason M. Wirth et al., eds., *Engaging Dōgen's Zen: The Philosophy of Practice as Awakening* (Boston: Wisdom, 2017).

8. RITUALITY AND CAUSALITY

1. According to a scripture Dōgen cites, a monk should always have for personal use eighteen indispensable items, including a tooth-cleaning willow twig, soap, three monastic robes, a water jug, an alms bowl, a bowing mat, a mendicant's traveling staff, an incense burner, a clothes box, a water filter, a towel, a razor, something to light a fire with, tweezers, a hammock, a sūtra and a rules text, an image of Buddha, and an image of a bodhisattva (Senmen: Dōgen 47, Nearman 675, Tanahashi 65).
2. Zuzana Kubovčáková, "Believe It or Not: Dōgen on the Question of Faith," *Studia Orientalia Slovaca* 12, no. 1 (2018): 214–215.
3. Kaoru Nonomura, *Eat Sleep Sit*, trans. Juliet Winters Carpenter (New York: Kodansha USA, 2015), based on an original 1996 publication.
4. The injunction is mentioned in the following writings listed in chronological order: (1) *Record of Hōkyō Era* (1226); (2) *Treasury* "Discerning the Way" (1231, with no mention of Rujing); (3) *Extensive Record* 9.85–86 (1236); (4) *Extensive Record* 1.33 (1240, with no mention of Rujing); (5) *Treasury* "Sustained Exertion" (1242); (6) *Treasury* "Sounds of Valleys, Colors of Mountains" (1242); (7) *Treasury* "Buddhist Sūtras" (1243); (8) *Treasury* "The King of All Samādhis" (1244); and (9) *Extensive Record* 6.432 (1251). *Bendōwa* is included in the 95-fascicle version but not the 75-fascicle version of SH, so it can be considered an independent text. Also, *Hōkyōki*, a record of Dōgen's conversations conducted in the abbot's quarters of Rujing, may represent the first appearance of the passage; but some modern scholars have suggested that this text was actually compiled by Dōgen toward the end of his life.

8. RITUALITY AND CAUSALITY [273]

5. T. Griffith Foulk, "Just Sitting? Dōgen's Take on Zazen, Sutra Reading, and Other Conventional Buddhist Practices," in *Dōgen: Textual and Historical Studies*, ed. Steven Heine (New York: Oxford University Press, 2012), 75.
6. Foulk, "Just Sitting?" suggests that the practice of *nembutsu*, which Dōgen likens in "Discerning the Way" to the croaking of a frog, can alternately suggest the state of mindful awareness or visualization while concentrating on Buddha in ways that are quite similar to seated meditation.
7. Pei-Ying Lin, "Precepts and Lineage in Chan Tradition: Cross-Cultural Perspectives in Ninth Century East Asia," Ph.D. diss., SOAS, University of London, 2011, 3.
8. Lin, "Precepts and Lineage in Chan Tradition," 3.
9. Foulk, "Just Sitting?," 75.
10. Dōgen 4.22; Taigen Dan Leighton and Shohaku Okumura, *Dōgen's Extensive Record* (Boston: Wisdom, 2010), 389.
11. See Yifa, *The Origins of Buddhist Monastic Codes in China: An Annotated Translation and Study of the Chanyuan Qinggui* (Honolulu: University of Hawaii Press, 2002), 43–45.
12. Ann Heirman and Mattieu Torck, *A Pure Mind in a Clean Body: Bodily Care in the Buddhist Monasteries of Ancient India and China* (Gent, Belgium: Academia Press, 2002), 44; the authors point out that Dōgen's primary concern is with cleanliness of the mouth.
13. Heirman and Torck, *A Pure Mind in a Clean Body*, 44.
14. Natasha Heller, *Illusory Abiding: The Cultural Construction of the Chan Monk Zhongfeng Mingben* (Cambridge, MA: Harvard University Press, 2014), 220. Mingben was sought out for abbotships at Jingshan and Lingyin monasteries in Hangzhou, and officials of the Bureau of Tibetan and Buddhist Affairs were ordered to treat him with special deference. Today, the Mount Tianmu area is barely a two-hour drive from the city but still feels like a very different, more remote Buddhist world.
15. Dōgen provides an innovative interpretation of *ehō shōhō* (lit., "dependent effects and primary effects"), a traditional Buddhist term for the results of past karma that are reflected in the interiority or character of the individual (*shōhō*) in terms of how he or she is born into particular external circumstances (*ehō*); see Ōtani Tetsuō, *Dictionary of Key Terms in the Treasury of the True Dharma-Eye and Dōgen's Extensive Record* [*Shōbōgenzō-Eihei kōroku yōgo jiten*] (Tokyo: Daihōrinkan, 2012), 38.
16. Dōgen also says, "There is certainly a difference between them that surpasses the separation of the heavens and the earth" (Sanjūshichihon bodaibunpō: Dōgen 2.149, Nearman 804, Tanahashi 690).
17. The sixteen precepts advocated by Dōgen include: taking refuge in Buddha, Dharma, and Samgha; ceasing evil, doing only what is good, and doing good for the sake of all beings; not killing; not stealing; not lying; not coveting; not deluding; not betraying; not having pride; not possessing objects; not showing anger; and not defaming the three jewels.
18. The six *pāramitās* in Sanskrit are: *dāna-pāramitā*, *śīla-pāramitā*, *kṣānti-pāramitā*, *vīrya-pāramitā*, *dhyāna-pāramitā*, and *prajñā-pāramitā*. But *dāna* is not necessarily the first, nor is *prajñā* the last; also *kṣānti* or *dhyāna*, for example, could come at the beginning.
19. Philip B. Yampolsky, trans., *The Platform Sutra of the Sixth Patriarch: The Text of the Tun-huang Manuscript with Translation, Introduction, and Notes* (New York: Columbia University Press, 1967), 125–142.

20. For a discussion of the notion of intentionality in Buddhist philosophy, including Zen and the martial arts, see Jay L. Garfield, "Hey, Buddha! Don't Think! Just Act!—A Response to Bronwyn Finnigan," *Philosophy East and West* 61, no. 1 (2011): 74–183 (esp. 179). Regarding Dōgen's standpoint, I agree with the analysis of Eji Suhara, who argues, "if the practitioner lacks aspiration, there is neither a chance for him to practice *shikan taza* after realization, nor before realization. Not only that, for those people with a half-baked aspiration, any practice, even *nembutsu* as an easy practice, cannot be carried out for any preferable fruits." "Re-Visioning Dōgen Kigen's Attitude Toward the System (*Kenmitsu Taisei* 顕密体制) in Considering the Concept of Aspiration (*Kokorozashi* 志) and Just-Sitting Mediation (*Shikan taza* 只管打坐)," *Journal of Buddhist Philosophy* 2 (2016): 187–213.
21. Perhaps the main example from Dōgen's traditional biography occurs when he ostracizes the monk Gemmyō, one of several prominent former members of the Daruma school, for violating his instructions by accepting an offer of land from the shogun that Dōgen implicitly rejected when he left Kamakura to return to Eiheiji. In addition to all his possessions being removed, it is said that Gemmyō's meditation platform was dug up and discarded so that nobody could ever sit there again; see Nara Yasuaki et al., eds. *Anata dake no Shushōgi* (Tokyo: Shōgakukan, 2001), 121.
22. In sum, Dōgen felt that in China monks were washing their face in a way that was not being done in Japan, but conversely, in Japan monks brushed their teeth with a willow twig not commonly used in China; both practices, he says, represent the "true pathway of ancient buddhas" (Senmen: Dōgen 2.52, Nearman 679, Tanahashi 70).
23. Other precious Zen objects used by Dōgen and evoked frequently in the *Treasury* include the staff (*shujō*) and ceremonial fly whisk (*hossu*), which are emblematic of a master's authority and authenticity, and a pine branch (*shōshi*) used in Dharma succession rituals.
24. Giun, *Verse Comments on the Treasury* [*Shōbōgenzō hinmokuju*], in *Taishō shinshū daizōkyō*, 82:477.
25. Takeuchi Michio, *Dōgen* (Tokyo: Yoshikawa kobunkan, 1992), 103.
26. See Andrew Hill with John Wooden, *Be Quick, But Don't Hurry: Finding Success in the Teachings of a Lifetime* (New York: Simon and Schuster, 2001).
27. "Sustained Exertion" is a two-part fascicle, and the second part that focuses on Rujing was written first; in the 60-fascicle edition, the two parts are considered a single fascicle.
28. The five petals image alludes to the Five Houses of Song-dynasty Chinese Chan. According to an Edo period tradition, the 95-fascicle edition was divided into 20 subsections based on words from sayings of Bodhidharma; these contained three to seven fascicles each and were printed, bound, and sold separately. One example of such a publication is shown in figures 0.1 and 0.2.
29. Dōgen 3.168; Leighton and Okumura, *Dōgen's Extensive Record*, 246.
30. Examples include case 2 in the *Gateless Gate* and case 8 in the *Record of Serenity*. The importance of this case for Dōgen is demonstrated by its inclusion as case 102 in his own kōan compilation, the *300-Case Treasury*, as well as interpretations suggested in *Miscellaneous Talks* and in numerous passages in the *Extensive Record*, such as a verse remark that appears in the ninth volume.
31. Ironically, the term *hinin* was traditionally used not only for spirits and gods but also as an epithet for outcasts.

32. Robert Aitken, trans., *The Gateless Barrier Barrier: The Wu-Men Kuan (Mumonkan)* (New York: North Point Press, 1991), 21 (modified); according to the verse in the *Record of Serenity*, arguing over not falling and not ignoring causality is laughable.
33. In this freewheeling section of the fascicle, Dōgen explores many standpoints, and he does say, "Those who feel that this case is based on denying causality ... are in the dark" (Daishugyō: Dōgen 2.190, Nearman 828, Tanahashi 709). But this view is not consistently followed, according to Critical Buddhism, especially since he also suggests several times that "any statement is correct only 80 or 90 percent of the time."
34. Yuanwu's view of the kōan is also criticized in this fascicle.
35. One scholar suggests using the term "licensed evil," which has been applied to discussions of behavior generated by Pure Land Buddhist thought; see Carl Alexander Leslie, "Zen Body, Zen Mind: Dōgen and the Question of Licensed Evil," M.A. thesis, McGill University, 2007, 2–3.
36. William M. Bodiford, *Sōtō Zen in Medieval Japan* (Honolulu: University of Hawaii Press, 1993), 57.
37. Dōgen 4.26–28; Leighton and Okumura, *Dōgen's Extensive Record*, 392–394. This is sermon 6.437, which portrays Rujing's injunction to cast off body-mind as a confessional experience.
38. An intriguing modern example of an apparent conflict between ethical ideals and real-world applications of Zen thought is represented at Sengakuji temple in the Shinagawa district of Tokyo. A prominent Edo-period Sōtō monastery affiliated with other provincial temples, in 1703 Sengakuji came to house the graves of the famous 47 Ronin, who committed mass suicide after avenging the death of their warlord, who was a member of the sect. The annual December 14th festival commemorating the historic event is still the temple's biggest attraction, but to mitigate celebrating violence, recent abbots have established a series of lectures given by priests on topics from the *Treasury* highlighting the role of zazen.
39. Nakano Tōzen, *Sunday Treasury [Nichiyōbi Shōbōgenzō]* (Tokyo: Tōkyōdō shuppan, 2012).
40. A very different way of applying Dōgen's medieval Buddhist thought to the current environmental crisis following the 2011 Fukushima Triple Disaster is found in Masato Ishida, "Nondualism After Fukushima? Tracing Dōgen's Teaching vis-à-vis Nuclear Disaster," in *Japanese Environmental Philosophy*, ed. J. Baird Callicott and James McRae (New York: Oxford University Press, 2017), 243–270. Ishida links Dōgen's discussion of the kōan about cutting a cat in half in the *Treasury of Miscellaneous Talks* with his analysis in the "Buddha Nature" fascicle of another case about chopping a worm, since in that situation both halves survive.

BIBLIOGRAPHY

COLLECTIONS AND THEIR ABBREVIATIONS

Dōgen Zenji zenshū 道元禪師全集. 7 vols. Ed. Kawamura Kōdō 河村孝道, et al. Tokyo: Shunjūsha, 1988–1993. Abbreviated as *Dōgen*.

Dōgen Zenji zenshū 道元禪師全集. 3 vols. Ed. Ōkubo Dōshū 大久保道舟. Tokyo: Chikuma shobō, 1969–1970; Tokyo: Rinsen Shoten, rpt. 1989. Abbreviated as *DZZ Ōkubo-1*.

Dōgen Zenji zenshū: Genbun taishō gendaigoyaku 道元禪師全集―原文対照現代語訳. 17 vols. Ed. Kagamishima Genryu 鏡島元隆, et al. Tokyo: Shunjūsha, 1999–2009. Abbreviated as *DZZ Genbun*.

Eihei Shōbōgenzō shūsho taisei 永平正法眼藏蒐書大成. 27 vols. Ed. Dai Honzan Eiheijinai Eihei Shōbōgenzō shūsho taisei kankōkai 大本山永平寺内永平正法眼藏蒐書大成刊行会. Tokyo: Taishūkan shoten, 1974–82. Abbreviated as *SBGZ Shūsho*.

Sawaki Kōdō zenshū 澤木興道全集. 18 vols. Ed. Sawaki Kōdō 澤木興道 (1880–1965). Tokyo: Daihōrinkan, rpt. 1963.

Shōbōgenzō chūkai zensho 正法眼藏注解全書. 11 vols. Ed. Jinbo Nyoten 神保如天 and Andō Bun'ei 安藤文英. Tokyo: Nihon bussho kankōkai, rpt. 1956–1957. Abbreviated as *SBGZ Chūkai*.

Sōtōtshū zensho 曹洞宗全書. 18 vols. Ed. Sōtōshu Zensho jōkankōkai 曹洞宗全書成刊行会. Tokyo: Sōtōshū shūmuchō, 1970–1973. Abbreviated as *SSZ*.

Taishō shinshū daizōkyō 大正新脩大藏經. 100 vols. Ed. Takakusu Junjirō 髙楠順次郎 and Watanabe Kaigyoku 渡邊海旭. Tokyo: Taishō issaikyō kankōkai, 1924–1932. Abbreviated as *T*.

Teihon Dōgen Zenji Zenshū 定本道元禪師全集. 2 vols. Ed. Ōkubo Dōshū 大久保道舟. Tokyo: Shunjūsha, 1944. Abbreviated as *DZZ Ōkubo-2*.

Xu zangjing 續藏經. 150 vols. Taipei: Xinwenfeng chuban gongsi, rpt. 1976. Abbreviated as *X*.

Zoku Sōtōshū zensho 續曹洞宗全書. 10 vols. Ed. Zoku Sōtōshō zensho jō kankōkai 續曹洞宗全成刊行会. Tokyo: Sōtōshū shūmuchō, 1974–77.

PRIMARY SOURCES

Japanese Editions of the *Treasury*

Original Edition (75 + 12 plus miscellaneous fascicles)

Kohon kōtei Shōbōgenzō 古本校訂正法眼蔵. Ed. Ōkubo Dōshū 大久保道舟. Tokyo: Chikuma shobō, 1971.
Shōbōgenzō 正法眼蔵. In *SBGZ Chūkai*, vols. 1–10.
Shōbōgenzō 正法眼蔵. In *Dōgen*, vols. 1–2. Ed. Kawamura Kōdō 河村孝道.
Shōbōgenzō 正法眼蔵. In *DZZ Genbun*, vols. 1–7. Ed. Mizuno Yaoko 水野弥穂.
Shōbōgenzō 正法眼蔵. 4 vols. Ed. Mizuno Yaoko 水野弥穂. Tokyo: Iwanami bunko, 1990–1993.
Shōbōgenzō 正法眼蔵. In *DZZ Ōkubo-1*, vol. 1.
Shōbōgenzō 正法眼蔵. 2 vols. Ed. Terada Tōru 寺田透 and Mizuno Yaoko 水野弥穂. Nihon shisō taikei. Tokyo: Iwanami shoten, 1970–1972.
Shōbōgenzō 正法眼蔵. http://www.shomonji.or.jp/soroku/genzou.htm.

Main Temple Edition (95 fascicles)

Shōbōgenzō 正法眼蔵. 3 vols. Ed. Etō Sokuō 衛藤即応. Tokyo: Iwanami bunko, 1939–1943.
Shōbōgenzō 正法眼蔵. In *T* no. 2582; vol. 82:7–309.
Shōbōgenzō 正法眼蔵. In *DZZ Ōkubo-2*, vol. 1.
Dōgen gendaigoyaku Shōbōgenzō 道元現代語訳正法眼蔵. 12 vols. Ed. Nishijima Gudō Wafu 西嶋愚道和夫. Tokyo: Bukkyōsha, 1970–1979.
Shōbōgenzō 正法眼蔵. In *SSZ* vol. 1:13–585.

OTHER PRIMARY SOURCES

Baoji jing 寶積經 (Jp. *Hōsekikyō*). Bodhiruci 菩提流志 (562–727). *T* no. 310.
Biyan lu 碧巖錄 (Jp. *Hekiganroku*). Yuanwu 圓悟 (1063–1135). *T* no. 2003.
Chanyuan qinggui 禪苑清規 (Jp. *Zen'en shingi*). Changlu Zongze 長蘆宗賾 (-1107?). Translated as *Zen'en shingi: Yakuchū* 禅苑清規—訳註. Ed. Kagamishima Genryū 鏡島元隆, Satō Tatsugen 佐藤達玄, and Kōsaka Kiyū 小坂機融. Tokyo: Sōtōshū shūmuchō, 1972.
Congrong lu 從容錄 (Jp. *Shōyōroku*). Wansong 萬松 (1166–1246). *T* no. 2004.
Da Mohebore jing 大般若波羅蜜多經 (Jp. *Dai Makahannyakyō*). Xuanzang 玄奘 (602–664). *T* no. 220.
Dōgen shū 道元集. Ed. Ishii Shūdō 石井修道. Tokyo: Rinsen shoten, 2015.
Dongshan yulu 洞山語錄 (Jp. *Tōzan goroku*). Dongshan 洞山 (807–869). *T* no. 1986A.
Fahuajing 蓮華經 (Jp. *Hokkekyō*). 妙法. Kumarajiva 鳩摩羅什 (334–413). *T* no. 262.
Fanwang jing 梵網經 (Jp. *Bonmōkyō*). Kumarajiva 鳩摩羅什 (334–413). *T* no. 1484.
Hongzhi guang lu 宏智禪師廣錄 (Jp. *Wanshi kōroku*). Hongzhi 宏智 (1091–1157). *T* no. 2001.
Huayan jing 華嚴經 (Jp. *Kegonkyō*). Buddhabhadra 佛陀跋陀羅. *T* no. 278.
Jingang jing 金剛經 (Jp. *Kongōkyō*). Kumarjiva 鳩摩羅什 (334–413). *T* no. 235.
Jingde chuandeng lu 景德傳燈錄 (Jp. *Keitoku dentōroku*). Daoyuan 道原 (n.d.). *T* no. 2076.
Kōzen gokokuron 興禪護國論. Eisai 榮西 (1141–1215). *T* no. 2543.
Linji yulu 語錄 (Jp. *Rinzai goroku*). Linji 臨濟 (d. 866). *T* no. 1985.
Niepan jing 涅槃經 (Jp. *Nehangyō*). Dharmaksema 曇無讖 (385–433). *T* no. 374.

Rentian yanmu 人天眼目 (Jp. *Ninden Gammoku*). Huian Zhizhao 晦庵智昭 (fl. 12th c.). *T* no. 2006.
Rujing yulu 如淨語錄. (Jp. *Nyojō goroku*). Rujing. 如淨 (1163–1227). *T* no. 2002A.
Shamon Dōgen 沙門道元. Watsuji Tetsurō 和辻哲郎 (1889–1960). Tokyo: Iwanami bunko, rpt. 1982.
Shōbōgenzō hinmokuju 正法眼蔵品目頌. Giun 義雲 (1253–1333). *T* no. 2591, vol. 82:460–478, and *SBGZ Shūsho* vol. 20.
Shōbōgenzō keiteki 正法眼蔵啓迪. 3 vols. Nishiari Bokusan 西有穆山 (1821–1910). Tokyo: Daihōrinkan, rpt. 1965.
Shōbōgenzō kikigakishō 正法眼蔵聞書抄. Senne 詮慧 (n.d.) and Kyōgō 經豪 (n.d.). *SSZ* vols. 10–11.
Shōbōgenzō shōtenroku 正法眼蔵渉典録. Menzan Zuihō 面山瑞方 (1683–1769). *SBGZ Shūsho* vol. 21.
Shōbōgenzō zenkō 正法眼蔵全講. 24 vols. Kishizawa Ian 岸沢惟安 (1865–1955). Tokyo: Daihōrinkan, rpt. 1972–1974.
Shoulenyan jing 首楞嚴經 (Jp. *Shuryōgenkyō*). Paramiti 般剌蜜帝 (8th c.). *T* no. 945.
Shūso toshite no Dōgen Zenji 宗祖としての道元禅師. Etō Sokuō 衞藤即応 (1888–1958). Tokyo: Iwanami shoten, 1944.
Tan jing 壇經 (Jp. *Dankyō*). Zongbao 宗寶 (fl. 13th c.). *T* no. 2008.
Weimojie jing 佛說維摩詰經 (Jp. *Yuimagyō*). Zhiqian 支謙 (fl. 222–252). *T* no. 474.
Wumenguan 無門關 (Jp. *Mumonkan*). Wumen 無門 (1183–1260). *T* no. 2005.
Yuanwu yulu 圓悟語錄 (Jp. Engo goroku). Yuanwu 圓悟 (1163–1135). *T* no. 1997.
Zhengfayanzang 正法眼蔵 (Jp. *Shōbōgenzō*). Dahui 大慧 (1089–1163). *X* no. 1309.
Zhiguan fuxing zhuan hongjue 止觀輔行傳弘決 (Jp. *Shikan fudenkōdetsu*). Zhanran 湛然 (711–782). *T* no. 1912.

Translations of the *Treasury*

Complete Translations

Ferreras, Pedro Piquero, trans. *Shōbōgenzō: Tesoro del verdadero ojo del Dharma*. 4 vols. Málaga, SP: Sirio, 2013–2016.
He Yansheng 何燕生, trans. *Zhengfayanzang* 正法眼蔵 (Jp. *Shōbōgenzō*). Beijing: Zongjiao wenhua chubanshe, 2003.
Kristkeitz, Werner, trans. *Shōbogenzo. Die Schatzkammer des wahren Dharma-Auges*. 8 vols. Heidelberg: Werner Kristkeitz Verlag, 2008–2012.
Nearman, Hubert, trans. *Shōbōgenzō: The Treasure House of the Eye of the True Teaching, A Trainee's Translation of Great Master Dōgen's Spiritual Masterpiece*. Mount Shasta, CA: Shasta Abbey Press, 2007.
Nishijima, Gudō Wafu 西嶋愚道和夫, and Chodo Cross, trans. *Master Dogen's Shōbōgenzō*. 4 vols. Woods Hole, MA: Windbell Publications, 1994–1999.
———, trans. *Shōbōgenzō: The True Dharma-Eye Treasury*. 4 vols. Berkeley: Numata Center for Buddhist Translation and Research, 2007–2009.
Nishiyama, Kōsen 西山廣宣, and John Stevens, trans. *Shōbōgenzō: The Eye and Treasury of the True Law*. 4 vols. Tokyo: Nakayama Shobō, 1975–1983.
Orimo, Yoko, trans. *Shōbōgenzō: la vraie Loi, Trésor de l'Oei*. 8 vols. Vannes, FR: Sully, 2007–2016.
Sōtō Zen Translation Project, trans. *Shōbōgenzō* 正法眼蔵, *Treasury of the True Dharma Eye by Dōgen* 道元: *An Annotated Translation by the Soto Zen Text Project*. Tokyo: Sōtōshū Shūmuchō, forthcoming.

Tanahashi, Kazuaki 棚橋一晃, ed. and trans. *Treasury of the True Dharma Eye: Zen Master Dogen's Shobo Genzo.* Boston: Shambhala, 2010.
Villalba, Dokushō, trans. *Shōbōgenzō: La preciosa visión del verdadero.* Barcelona: Editorial Kairós, 2016.
Yokoi, Yūho 横井雄峯, trans. *Shōbō-genzō.* Tokyo: Sankibō Buddhist Bookstore, 1986.
Yokoi, Yūho 横井雄峯, with Daizen Victoria, trans. *Zen Master Dōgen: An Introduction with Selected Writings.* Tokyo: Weatherhill, 1976.

Partial Translations

Cleary, Thomas, trans. *Shōbōgenzō: Zen Essays by Dōgen.* Honolulu: University of Hawaii Press, 1986.
Cook, Francis, trans. *How to Raise an Ox: Zen Practice as Taught in Zen Master Dōgen's "Shōbōgenzō."* Boston: Wisdom, 2002.
———, trans. *Sounds of Valley Streams: Enlightenment in Dōgen's Zen.* Albany: State University of New York Press, 1989.
Elberfeld, Rolf, and Ryōsuke Ōhashi, trans. *Dōgen Shōbōgenzō: Ausgewählte Schriften. Anders Philosophieren aus dem Zen. Zweisprachige Ausgabe.* Tokyo: Keio University, 2006.
Kennett, Jiyu, trans. *Selling Water by the River: A Manual of Zen Training.* New York: Vintage, 1972.
Kim, Hee-Jim, trans. *Flowers of Emptiness: Selections from Dōgen's Shōbōgenzō.* New York: Edwin Mellen Press, 1985.
Maezumi Taizen Hakuyu 前角大山博雄, trans. *The Way of Everyday Life: Zen Master Dogen's Genjokoan.* Los Angeles: Zen Center of Los Angeles, 1978.
Masunaga Reihō, trans. *The Sōtō Approach to Zen.* Tokyo: Layman Buddhist Society Press, 1958.
Nishiari Bokusan, et al., trans. *Dōgen's Genjo Koan: Three Commentaries.* Berkeley, CA: Counterpoint, 2011.
Okumura, Shohaku 奥村正博, trans. *The Mountains and Waters Sutra: A Practitioner's Guide to Dōgen's Sansuikyo.* Somerville, MA: Wisdom, 2018.
———, trans. *Realizing Genjokoan: The Key to Dogen's Shobogenzo.* Somerville, MA: Wisdom, 2010.
Okumura, Shohaku 奥村正博 and Taigen Dan Leighton, trans. *The Wholehearted Way.* Boston: Tuttle, 1997.
Tanahashi, Kasuaki 棚橋一晃, ed. and trans. *Enlightenment Unfolds: Life and Work of Zen Master Dōgen.* Boston: Shambhala, 1998.
———, ed. and trans. *Moon in a Dewdrop: Writings of Zen Master Dōgen.* San Francisco: North Point Press, 1985.
Tanahashi, Kazuaki 棚橋一晃, and Peter Levitt, eds. *The Essential Dogen: Writings of the Great Zen Master.* Boston: Shambhala, 2013.
Warner, Jisho, Shohaku Okumura 奥村正博, John McRae, and Taigen Dan Leighton, eds. *Nothing Is Hidden: Essays on Zen Master Dōgen's Instructions for the Cook.* New York: Weatherhill, 2001.
Yasutani Hakuun 安谷白雲. *Flowers Fall: A Commentary on Zen Master Dōgen's Genjōkōan.* Boston: Shambhala, 1996.
Waddell, Norman, and Masao Abe 阿部正雄, trans. *The Heart of Dōgen's Shōbōgenzō.* Albany: State University of New York Press, 2002.

SECONDARY SOURCES

Abe, Masao 阿部正雄. *A Study of Dōgen: His Philosophy and Religion*. Ed. Steven Heine. Albany: State University of New York Press, 1994.
Aitken, Robert, trans. *The Gateless Barrier: The Wu-Men Kuan (Mumonkan)*. New York: North Point Press, 1991.
Arai, Paula. *Women Living Zen: Japanese Sōtō Buddhist Nuns*. New York: Oxford University Press, 1999.
Araki Kengo 荒木見悟, ed. *Daie sho* 大慧書. Tokyo: Chikuma shobō, 1969.
Bashō 芭蕉. *Narrow Road to the Far North and Other Travel Sketches*. Trans. Nobuyuki Yuasa. London: Penguin, 1966.
Bein, Steve, trans. *Purifying Zen: Watsuji Tetsurō's Shamon Dōgen*. Honolulu: University of Hawaii Press, 2011.
Bielefeldt, Carl. *Dōgen's Manuals of Zen Meditation*. Berkeley: University of California Press, 1988.
———. "Recarving the Dragon: History and Dogma in the Study of Dōgen." In *Dōgen Studies*, ed. William R. LaFleur, 21–53. Honolulu: University of Hawaii Press, 1985.
Bodiford, William M. "The Rhetoric of Chinese Language in Japanese Zen." In *Zen Buddhist Rhetoric in China, Korea, and Japan*, ed. Christoph Anderl, 285–314. Leiden: Brill, 2012.
———. *Sōtō Zen in Medieval Japan*. Honolulu: University of Hawaii Press, 1993.
———. "Textual Genealogies of Dōgen." In *Dōgen: Textual and Historical Studies*, ed. Steven Heine, 15–41. New York: Oxford University Press, 2012.
Bolokan, Eitan. "Dimensions of Nonduality in Dōgen's Zen: A Study in the Terminology of the *Shōbōgenzō* and the *Eihei-Kōroku*." Ph.D. diss., Tel Aviv University, 2017.
Breugem, Vincent Michaël Nicolaas. "From Prominence to Obscurity: A Study of the Darumashū: Japan's First Zen School." Ph.D. diss., Leiden University, 2012.
Buswell, Robert E., and Donald S. Lopez, eds. *The Princeton Dictionary of Buddhism*. Princeton, NJ: Princeton University Press, 2013.
Cleary, Thomas, trans. *The Blue Cliff Record*. Berkeley, CA: Bukkyo Dendo Kyokai, 1998.
———, trans. *Book of Serenity: One Hundred Zen Dialogues*. Boulder, CO: Shambhala, rpt. 2005.
———, trans. *Transmission of Light: Zen in the Art of Enlightenment by Zen Master Keizan*. San Francisco: North Point Press, 1990.
Cohen, Jundo. "Dogen: A Love Supreme." http://www.treeleaf.org/forums/showthread.php?9332-SIT-A-LONG-with-JUNDO-Dogen-A-Love-Supreme (accessed April 20, 2018).
Collcutt, Martin. *Five Mountains: The Rinzai Zen Monastic Institution in Medieval Japan*. Cambridge, MA: Harvard University Press, 1981.
"Dōgen Kigen (1200–1253)." https://terebess.hu/zen/dogen/index.html.
Dumoulin, Heinrich. *Zen Buddhism: A History, Japan*. Vol. 2. New York: Macmillan, 1988.
———. *Zen Enlightenment: Origins and Meaning*. New York: Weatherhill, 1979.
Eberstadt, Mary. "The Prophetic Power of Humanae Vitae: Documenting the Realities of the Sexual Revolution." *First Things* (April 1, 2018), n.p.
Eliot, T. S. *The Four Quartets*. Orlando, FL: Harcourt, rpt. 1971.
Etō Sokuō 衞藤即応. *Zen Master Dōgen as Founding Patriarch*. Trans. Ichiumura Shohei. Washington, DC: North American Institute of Zen and Buddhist Studies, 2001.

Eubanks, Charlotte. "Performing Mind, Writing Meditation: Dōgen's *Fukanzazengi* as Zen Calligraphy." *Ars Orientalia* 46 (2016): 173–197.

Faure, Bernard. *La Vision immédiate: Nature, éveil et tradition selon le Shobogenzo*. Paris: Le Mail, 1987.

———. "The Daruma-shū, Dōgen, and Sōtō Zen." *Monumenta Nipponica* 42, no. 1 (1987): 25–55.

Foulk, T. Griffith. "Just Sitting? Dōgen's Take on Zazen, Sutra Reading, and Other Conventional Buddhist Practices." In *Dōgen: Textual and Historical Studies*, ed. Steven Heine. New York: Oxford University Press, 2012.

———, ed. *Record of the Transmission of Illumination by the Great Ancestor, Zen Master Keizan* 太祖瑩山禪師撰述傳光録 *Taiso Keizan Zenji senjutsu Denkōroku, Volume Two: Introduction, Front Matter, Glossary, and Bibliography*. Tokyo: Sōtōshū Shūmuchō, 2017.

———. "The 'Rules of Purity' in Japanese Zen." In *Zen Classics: Formative Texts in the History of Zen Buddhism*, ed. Steven Heine and Dale S. Wright, 137–169. New York: Oxford University Press, 2006.

Fu, Charles Wei-hsun 傅偉勳. *Daoyuan* 道元 (Jp. *Dōgen*). Taipei: Tungta, 1994.

Furuta Shōkin 古田紹欽. *Shōbōgenzō no kenkyū* 正法眼蔵の研究. Tokyo Sōbunsha, 1972.

Garfield, Jay L. "Hey, Buddha! Don't Think! Just Act!—A Response to Bronwyn Finnigan." *Philosophy East and West* 61, no. 1 (2011): 74–183.

Girard, Frédéric. *The Stanza of the Bell in the Wind: Zen and Nenbutsu in the Early Kamakura Period*. Tokyo: The International Institute for Buddhist Studies of The International College for Postgraduate Buddhist Studies, 2007.

Hakamaya Noriaki 袴谷憲昭. *Dōgen to Bukkyō: Jūnikanbon Shōbōgenzō no Dōgen* 道元と仏教—十二巻本正法眼蔵の道元. Tokyo: Daizō shuppan, 1992.

Hakuin 白隠. *Poison Blossoms from a Thicket of Thorn*. Trans. Norman Waddell. Berkeley, CA: Counterpoint, 2014.

He Yansheng 何燕生. *Dōgen to Chūgoku Zen no shisō* 道元と中國禪思想. Kyoto: Hōzōkan, 2001.

Heidegger, Martin. *Being and Time*. Trans. John Macquarrie and Edward Robinson. Oxford: Blackwell, 1962.

———. *The Event*. Trans. Richard Rojcewicz. Bloomington: Indiana University Press, 2012.

Heine, Steven. "Abbreviation or Aberration: The Role of the *Shushōgi* in Modern Sōtō Zen Buddhism." In *Buddhism in the Modern World: Adaptations of an Ancient Tradition*, ed. Steven Heine and Charles S. Prebish, 169–192. New York: Oxford University Press, 2003.

———. "After the Storm: Matsumoto Shirō's Transition from 'Critical Buddhism' to 'Critical Theology.'" *Japanese Journal of Religious Studies* 28, no. 1–2 (2001): 133–146.

———. *Chan Rhetoric of Uncertainty in the Blue Cliff Record: Sharpening a Sword at the Dragon Gate*. New York: Oxford University Press, 2016.

———. "Critical Buddhism (*Hihan Bukkyō*) and the Debate Concerning the 75-fascicle and 12-fascicle Shōbōgenzō Texts." *Japanese Journal of Religious Studies* 21, no. 1 (1994): 37–72.

———. *Did Dōgen Go to China: What He Wrote and When He Wrote It*. New York: Oxford University Press, 2006.

———. "Dōgen: His Life, Religion, and Poetry." *Education About Asia* 20, no. 2 (2015): 32–36.

———, ed. *Dōgen: Textual and Historical Studies*. New York: Oxford University Press, 2012.

———, ed. *Dōgen and Sōtō Zen*. New York: Oxford University Press, 2015.

———. "The Dōgen Canon: Dōgen's Pre-Shōbōgenzō Writings and the Question of Change in His Later Works." *Japanese Journal of Religious Studies* 24 (1997): 39–85.

———. *Existential and Ontological Dimensions of Time in Heidegger and Dōgen*. Albany: State University of New York Press, 1985.

———. *Opening a Mountain: Kōans of the Zen Masters*. New York: Oxford University Press, 2002.

———. *Shifting Shape, Shaping Text: Philosophy and Folklore in the Fox Kōan*. Honolulu: University of Hawaii Press, 1999.

———, trans. *The Zen Poetry of Dōgen: Verses from the Mountain of Eternal Peace*. Mt. Tremper, NY: Dharma Communications, 2005.

———. *Zen Skin, Zen Marrow: Will the Real Zen Buddhism Please Stand Up?* New York: Oxford University Press, 2008.

Heine, Steven, with Katrina Ankrum. "Outside of a Small Circle, Sōtō Zen Commentaries on Dōgen's *Shōbōgenzō* and the Formation of the 95-Fascicle Honzan (Main Temple) Edition." *Japan Studies Review* 21 (2017): 85–127.

Heirman, Ann, and Mattieu Torck. *A Pure Mind in a Clean Body: Bodily Care in the Buddhist Monasteries of Ancient India and China*. Gent, Belgium: Academia Press, 2002.

Heller, Natasha. *Illusory Abiding: The Cultural Construction of the Chan Monk Zhongfeng Mingben*. Cambridge, MA: Harvard University Press, 2014.

Hill, Andrew, with John Wooden. *Be Quick, But Don't Hurry: Finding Success in the Teachings of a Lifetime*. New York: Simon and Schuster, 2001.

Hokenson, Jan. *Japan, France, and East-West Aesthetics: French Literature, 1867–2000*. Teaneck, NJ: Fairleigh Dickenson University Press, 2004.

Hubbard, Jamie, and Paul L. Swanson, eds. *Pruning the Bodhi Tree: The Storm Over Critical Buddhism*. Honolulu: University of Hawaii Press, 1997.

Ikeda Rōsan 池田魯参. *Dōgengaku no yōran* 道元学の揺籃. Tokyo: Daizō shuppan, 1991.

Imaeda Aishin 今枝愛真. *Dōgen: Zazen hitosuji no shamon*. 道元 坐禅ひとすじの沙門. Tokyo: Nihon hōsō shuppan kyōkai, 1976.

Ishida, Masato. "Nondualism After Fukushima? Tracing Dōgen's Teaching vis-à-vis Nuclear Disaster." In *Japanese Environmental Philosophy*, ed. J. Baird Callicott and James McRae, 243–270. New York: Oxford University Press, 2017.

Ishii Seijun 石井清純. "Kenkon'in bon 'Senmen' to Tōunji bon 'Senmen' ni tsuite: ichi" 乾坤院本洗面と洞雲寺本洗面について(一). *Komazawa Daigaku Bukkyōgakubu kenkyū kiyō* 48 (1991): 76–90.

———. *Kōchiku sareta Bukkyō shisō: Dōgen—butsu de aru ga yuheni ni zasu* 構築された仏教思想 道元―仏であるがゆえに坐す. Tokyo: Kōsei shuppansha, 2016.

Ishii Seijun 石井清純 and Tsunoda Tairyū 角田泰隆. *Zen to Ringo: Suteebu Jobuzu to iu ikikata* 禅と林檎 スティーブ・ジョブズという生き方. Tokyo: MP, 2012.

Ishii Shūdō 石井修道. *Chūgoku Zenshūshi wa: Mana Shōbōgenzō ni manabu* 中国禅宗史話:漢字正法眼蔵に学ぶ. Kyoto: Zen bunka kenkyūsho, 1988.

———. "On the Origins of *Kana Shōbōgenzō* / *Kana Shōbōgenzō* wa itsu seiritsu shitta ka 仮名正法眼蔵わ成立しった か." *Komazawa Daigaku kenkyūsho nenpō* 28 (2016): 234–280.

———. "Saigo no Dōgen: Jūnikanbon *Shōbōgenzō* to *Hōkyōki* 最後の道元―十 二巻本正法眼蔵と宝慶記." In Jūnikanbon Shōbōgenzō no shomondai 十二巻本正法眼の諸問題], ed. Kagamishima Genryū 鏡島元隆 and Suzuki Kakuzen 鈴木格禅, 319–374. Tokyo: Daizō Shuppan, 1992.

———. *Shōbōgenzō [Gyōji] ni manabu* 正法眼蔵行持に学ぶ. Kyoto: Zen bunka kenkyūsho, 2007.
Kagamishima Genryū 鏡島元隆. *Dōgen Zenji no in'yō kyōten-goroku* 道元禅師の引用経典・語録の研究. Tokyo: Mokujisha, 1965.
Kagamishima Genryū 鏡島元隆 and Suzuki Kakuzen 鈴木格禅編, eds. *Jūkanbon Shōbōgenzō no shomondai* 十二巻本正法眼蔵の諸問題. Tokyo: Daizō shuppan, 1991.
Kasulis, Thomas P. "The Incomparable Philosopher: Dōgen on How to Read the *Shōbōgenzō*." In *Dōgen Studies*, ed. William R. LaFleur. Honolulu: University of Hawaii Press, 1985.
———. *Zen Action, Zen Person*. Honolulu: University of Hawaii Press, 1979.
Kawamura Kōdō 河村孝道. "Shōbōgenzō 正法眼蔵." In eds. *Dōgen no chosaku* 道元の著作, 7 vols., ed. Kagamishima Genryū 鏡島元隆 and Tamaki Kōshirō 玉城康四郎, 3:1–74. Tokyo: Shunjūsha, 1980.
———. *Shōbōgenzō no seiritsu-shiteki no kenkyū* 正法眼蔵の成立史的研究. Tokyo: Shunjūsha, 1986.
Kenko and Chōmei. *Essays in Idleness and Hōjōki*. Trans. Meredith McKinney. New York: Penguin Classics, 2014.
Kim Hee-Jin. *Dōgen Kigen—Mystical Realist*. Tucson: University of Arizona Press, 1975.
———. *Dōgen on Meditation and Thinking: A Reflection on His View of Zen*. Albany: State University of New York Press, 2007.
———. "The Reason of Words and Letters: Dōgen and Kōan Language." In *Dōgen Studies*, ed. William R. La Fleur, 54–82. Honolulu: University of Hawaii Press, 1985.
Kimura Kiyotaka 木村清孝. *Shōbōgenzō zenbon kaidoku* 正法眼蔵全巻解読. Tokyo: Kōsei shuppan, 2015.
Kodera, Takashi James. "The Buddha Nature in Dōgen's *Shōbōgenzō*." *Japanese Journal of Religious Studies* 4, no. 4 (1977): 267–298.
———. *Dogen's Formative Years in China*. Boulder, CO: Prajña Press, 1980.
Kopf, Gereon. *Beyond Personal Identity: Dōgen, Nishida and a Phenomenlogy of No-Self*. Richmond, Surrey, UK: Curzon Press, 2001.
Kraft, Kenneth. *Eloquent Zen: Daitō*. Honolulu: University of Hawaii Press, 1993.
Kubovčáková, Zuzana. "Believe It or Not: Dōgen on the Question of Faith." *Studia Orientalia Slovaca* 12, no. 1 (2018): 193–215.
Kurebayashi Kōdō 樺林皓堂, ed. *Dōgen Zen shisōteki kenkyū* 道元禅の思想的研究. Tokyo: Shunjūsha, 1973.
LaFleur, William, ed. *Dōgen Studies*. Honolulu: University of Hawaii Press, 1985.
Leighton, Taigen Dan, and Shohaku Okumura 奥村正博, trans. *Dōgen's Extensive Record*. Boston: Wisdom, rpt. 2010.
———, trans. *Dōgen's Pure Standards for the Zen Community: A Translation of Eihei Shingi*. Albany: State University of New York Press, 1995.
Leighton, Taigen Dan. *Visions of Awakening Space and Time: Dōgen and the Lotus Sūtra*. New York: Oxford University Press, 2008.
Leslie, Carl Alexander. "Zen Body, Zen Mind: Dōgen and the Question of Licensed Evil." M.A. thesis, McGill University, 2007.
Levering, Miriam L. "'Raihaitokuzui' and Dōgen's Views of Gender and Women: A Reconsideration." In *Dōgen and Sōtō Zen*, ed. Steven Heine, 46–73. New York: Oxford University Press, 2015.
Li, Puqun. *A Guide to Asian Philosophy Classics*. New York: Broadway Press, 2012.
Lin, Pei-Ying. "Precepts and Lineage in Chan Tradition: Cross-Cultural Perspectives in Ninth Century East Asia." Ph.D. diss., SOAS, University of London, 2011.

Matsumoto Shirō 松本史朗. *Dogen shiso ron* 道元思想論. Tokyo: Daizo Shuppan, 2000.
——. "Japanese Philosophy and Buddhism." *Komazawa Daigaku Bukkyōgakubu kenkyū kiyō* 76 (2018): 202–228.
Matsunami Naohiro 松波直弘. *Kamakura ki Zenshū shisōshi no kenkyū* 鎌倉期禅宗思想史の研究. Tokyo: Pelikan, 2011.
Matsuoka Yukako 松岡由香子. *Kobutsu Dōgen no shii* 古仏道元の思惟. Kyōto: Hanazono Daigaku kokusai zengaku kenkyūjo, 1995.
McCutcheon, Russell T. "In Memoriam: Jonathan Z. Smith (1938–2017)." *Religious Studies News* (January 5, 2018), n.p.
McRae, John R. *Seeing Through Zen: Encounter, Transformation, and Genealogy in Chinese Chan Buddhism.* Berkeley: University of California Press, 2003.
Miura, Isshu, and Ruth Fuller Sasaki. *Zen Dust: The History of the Koan and Koan Study in Rinzai (Linji) Zen.* Quirin Press, rpt. 2015.
Mizuno Yaoko 水野弥穂子, ed. *Daichi: Geju, Jūni hōgo, kana hōgo* 大智―偈頌・十二時法語・仮名法語. Tokyo: Kōdansha, rpt. 1994.
Morimoto Kazuo 森本和夫. *Derrida kara Dōgen e: datsu-kochiku to shinjin datsuraku* デリダから道元へ―脱構築と身心脱落. Tokyo: Fukutake Books, 1989.
Müller, Ralf. "Watsuji's Reading of Dōgen's *Shōbōgenzō*." *Frontiers of Japanese Philosophy* 6 (2009): 109–125.
Nagahisa Gakusui 永久岳水. *Shōbōgenzō no ihon to denpashi no kenkyū* 正法眼蔵の異本と伝播史の研究. Tokyo: Nakayama shobō, 1973.
Nakano Tōzen 中野東禅. *Dōgen* 道元. Tokyo: Natsumesha, 2004.
——. *Nichiyōbi Shōbōgenzō* 日曜日の正法眼蔵. Tokyo: Tōkyōdō shuppan, 2012.
Nakao Ryōshin 中尾良信, ed. *Lofty Zen Master Dōgen* [*Kokō no Zenji: Dōgen* 孤高の禅師道元]. Tokyo: Yoshikaw kobunkan, 2003.
——. *Zen* 禅. Tokyo: Natsumesha, 2005.
Nara Yasuaki, ed. *Budda kara Dōgen e* ブッダから道元へ. Tokyo: Tōkyō shoseki, 1992.
Nara Yasuaki 奈良康明, et al., eds. *Anata dake no Shushōgi* あなただけの修証義. Tokyo: Shōgakukan, 2001.
Nishijima, Gudo Wafu. *Understanding the Shobogenzo.* Woods Hole, MA: Windbell Publications, 1992.
Nishio Minoru 西尾実. *Dōgen to Zeami* 道元と世阿弥. Tokyo: Iwanami shoten, 1965.
Nishitani, Keiji 西谷啓治. *Religion and Nothingness.* Trans. Jan van Bragt. Berkeley: University of California Press, 1982.
Nonomura, Kaoru. *Eat Sleep Sit.* Trans. Juliet Winters Carpenter. New York: Kodansha USA, 2015.
Ogawa Yoshio 小川義男, ed. *Nihon no koten* 日本の古典. Tokyo: Sekai bunkasha, 2007.
Ōkubo Doshū 大久保道舟. *Dōgen Zenji den no kenkyū* 道元禅師伝の研究. Tokyo: Chikuma shobō, 1966.
Okumura Shohaku 奥村正博, trans. *The Heart of Zen: Practice Without Gaining-Mind.* Tokyo: Sōtōshū Shūmuchū, 1988.
Okumura Shohaku 奥村正博, and Tom Wright, trans. *Shōbōgenzō Zuimonki: Sayings of Eihei Dōgen Zenji Recorded by Koun Ejō.* Tokyo: Sōtōshū Shūmuchū, rpt. 2004.
Ōtani Tetsuō 大谷哲夫. *Shōbōgenzō and Eihei kōroku yōgo jiten* 正法眼蔵―永平広録用語辞典. Tokyo: Daihōrinkan, 2012.
Otogawa, Kobun 乙川弘文. *Embracing Mind: The Zen Talks of Kobun Chino Otogawa.* Ed. Judy Cosgrove. Los Gatos, CA: Jikoji Zen Center, 2016.
Ozeki, Ruth. *A Tale for the Time Being.* New York: Penguin, 2013.

Putney, David. "Some Problems in Interpretation: The Early and Late Writings of Dōgen." *Philosophy East and West* 46 (1996): 497–531.

Raud, Rein. "The Existential Moment: Rereading Dōgen's Theory of Time." *Philosophy East and West* 62, no. 2 (2012): 153–173.

Reader, Ian. "Zazenless Zen? The Position of Zazen in Institutional Zen Buddhism." *Japanese Religions* 14, no. 3 (1986): 7–27.

Riggs, David E. "The Life of Menzan Zuihō, Founder of Dōgen Zen." *Japan Review* 16 (2004): 67–100.

Rogacz, David. "Knowledge and Truth in the Thought of Jizang (549–623)." *The Polish Journal of the Arts and Culture* 16 (2015): 125–138.

St. Augustine. *The Confessions*. Ed. Michael P. Foley. Indianapolis: Hackett, 2002.

——. *On Genesis*. Ed. John E. Rotelle. Hyde Park, NY: New City Press, 2006.

Sasaguichi, Rei. "Zazen and the Art of Playwriting: A New Kabuki Drama Shows the Path to Enlightenment." *The Japan Times* (March 20, 2002), n.p.

Shōbōgenzō shuppan no sokuseki: tenji kaisetsu leaflet 正法眼蔵の足跡―展示解説リーフレット. The Museum of Zen History and Culture at Komazawa University, 2009.

Souyri, Pierre. *The World Turned Upside Down: Medieval Japanese Society*. New York: Columbia University Press, 2003.

Springer, Kate. "Woljeongsa Temple: Spend the night in a South Korean landmark." CNN Travel (February 19, 2018), n.p.

Stambaugh, Joan. *Impermanence Is Buddha-Nature: Dōgen's Understanding of Temporality*. Honolulu: University of Hawaii Press, 1990.

Steineck, Christian. "Time Is Not Fleeting: Thoughts of a Medieval Zen Buddhist." *KronoScope* 7 (2007): 33–47.

Suhara, Eji. "Re-Visioning Dōgen Kigen's Attitude Toward the System (*Kenmitsu Taisei* 顕密体制) in Considering the Concept of Aspiration (*Kokorozashi* 志) and Just-Sitting Meditation (*Shikan taza* 只管打坐)." *Journal of Buddhist Philosophy* 2 (2016): 187–213.

Suzuki, D. T. (Daisetsu) 鈴木大拙, trans. *The Lankavatara Sutra*. London: George Routledge and Sons, 1932.

Suzuki, Shunryu 鈴木俊隆. *Zen Mind, Beginner's Mind*. Boulder, CO: Shambhala, rpt. 2011.

Takasaki Jikidō 高崎直道 and Umehara Takeshi 梅原猛. *Kobutsu no manebi (Dōgen)* 古仏のまねび (道元). Tokyo: Kadokawa shoten, 1969.

Takemura Mikio 竹村牧男. "Bannen no Dōgen no zazen-kan 晩年の道元の坐禅観." *Zen kenkyūsho kiyō* 31 (1994): 13–30.

Takeuchi Michio 竹内道雄. *Dōgen* 道元. Tokyo: Yoshikawa kobunkan, 1992.

Tamura Yoshirō 田村芳朗. "Critique of Original Awakening Thought in Shōshin and Dōgen." *Japanese Journal of Religious Studies* 11 (1984): 243–266.

——. *Kamakura shin-Bukkyō shisō no kenkyū* 鎌倉新仏教思想の研究 Kyoto: Heirakuji shoten, 1965.

Tanabe Hajime 田辺元. "Memento Mori." Trans. V. H. Viglielmo. *Philosophical Studies of Japan* I (1959): 1–12.

——. *Shōbōgenzō no tetsugaku shikan* 正法眼蔵の哲学私観. Tokyo: Iwanami shoten, 1939.

Tanahashi, Kazuaki 棚橋一晃. "Dogen: A Thirteenth-Century Post-Existentialist." *Dharma Eye* 9 (2001): n.p.

Tanahashi, Kazuaki 棚橋一晃, and John Daido Loori, trans. *The True Dharma Eye: Zen Master Dōgen's Three Hundred Kōans*. Boston: Shambhala, 2005.

Tatematsu Wahei 立松和平. *Dōgen no tsuki* 道元の月. Tokyo: Shodensha, 2002.

Terada Tōru 寺田透. *Dōgen no gengo uchū* 道元の言語宇宙. Tokyo: Iwanami shoten, 1974.
Tsunoda Tairyū 角田泰隆. *Dōgen Zenji no shisōteki kenkyū* 道元禅師の思想的研究. Tokyo: Shunjūsha, 2015.
——, ed. *Dōgen Zenji ni okeru no shomondai: Kindai no shūgaku ronsō wo chūshin toshite* 道元禅師研究における諸問題近代の宗学論争を中心として. Tokyo: Shunjūsha, 2017.
Uchiyama Kōshō 内山興正. *Zen Teaching of Homeless Kodo*. Boston: Wisdom, 2014.
Victoria, Brian. *Zen at War*. 2nd ed. Lanham, MD: Rowman and Littlefield, 2006.
Warner, Brad. *Don't Be a Jerk: And Other Practical Advice from Dogen, Japan's Greatest Zen Master*. San Francisco: New World Library, 2016.
Wirth, Jason M. *Mountains, Rivers, and the Great Earth: Reading Gary Snyder and Dōgen in an Age of Ecological Crisis*. Albany: State University of New York Press, 2017.
Wirth, Jason M., et al., eds. *Engaging Dōgen's Zen: The Philosophy of Practice as Awakening* Boston: Wisdom, 2017.
Wu, Kuang-ming. *The Butterfly as Companion*. Albany: State University of New York Press, 1990.
Yampolsky, Philip B., trans. *The Platform Sutra of the Sixth Patriarch: The Text of the Tun-huang Manuscript with Translation, Introduction, and Notes*. New York: Columbia University Press, 1967.
Yanagida Seizan 柳田聖山. *Shoki zenshū shisho no kenkyū* 初期禅宗史書の研究. Kyoto: Hōzōkan, 1967.
——, ed. *Zen no yuige*. Tokyo: Chōbunsha, 1973.
Yasuraoka Kōsaku 安良岡康作. *Shōbōgenzō "Gyōji"* 正法眼蔵行持. 2 vols. Tokyo: Kodansha, 2002.
Yifa. *The Origins of Buddhist Monastic Codes in China: An Annotated Translation and Study of the Chanyuan Qinggui*. Honolulu: University of Hawaii Press, 2002.
Yorizumi Mitsuko 賴住光子. *Dōgen no shisō* 道元の思想. Tokyo: NHK bukkusu, 2011.
——. *Shōbōgenzō nyūmon* 正法眼蔵入門. Tokyo: Kadokawa sofia bunko, rpt. 2014.
Yu, Anthony C. "The Quest for Brother Amor: Buddhist Intimations in *The Story of Stone*." *Harvard Journal of Asiatic Studies* 49, no. 1 (1989): 55–92.
Yusa, Michiko. "Dōgen and the Feminine Presence: Taking a Fresh Look Into His Sermons and Other Writings." *Religions* 9 (2018): 1–22.
Zengaku daijiten hensanjo 禪學大辭典編纂所, ed. *Zengaku daijiten* 禪學大辭典. Tokyo: Taishūkan, rpt. 1985.

INDEX

Bashō, 35, 75; visit to Eiheiji, 35, 75
being-time. *See under* temporality; *Treasury*, fascicles of
Blue Cliff Record. *See under* kōan
Buddha nature (*busshō*), 68, 109–113; and buddhahood (*jōbutsu*), 97–98, 112; and original awakening/enlightenment, 13, 69–71, 95, 96f4.1, 111, 123–124, 184; and negation, 104, 109, 111–112, 122–123, 149, 191; and *Nirvāṇa Sūtra*, 110, 122; and sentient and insentient beings, 37, 92, 103, 110–111, 114–115, 131, 165, 176–177, 211; and time, 6, 37, 110–111, 113, 120, 122–124, 126, 130–132, 165, 173; theories about, 23, 40, 71, 110, 112–113, 124, 131, 172, 220; unity of, 5–6, 55, 74, 92, 103–105, 109, 112, 118, 175, 211; and whole-being Buddha nature, 109–112, 123–124, 126, 131. *See also Treasury*, fascicles of; reality; temporality

casting off body-mind (*shinjin datsuraku*), 56, 104, 122, 136, 156, 179t7.1, 195; and awakening, 16, 127, 136, 165, 195, 205, 214; and casting off dust from the mind, 16, 20; Dōgen's experience of, 15–17, 23, 47, 68, 71, 73, 95, 184. *See also* just sitting; zazen
causality, 201; and the Fox Kōan, 30, 221–222; and karma, 12, 40, 48, 201, 203, 220–222, 273n15; and merit, 9, 39, 45, 203, 208, 220; and motivation, 49, 166, 176, 194, 208–210, 214; and repentance, 38, 78, 86, 166, 201, 203, 220–224; and retribution, 9, 34, 38, 57, 78, 86, 201, 220–222. *See also* Critical Buddhism under *Treasury*, interpretations of

Dahui, 152–53, 259n5; Dōgen's criticism of, 31, 46, 74, 183, 222, 265n12, 272n19; and *Zhengfayanzang* (Jp. *Shōbōgenzō*), 31, 46
Daruma school, 72, 77, 265n12; impact on early Sōtō Zen, 73, 223; and monks who joined Dōgen, 73–74, 77, 79, 83, 274n21
deceptivity, 92, 104, 145, 148, 167; and delusion, 105, 149, 151, 158, 164, 167–168, 170–173, 179t7.1; as Dharma, 167–168; and dreams, 29, 93, 148–149, 168, 170–171, 173; and "dream within a dream," 29, 149, 170–171; and four levels of awareness, 171–173;

deceptivity (continued)
    and language, x, 21, 37, 92, 112,
        145–147, 149–151, 155, 158, 169, 172;
    and mistakes, 6, 21, 67, 117, 130, 169,
        172; and nondualism, 19, 38, 94,
        96–97, 124, 132–134, 158, 164, 168, 184,
        194, 222; overcoming of, 6, 37, 104,
        112, 126, 128–129, 150, 185, 189, 219;
        and temporality, 22, 102, 124, 126, 135,
        148–150, 154, 165, 171–172, 208
Dharma, 35, 62, 69, 71, 91, 95, 98, 159, 164,
    170, 185, 194–195, 201, 203, 213–214; and
    language, 10, 32, 47, 92, 146, 151–152,
    166; and nonverbal symbols, 45,
    114–116, 146, 166, 169, 197, 223, 268n21;
    transmission of, 41–42, 46, 52, 147–148,
    151, 156, 167–168, 211, 218, 222, 274n23
Dōgen: basic interpretative standpoint of,
    6–7, 13, 21, 34, 94, 98–102, 192f7.1,
    266nn5–6; basic standpoint, and
    hermeneutics of intrusion, 99–101,
    107, 115, 123, 149, 159, 174, 191, 196;
    career stages of, 12–15, 29, 40–41, 57,
    68–70, 75, 77, 85–87, 143, 220, 223; and
    coming back empty-handed, 11, 17;
    death of, 27–28, 40, 61, 63–64, 84,
    143–144, 167, 269n18; and doubt, 11, 13,
    41–42, 68–71, 95, 184; early life of,
    11–13, 40, 68; and Eisai, 12–14, 41–42,
    69–70, 72, 183, 210–211, 223, 260n20;
    legends about, 18, 40–41; and Myōzen,
    14, 41–42, 69–70, 95, 121; poetry of, 52,
    78, 95, 113, 121, 144–146, 266n22,
    267n20, 269n18; and question of
    changing views, 66–67, 85–86, 220,
    222, 224; and relocation to Echizen, 11,
    43, 63–64, 73, 75, 78, 85–86, 113;
    sermons of. See Treasury, fascicles of;
    temples established by, 38, 41, 47, 64,
    68, 72–75, 77, 79, 184, 224; temples
    established by, and Eiheiji, 45, 60–61,
    63, 75, 81, 83, 113, 121, 181, 185, 203, 207,
    224, 260n18; and Western thought, 8,
    26–27, 55, 57–58, 177, 264n25, 266n1;
    works by, 68, 70, 80t3.1, 86, 91, 175, 184,
    179t7.1, 272n4, 274n30: 300-Case
    Treasury, 47, 73, 153, 274n30; Dōgen's
    Monastic Rules, 73, 79, 81, 86, 91, 175,
    178, 182, 207; Extensive Record, 53–54,
    64, 70, 73, 78, 186, 220, 223; Record of
    the Hōkyō Era, 42, 70, 185; Treasury of
    Miscellaneous Talks, 47, 73, 178,
    185, 194, 275n40; Universal
    Recommendation of the Principles of
    Zazen, 70–71, 178, 181, 184. See also
    Treasury of the True Dharma Eye
    (Shōbōgenzō)

Ejō, 143; as Dōgen's scribe, 28, 47, 63, 64,
    73, 204; editorial role of, 61–65, 67, 72,
    77, 79, 81–82t3.2. See also under
    Treasury, editions of
enlightenment, x, 3, 23, 31, 121, 163, 170,
    176, 194, 197, 206–207, 210, 220–221,
    268n1; and realization here and now
    (genjōkōan), 103, 150, 198, 212, 214,
    216; and everyday reality, 6, 24, 51,
    102, 111, 124–127, 127f5.1, 147–149,
    165, 198; and nirvāṇa, 45, 95, 97, 103,
    130, 132–133, 140, 212, 270n23; and
    practice-realization 53, 58, 94, 71, 74,
    94, 96–98, 100, 102, 110, 176–177, 208;
    and postrealization cultivation
    (shōtaichōyō), 53, 93, 95, 97, 113,
    171–174, 184, 209; and spontaneous
    illumination (satori), 37, 46, 158,
    185, 189, 191, 222; and original
    enlightenment thought, 13, 69–71,
    73, 95, 96f4.1, 124, 184, 196. See also
    awakening under expressivity;
    ephemerality; practice
ephemerality, 119, 170; and change, 22,
    103, 110, 117, 119, 122–123, 125, 132–133,
    170, 268n8; contemplation of, 119, 121,
    125–126, 130–131, 140, 171, 215, 268n1;
    and detachment, 120, 144, 154; and
    dualistic view of reality, 96, 110–111,
    121–122, 124–125, 131–132, 140, 172;
    and enlightenment, 130, 133–134, 139,
    143–144; and environment, 121–122,
    138, 144; and impermanence, x, 12,
    37, 40, 68, 112, 120, 129–133, 135, 144,
    173; and mortality, 38, 92, 126, 132,
    139–140; and the self, 118, 135, 140;
    and unity of birth-and-death, 132–133,
    140. See also temporality
expressivity, x, 92, 145, 148, 154, 171–172;
    and awakening, 21, 37, 45–49, 149,

151–152, 154, 156–158, 160, 172; and entangled vines (*kattō*), 6, 21, 67, 117, 146–147, 151, 168–169, 172, 213, 219; and changed readings, 13, 16–17, 20–21, 51, 74, 106–107, 125, 131, 191, 197–198; and Chinese approaches to, 4, 8, 20, 49, 54, 150, 152–154, 156–157, 163, 196; and Dōgen's distinctive rhetoric, 6, 9, 18–21, 23, 48, 78, 87, 98–100, 110, 145–148, 150; and everyday life, 6, 20–21, 24, 100, 126, 149, 159, 182; and language, x, 4, 21, 37, 47, 92, 56, 112, 145–147, 149–152, 155, 166–167, 175; and literary Zen versus nonliterary Zen, 4–5, 10, 48–49, 92, 152–153, 270n10; and literature, 9, 56, 145, 177; and nonspeaking (*higogen*), 47, 49, 92, 103, 145–147, 152, 156, 171, 191, 193; as pedagogical device, 146–47, 149–150, 154, 156; and poetry, 18, 34, 43–44, 60–61, 81–82, 85, 92, 101, 115, 146–147, 149, 170, 197–198; and reality, 22, 38, 94, 100–104, 109, 113, 132, 149–152, 154, 164, 168–171, 174; and ten directions, 157, 164; utility of, 5, 151–152, 157, 217; and waka, 35, 39, 113, 121, 143, 267n20, 268n7; and wordplay, 3, 11, 21, 94, 100, 121, 146, 154–156, 158–161. *See also* kōan; practice; sūtras

Heidegger, Martin, 55–56, 120
Hōjō Tokiyori, 69, 263n4; and meeting Dōgen, 72, 77–78
Huineng, 34, 46, 162, 164, 167–168, 182, 214, 216, 262n1, 267n10; Dōgen's critique of, 49, 124

just sitting, 5, 16–17, 37, 61, 70, 73, 86, 92–93, 104, 162, 174–175, 188, 214; and Kaoru Nonomura, 203, 272n3; Rujing on, 16–17, 162, 205–207; and Sawaki Kōdō, 198–199. *See also* casting off body-mind; reflexivity; zazen

Kamakura Buddhism, 12–13, 19, 69, 82, 91, 210; and Decline of the Dharma (*mappō*), 39, 48; and Pure Land, 12, 25, 37, 48, 110, 134, 182, 275n35; and Rinzai, 12, 19, 28, 30–31, 36–37, 48–49, 75, 153–154, 263n4; and selectionism, 37, 183, 206–207; and social changes, 61, 66, 68–69, 119, 180, 224; and Tendai, 37, 110, 161, 183: and Tendai and Dōgen, 12–13, 68–69, 71, 75–77, 95, 162, 183; and Tendai and role of Mount Hiei, 12, 41, 68, 210. *See also* just sitting
kōan, 18, 40, 47, 73, 162, 179t7.1, 180, 187, 190–191, 212, 220, 259n5, 264n10, 274n30; approaches to in the *Treasury*, 44, 46, 48, 50, 99–100, 110, 126, 148, 153–159, 176, 221; and *Blue Cliff Record*, 18, 70, 99, 106, 109, 152–153, 270n15; Chinese Zen approaches to, 17–18, 31, 34, 45–46, 70, 106, 115, 142, 152–154, 183, 185; commentaries on, 31, 33, 70, 78, 142, 152–153; and dialogues, 32, 93, 99, 125, 154, 166, 184, 192f7.1; and *Gateless Gate*, 45–46, 70, 153; interpretations of, 55, 115, 151, 154, 178, 182–183, 192f7.1, 194, 209, 275n34, 275n40; and Korean Zen, 70; Rinzai approaches to, 37, 48; and Zhaozhou exchange, 101–102. *See also* expressivity; Fox Kōan *under* causality
Komazawa University, 84, 262n42, 262n50; and Dōgen studies, xii, 26, 57

Lingyun, 121–122, 141, 185
Lotus Sūtra. See under sūtras

meditation. *See under* reflexivity
mentality, 91, 141; and perceptivity, 7, 26, 38, 40, 91–92, 100, 103–104, 115–117, 140–142, 144, 150, 188, 197; and the individual, 7, 55, 91–93, 103, 111, 113, 165, 182, 189, 213; and mind itself is Buddha, 23, 51, 131, 179t7.1; and thusness, 105–106, and "walls and fences," 52, 118, 150, 158. *See also* Buddha nature; nature; reality
Mount Hiei. *See under* Tendai *under* Kamakura Buddhism

nature, 5, 12, 39, 113–114, 116, 120–121, 157, 189, 260n17, 267n21; and anthropocentrism, 95, 112–113, 115, 117–118; and environment, 35, 38,

nature (continued)
58–59, 78, 108, 113, 117–118, 121, 275n40; and human behavior, 34, 57, 74, 91, 108, 113, 125, 171, 175, 187, 189, 225; imagery of, 22, 44, 105, 117, 122, 133–135, 143–144, 146–147, 152, 154, 170, 202, 269n6; and Korean Zen, 113; and reclusion, 5, 41, 43, 85, 93, 113, 134, 163, 176, 210, 212; and seasons, 22, 35, 113, 121, 134, 179t, 270n24; and sounds, 20, 46, 52, 101, 107–108, 114–115, 121–122, 142; and Su Shi, 35, 115; and water, 44, 58, 105, 108–109, 116, 118, 124, 128, 134, 138, 198. *See also* sentient and insentient beings *under* Buddha nature

practice, 11–13, 16, 23, 43, 48, 61, 69, 86, 142, 145, 165–166, 173, 180, 209, 261n25; and authenticity, 17, 30, 41, 44, 47, 57, 59, 92, 97, 126, 152, 154–155, 168, 177, 209, 210; and cleanliness, 5, 38, 73, 181, 201–203, 208–209, 214, 216, 272n1, 273n12; daily activities as, 4–5, 38, 73, 79, 92, 102, 201–205, 213, 266n17; and dignified demeanor, 189–190, 201–203, 204f8.1, 216; and continuity of, 125, 132, 140, 142, 174–175, 184, 186, 188, 194, 263n3; instructions for, 4, 54, 61, 64, 70–71, 91, 166, 175, 179t7.1, 181, 184, 201, 205, 207, 211; monastic activities as, 5, 18, 40, 63, 79, 92, 104, 181t7.2, 202–204, 210; and motive, 49, 93, 135–136, 164, 166, 176, 194–195, 207, 214, 274n20; and precepts, 40, 73, 93, 183, 185, 201, 206, 209–212, 214–215, 223, 273n17; and precepts and formlessness, 204, 210, 214–218, 222–223; and ritual, 17, 53–54, 77, 93, 122, 162, 166, 177, 201, 203, 205–206, 209, 212, 272n1; rituality, and daily chores, 5, 53, 73, 92, 181t7.2, 182, 202, 204f8.1, 213; rituality, ethics of, 57, 74, 201–202, 224; rituality, and lineal transmission, 15, 18, 45–46, 50, 93, 185, 206, 218, 260n20, 265n12; rituality, and purity, 16, 38, 93, 205, 208–211, 215, 218, 223; rituality, and ceremonies, 27, 53, 61, 92–93, 136, 166–167, 199–200, 206, 211, 215–217; rituality, and six perfections, 212–213, 273n18; rituality, and summer retreats, 14, 39, 79, 137, 155, 203, 217–218; rituality, and tea, 100–102, 267n17; and role of ethics, x, 74, 92, 175, 201–202, 224; and Rujing's injunction, 52, 75, 162, 205, 207, 220, 267n17, 272n4; and *samādhi*, 176, 179t7.1, 180, 187; and the self, 6, 49, 135, 188–189; Tendai approaches to, 12–13, 37, 95, 162, 167, 183, 206, 210; theory of, 33, 37, 39, 49, 53, 74, 91, 94, 113, 119–120, 123, 131, 141, 176–178, 196–199; and Zongze, 180–182; and Zongze, *Rules for Purity in Zen Monasteries*, 180, 182, 208–209. *See also* enlightenment; reflexivity

reality, x, 91, 125, 151–152, 168, 172–174, 186; and Buddha nature, 92, 95, 109–112; and everyday actions, 6, 51, 93, 100–102, 127f5.1, 147, 149, 159, 213, 217; Dōgen's views of, 6, 52, 71, 94, 103–105, 113, 123, 132, 144, 150, 154, 187; and metaphysics, 20, 51, 55, 86, 91, 97, 111, 122, 268n1; and polarities, 5, 93–94, 102–103, 106, 130, 133–134, 171, 173, 188, 223, 225; and the senses, 7, 106–107, 114, 116, 118, 122, 142, 163, 167, 169, 185, 215; and unity of, 19, 92, 96f4.1, 97, 103–104, 110, 124–125, 158, 194, 222, 275n40; views of, 21, 23, 26, 39, 130, 149, 157, 170–171, 177, 206–207; and Zhaozhou, 34, 101–102, 166, 262n1. *See also* expressivity; mentality; nature

reflexivity, x, 93, 175, 179t7.1, 188–191; and just sitting, 175–176, 178, 181–182, 186, 188, 193–194, 196–199, 208, 210, 213–215; and Hongzhi, 74, 97, 124–125, 142–143, 183, 194, 197–198, 222, 261n24, 262n1; and Mazu, 51, 125–126, 128, 151, 163–164, 179t7.1, 194–196, 214, 262n1; and meditation, 12, 30, 33, 37, 40–41, 46–47, 77–78, 106, 162, 176–178, 195, 199–200, 210; meditation and purposelessness, 53, 172–173, 175, 194, 207, 214; and the mind, 16, 38, 93,

107, 118, 164, 184–185, 187–189, 209–211; and nonthinking, 5, 23–24, 39, 92–94, 117, 146–147, 175–179, 188, 190–194, 215; and Yaoshan dialogue, 21, 190–194, 192f7.1, 262n1. *See also* zazen

Rujing, 14–15, 17, 41–42, 46, 68–69, 95, 101, 122, 159, 184–185, 218, 262n1, 267n11, 272n1; Dōgen's views of, 16, 20, 31, 34, 42–43, 72, 74, 91, 107, 114, 157, 197, 263n7; and Mount Tiantong, 14–15, 42–43, 68, 205; recorded sayings of, 42–43, 74; on training, 15–16, 43, 44, 52, 70, 75, 102, 162, 179t7.1, 183, 195, 205–207, 218, 220. *See also* Rujing's injunction *under* practice

Senika heresy, 49, 71, 73; and Critical Buddhism, 222–223; and Dōgen's criticism of, 23–24, 98, 124

Snyder, Gary, 55, 58

Song Dynasty, 13–15, 50, 72; culture of, 14–15; literature of, 98–99, 106, 115, 152; role of Zen in, 13, 18, 41–42, 64, 66, 69, 141, 152, 180, 194, 222, 274n28

Sōtō/Caodong sect, 24, 35, 37, 49, 60–61, 74, 79, 113, 203, 218, 259n5, 262n1, 263n3, 275n38; in contemporary Japan, xiii, 55, 57, 65, 120, 181, 199–200, 203, 207, 211, 224–225, 263n; after Dōgen, x, 9, 25–28, 36, 52, 82–86, 91, 167, 191, 198, 200, 264n10; Dōgen's views of, 19, 30–31, 48, 74, 143, 197, 222, 272n19; origins in China, 14, 34, 48, 70, 218; and realization, 124, 183, 261n24; and transition to Japan, 3, 11–12, 46. *See also* Zen

sūtras, 9, 13, 17, 33–34, 50, 93, 161, 180, 219; attachment to, 152, 159–161, 167; and buddhas and ancestors, 141, 163–164; Dōgen's views on, 3, 15, 55, 149, 151, 161–164, 166–167, 181t7.2, 185, 202, 206; interpretations of, 66, 163, 165–166; the *Lotus Sūtra*, 33, 37, 46, 48, 66, 115, 161–166, 168, 270n23; and practice, 161–163, 167; and realization, 15–16, 33, 38, 93, 141, 160–168, 185, 205–206, 211; recitation of, 15–16, 38, 161–162, 164, 167, 182, 202; in rituals, 38, 162, 166; role in Zen, 162, 164, 166, 205; as sacred objects, 38, 162, 166; Tendai approaches to, 162. *See also* expressivity

temporality, x, 21–22, 56, 92, 119–120, 122, 128–130, 132, 135–136, 139, 171–172, 177, 208; and being-time, 24, 71, 92, 94, 108, 110, 123, 128–129, 131, 135, 137–138, 212, 217; being-time, realization of, 101–102, 120, 126–127, 130, 134, 139–141, 174, 176, 215, 219; being-time, unity of, 21–24, 55, 58, 103, 119, 122, 125 127f5.1, 129f5.2, 132, 136, 148, 171; and continuity, 21, 37, 92, 129, 136, 138; and everyday life, 127f5.1, 129f5.2; here and now (*nikon*), 95, 101, 111, 120, 123, 126, 131, 136–137, 139, 141, 172–173, 214; in Indian Buddhism, 23, 40, 124, 130, 213; and momentariness (*setsuna*), 21, 51, 92, 126, 130, 132, 137, 217; and ordinary time, 22, 123, 125, 136; and sometimes (*uji*), 21–22, 110. *See also* Buddha nature; ephemerality

Treasury of the True Dharma Eye (*Shōbōgenzō*), commentaries on: and Giun, 9–10, 28, 79, 81–82, 82t, 173, 217, 260n15, 266n20, 266n22; and Gudō Wafu Nishijima, vii–x; and Manzan, 83–84; and Menzan, 10, 84, 193–194, 261n21; and Nishiari Bokusan, 84, 265n11; and Nishitani Keiji, 55; and non-Buddhist studies scholars, 9, 58, 146, 269n4; and Senne-Kyōgō, 81–82, 82t3.2, 173, 266n22; and Tenkei, 84, 262n44

Treasury, editions of, x, 29, 31, 65–66, 79, 80t3.1, 83, 87, 177, 233; composition of, 10, 62, 65, 68, 71–73, 77, 80t3.1, 83, 221, 224, 234–237; and Ejō, 233, 234, 236, 237, 265n2, 266n22; and Gien, 28, 79, 81, 266n22; and Giun, 9–10, 28, 79, 81–82, 82t3.2, 173, 217, 233, 260n15, 266n20; inconsistencies of, 7, 11, 29–30, 32, 57, 62, 204, 267n9; New (or Later) Draft, 61, 78, 143, 221; Old (or Early) Draft, 78, 222–223;

[294] INDEX

Treasury, editions of (*continued*)
75-, 60-, 12-, 95-fascicle editions, 28–29, 65–67, 71–72, 75, 79–84, 133, 164, 208, 220

Treasury, fascicles of, 227–234, 236–237, 265nn11,12,13; Arousing the Aspiration for Enlightenment, 126, 132–133, 229; Being-Time, 21, 74, 115, 123, 126, 128, 138, 228; Buddha Nature, 23, 74, 86, 109–110, 112, 124, 130, 187, 191, 227, 275n40; Deep Faith in Causality, 30, 220–222, 266n18; Discerning the Way, 23, 41, 66, 71–73, 83–84, 158, 230; Discerning the Way, and practice, 4, 16, 53, 94–95, 97, 162, 176–177, 184–185, 205, 261n25; Disclosing a Dream Within a Dream, 29, 35, 170–171, 228; Empty Space, 107, 158, 162, 225, 229, 266n22, 267n11; Expressing the Way, 47, 148, 228; Extensive Studies, 155; Face-to-Face Transmission, 15, 42, 229, 265n4; Great Awakening, 57, 86, 173, 180, 195, 228, 230; Great Cultivation, 30, 220–222; Insentient Beings Preaching the Dharma, 114, 228; The King of All Samādhis, 180, 186–188, 229; The Lancet of Zazen, 51, 125, 178, 184, 186, 188, 190, 194, 196–198, 228; The Moon, 23, 105, 228, 265n12; Mountains and Rivers Proclaiming the Sūtras, 44, 49, 74, 115, 123, 150, 153, 228; The Nature of Things, 100, 124, 213, 229; The Perfection of Great Wisdom, 20, 72, 107, 227; Plum Blossoms, 43–44, 114, 229, 265n4; Radiant Light, 44, 216, 228, 263n9; Realization Here-and-Now, 49, 71–72, 108, 117, 133–137, 171, 189, 227; Reciting Sūtras, 208, 228; Sounds of Valleys, Colors of Mountains, 35, 222, 272n4; Spring and Autumn, 35, 106, 228; Summer Retreat, 137, 205, 208, 217, 229, 266n22; Sustained Exertion, 97, 142, 180, 207, 218, 228, 266n21, 269n4, 272n4, 274n27; Taking Refuge in the Three Jewels, 79, 163, 208, 230, 266n22; Total Activity, 75–77, 108; The Ungraspable Mind, 159, 224, 227, 230, 268n10;

Washing the Face, 38, 73, 78, 208, 211, 215, 229, 230, 262n45, 265n3

Treasury, interpretations of: in comparative religious thought, 3, 26, 33, 36, 54–58, 102, 120, 223; Edo period approaches to, 28, 36, 71, 78, 83–84, 190–191, 207–209, 274n28; ethical controversies regarding, 57, 85–86, 202, 220, 222–225, 275n38; and *Genzō-e*, 27, 84; and *Genzō-ka*, 26, 64; and Hee-Jin Kim, 17, 50, 114, 145, 178; influence of, 9–10, 25–26, 32, 35, 39, 55–58, 199, 225; in relation to Japanese arts, 27, 121, 262n43, 265n6, 269n3; and Kagamishima Genryū, 34, 262n1; and myths surrounding, 40, 60, 62–63; and Nakano Tōzen, 225; neglect of, 27–28, 31, 36, 63, 84; and Ozeki, Ruth, 56, 261n35; as pedagogical device, 9, 24, 32, 36, 54, 186; popularity of, 8, 10–11, 20, 27–28, 54–56, 198; postwar studies of, 20, 31, 34, 54, 81, 84, 146, 199, 217; and prohibition of publication, 28, 84; rhetorical style of, 9, 18–23, 34, 48, 50, 87, 92, 98–99, 105, 145, 148, 156, 215; sources for, 19–22, 34–36, 50, 70, 84, 94, 99, 101, 110, 131, 142, 155, 159, 180, 195; and Tanabe Hajime, 25, 54; theories about, 87t3.3: theories, Critical Buddhism, 57–58, 86, 202, 220, 222–225, 275n33; theories, Decline Theory, 63, 67, 85–87; theories, Renewal Theology, 63, 67, 85–87; theories, Traditional Theology, 85–87; translations of, x–xiii, 11, 19, 27, 29, 54, 57, 227, 239–242, 260n14, 271n9, 272n18; and Watsuji Tetsurō, 25, 54, 151; and women, 9, 57, 66–67, 76f3.1, 85, 185, 220, 224, 264nn23–24; works on, 84, 146

zazen, 8, 13, 54, 69, 71–72, 113, 115, 143, 201, 204f8.1; Dōgen's views on, 4–5, 92, 162, 175–176, 178, 179t7.1, 180–187, 181t7.2, 195–198, 208, 214; interpretations of, 25, 177–178, 180, 182, 194, 198, 202, 204, 207, 209; and role in contemporary Zen, 199,

272n23, 275n38; and sustained exertion, 4, 13, 16, 53, 117, 120, 140–143, 174, 184–186, 194, 202, 210. *See also* casting off body-mind (*shinjin datsuraku*); just sitting; reflexivity

Zen: and history of institution, 4, 12, 35, 41, 45–46, 84, 98, 206, 209, 265n12; and Five Houses, 42, 274n28; and Five Mountains, 15, 261n22; lineages of, 7, 13–14, 30–31, 46, 49, 60, 72, 74, 82t3.2, 84, 139, 218; transplantation to Japan, 4, 12, 30, 37, 46, 69, 94–95, 148, 152, 180, 185, 210; Zen patriarchs, 15, 34, 46, 79, 99, 142, 155–156, 164, 182, 216, 222, 262n1; Zen patriarchs, and Śākyamuni Buddha, 30, 34, 45–46, 110, 153, 163, 185, 211. *See also* Sōtō/Caodong sect

Zongze. *See under* practice

GPSR Authorized Representative: Easy Access System Europe, Mustamäe tee
50, 10621 Tallinn, Estonia, gpsr.requests@easproject.com

www.ingramcontent.com/pod-product-compliance
Lightning Source LLC
Chambersburg PA
CBHW021936290426
44108CB00012B/862